International acclaim for *Fernand* L

MEMORY AND THE MEDITERRANEAN

"Highly ambitious. . . . Braudel's handling of this early period is fascinating." — *The Spectator*

"An awesome panorama recited in a most memorable narrative by a true scholar. . . . Prodigious. . . . Compelling. . . . A majestic tapestry." — *Anniston Star*

"Not enough can be said about [*Memory and the Mediterranean*]. . . . [Braudel's] approach to the Mediterranean will fascinate modern students of ancient history." — *Library Journal*, starred review

"Braudel's enthusiasm is often catching. . . . His greatness shows through." — *Daily Telegraph*

"*Memory and the Mediterranean* forms a natural overture to [Braudel's] most famous magnum opus . . . the perfect prequel. . . . [It] plays to all its author's best qualities: the encyclopedic yet never oppressive knowledge [and] the bold panoramic grasp of vast periods. . . . This, certainly, is one book by Braudel that has the capacity to provoke and stimulate everyone, from the young student to the seasoned general reader." — *The New Republic*

"Highly readable. It is hard to imagine anyone but Braudel taking on such a vast period and maintaining a sense of structure and direction. Nothing like it exists." — *Books Direct*

"Braudel's venture into global history ranks among the most impressive demonstrations yet conceived and carried through of how a single author can create an elegant, intelligible portrait of several centuries of the world's history. . . . Braudel, in short, was an authentic heir of Herodotus and deserves his reputation as the most influential historian of his time."
— *The Journal of Modern History*

Fernand Braudel

MEMORY AND THE MEDITERRANEAN

Fernand Braudel was the most celebrated French historian of the post-war era. He taught at the Collège de France and was the leader of the Annales school, serving as a member of the editorial board of Annales and of the École Pratique des Hautes Études, as well as chief administrator of the Maisons des Sciences de l'Homme. His widely acclaimed works include *The Mediterranean and the Mediterranean World in the Age of Philip II, A History of Civilizations*, and *The Structures of Everyday Life*. Braudel died in 1985.

MEMORY
and the
MEDITERRANEAN

MEMORY
and the
MEDITERRANEAN

Fernand Braudel

TEXT EDITED BY ROSELYNE DE AYALA
AND PAULE BRAUDEL

TRANSLATED FROM THE FRENCH
BY SIÂN REYNOLDS

VINTAGE BOOKS

A DIVISION OF RANDOM HOUSE, INC.

NEW YORK

CONTENTS

List of Illustrations   vii
Introduction by Oswyn Murray   ix
Preamble by Christopher Logue   xxi
Editors' Foreword to the French Edition   xxiii
Author's Preface   xxv

PART ONE

CHAPTER ONE: *Seeing the Sea*   3

CHAPTER TWO: *The Long March to Civilization*   17
    The Lower Paleolithic: the first artefacts, the first people   18
    Fire, art and magic   27
    The Mediterranean strikes back: the first agrarian
        civilization   37
    Conclusion   45

CHAPTER THREE: *A Twofold Birth*   47
    Mesopotamia and Egypt: the beginnings   47
    Boats on the rivers, ships on the sea   73
    Can the spread of megaliths explain the early
        history of the Mediterranean?   85

CHAPTER FOUR: *Centuries of Unity: The Seas of the Levant 2500–1200 B.C.* 95
    Ever onward and upward?   96
    Crete: a new player in the cosmopolitan civilization
        of the Mediterranean   108
    Accidents, developments and disasters   134

CHAPTER FIVE: *All Change: The Twelfth to the Eighth Centuries B.C.*   159

Contents

PART TWO

CHAPTER SIX: *Colonization: The Discovery of the Mediterranean*
"Far West" in the Tenth to Sixth Centuries B.C.   179

The first in the field: probably the Phoenicians   180

The Etruscans: an unsolved mystery   199

Colonization by the Greeks   212

CHAPTER SEVEN: *The Miracle of Greece*   227

Greece: a land of city-states   228

Alexander's mistake   244

Greek science and thought
(eighth to second centuries B.C.)   251

CHAPTER EIGHT: *The Roman Takeover of the Greater Mediterranean*   271

Roman imperialism   272

Rome beyond the Mediterranean   289

A Mediterranean civilization: Rome's real achievement   297

Appendix I: Table of Prehistoric Ages and Anthropoids   317

Appendix II: Maps   321

Notes   341

Bibliography   345

Translator's Note   349

Index   351

ILLUSTRATIONS

FIGURES

Figure 1 Hunters from the caves of the Spanish *Levante* 34

Figure 2 Deerhunt, Cueva de los Caballos 34

Figure 3 Çatal Höyük—inside a sanctuary 44

Figure 4 A district in Çatal Höyük 44

Figure 5 The Narmer Palette 64

Figure 6 Phoenician warships and roundships 176

Appendix 1 Table of Prehistoric Ages and Anthropoids 318

MAPS

1. The Mediterranean (geographical overview) 322

2. The Fertile Crescent 324

3. Mesopotamia 325

4. Ancient Egypt 326

5. "Phoenicia" 327

6. The eastern basin of the Mediterranean (2500–1200),
   showing Hittite expansion and the rise of Crete 328

7. Phoenician colonization 330

8. Greek colonization 332

9. Etruscan settlements 334

10. The urn-field burial people 335

11. Celtic migrations 336

12. Julius Caesar's conquest of Gaul 337

13. The Empire of Alexander the Great 338

14. The Roman Empire in the reign of Septimius Severus 339

INTRODUCTION

Fernand Braudel (1902–1985) was the greatest historian of the twentieth century. So universal has his influence been on the study of history since the publication of his first major work fifty years ago that it is almost impossible for us to remember what history was like before Braudel. For that reason we often tend to forget how important was this revolution in historical method: it takes a discovery like that presented here, of a lost work by the master on his favourite theme, to remind us of our debt to him.

Braudel liked to think of himself as a typical Frenchman from the provinces. In his memory he belonged to a peasant family from Lorraine, on the borders of France and Germany. Because of poor health he had indeed spent his early years in the village of Luméville-en-Ornois at his paternal grandmother's smallholding, with its chickens, stone walls, and espaliered fruit trees, in a world that (as he described it) was still centred on the blacksmith, the wheelwright, the itinerant woodcutters and an ancient mill. He subsumed the contemporary realities of industrial Lorraine and the ever-present threat from Germany into this idyllic picture, along with the fact that his later childhood and adolescence were spent in Paris and its suburbs, where his father was a teacher of mathematics. On leaving school Braudel did not compete for entry to the elite institution of the École Normale Supérieure but instead went to the Sorbonne. There he was attracted to economic and social history and the study of ancient Greece, and to the lectures of history professors outside the mainstream, which usually had audiences of only four to seven people. He chose resolutely to identify himself with the margins of French society and to escape from his Parisian bourgeois background to a career in the provinces. In 1923, at the age of twenty-one, he travelled to his first post as a history teacher, at the grammar school of Constantine in Algeria, and here he saw the Mediterranean for the first time.

His true intellectual formation began in Algeria, a world in which a young man could take himself seriously. He turned from studying the past of

Lorraine (which he came to think was too full of national problems) to that of Spain, and he began to contemplate a traditional historical thesis on the Mediterranean policy of Philip II between 1559 and 1574; by 1927 he was publishing reviews of books on Spanish history. But he was also fascinated by the new history of Lucien Febvre, based on the science of human geography, as exemplified in a book written in 1913 but not published until 1922, *La Terre et l'évolution humaine,* translated as *A Geographical Introduction to History* (London, 1932). Braudel read the book in 1924. As usual his approach was cautious: it was three years before he began to write to Febvre, and their close personal friendship did not begin for another ten years. Meanwhile, in his first reply to Braudel, Febvre had planted a serious doubt about Braudel's subject of research:

> Philip II and the Mediterranean, a good subject. But why not the Mediterranean and Philip II? A much larger subject. For between these two protagonists, Philip and the middle sea, the division is not equal.

Braudel was a successful schoolteacher and became known as an expert in his chosen area. In 1932 he returned to Paris and was nominated to a series of more and more prestigious *lycées;* in 1933 he married one of his earliest pupils from Algiers. Then he made a decision that was to change his life: in 1935 he accepted the offer of a five-year secondment to the new university being established with French help at São Paolo, Brazil. It was a golden chance for him and for others of his generation who had not followed the easy road to break into French academic life; at least one of his contemporaries and friends in that enterprise is now equally famous—the anthropologist Claude Lévi-Strauss.

"It was in Brazil that I became intelligent." Braudel was always an eminently practical man. He managed to rent a large mansion, complete with a Chevrolet and an Italian chauffeur, from someone who conveniently spent the period of the university terms in Europe. Each winter Braudel returned to Europe and worked in the archives of the great Mediterranean trading cities, such as Venice and Dubrovnik (Ragusa). He was an innovative researcher in two respects, conceptual and practical. He made the move from government archives to commercial archives, and by chance he invented the microfilm, which he used in order to copy two or three thousand documents a day, to be read during the university year in Brazil.

I bought this machine in Algiers: it belonged to an American cameraman and was used to make rough images of scenes for films. On it you had a button that allowed you to take one photo at a time, or you pressed it and you took the whole shoot at once. When I was offered it, I said to the cameraman, "Photograph me that: if I can read it, I'll buy it." He made me a magnificent photo. And that's how I made kilometres of microfilms. It worked so well that when I was in Brazil I could spend whole days reading documents.

In 1936, during the long voyage back to Brazil in a cargo boat, he told his wife that he had decided to make the Mediterranean the centre of his research. A year later he was offered and accepted a post with a much lower salary at the main research centre in Paris, the École Pratique des Hautes Études, in one of the two nonscientific sections, the IVe Section (historical and philological sciences). By chance the boat on which he and his wife travelled home from Brazil in 1937 was carrying Lucien Febvre back from a lecture tour in Buenos Aires; during the two-week voyage they became close friends. Febvre, now aged sixty and a professor at the Collège de France, had been one of the two young professors at Strasbourg who founded the polemical journal *Annales* in 1929. The journal sought to create a new and more open approach to history in a provocatively colloquial style, an approach defined mostly by its search for "a larger and a more human history" (Marc Bloch), by its denial of all historical barriers and by its rejection of the traditional history of politics and government in favour of a deeper analysis of social and economic forces. From this time on Febvre became Braudel's friend, intellectual adviser and confidant.

When war began, Braudel was mobilised in the artillery and stationed on the frontier in Alsace; he saw no fighting, but he was forced to surrender after the Germans encircled the French army. Despite the armistice, in 1940 he was imprisoned at Mainz, where he remained until 1942. Then he was denounced by fellow officers as being a supporter of De Gaulle rather than Pétain and sent to a special "discipline camp" for "enemies of Germany" at Lübeck. He remained until 1945. He was reasonably happy amid all sorts of "dissidents"— partisans of De Gaulle, French Jewish officers, sixty-seven French priests of all descriptions, escapees, "all the best types in the French army," together with English airmen and Dutch, Swedish and Polish officers. He only missed the German books that he could find in the municipal library of Mainz.

It was during these four years of captivity that Braudel wrote the first draft of his monumental work, *The Mediterranean and the Mediterranean World in the Age of Philip II.* Assisted by a few books, but using mainly his prodigious memory of his prewar researches, he constructed a work that combined a vast chronological and historical sweep with a mass of minute details, covering the entire Mediterranean world from the Renaissance to the sixteenth century. This immense intellectual achievement was written in exercise books on a small plank in a room shared with twenty prisoners. At intervals parcels of the manuscript would arrive in Paris for criticism by Febvre; by the end of the war the work was finished, only to be rewritten at the rate of thirty to fifty pages a day until it was finally presented in 1947 as a thesis of 1,160 pages.

The transformation of Braudel's thought in captivity remains a mystery, although recent publications of writing from this period offer some insights. In one sense *The Mediterranean* was, as he said, "a work of contemplation," his escape into a world that he could control and whose detailed realities he could believe in with greater ease than the artificial world of prison life. In 1941 he wrote a rare letter from Mainz to his wife (who was living in Algeria): "As always I am reading, writing, working. I have decided to expand my work to the period from 1450 to 1650: one must think big, otherwise what is the point of history?" In the two camps he gave miniature university lectures to his fellow prisoners. Notebooks containing the text of some of these have been discovered and were published in 1997. They show that the reflective experience of prison was crucial to his historical thought, for in these lectures he sets out virtually all the great themes that he presented after the war.

Shortly before the presentation of his thesis, Braudel had been passed over as Professor of History at the Sorbonne in favour of a more conventional historian. At his rival's viva voce examination, he sought to justify the choice, telling Braudel: "You are a geographer; allow me to be the historian." In retrospect it is clear that this moment marked a turning point in the intellectual history of France: over the next thirty years the Sorbonne stagnated as a conservative backwater, while outside the university system Braudel proceeded to construct his great empire of "the human sciences," and to open a series of vistas that could perhaps never have found their place within a more conventional university atmosphere, where orthodoxy in teaching was valued above originality of ideas.

Braudel made his reputation with *The Mediterranean,* which was published in 1949; a second revised and reorganised edition was published in 1966, in preparation for the American edition of 1973, in the magnificent translation of Siân Reynolds (who takes leave of Braudel with the present book). With this new edition Braudel became the best-known historian in the world. My generation was brought up to believe in the words of its preface: the old history of events was indeed dead, "the action of a few princes and rich men, the trivia of the past, bearing little relation to the slow and powerful march of history . . . those statesmen were, despite their illusions, more acted upon than actors." In their place Braudel offered not "the traditional geographical introduction to history that often figures to so little purpose at the beginning of so many books, with its description of the mineral deposits, types of agriculture and typical flora, briefly listed and never mentioned again, as if the flowers did not come back every spring, the flocks of sheep migrate every year, or the ships sail on a real sea that changes with the seasons," but a whole new way of looking at the past, in which the historian re-created a lost reality through a feat of historical imagination based on detailed knowledge of the habits and techniques of the ploughman, the shepherd, the potter, and the weaver, the skills of the vintage and the olive press, the milling of corn, the keeping of records of bills of lading, tides and winds. It began to seem as important for a historian to be able to ride a horse or sail a ship as to sit in a library. Only the third section of Braudel's book returned to the history of events, "surface disturbances, crests of foam that the tides of history carry on their strong backs." Braudel taught us to see that historical time was divided into three forms of movement—geographical time, social time, and individual time—but that beyond all this the past was a unity and a reality. All these movements belonged together: "history can do more than study walled gardens."

This was the ultimate expression of the intellectual ambitions of the *Annales* school, which was reborn after the war and the Nazi execution of Marc Bloch, one of its two founders and a hero of the resistance. Braudel became a member of the *Annales* editorial board. Meanwhile, in 1947, a new section of the École Pratique des Hautes Études had been formed (with the help of money from the Rockefeller Foundation): the famous VIe Section in social sciences, with Febvre as its president and Braudel as his assistant. In 1949 Braudel was elected to the Collége de France, and in the same year he was given the immensely powerful position of president of the *agrégation* in history, the general qualifying examination for teaching in secondary schools. His reforms were resisted by the conservatives, but they could not dislodge him until 1955. The record of what he sought to achieve is contained in his little textbook for teachers called *Grammar of Civilizations* (written between

1962 and 1963, republished in 1987), designed to introduce contemporary history and world history to the school curriculum. History was divided into six civilizations—Western, Soviet, Muslim, the Far East, southeast Asia, and black Africa, all of course of relevance to a France still, at least in memory, committed to its status as a colonial power. Braudel's attempts at reform were destroyed by an unholy alliance of right and left, for he was one of the few French intellectuals who belonged to neither camp. He was therefore hated by Georges Pompidou, who held proto-Thatcherite views on the unimportance of all history apart from the history of one's own country and who irrationally regarded Braudel as responsible for the events of 1968. At the same time Braudel was denounced by orthodox communists as "a willing slave of American imperialism."

Lucien Febvre died in 1956, and Braudel inherited the direction of both the Ecole Pratique and the journal *Annales*. In the first institution he created and fostered one of the most extraordinary collections of talent in the twentieth century through his appointments: to mention only the most famous of his colleagues, they included the historians Georges Duby, Jacques Le Goff, Emmanuel Le Roy Ladurie and Maurice Aymard; the philosophers Roland Barthes and Michel Foucault; the psychologists Jacques Lacan and Georges Devereux; the sociologist Pierre Bourdieu; the anthropologist Claude Lévi-Strauss; and the classical scholars Jean-Pierre Vernant and Pierre Vidal-Naquet. Braudel worked hard to create a separate institution or building where all his colleagues could work together, and where a succession of foreign visitors could be invited as associate professors; this idea, begun about 1958, did not achieve physical shape until the opening of the Maison des Sciences de l'Homme in 1970. And it was only after he retired in 1972 that the VIe Section finally metamorphosed into its present status as a new and independent teaching institution, the École des Hautes Études en Sciences Sociales.

In and through *Annales* Braudel sought to promote and defend his conception of history. For thirty years the great debates on the nature of history took place in its pages. In retrospect one can see four successive but overlapping issues with which he engaged.

The first debate was provoked by the anthropologist Claude Lévi-Strauss's claims that the theory of structuralism offered an explanation of human social organisation. Braudel had been possibly the first historian to use the word *structure* in his original thesis, but he saw that the structuralism of Lévi-Strauss was fundamentally antihistorical, in that it sought to explain all human societies in terms of a single theory of structures. The notions of difference and of change that are basic to all historical thought were simply dismissed as irrelevant to the search for a universal underlying structure, which existed in the human mind if not in the physical universe itself. Against this, in a famous article in *Annales* (1958) on the "*longue durée*," Braudel sought to explain his own historical conception of the varieties of underlying forces influencing human society, which he had already formulated during the writing of his thesis in relation to the static forces and the slow movements behind the ephemeral history of events. Braudel's conception of the *longue durée* (usually translated rather misleadingly as "the long perspective") is not easy to express in nonhistorical terms as a theoretical concept; it is the recognition that human society develops and changes at different rates in relation to different underlying forces, and that all the elements within any human situation interact with one another. There are underlying geographical constraints; there are natural regularities of behaviour related to every activity, whether climatic or seasonal or conventional; there are social customs; there are economic pressures; and there are short-term events in history with their resulting consequences— battles, conquests, powerful rulers, reforms, earthquakes, famines, diseases, tribal loves and hatreds. To translate the messy complications that constitute the essence of history into a general theory is impossible, and this fact represents the ultimate problem of trying to subsume history within any abstract theory, from whatever philosophical or sociological or anthropological source it is derived.

The second debate concerned quantitative history: after *The Mediterranean* Braudel became more and more attracted to the idea of quantification in economic history, the notion that history could become scientifically respectable through the use of graphs and tables and the collection of hard quantifiable data. It took the example of his disciple Pierre Chaunu, who sought to surpass Braudel with his immense work of 7,800 pages on Seville and the Atlantic trade (finally published in 1963) to convince Braudel that something was missing from this type of statistical history. History was something more than the effect of the fluctuations in the Spanish-American trade or the economic boom and decline of the sixteenth and seventeenth centuries. It was in response to this debate that Braudel wrote his second great work, translated as *Civilization and Capitalism, 15th–18th Century* (1982). The first volume of this work was originally published in 1967 and translated into English as *Capitalism and Material Life, 1400–1800* (1973). It presented a vivid picture of social life and its structures before the Industrial Revolution, in terms of population, bread, food and drink, fashion, housing, energy sources, technology, money, cities and towns. This was revised and incorporated into a three-volume work with a one-word addition to the title: *Material Civilization, Economy and Capitalism* (1979). The work now approached the whole question of the origins of modern world capitalism. The second volume dealt with the organisation of commerce, manufacture and capitalism, the third with the growth of a world economy and world trade. His conclusion was both historical and practical: it is small-scale business and freedom of trade that both produce and sustain capitalism, not state enterprise or large-scale capitalism. Without the independent small artisan and the merchant-shopkeeper no economic system can survive, and these smaller entities are embedded in the social fabric so that society and economy can never be separated from each other. His work stands therefore as a refutation through the study of history of both communism and capitalism.

The third issue with which Braudel was involved was a consequence of his growing distance from the most talented historians whom he had called to join him in the management of *Annales*. The new history of the sixties turned away from the factual certainties of economic and descriptive social history, and explored the "history of mentalities." The historical world was created out of perceptions, not out of events, and we needed to recognise that the whole of history was a construct of human impressions. The crucial problem for a history that still sought a degree of certainty and an escape from arbitrariness or fiction was to analyse the mental world that created an age or a civilisation. It was the medieval historians Duby, Le Goff and Ladurie who pioneered this approach from 1961 onward; it meant a whole-scale return to the old German conceptions of cultural history, and to the use of literary and artistic sources alongside archival material. This was perhaps one of Braudel's blind spots: to him, it was the realities of peasant or merchant existence that mattered, not the way that they might be expressed in artistic or literary form. He was also more and more interested in the global sweep and saw the detailed studies of the mental world of small communities undertaken by his colleagues as a betrayal of the grand vision. As he said to Ladurie in relation to his famous book *Montaillou,* "We brought history into the dining room; you are taking it into the bedroom." His disapproval of these trends cost him the direction of his journal, and by 1969 he had abandoned *Annales,* sidelined by those whose careers he had started and whom he had originally invited to join him.

Braudel's reply to this development was long in coming and remains incomplete; it was his last great projected work, *The Identity of France.* Three volumes were published before his death, comprising the first two parts on geography and demography and economy: these were for him traditional territory. With the third and fourth he would be entering new territory by writing about the state, culture, and society, and in the fourth about "France outside France." Fragments of the third volume were published in 1997. They suggest that in this last work he intended to confound his critics by proving that the "mentality" of France was contained within its physical, social and economic history. The peasant was the key to the history of France, and a true history of mentalities could only be written in the *longue durée* and from a long perspective. History must do more than study walled gardens.

The difficulty of translating *longue durée* with the phrase "the long perspective" reveals another problem that was perhaps to emerge in the later debates with Michel Foucault. Braudel never claimed that his categories were absolute. They were only means of organising the explanatory factors in any situation, but equally he was not prepared to see them simply as constructs fashioned by the observer for his immediate purposes. However indeterminate and changeable, they did possess a real existence as forces in the field of history. This was challenged by the theories and methods of Foucault in his *Words and Things* (1966), and *The Archaeology of Knowledge* (1969). The idea of historical relativity introduced in these works and adopted by postmodern historians took one step beyond the history of mentalities. Not only did the uncertainty contained in the study of history rest on its derivation from a set of human impressions rather than facts: the crucial role in this process belonged to the historian as interpreter. Indeed, the whole organisation of knowledge could be seen as a construction designed to control the world. History, like all the social sciences, was an aspect of power, so that history was both the history of forms of control and itself a form of control, not an innocent activity. All this is still highly controversial today, but it was of course one step worse for Braudel than the history of mentalities. The historian was no longer the innocent observer but himself complicitous in society's attempt to marginalize groups such as the women, aboriginal peoples, the mad, criminals, and homosexuals, and through its control of the psychology of humanity to construct mechanisms of social power—or ultimately (in Foucault's last work) a more beneficent form of the control of the self. Moreover, Foucault singled out the Braudelian conception of history for special attack: it was ideas and the sudden rupture created by them (exemplified in his own books), not the long perspective, which mattered in a history dominated by random change, by discontinuities instead of structures.

This theoretical debate had just begun in 1968. Braudel was giving a lecture series in Chicago when he was recalled to face—at the age of sixty-two—the revolutionary student movement, Like many radical professors he was sympathetic but uncomprehending of the anarchic streak in youthful protest; his interventions were paternalistic and not well received, and later he condemned the revolution because it made people less rather than more happy. He could not understand the desire to destroy everything that he had personally tried to build outside the university system of which both he and they disapproved, or their contempt for facts and research in face of neocommunist and anarchist ideas.

More dangerous still for Braudel was the reaction, which brought the conservatives under Pompidou to power, and which placed the blame, not on their own resistance to change, but on those who had tried to encourage change. Had not the "events" of 1968 proved the importance of the history of events? Where now was the long perspective? "Has Structuralism Been Killed by May '68?," as a headline in *Le Monde* put it in November of that year. Either the new history (whatever it was) was responsible for the "events," or it was disproved by them. As a conservative you could have it both ways, and both implicated Braudel along with all his intellectual opponents. This was of course to accuse the Enlightenment of causing the French Revolution, but the claim was successful in blocking Braudel's access to government circles almost for the first time in his career. The university conservatives had indeed lost, and the old Sorbonne was swept away, but they also had their revenge on the man who was most responsible for establishing their irrelevance to modern life.

Braudel ended his life as he began it, as an outsider, but not unhappy with this fate. He had always believed in the importance of accepting reality and the relative powerlessness of the individual in the face of his circumstances, even though he had himself ruled French intellectual life "as a prince" for a generation. Above all, despite his recognition of the importance of the grand vision and the power of the *longue durée* and of structures, he had always upheld that crucial historical value, the centrality of the individual as the subject of history; not the individual great man but the anonymous yet real peasant, the ordinary unknown man. In this sense he remains more truly revolutionary than any of his opponents on the left or the right.

How powerful the legacy of Braudel, and especially of his *Mediterranean,* still is and how modern its conception still appears, can be seen by considering its impact on two recent books. The first is Barry Cunliffe's *Facing the Ocean: The Atlantic and Its Peoples* (2001), in which Cunliffe seeks to do for the Atlantic what Braudel once did for the Mediterranean. The title of his last chapter makes explicit reference to Braudel's *longue durée*. The second is the latest book on the Mediterranean, whose first volume appeared in the year 2000, Peregrine Horden and Nicholas Purcell's *The Corrupting Sea: A Study of Mediterranean History*. For all its immense learning and resolute up-to-dateness, this work too is inconceivable without the example of Braudel: it is an attempt to answer the same questions as Braudel for the centuries before the age of Philip II. When we were young we all of us indeed dreamed of writing a book on the Mediterranean that would replace in its title Philip II of Spain with that earlier Philip II of Macedon.

It is not therefore surprising that this work, Braudel's *Memory and the Mediterranean*, although it was originally written a generation ago, can still serve as a model. This little book exemplifies all the ideas that Braudel believed in, and for that reason it is richer than most of the detailed books by experts written both before and since its composition. It contains all those elements that he taught us to respect, and offers new surprises. The first is its scope and its exemplification of the meaning of the *longue durée*. A history of the ancient Mediterranean would normally begin with the Minoan age, or not earlier than 2000 B.C.; Braudel invites us to consider the Mediterranean, not geographically, but as a historical phenomenon beginning in the Paleolithic age or even with the start of geological time; as he points out, the historical period of classical civilization belongs in the last two minutes of the year, and the last two chapters of his book. How Braudel would have relished the new perspectives on the early stages of evolution and the biological history of the universe that are being revealed by the new uses of genetics in archaeology and evolutionary biology. How he would have loved the enrichment of our knowledge of the origins of human art in the Paleolithic age with the new discoveries of the Grotte Chauvet in the Ardèche.

Braudel's picture also invites us to consider the Mediterranean in its broadest geographical context, inclusive of the great civilisations of Iraq and Egypt, the steppes of Russia, the forests of Germany, and the deserts of the Sahara. For him Mediterranean history is an aspect of world history. Within the context of human history he emphasises two themes. The first is what I would call the reality principle. Human history is a history of technological mastery and the development of the skills basic to ancient civilisation: fire and water technology, pottery, weaving, metalworking, seafaring and finally writing. This emphasis on the physical realities of early civilisations brings out the actual quality of life with a vividness that no amount of reading other books can achieve. The second is the importance of exchange, especially long-distance exchange: "Our sea was from the very dawn of its protohistory a witness to those imbalances productive of change which would set the rhythm of its entire life." It is imbalance that creates exchange and therefore leads to progress. These two ideas, first formulated in *The Mediterranean* and subsequently explored in depth in for the preindustrial world in *Civilization and Capitalism,* are here applied to the ancient Mediterranean with magnificent effect. This deceptively modest book is indeed the work of the greatest historian of the twentieth century, and the new poem by Christopher Logue will serve as a fitting preamble.*

Oswyn Murray

---

*In writing this essay I have been helped of course by Braudel's own brief description of his historical development published in English in the *Journal of Modern History* for 1972, but more especially by the magnificent biography of Pierre Daix, *Braudel* (Flammarion, 1995). The lectures from the period of the Second World War and the fragments related to the third volume of Braudel's *L'Identité de la France* are published in *Les ambitions de l'Histoire* (Editions de Fallois, 1997).

Christopher Logue's poem was first published in Harold Berliner's deluxe edition of *War Music* (Nevada City, California, 1999). It is reprinted here for the first time as fitting homage to Braudel, for which privilege I thank my friend Christopher Logue.

PREAMBLE

Two limestone plates support the Aegean world.
The greater Anatolian still lies flat,
But half an eon past, through silent eyes
    "Ave!"
God watched the counterplate subside, until,
Only its top and mountain tops remained
Above His brother, Lord Poseidon's, sea:
    "And that, I shall call Greece. And those,
Her Archipelago," said He. Then turned away
To hear Apollo and the Nine perform
Of Creation, *from the stage at Table Bay.*

    They enter. They attend. They bow.
The Lord of Light and Mice gives them their note.
    And then they sing:

    "In the beginning there was no Beginning,
And in the end, no End . . ."

                             Christopher Logue

EDITORS' FOREWORD TO
THE FRENCH EDITION

This book has a history. Early in 1968, a representative of the Swiss publisher Albert Skira arrived from Geneva to see Fernand Braudel. Skira had planned a series of illustrated volumes in large format narrating the history of the Mediterranean. His agent had been asked to persuade Braudel to take on not only the volumes on the sixteenth and seventeenth centuries—as he was expecting since that was the period of his own research—but also the first volume in the series, on the Mediterranean in prehistory and antiquity. Initially surprised but immediately tempted, Braudel quickly became fascinated by prehistory, a field that was quite new to him and was going through revolutionary change at the time. He sat down and wrote his manuscript in a short time and with great enjoyment.

But by 1970 Albert Skira was in very poor health. This may explain why in 1971–2 the project was held up, and there were uncertainties over the choice of illustrations. Then, after Skira's death in 1973, the whole expensive series was cancelled almost before it had begun. By this time, Fernand Braudel was too absorbed in his work on the second volume of *Civilization and Capitalism* to consider revising for separate publication a text originally written as part of a larger project. It would also have meant the extra task of finding the necessary maps and illustrations. So he set aside the manuscript and thereafter more or less forgot about it.

Still unpublished ten years or more after the author's death, this text had become problematic. Those who knew of its existence were anxious that it should not be lost. But to publish it as it stood seemed inappropriate, since in the years since 1970 archaeology had made a great deal of progress; in particular, carbon dating had thrown into question earlier attempts at chronology. On the other hand, finding a co-operative expert who could bring up to date a book written essentially for the general reader would also be difficult. What could be done? We appealed to Jean Guilaine, whose expert knowledge would enable him to make an informed judgement. He unhesitatingly declared that the tone of the book was so captivating that he favoured publishing the text as it stood. The important thing in his view was to avoid disrupting the book's narrative and stylistic flow. The original problem could be solved by adding notes informing the reader wherever modern scholarship had revised certain dates or interpretations in the interval, and by providing references to recent publications. The task remained of finding a scholar prepared to take on this work. Jean Guilaine volunteered to cover his own field, prehistory, while Pierre Rouillard, assisted by two colleagues,[1] agreed to cover the period from 1000 B.C. Publisher and editors wish to thank all those concerned for their generous assistance.

The text of which a translation is published here is therefore the same manuscript which was sent to the Skira publishing house in 1969, and which the author received back a few years later. Notes by Jean Guilaine and Pierre Rouillard (recognizable by their initials) appear after the text. The maps in Appendix II identify place-names mentioned in the text. Since the maps do not need to be consulted in order to follow the argument, it was decided not to incorporate them into the body of the book, especially since they refer to more than one chapter. There is also a full index.

AUTHOR'S PREFACE

As the reader may know, I am a specialist on the Mediterranean in the sixteenth century. Out of curiosity, and indeed necessity, I have explored the whole of the sea's past, and have read almost all the serious works I could find on it in ancient and modern times. For all that, my personal research really covers only the period 1450–1650.

Why then did I rashly accept Albert Skira's request to write the first volume in a series on the past of the Mediterranean, since it indubitably lay outside the usual range of my competence?

To move into new territory without really leaving home is a temptation, a delight comparable to a taste for travel. Perhaps I yielded to it once more out of that sin of curiosity, and also because I have always believed that history cannot be really understood unless it is extended to cover the entire human past. Perhaps it is only right, as well, to measure one's ideas and explanations against unfamiliar historical landscapes. The present work, which is intended for the educated general reader, offered me the chance to take my own fabulous journey through the long expanse of history, *la très longue durée*. So I seized the chance.

I must say that it has given me enormous pleasure to follow the discoveries, hypotheses and running debates in archaeology and ancient history, disciplines which have been completely revolutionized over the last half-century—while also, naturally, being reminded quite often of the historical periods and problems I knew well from devoting a lifetime to them. For in the long and dazzling past of the Mediterranean, history may not repeat itself, but it is all part of a single fabric.

F. B.
29 July 1969

PART ONE

CHAPTER ONE

Seeing the Sea

The best witness to the Mediterranean's age-old past is the sea itself. This has to be said and said again; and the sea has to be seen and seen again. Simply looking at the Mediterranean cannot of course explain everything about a complicated past created by human agents, with varying doses of calculation, caprice and misadventure. But this is a sea that patiently recreates for us scenes from the past, breathing new life into them, locating them under a sky and in a landscape that we can see with our own eyes, a landscape and sky like those of long ago. A moment's concentration or daydreaming, and that past comes back to life.

But if that is true, if the Mediterranean seems so alive, so eternally young in our eyes, "always ready and willing," what point is there in recalling this sea's great age? What does it matter, the traveller may think, what can it possibly matter, that the Mediterranean, an insignificant breach in the earth's crust, narrow enough to be crossed at contemptuous speed in an aeroplane (an hour from Marseille to Algiers, fifteen minutes from Palermo to Tunis, and the rest to match) is an ancient feature of the geology of the globe? Should we care that the Inland Sea is immeasurably older than the oldest of the human histories it has cradled? Yes, we should: the sea can be only be fully understood if we view it in the long perspective of its geological history. To this it owes its shape, its architecture, the basic realities of its life, whether we are thinking of yesterday, today or tomorrow. So let us look at the record.

In the Paleozoic era, millions and millions of years ago, removed from us by a chronological distance that defies the imagination, a broad band of sea known to geologists as Tethys ran from the West Indies to the Pacific. Following the lines of latitude, it bisected what would much later become the landmass of the Ancient World. The present-day Mediterranean is the residual mass of water from Tethys, and it dates back almost to the earliest days of the planet.

The many violent foldings of the Tertiary era took place at the expense of this very ancient Mediterranean, much larger than the present one. All the mountains, from the Baetic Cordillera to the Rif, the Atlas, the Alps and the Apennines, the Balkans, the Taurus and the Caucasus, were heaved up out of the ancient sea. They reduced its area, raising from the great sea bed not only sedimentary rocks—sands, clays, sandstones, thick layers of limestone—but also deeply buried primitive rocks. The mountains surrounding, strangling, barricading and compartmentalizing the long Mediterranean coastline are the flesh and bones of the ancestral Tethys. Everywhere the sea water has left traces of its slow labour. The sedimentary limestones outside Cairo, "so fine-grained and of such milky whiteness that they allow the sculptor's chisel to give the sensation of volume by working to a depth of only a few millimetres"; the great slabs of coraline limestone from which the megalithic temples in Malta were built; the stone of Segovia which is easier to work when wet; the limestone of the Latomies (the huge quarries of Syracuse); the Istrian stones of Venice and many other rock formations in Greece, Italy and Sicily—all these came from the sea bed.

At the end of this process, since the series of Mediterranean trenches was never filled in, the sea was left as a deep basin, its hollows as if scooped out by some desperate hand, its depths in places equal or superior to the heights of the tallest Mediterranean mountains. Near Cape Matapan runs a sea-trench 4600 metres deep, easily enough to drown the tallest peak in Greece: Mount Olympus, 2985 metres high. Whether under the water or on land, the relief of the whole area is unstable. Networks of long fault lines are visible everywhere, some reaching as far as the Red Sea. The narrow passage of the Pillars of Hercules between the Mediterranean and the Atlantic Ocean is the result of at least a twofold fault.

All this suggests a tortured geology, a process of orogenesis not yet stable even today. It accounts for the frequent and often catastrophic earthquakes, for the hot springs which the Etruscans had already discovered in Tuscany, and for the broad volcanic zones, with their strings of volcanoes, extinct, active or potentially active. Mount Etna was the fabled home of the Cyclops, blacksmiths and makers of thunderbolts, wielding their mighty bullhide bellows; here, much later, the philosopher Empedocles is supposed to have cast himself into the crater, from which a lone sandal was recovered. "How often we have seen boiling Etna spill forth balls of fire and molten rock!" remarked Virgil. Vesuvius really did destroy Pompeii and Herculaneum in AD 79. And in the years before 1943 its plume of smoke could be seen hanging over Naples. Every night, in the Lipari archipelago, between Sicily and Italy, Stromboli still lights up the sea with its incandescent lava displays. Earthquakes and eruptions have continually punctuated the past and still threaten the present in Mediterranean countries. One of the most ancient of mural paintings (and I mean mural, not cave painting) in a temple at Çatal Höyük in Anatolia dating from 6200 B.C., represents a volcanic eruption, probably of the nearby Hasan Dag.

We shall have occasion to return to the "Plutonian" convulsions of the earth's crust apropos of Minoan Crete, notably the cataclysmic explosion of the nearby island of Thera (known today as Santorini) in about 1470–1450 B.C. Half the island was hurled into the air, creating a massive tidal wave and an apocalyptic rain of ash. Today the strange island of Santorini is a semi-crater, partially submerged under the sea. According to the archaeologist Claude Schaeffer earthquakes and seismic shocks also contributed to the swift and unexpected destruction of all the Hittite cities in Asia Minor in the early twelfth century B.C. In this instance, nature rather than human intervention may have been responsible for a cataclysm that still puzzles historians.

Mountains are all around in the Mediterranean. They come right down to the sea, taking up more than their share of space, piling up one behind another, forming the inescapable frame and backdrop of every landscape. They hinder transport, turn coast roads into corniches and leave little room for serene landscapes of cities, cornfields, vineyards or olive-groves, since altitude always gets the better of human activity. The people of the Mediterranean have been confined not only by the sea—a potential means of escape, but for countless ages so dangerous that it was used little if at all—but also by the mountains.

Up in the high country, with few exceptions, only the most primitive ways of life could take hold and somehow survive. The Mediterranean plains, for lack of space, are mostly confined to a few coastal strips, a few pockets of arable land. Above them run steep and stony paths, hard on the feet of men and the hooves of beasts alike.

Worse still, the plains, especially those of any size, were often invaded by floodwaters and had to be reclaimed from inhospitable marshland. The fortunes of the Etruscans depended in part on their skill at draining the semi-flooded flatlands. The larger the plain, of course, the harder and more backbreaking the task of drainage, and the later the date at which it was undertaken. The great stretches of the Po valley, watered by the wild rivers of the Alps and Apennines, were a no man's land for almost the entire prehistoric period. Humans hardly settled there at all until the pile-based dwellings of the *terramare*, in about 1500 B.C.

On the whole, human settlement took more readily to the hillsides, as being more immediately habitable than the plains. Lowland sites, which called for land improvement, could be occupied only by hierarchical societies, those able to create a habitable environment by collective effort. These were the opposite of the high-perched hill settlements, poor but free, with which they had contacts born of necessity, but always tinged with apprehension. The lowlanders felt and wished themselves to be superior: they had plenty to eat and their diet was varied; but their wealth, their cities, their open roads and their fertile crops were a constant temptation to attackers. Telemachus had nothing but contempt for the acorn-eating mountain-dwellers of the Peloponnese. It was logical that Campania and Apulia should dread the peasants of the Abruzzi, shepherds who at the first sign of winter swarmed down with their flocks to the milder climate of the plains. Given the choice, the Campanians would rather face the Roman barbarians than the barbarians from the local mountains. The service Rome rendered southern Italy in the third century B.C. was to bring the wild and threatening massif of the Abruzzi to heel.

Dramatic descents from the mountains took place in every period and in every region of the sea. Mountain people—eaters of acorns and chestnuts, hunters of wild beasts, traders in furs, hides or young livestock, always ready to strike camp and move on—formed a perpetual contrast to lowlanders who remained bound to the soil, some as masters, some as slaves, but all part of a society based on working the land, a society with armies, cities, and seagoing ships. Traces of this dialogue remain even today, between the ice and snow of the austere mountain tops and the lowlands where civilizations and orange-trees have always blossomed.

Life was simply not the same in the hills as in the plains. The plains aimed for progress, the hills for survival. Even the crops, growing at levels only a short walk apart, did not observe the same calendar. Wheat, sown as high up the mountainside as possible, took two months longer to ripen there than at sea level. Climatic disasters meant different things to crops at different altitudes. Late rains in April or May were a blessing in the mountains but a disaster lower down, where the wheat was almost ripe and might rust or rot on the stalk. This was as true of Minoan Crete as of Syria in the seventeenth century A.D. or Algeria in our own time.

The one exception, where the mountains do not come right down to the sea, is the very long and unusually flat seaboard starting at the edge of the Sahara and running hundreds of kilometres, from the Tunisian *sahel* or coastal hills and the round island of Jerba (home of the Lotus-Eaters) to the Nile delta, which empties its fresh, muddy waters far out into the sea. The flat coastline runs even further round, as far as the mountains of Lebanon, which lent the cities of the Phoenicians, on their crowded islands and terraces overlooking the sea, their thoroughly Mediterranean character. Viewed from the air, when landscapes appear in brutal simplicity, the sea and the Sahara come into stark contrast: two great immensities, one blue, the other white shading away into yellow, ochre and orange.

In fact, the desert has had a powerful impact on the physical and human life of the sea. In human terms, every summer saw the desert nomads, a devastating multitude of men, women, children and animals, descend on the coast, pitching camp with their black tents woven from goat or camel hair. As neighbours, they could be troublesome, at times marauding. Like the mountain people, high above the fragile strips of civilization, the nomads were another perpetual menace. Every successful civilization on the Mediterranean coast was obliged to define its stance towards the mountain-dweller and the nomad, whether exploiting them, fighting them off, reaching some compromise with one or other, sometimes even keeping both of them at bay.

In spite of its great size, the desert never completely contained the peoples who inhabited it, but usually propelled them at regular intervals towards the coast, or on to the *sahels*. Only small numbers of people took the caravan routes which criss-crossed the deserts like so many slow sea-passages across the stony and sandy wastes of Africa and Asia—oceans incomparably greater than the Mediterranean. But in the long run, these caravan routes created a fantastic network of connections reaching out to sub-Saharan Africa and the primitive gold-panning of the Senegal and Niger rivers, or the great civilizations bordering the Red Sea, the Persian Gulf and the Indian Ocean, the sites of the earliest experiments in ceramics, metal-working, jewellery, perfumes, miraculous medicines, spices and strange foods.

Physically, too, the desert has always invaded the Mediterranean. Every summer, the hot dry air above the Sahara envelops the entire sea basin, extending far beyond its northern shores. This is what creates those dazzling skies of startling clarity to be seen over the Mediterranean, and a starry night sky found nowhere else in such perfection. The dominant north-easterlies, from April to September, the Aetesian winds as the Greeks called them, bring no relief, no real moisture to the Saharan furnace. There, the summer sky is clouded only for a few short days when the *khamson* blows, or the sirocco, the wind Horace called the *plumbeus Auster*, heavy as lead. These southerly winds carrying grains of sand sometimes dropped from the sky that "rain of blood" which made sages wonder and simple mortals tremble.

Six months of drought, without a drop of rain, is a long time to wait, whether for plants, animals or humans. The forests, the indigenous vegetation of the Mediterranean mountains, could only survive if the inhabitants left them alone and did not build too many roads through them, burn too many clearings for crops, send flocks to graze in them, or fell too many trees for fuel or shipbuilding. Ravaged forests declined fast: maquis and scrub, with their rocky outcrops and fragrant plants and bushes, are the decadent forms of these mighty forests, which were always admired in the ancient Mediterranean as a rare treasure. Carthage, disadvantaged by its African site, sent to Sardinia for timber to build ships. Mesopotamia and Egypt were even worse placed.

The desert retreats only when the ocean advances. From October onwards, rarely earlier and often later, Atlantic depressions, heavy with moisture, begin to roll in from the west. As soon as a depression crosses the Straits of Gibraltar, or makes its way from the Bay of Biscay to the Gulf of Lions, it heads east, attracting from every compass point winds that propel it further eastwards. The sea grows dark, its waters take on the slate-grey tones of the Baltic, or are whipped up by gales into a mass of spray. And the storms begin.

Rain starts to fall, sometimes snow: streams which have been dry for months become torrents, cities disappear behind a curtain of driving rain and low cloud, giving the dramatic skyline of El Greco's paintings of Toledo. This is the season marked by the *imbribus atris* of the ancients, "dark rains" cutting off the light of the sun. Floods are frequent and sudden, rushing down through the plains of Roussillon, or the Mitidja of Algeria, striking Tuscany or Spain, or the countryside round Salonika. Sometimes this torrential rainfall invades the desert, swamping the streets of Mecca, and turning the tracks through the northern Sahara into torrents of mud and water. At Aïn Sefra, south of Oran, Isabelle Eberhardt, a Russian exile fascinated by the desert, was killed in 1904 when a flash flood swept down the wadi.

But the Mediterranean winters have their gentle side too. Snow falls only rarely in the low-lying plains; there can be days of bright sunshine without the cold mistral or bora winds; the sea itself can become unexpectedly calm and the galleys of former times would have been able to risk a brief sortie. And the rain of the stormy season is much needed. The peasants of Aristophanes' plays make merry, drinking and talking the time away while Zeus, with mighty rainstorms, "makes the earth fertile." In cold weather, let us heap logs on the fire and drink, advises Alcaeus, the ancient poet of Mytilene. There will always be time for the few tasks of the winter season: crushing grain or roasting it to keep it edible, heating and reducing sweet wine, cutting vine props, finding a curved branch of evergreen oak to make the plough handle, trapping migrating birds, weaving baskets, taking the mule into town to market.

Real work could only begin again after the last of the spring rains, when the swallows returned, as the old song of Rhodes recalled:

> *Swallow, swallow,*
> *Bringer of spring,*
> *Swallow, white of throat,*
> *Swallow, black of back . . .*

But spring is short-lived, almost over by the time the hyacinths or lilies bloom, or when the tiny flowers appear on the olive trees. The "dragging months of summer" begin, with their interminable round of tasks. The full farming calendar will be interrupted only in autumn, when, according to Hesiod, "the voice of the crane sends its call from the clouds," heralding the time of planting and "the coming of rain-drenched winter."

I have of course simplified the mechanisms of the Mediterranean climate. It is certainly not a perfect agricultural model with two clear seasons; other influences play their part. But this account is not too misleading, so long as we remember that the mechanism can malfunction at times: rain can arrive too early or too late, there can be too much of it or too little, "winter can become like spring," wayward winds may bring an untimely drought or too much water, spring frosts may burn up the young wheat or the vine shoots, and the hot sirocco can parch the grain before it has had time to ripen. Peasant societies in the Mediterranean have always dreaded these surprises which can destroy everything in the twinkling of an eye, as fast as the "plagues of locusts"—and these too were frequent. In Kabylia, when the "gates of the year" opened (equinoxes and solstices), they used to say it was the signal for a new season "with its fortunes: barley bread or famine."

Was the only remedy artificial irrigation, the solution adopted by the earliest civilizations on the banks of rivers such as the Nile, the Euphrates or the Indus? In theory, yes. But even in these cases, some necessary circumstance had to make irrigation imperative. For it was a costly solution, requiring immense effort. Limited in extent, it brought help only to a few regions.

Claudio Vita-Finzi's book *The Mediterranean Valleys* (1969) reminds us that the most spectacular events—volcanic eruptions, earthquakes, climate change—are not the only ones we should notice in retrospective geography. The waterways too have had a role to play, even the coastal streams which so often run dry in the Mediterranean.

Their role is twofold: as carriers of water, debris or alluvial clay, they were basically responsible for creating the arable plains which humans would laboriously cultivate; or as instruments of erosion, they might attack their own valley beds, cutting channels through their own flood plains and shifting them once more. Plato imagined that the waters had carried off "the soft thick layers" of earth in Attica: "all that remains is the bare carcass."

The value of Vita-Finzi's book is not so much that it distinguishes between these two types of long-term action, but that it historicizes their past, suggesting a kind of human history of the waterways that run down to the

Mediterranean. It is an exciting and eventful history, since flowing water mingles with every kind of natural phenomenon; and, more than one might imagine, it has also mingled with the particular destiny of mankind.

In the Paleolithic era, there began a long period of sedimentation, which was also responsible for the layers of ancient alluvial mud, the soils reddened by iron oxide. Between 30,000 and 10,000 B.C., the Nile flowed more abundantly than in the time of the Pharaohs, and accumulated its greatest volumes of mud. The Neolithic Age, when agriculture began, coincided unfortunately with a time of erosion, damaging to arable lands. This carried on until and during the Roman Empire, which sought to combat it by every means, building dykes, dams, and retaining terraces throughout North Africa, from Cyrenaica to Morocco. Halting only briefly, erosion made further advances towards the end of the Empire: water poured in to break the dams and dykes, and fertile soil was washed away. The Middle Ages, in the Mediterranean and elsewhere, were more fortunate: the waterways were more abundant and became once more the source of good river-valley soil. The Arabian geographers of the eleventh, twelfth and thirteenth centuries were even able to compare the Sous, or the Shelif, with its regular flooding, to the Nile. We may think this an exaggeration, but these rivers were not then as they are today. It was in about the sixteenth century that the balance swung back the other way. Erosion began once more, the rivers cut channels through the ancient flats (sometimes forty metres deep) and carried off into the sea all the sand and mud accumulated there. The deltas expanded, but their fertile land was not easy to bring into cultivation. And it seems there is little hope today of finding an effective remedy to this general erosion of the land, which has been going on down to our own time.

The alternation between sedimentation and erosion is explained by changes in the sea level, by variations in the climate (more rainfall brings more erosion) and by human activity which may interfere with the composition of the layers of soil and modify the conditions of flow. This has been part of the equation since the Paleolithic era, when humans first caused forest fires (there are 5000 cubic metres of ash on one Algerian site from the Caspian era); and since Neolithic times, when the critical factors were slash-and-burn agriculture and grazing livestock.

These considerations open up new perspectives and oblige us to revise previous hypotheses. If the Roman Campagna was depopulated and became wasteland in the fourth century A.D., the reason may be sought not only in human negligence but in the increased waterflow which washed gravel and unhealthy waters down to the low-lying regions. Similarly, when malaria became virulent there in the sixteenth century, it was because water had flooded the flatlands and stayed there, obliging the residents either to wage war unremittingly against floodwaters, or to abandon the site.

All this helps to explain too why hill farming persisted and came to be of exceptional value in the Mediterranean: up above the waterlogged valleys, on the mountain slopes, a combination of wheat, olives, vines and fig-trees was cultivated from earliest times.

Let me sum up. We are too inclined to think of Mediterranean life as *la dolce vita*, effortlessly easy. But we are allowing the charms of the landscape to deceive us. Arable land is scarce there, while arid and infertile mountains are everywhere present ("plenty of bones, not enough meat" as one geographer has put it). Rainfall is unevenly distributed: plentiful when the vegetation is hibernating in winter, it disappears just when plant growth needs it. Wheat, like other annual plants, has to ripen quickly. Human labour is not relieved by the climate: all the heavy work has always had to be done when the summer heat is at its fiercest, and the resulting harvest crop is all too often meagre. Hesiod's advice in summer was to go "naked to sow, naked to plough, naked to reap," and Virgil repeated the tag: *nudus ara, sere nudus*. If the grain is in short supply at the end of the year, he adds, "then shake the oak tree of the forests to satisfy your hunger."

To all this, it should be added that the water of the Mediterranean, always quite warm, near 13 degrees centigrade over most of its area (hence the warm winter climate), is biologically very poor. The naturalist who knows the Atlantic, and then witnesses the "hauling up of pots and nets" in the Mediterranean, is astonished not to find there "that squirming variety of sea life that characterizes the rich ocean deeps." There are few species of fish and shellfish and most of them are small. There are of course some famous fishing-grounds, the lagoon of Comacchio, the lake of Bizerte, the Riviera of the Bosphorus and in the Hellespont the "passes of Abydos, rich in oysters." Shoals of tuna are hunted every year off the coast of Sicily, North Africa, Provence and Andalusia. But for all that, the overall harvest is lean. The *frutti di mare* may be exquisite perhaps, but their stocks are limited. There are several reasons for the shortfall. The coasts plunge abruptly into the water without shelving—and coastal shelves are the habitat of sea creatures. The animal and vegetable plankton is very poor—almost as bad as in the Sargasso Sea, where the surface water for that very reason has the same blue transparency as the Mediterranean. And lastly there is the complicated marine history, which is responsible for frequent sudden shifts of salinity and temperature: the local species have been decimated one after another.

It is its narrow opening into the Atlantic that has been the Mediterranean's lifeline. Imagine if a dam were to seal up the Strait of Gibraltar: the Mediterranean would be transformed into a salt lake from which all life would disappear. If on the other hand it was more open to the Atlantic, the sea would be reinvigorated, revived by the traffic of the tides, invaded by oceanic fauna. The surface water would be disturbed, the exceptional warmth in winter would vanish. Which would we prefer? Perhaps we should be resigned to eating frozen fish from the Atlantic, which is brought regularly to the Mediterranean. Then when we visit Venice, it will be a great luxury to order an *orata di ferri* not from the lagoon but from the free waters of the Adriatic, landed from one of those beautiful fishing smacks from Chioggia with their painted sails.

But what about the riches of the sea itself, the reader may wonder. We can all conjure up images of a Mediterranean jewelled with islands, its coastlines indented by harbours, those schools for mariners, an invitation to travel and trade. In fact the sea did not always in the past provide that "natural link" between countries and peoples so often described. A very long apprenticeship had to be served. Almost as daunted by the sea as later generations would be by the sky, primitive peoples did not risk taking to the waves in the Mediterranean until the twelfth and eleventh millennia B.C. at the very earliest, more likely the sixth and fifth (dates of which we are much more certain)—and even then it was a brave venture. But starting an apprenticeship does not mean attaining mastery all at once. Only with the third millennium B.C., if then, did fleets become of practical importance; in the second, effective trade became possible, and not until the first did ships sail out beyond the Pillars of Hercules on to the trackless waters of the Sea of Darkness.

So although they were attempted very early, these "haphazard voyages" did not become regular and civilized (though not always safe) shipping roads until very late in the day. While the network of maritime links was comparatively dense, it operated only on certain coasts, from certain ports. Crossings were mostly made across narrow stretches of the sea, or in one of the sea-basins into which the Mediterranean is divided and which acted as so many semi-insulated economies. "He who sails beyond Cape Malea," said a Greek proverb, "must forget his native land."

As a result, the Mediterranean world was long divided into autonomous areas, only precariously linked. The entire globe is today far more united as between its constituent parts than the Mediterranean was in the age of Pericles. This is a truth one should never lose sight of even when contemplating the apparent tranquillity and unity of the Pax Romana. The plural always outweighs the singular. There are ten, twenty or a hundred Mediterraneans, each one sub-divided in turn. To spend even a moment alongside real fishermen, yesterday or today, is to realize that everything can change from one locality to another, one seabed to another, from sandbank to rocky reef. But the same is equally true on land. Yes, we can always tell that we are somewhere near the Mediterranean: the climate of Cádiz is quite like that of Beirut, the Provençal riviera looks not unlike the south coast of the Crimea, the vegetation on the Mount of Olives near Jerusalem could equally well be in Sicily. But we would find that no two areas are actually farmed alike, no two regions bind and stake the vines the same way—in fact we would not find the same vines, the same olive-trees, fig-trees or bay-trees, the same houses or the same kind of costume. To understand the essentially dual character of Dalmatia, one would have to have seen the port of Ragusa (Dubrovnik) in February during the Feast of Saint Blaise, when the city was transformed by music and dancing, and thronged by men and women from the mountains. These differences have often only been partly created by geography. It is the historical past, persistently creating differences and particularities, that has accentuated these variations, leaving colourful traces which still delight us.

The unified image of the sea is in any case belied by some major contrasts. The north can never be taken for the south; *a fortiori* the eastern Mediterranean is not the same as the west. The Mediterranean stretches out so far along the parallels that the Sicilian bar bisects it rather than bringing the fragments together.

Between the south coast of Sicily and the low-lying shores of Africa, the sea is not very deep. It seems to heave up its bed: one more effort and a barrier would run from north to south. These shallow waters are signalled by the string of islands stretching from Sicily to the Tunisian coast with its coral and sponges: Malta, Gozo, Pantelleria, Lampedusa, Zembra, the Kerkennah islands, Jerba. I can remember flying from Tunisia to Sicily, or between Greece and Italy, in the days of flying-boats which took you low over the sea: you could make out even the white edge of the Trapani saltmarshes in western Sicily, the shadows of the boats on the seabed close in to shore, and the channels of deeper blue water marking the surface currents. You could even see Corfu and the Gulf of Taranto at the same time! I always imagine the dividing line between the two Mediterraneans on this imaginary aerial map, made up of memories laid end to end. It is a line marked by some of the stirring episodes in Mediterranean history. But that is hardly surprising. North against south meant Rome against Carthage; east against west meant the Orient against the Occident, Islam against Christendom. If all the battles of the past were to be plotted together on the map, they would describe a long combat zone stretching from Corfu through Actium, Lepanto, Malta and Zama to Jerba.

History has demonstrated over and again that the two basins of the Mediterranean, the east and west, have been comparatively self-contained worlds, even if they have at times exchanged ships, commodities, people and even beliefs. In the end, the sea itself obliged them to co-exist, but they have always been quarrelling brothers, opposed to each other in everything. Even the sky and its colours look different either side of Sicily. The east is lighter: in a sea more purple than blue, or wine-dark as Homer called it, the Cyclades are patches of luminous orange, Rhodes a black mass, Cyprus a shape of intense blue. Or that is how I saw them, one afternoon, flying from Athens to Beirut. We may criticize progress, but if you want to see the Mediterranean, the best thing you could do as an introduction would be to fly over it on a clear day in a little plane which is not travelling too high or in too much of a hurry.

Immense though the Mediterranean was if measured by the travelling speeds of the past, it has never been confined inside its own history. It rapidly outstripped its own borders, looking westward to the Atlantic, eastward to the Levant which was to fascinate it for centuries on end, south to the desert marches beyond the palm groves, north one way to the rolling Eurasian steppes that border the Black Sea, and north the other way to the slow-developing Europe of forests, beyond the traditionally sacrosanct northern limit of the olive tree. The life and history of the Mediterranean do not stop—as the geographer, the botanist or even the historian might have imagined—at the point where the last olive tree has been left behind.

It is in fact the major feature of the sea's destiny that it should be locked inside the largest group of landmasses on the globe, the "gigantic linked continent" of Europe-Asia-Africa, a sort of planet in itself, where goods and people circulated from earliest times. Human beings found a theatre for their historical drama in these three conjoined continents. This was where the crucial exchanges took place.

And since this human history was in perpetual motion, flowing down to the shores of the Mediterranean where it regularly came to a halt, is it any wonder that the sea should so soon have become one of the living centres of the universe, and that in turn it should have sent resonant echoes through these massive continents, which were a kind of sounding-board for it? The history of the Mediterranean lent an ear to the distant sounds of universal history, but its own music could be heard from far away too. This two-way flow was the essential feature of a past marked by a double movement: the Mediterranean both gave and received—and the "gifts" exchanged might be calamities as well as benefits. Everything was in the mixture and, as we shall see, the brilliant arrival of the earliest civilizations in the Mediterranean can already be explained as the coming together of different elements.

CHAPTER TWO

The Long March to Civilization

Taking our bearings within the familiar spatial compass of the Mediterranean calls for little effort. We have only to close our eyes and memories flood in: we can picture Venice, Provence, Sicily, Malta or Istanbul. But taking our bearings across the total span of lived time in the same Mediterranean raises problems of a quite different order. Going in search of lost time is like unrolling an endless ribbon: the further back we go, the harder it is to keep hold of it.

When we embark on this backward journey, should we stop at the turn of the third millennium B.C.? For this was when truly established civilizations first appeared in the Middle East—with their fields, domestic animals and clustered villages, their towns, gods, princes, scribes, ships and trade. These are the classic civilizations, recognizable from our schoolbooks, and still the normal starting point for all teaching about history. Egypt and Mesopotamia seem almost familiar territory. But perhaps it is misleading to grant them this status as the take-off point in human history?

Their era did indeed mark a sensational turning point. The great watershed in human history was not the fall of the Roman Empire, as leading historians of a former generation used to think (Fustel de Coulanges, Ferdinand Lot, Henri Pirenne) but the emergence of two key developments: agriculture and writing. This is where the waters of the world divide, with "prehistory" on one side and "history" in the *traditional* (and too narrow) meaning of the term, on the other. We can agree on this; but contrary to what was once thought, agriculture and writing did not appear at the same moment.

From the most recent archaeological discoveries, we now know that the earliest forms of agriculture, the earliest domestication of wild animals, the first signs of awareness of the human condition, the first pottery and bronze artefacts, the first sea voyages, did not begin with the Sumerians, or with Menes-Harmer, the first legendary pharaoh of Egypt, but some two, three or four millennia earlier, in Asia Minor, Palestine and Iraq. We would probably no longer dare agree with the author of a (nevertheless rather good) book published in 1958 that *History Begins at Sumer*. Sumerian civilization did not spring from nowhere. And since we are beginning to find out more about what happened centuries or even millennia before that civilization, the urge to penetrate further into the earlier past becomes more pressing.

I

THE LOWER PALEOLITHIC: THE FIRST ARTEFACTS, THE FIRST PEOPLE

I shall therefore follow the advice of Alfred Weber, a sociologist who cared passionately about history. As early as 1935, he was saying that if we really wanted to know what human beings are and where they come from, we would have to start from prehistory in its entirety. But we should recognize that that is easier said than done. In those timeless ages before writing was invented, there was no Herodotus to describe the Egypt of his day, no cuneiform or hieroglyphic script for scholars to decipher. Once human beings start to speak and write down their words, there is some chance that we might understand them. But without any written documents, how are we to imagine their life, their legends, their religions?

Our only recourse is archaeology, of course, a special kind of science and even more complicated when applied to prehistory, since that compounds one uncertain science with another. The talented popularizer C. W. Ceram once described archaeologists as detectives, looking not for corpses and murderers but for skeletons, shards of pottery and fragments of tools. These detectives will never succeed in uncovering the whole truth, but may patiently piece together the fragments, devising overall explanations if they have a bent for generalizations—and that is always dangerous. New excavations can at any moment demolish what might have seemed a very plausible version of the past.

Every archaeological site uncovers a series of layers from different ages, each with its traces of human activity. Ideally, one would wish to dig down to virgin soil, to the earliest occupation of the site. In Crete for example, on the site of Knossos, fifteen metres represents the vertical distance between the present day and the seventh millennium B.C. (the beginning of the Neolithic, when the island was apparently first occupied by humans). Every excavation therefore creates its own chronology: "this" must have happened before "that." The difficulty lies in matching one chronology with those from other sites and in charting that elusive "absolute" chronology which is the dream of every archaeologist.

There are several approaches to this task, the most sensational of which has been radio-carbon dating, devised by the American chemist William F. Libby in 1946. This enables us to date things as far back as 60,000 years ago. Plants, animals and humans all absorb during their lifetime a certain amount of radioactive carbon, which is progressively lost from their remains. This loss is measurable and becomes a sort of retrospective clock, with some margin of error, some exceptions, generally self-evident, and some astonishing results, which can be verified when they coincide with those obtained by other means. The problem is that carbon dating has not been applied to all sites, and the results of excavations still under way may not be published for some time. So archaeological knowledge is always in a state of flux. But even Sherlock Holmes sometimes had to abandon his first hypotheses and start again.

From the earliest days, the human species was present across the whole surface of the Ancient World. Essentially, then, the early history of the Mediterranean and the early history of mankind went hand in hand from the start. This history moved slowly, so slowly that its chronological stages are measured not even in millennia—which would be meaningless—but in tens and hundreds of millennia. It is not easy for us even to begin to understand the dimensions of such a fabulous, unthinkable stretch of time.

There were probably "three stages in human evolution, starting from our hominid ancestors: Australopithecus, Pithecanthropus and the Hominoidae." Pithecanthropus, who is found all over the Ancient World, is often called *Homo erectus*: in other words, the emergence of the human species is traced back to this stage. But on what criteria, and at what stage can we see mankind beginning? The use of tools was once regarded as the defining moment, but we now know that Australopithecus, who is found all over Africa, was already able to fashion tools out of stone and to use them, possibly as many as three million years ago. That takes us to the beginning of the Quaternary era. Before that, the hominids of the Miocene and Pliocene eras, ancestors of Australopithecus, were links in a chain of primates and, like them, were in turn related to other species. In this endless sequence of evolution, "mankind" was just an accident, an infinitely precious one in view of what was to follow, but certainly belated and of small significance if viewed on the scale of the earth's existence. One prehistorian famously used a telling metaphor to describe it: if we imagine the entire biological evolution of life on earth as contained within the cycle of one solar year, with the very first signs of life appearing on 1 January, the earliest prehominid species would appear at about five thirty on the afternoon of 31 December; Neanderthal man would show up at about twenty minutes to midnight; and the entire existence of *Homo sapiens*, from the Stone Age to our own time, would be contained in the last few minutes of the year.

For our present purpose, we shall be concerned with mankind only from the point at which the species had embarked on its human destiny, had converted to walking upright on two legs (*Homo erectus*) and thus had full use of its hands, making it possible to pit its intelligence and the tools it could now handle against the combined obstacles of a hostile natural environment. These tools, made from crude stone, whether hewn, split or much later polished, offer us almost the only clue as we trace the steps of a long technological journey, with recognizable stages at very long intervals.

We are faced with a huge time-span: at least a million years.[1] How are we to find any bearings in this vast expanse of time? Traditionally, history has used the terms Antiquity, the Middle Ages and Modern Times. We can distinguish a similar tripartite division in prehistory: the Paleolithic (the Old Stone Age); Mesolithic (Middle Stone Age); and Neolithic (New Stone Age). But these three ages are of enormously uneven lengths. The Paleolithic runs from at least a million years B.C. to 10,000 or 8000 B.C.[2] Over the next four or five millennia came the decisive ages of the Mesolithic and Neolithic, varying greatly between regions however, and eventually leading to the Bronze Age, which broadly corresponds to the age of writing. This disproportion in duration is of capital importance. The Paleolithic lasted a very long time indeed: 99 per cent of human existence so far took place then.

Logically, then, scholars have taken to distinguishing several periods within the long Paleolithic era: Lower, Middle and Upper. Here too, the difference in time-scale is fantastic: in round figures about one million years for the Old or Lower Paleolithic; 40,000 for the Middle,[3] less than 30,000 for the Upper. Nothing indicates more clearly the late appearance of progress. First came an empty monotonous age, marked only by the very slow evolution of the species; then the process speeded up, punctuated by new developments and by what can almost be called events, especially after the crucial emergence of Neanderthal man in about 100,000 B.C., and of *Homo sapiens*, who may have appeared at about the same time, but who became widespread only in about 30,000 B.C.

But it is above all the tools that these early humans made, and their successive refinements, which have become markers for the traditional chronological divisions. Here we shall have to use a terminology which may seem odd to the layman, and lacking any obvious logic, since the stages in prehistoric tool-making have been named after the archaeological sites where the first characteristic discoveries were made. Since France was the location of many finds, and since numerous pioneers of prehistorical studies were French, many of these names come from French sites: Abbeville, Saint-Acheul, Levallois, La Gravette, Solutré, La Madeleine—but there are English ones too (Clacton-on-Sea) as well as variants found in North Africa, Palestine, etc. A table in Appendix I lists this long series of names, which is not repeated here; rather we need to understand its symbolic meaning. It would certainly be preferable to have some kind of systematic typology synthesizing all the finds. But is that possible? It would mean jettisoning the scientific language which has now been used regularly for over a hundred years.

The Lower and Middle Paleolithic, which many specialists prefer not to separate, consisted first of all of countless ages when a mere split pebble with one or two cutting edges was the only implement (the so-called Pebble Culture). After that we can begin to speak of the Abbeville, Saint-Acheul, Clacton, Levallois or Mousterian periods. Each of these refers to a different kind of stone-age technology: double-sided hand-axes, made by chipping both sides of a large lump of flint to reduce it in size and narrow it to a triangular piercing point; choppers cut by the same method, but ending in an edge not a point; and then all the tools based on splinters of flint. With the Mousterian-Levallois period, which corresponds to a long plateau in the Middle Paleolithic, improved techniques made it possible to obtain flakes rather than splinters of flint. The two-sided all-purpose tools came to have a more regular and functional shape. The splinter-tools were refined by fine bevelling, giving them sharp edges and making them into specialized items. This skill would soon enable Neanderthal men, who flourished in the Middle Paleolithic, to combine wooden handles and stone tools: by fixing a stone arrow-head to a wooden stake, they could arm themselves more effectively against wild beasts.

But this breakthrough, heralding the crucial advances made during the Upper Paleolithic (sometimes known as the Leptolithic or "light" Stone Age), was a late development. For long ages, the primitive tools used by the human species meant that men were ineffective predators, poorly equipped hunters who had to be content with catching slow or immature animals; they sometimes fell prey themselves to wild beasts who were stronger and faster. Fishing, gathering or scavenging, human beings were nomads, living in tiny groups constantly on the move from one hunting-ground to another, subject to hunger since they had few reserves, and only occasionally meeting other groups of humans with whom they might fight or barter a few objects.

As time went by, these small bands of people began to travel very far afield. Although we cannot reconstruct even approximate itineraries, we know that their possessions, especially stone tools with their easily recognized manufacture, must have been carried over fabulous distances. We can detect the same "civilization" or rather the same method of stone-cutting all round the Mediterranean at periods which more or less concur, at least in the early stages of the Lower Paleolithic: tools of the Abbeville or Saint-Acheul type have been found in North Africa, Spain, Syria and the Balkans. Later, especially from the Upper Paleolithic onwards, there would be irregular developments, with some regions forging ahead while others lagged behind. The western Maghreb seems to have been a region slow to develop in the late Paleolithic or early Neolithic Age, although the experts are not all agreed on this.

Certainly the working of small flints, the microliths which developed in Europe at the end of the Paleolithic and especially in the Mesolithic, as well as the use of a whole range of small tools each devised for a special purpose, can be attested everywhere, from Scotland to the Cape of Good Hope, from the Atlantic to the Vindhya mountains in India, or to the Mongolian desert, over areas far exceeding the bounds of the Mediterranean. The taste for ornament—shell necklaces and bracelets, ochre body-paint—seems to have been very marked and was no doubt linked to belief in magic. We know that ornaments travelled long distances, since amber from the north has been found in the Pyrenees.

Sooner or later, all the accessible regions round the rim of the Mediterranean would witness the arrival of these tiny groups of primitive hunters. They have left traces almost everywhere of their passage or settlement. Corsica and Sardinia, as islands far out to sea, may have had to wait until the third millennium to be inhabited by seaborne settlers, but if so they were the exception that proved the rule.[4] Twenty or thirty years ago, it was thought that the immigrants who brought the "Neolithic revolution" to the Greek archipelago had also landed on soil previously untouched by human habitation. The Abbé Breuil was one of the sceptics: "Seek and ye shall find," as he put it. And indeed now that systematic excavation has been set in train in Greece, Paleolithic sites have one after another come to light. The hunting people of the early Stone Age did not leave many regions unexplored. Only wide expanses of sea could stop them.

Their presence almost everywhere was in fact achieved over time, over an almost unimaginable stretch of time, millennia after millennia. The early Stone Age culture had plenty of time to work its way round the Ancient World, spreading in waves of identical nature. It was only when progress began to be made (relatively) quickly at the end of the Paleolithic and above all the Neolithic that serious time-lags began to create privileged areas, introducing differences in the degree of development. But as is always the case, these imbalances were to result in increased compensatory exchanges between zones, leading in turn to further progress.

In this slow-motion past, there was one forceful, or at any rate dominant feature, capable of upsetting everything: the climate. For reasons still uncertain (see below) it was subject to constant change. From the beginning of the Villefranche period at the start of the Quaternary era, it was the cause of many upheavals. This was the most dramatic aspect of these far-off millennia. Geology has made it possible to detect past climatic change and almost to map its effects, but here, too, we should remember that these awesome fluctuations occurred over very long time-spans, with change accumulating long before its presence becomes visible.

The most spectacular sign of these worldwide disruptions was the accumulation, at four different periods, of enormous masses of ice to the north of the Ancient World and America, giant glaciers like those which still cover Greenland and the Antarctic today, up to two or three kilometres deep. The advance and retreat of these monster glaciers, the *inlandsis*, were traumatic. When they expanded, it meant that the cold landmasses and fronts of polar air moved southwards towards the Mediterranean. At such times, the sea must have been subject to very low temperatures. At the same time, the cold northern air also displaced towards the Mediterranean almost all the cyclonic Atlantic depressions. Colder weather was accompanied by long periods of heavy rain, so the Mediterranean must have experienced several cold "rainy periods," alternating with comparatively warm dry periods when the glaciers retreated northwards again. Rushing torrents in the valleys, frosts cold enough to split stone on the peaks—all these phenomena of the past are recorded in the ancient alluvial deposits of the Paleolithic era.

But this general explanation is probably not sufficient to account for all possible climatic variation, since the Sahara also witnessed alternate periods of drought and humidity, which do not exactly match the chronology of those in the Mediterranean. Experts have suggested that another system of winds, temperatures and rainfall was responsible, a monsoon system centred on equatorial and tropical Africa, which may also have moved north and south by turns. Its moisture-laden influence may have been extended northwards at the time of the third interglacial period, creating the anomalous Saharan landscapes of "Lake Chad and the hippopotamus"; then there may have been an extension even further north at the end of the Ice Ages, which would explain the extraordinary flowering of the Saharan Neolithic Age, with its pastoral peoples, probably black, its remarkable cave-paintings of giraffes, elephants and gazelles, and its surprising agricultural achievements, short-lived miniature Egypts on the banks of the rivers flowing through the desert.

It is naturally tempting to link such climatic crises with changes in the destinies of living organisms, whether humans, flora or fauna, and with the disappearance or evolution of different species. But caution is more appropriate: these climatic shifts, while certainly dramatic for Europe, where they must have had an impact on human evolution, were virtually unknown in other parts of the world. And while it is true that plants, animals and humans would all have suffered from these devastating and invariably long-lasting shifts in the climate, the human race has a "tendency to disobey"; in any case, all living things react and often adapt when faced with obstacles, sometimes simply moving away to escape them. So changes in the fauna do not inevitably provide incontrovertible evidence about climate change.

It is all the same surprising to find that there were reindeer in western Europe well before the last great Ice Age (the Würm) and particularly strange to think of them in the Paris basin or on the plateaux of Castile; it is equally amazing to find the "beady-eyed mammoth" in cave-paintings at Rouffignac in the Périgord in France. These are not isolated cases. What are we to make of the remains of northern birds, and of a giant penguin, at Romanelli near Lecce on the heel of Italy, or, coming from the other direction, remains of hippopotami in the Pontine marches? It is true that the "woolly hippopotamus," now extinct, was adapted to a cold climate! The history of the elephant (Atlantic, Asian and African), with quite separate species corresponding to different climates, is an example of the possibility that any living creature could adapt. The remains of ancient elephants on Delos proves that the island was once attached to the mainland. In Sicily, Sardinia, Crete, Cyprus and Malta, the bones of dwarf elephants point to the degeneration of an ancient species, literally trapped when the islands broke away. In 1960, excavations at Larissa in Thessaly brought to light "mammoth and hippopotamus bones as well as tools made of flint and bone of the Levallois-Mousterian type." And there are plenty of similar examples: in 1940, cave-paintings were discovered in La Baume-Latrone, probably from the Aurignac period: a frieze of elephants and rhinoceros, depicted schematically, almost like a comic strip.

But animal remains can sometimes provide almost unbroken evidence about past climatic changes. On Mount Carmel in Palestine, archaeologists have been able to trace the alternating fortunes of the gazelle, which thrives in a dry climate with plenty of sunshine, and the roe deer, "which is suited to living in forests" and to the damp and temperate climate of the rainy periods. An entertaining graph showing this seesaw relationship has been compiled from traces of both species in different archaeological layers. As the climate altered, each species, true to its nature, sought refuge further north or south, in search either of warmth or of moisture. But these involuntary migrants were faced with the barrier of the Mediterranean. When the ice spread south, the "cold-weather species" were pulled up short by the sea. When the ice retreated, the "warm-weather species" could not easily reach the north shore and its hinterland. It was only in the vast African continent, or more likely in the great landmass of Eurasia, that large-scale migration might lead to free competition between species and to unexpected cross-breeding. This was one of several advantages of the Middle East region.

Vegetation and its combinations could also provide evidence that may be clearer and less disconcerting, although not without complications. But the fascinating science of paleo-botany is still in its infancy. We shall have to wait, but there are surely surprises in store here.

———

Over the surface of the globe, water in all its forms, liquid, solid and vapour, forms a constant mass. The amount of water locked up in glaciers is therefore related to the overall sea level. The latter falls when the glaciers advance, and rises when they melt. The difference may be as little as ten metres, a hundred at most. But this is enough to cause major change to coastlines all over the globe, change which can be charted with some accuracy. Thus the Adriatic, which was once partly dry land, prolonged the Po valley as far as Ancona; the Gulf of Lions, similarly, was a shelf attached to the mainland; Corsica and Sardinia formed a single island landmass, possibly even a peninsula; the low-lying Suez isthmus (only 15 metres above sea level) has several times been flooded by the sea, turning Africa into an island; the Aegean was a landmass throughout the Paleolithic (Asia Minor being joined to Greece); and the Black Sea was a lake, linked by a narrow channel to the Caspian. But the Strait of Gibraltar, where the water is comparatively deep, has apparently never been a corridor of dry land. It is also doubtful whether Tunisia was ever linked to Sicily, though the latter was certainly once joined to Italy. These observations explain why some islands were settled in very ancient times, as well as some odd features of their flora and fauna. Above the present-day level of the Mediterranean, ancient sea shores mark what were once high sea levels and beaches. All those bell towers halfway up hills on the Genoese riviera, forming a sort of amphitheatre looking down on the sea, trace the shoreline of onetime beaches, where villages now perch as if on a balcony.

Changes in sea level also led invariably to further erosion of watercourses. The rivers dug down into their own alluvial plains, so ancient terraces mark the slopes of onetime river valleys. These frequent accidents played a part in the choice of site made by prehistoric peoples for their settlements. And since geologists are able to date these accidents, it becomes easier to propose a plausible chronology.

The term "geological revolution" to describe the cataclysms of prehistory was coined by Alfred Weber. It is a controversial expression: while we certainly know that the geographical environment varied dramatically during the years of prehistory, were the humans who lived on earth during the Aurignac or

Solutré periods ever really conscious of the instability of their physical sur-
roundings, season by season, year by year? Climatic variations extend over
many centuries and obey very long-term rhythms. Are they the result of local
or general disturbances? Are they, for instance, caused by variations in solar
activity as some experts think, or—as was once suggested, though I think no
one would dare hazard it today, since it seemed too good to be true—because
of a shift in the polar axis? According to this theory, the North Pole was originally located in what is now Greenland and gradually moved to its present
position: this would have benefited Europe and North America but would
have been bad news for Siberia. The disappearance of the Siberian mammoths, some of which are still to be found preserved in the permafrost, and
which were the source of a flourishing trade in ivory as late as the twelfth century A.D., might be evidence of such a shift.

Nothing of the kind has ever been proved. But we can still wonder at
these cosmic revolutions which are yet to be explained: awesome transformations which for once really did change the face of the world.

II
FIRE, ART AND MAGIC

In a universe where living creatures were the playthings of the blind forces of
nature for thousands of years, in which so many animal species drove one
another into extinction, man gradually came to occupy a special place. He
overcame the obstacle of a determinism which should in theory have defeated
him; he safeguarded his achievements and "capitalized" on them, committing
them to memory and thus improving the tools he had developed. Biologically
too, the human race evolved. The most impressive evidence is that the size of
the human brain increased steadily. "Human progress" had begun everywhere
simultaneously, at a snail's pace of course, but from now on it was unstop-
pable. The Upper Paleolithic was to witness some extraordinary developments.

During the Middle Paleolithic, from about 100,000 B.C.,[5] all of Europe and
the Mediterranean basin was occupied by the people we know by the name
"Neanderthal man." Biologists no longer consider this species as primitive
and brutish. Despite his heavy jaw, low and receding brow and ape-like pos-

ture, Neanderthal man was a fairly close relation of his conqueror, *Homo sapiens*, and possibly a sub-species of the same. In recent times, it has been thought that he might have been a cross between Pithecanthropus and *Homo sapiens*, although this would oblige us to rethink much of our data.[6] Neanderthal man was at any rate responsible for perfecting the techniques of flint-knapping in the Levallois era, thanks to a method of obtaining splinters by calculating the angle of strike to obtain a desired shape. A few finishing touches and the tool was ready for use. Wood and stone were now combined to make implements and for the first time humans began to bury their dead, something which implies that rituals already existed, and that people had the capacity to reflect on death and the afterlife, a mental step which many pre-historians consider to mark the true birth of humanity. It is true that Neanderthal man had not yet taken the step, crucial for a hunting species, of developing weapons to be thrown; nor had he yet discovered any form of artistic expression or indeed language (or so it is thought, but how do we know?). At any rate it seems highly probable that he was the inventor of arti-ficially created fire. Until then, naturally occurring blazes were the only source of flames for human use, and they had to be carefully preserved. But to be able to produce fire at will, to "manufacture" it, was a formidable step for-ward, a "means of production" and guarantee of security—the greatest revo-lution before the coming of agriculture.

The Neanderthalers died out, however, in about 40,000 B.C., during the upheavals which accompanied the last major cold strike, the so-called Würm Ice Age. Was the problem that they were in some sense a mistake, an "evolu-tionary dead end," or was it simply that their low numbers made them unsus-tainable? One expert suggests that there were no more than about twenty thousand individuals scattered over the area that is present-day France (a number which cannot of course be confirmed, but is based on the number of authenticated sites, so is not blind guesswork). In their stead, mixing with them and eliminating them—perhaps by force although we do not really know that—a different human population became established and took over on a global scale. This was *Homo sapiens*, that is our own species, with the var-ious racial differences which still distinguish us from each other today. This was a species already the result of cross-breeding, "like a mongrel dog" as Marcelin Boule put it. Since inter-breeding between different races appears to have produced greater intelligence, it was obviously a good thing. Certain experts have claimed that in the area occupied by France alone, traces can be found of a white race, Cro-Magnon, in the Dordogne; an Inuit-type Lagerie man, at Chancelade, also in the Dordogne; and a Negro-type man at Grimaldi near Menton. "They are all still very close to us," writes R.-L. Nougier. "The Guanches of the Canaries are living examples of Cro-Magnon, and many peasant families in the Dordogne and Charente, tall and dolicho-cephalic, still display some of the same features. The Inuit peoples are descended from the Magdalenian people of Chancelade, while the residual Bushmen and Hottentot people of distant South Africa have affinities with the people of the Grimaldi caves." This all sounds a bit too neat to be true. But S. Coon's remarkable book on *The Origin of Races* firmly states that all the races present in the world today were already present before the final stage of evolution which produced *Homo sapiens*. As for this last-named, does he go back a very long way, 100,000 years B.C., with much the same appearance as today—as a UNESCO symposium suggested in September 1969? Prehistorians make jokes like everyone else, and one of them, F. Bordes, tells us that if *Homo sapiens* from 100,000 years ago were to "be dressed in present-day clothes, no one would turn round in the street." Well, perhaps we can believe him . . .

To sum up, whether very ancient or not, *Homo sapiens* appeared at about the same time in Europe and the Mediterranean. With his emergence—though now showing substantial regional differences—the evidence points to an increase in the rate of progress, from the Aurignac to the Gravettian, Solutré and Magdalenian periods. The range of everyday implements was extended by the production of fine stone blades and before long the emergence of more specialized tools: knives, chisels, scrapers and so on. The new technology involved placing between the hammer and the lump of flint a "chisel" made of some material less hard than stone, usually wood. Flakes of flint were shaped into long, light sharp-edged blades. At the same time, the original two-sided axes, which had already become slimmer in the Neanderthal period, were fashioned in the shape of crescents or leaves, light and sharp. These finely honed tools made excellent spearheads; the invention of the haft, a wooden stick with a groove into which the spearhead fitted, would turn it into a valuable acquisition, a really long-distance weapon. This projectile can be dated to the Magdalenian period. By the end of the Paleolithic, it was being replaced by the bow and arrow, a landmark invention which would be the standard equipment for hunters and warriors for thousands of years to come.

In addition, other materials were now being worked on with flint chisels: horn, bone and ivory, substances which were easy to split, slice, carve and polish. They would be used to make arrowheads, harpoons, awls, bradawls, fish-hooks, eyed needles—all objects found in abundance in deposits from the Solutré period onward.

All these objects also began to be decorated with patterns, carvings and engravings. Art now appeared for the first time in human history, and in many different forms: a fantastic development!

This art of the Paleolithic era seems to have been a feature of Europe as far as the Urals. It is found in the western Mediterranean, though very little in the eastern half, with one exception: the carvings and objects discovered in the caves and rock shelters of Belbasi in southern Anatolia. So the Middle East, where some millennia later the first forms of agriculture would develop, followed by the first cities and densely settled societies—the cradle of many original civilizations and cultures, all rich in art and technology—was *not* the site of the earliest forms of artistic expression in the Paleolithic era. All the *technical* innovations of the Upper Paleolithic in the way of implements have been found in the eastern basin, as well as along the North African coast, sometimes (in Syria, Palestine and Cyrenaica) in more sophisticated form than in the French sites, as revealed by carbon dating. But it seems that apart from Belbasi, there are no surviving traces there of Paleolithic art. The cave paintings of the Sahara and Libya date from much later, so are not relevant here.

This early Paleolithic art even seems to be altogether foreign to the Mediterranean in origin. The so-called Gravettian culture probably origi-nated in central Europe and Russia, and from there spread to what are now France, Spain and Italy, at a time when the Adriatic was still partly dry land, providing overland access between Italy and the Balkans. It is from this period that we can date the amazing female figurines made of stone, clay or mammoth ivory which have been found in southern Russia and Siberia, at Modena and Ventimiglia, and in Austria, Moravia and the Dordogne. About sixty or so have been discovered, most of them unarguably of similar origin: the heavy breasts, massive thighs and rounded pregnant bellies of these so-called Venuses are unambiguously some kind of symbol of fertility and prosperity, foreshadowing the mother-goddesses who would be venerated by all the agricultural cultures of the Neolithic, from the Middle East to Portu-gal, from Siberia to the Atlantic and elsewhere.

Perhaps with these figures, we hold a piece of essential evidence. Can we say that this stage of human development, starting with the so-called Aurignac culture, represents the basic religious prototype of humanity? I am inclined to agree with Jean Przyluski's synthesizing theory: what was beginning to take shape here, after an immensely long period when the instinct to survive was paramount, was the first stage—ritual magic—in a religious life which would take many long ages to move beyond this. Art itself had its source in magic. In the Paleolithic, there is very little representation of the human form for its own sake, as distinct from symbolic rituals. There are a few exceptions: in Moravia, a tiny carving has been found, a mere five centimetres of carved stone, in which a miraculously powerful human torso is depicted. (To a French eye it is reminiscent of the sculptures of Maillol.) And a tiny ivory carving of a face, as moving as an unfinished portrait, has been found at Brassempouy in France. Both of these suggest that models of human beauty were the source of inspiration, as distinct from the steatopygic goddesses of fertility. But is there any reason why Paleolithic art should have to be related to magic? Do we have to exclude the possibility that the idea of pure beauty could have possessed some Stone Age sculptor?

I should hasten to say that thoughts like these are prompted only by a few isolated exceptions. They certainly do not follow from the cave paintings, the glory of the Paleolithic, however pleasing aesthetically we now find them. It was once thought that cave paintings were confined to France and Spain. But recent discoveries in mainland Italy and on the island of Levanzo (one of the Aegadian Islands) as well as in a cave at Kapovaya in the Urals, seem to indicate that they cover the same territory as the Venuses of the Gravettian era.

France and Spain are nevertheless (but why?) the unchallenged centres of an art which is thought to date from the Aurignac to the Magdalenian eras (from about 30,000 to 8000 B.C.), although these dates are still a matter of debate. Cave paintings are almost entirely devoted to animals, which are depicted in realistic and fantastic mode, with such mastery of draughtsmanship and movement that when the first ones were discovered at Altamira, less than a hundred years ago, and attributed by a Spanish archaeologist to stone-age hunters, there was an outcry to the effect that they must be fakes. Since then a whole series of caves in the Franco-Cantabrian region, from Altamira to Lascaux and Font-de-Gaume in the Dordogne, have revealed a host of engravings, reliefs and immense frescoes, all evidently related in some way. We can now date them with some confidence and classify them; we know what there is to know about their subject matter (which is rather monotonous) and the techniques used. Yet their message remains mysterious. Only the outer caverns or the entrances of these caves were inhabited, and then only for part of the year; so the context was almost certainly one reserved for ritual activities, "far inside the darkness, barely lit by an oil lamp made of stone, with lichen for a wick," in deep caves once occupied or reoccupied by hyenas or bears. So why do we find there this profusion of animal drawings— rhinoceros, bison, reindeer, horses, goats, saiga, bulls, deer, elephants and mammoths—depicted lying in wait, running or wounded, all with an extraordinary feel for movement? It seems virtually certain that these figures, which are almost never grouped in realistic fashion, and are sometimes superimposed on each other, on the same wall at different periods, must have their place in some kind of ancient ritual. The image itself is a form of possession. All primitive human society is marked by incantation, magic, an anguished dialogue with supernatural forces. Plentiful geometrical signs, which are also no doubt symbolic, decorate the same walls, and some analogies with the few hunter-gatherer peoples surviving in the twentieth century have suggested various ingenious and all-encompassing explanations. In fact we still do not know what the social, sexual and ritual context was for these images. Their extraordinary beauty does not correspond to aesthetic preoccupations among our prehistoric ancestors, at least in any sense that we would understand today. They do not represent a quest for beauty so much as obedience to the enchantment of an incantatory and inescapable magic.

Yet sooner or later, from the Gravettian period onward, art began to impinge on everyday life. Ordinary implements made of horn, stone or bone start to be decorated with carvings or engravings, patterns made of lines or dots, more sophisticated arabesques and lifelike images of fauna: horses, ibex, bison, birds, fish, bears, rhinos, reindeer. When one looks at one of these "pierced rods" or "wands," with its painstaking deeply engraved carvings, or at the curved handle of a spear in the shape of a bounding gazelle or a horse's head, one is irresistibly reminded of the many everyday wooden objects, also lovingly painted, polished, carved and sculpted, produced in the Middle Ages. Does that mean that some other aim, apart from the desire to make a satisfactory implement, has always guided the hand of certain kinds of craftsmen? We are entitled to wonder: *Homo ludens* may have been present in every era.

We have no clear evidence, nor is it likely we ever shall, about what made up the cultural universe of these hunting peoples who decorated their caves: nothing is known about their beliefs, their ceremonies, songs and dances, about the painted skins and tattoos suggested by certain remains, or by the deposits of ochres and other dyestuffs found at Neanderthal sites.

A quite different kind of art, another language altogether, is found in the second great zone of prehistoric art, known as that of the Spanish *Levante*. It is actually divided into three basic groups: the Catalonian coastline; the coastal region of Valencia-Albacete; and the region of Cuenca-Teruel. In these areas, most of the paintings have been found in rock shelters open to the air, rather than deep inside caves. It has been suggested that this corresponds to some kind of liberation. The images may well have continued to hold some magical meaning or intention, but their spirit and style appear very different. There is none of the majesty of the powerful heavy beasts of Lascaux in these little pictures showing men and animals in everyday situations: hunters chasing their quarry, a wounded animal charging, groups of warriors armed with bows and arrows, a peaceful flock of birds, a group of dancers, women gathering plants or collecting honey from a swarm of bees at the top of a cliff. What the style may have lost in vigour it makes up for in liveliness and movement. Its charm lies in the swift gestures so confidently suggested by these monochrome silhouettes, stylized to the point of being schematic. The latest in date are sometimes reduced to single strokes. The lifelike character of the gestures and scenes contrasts with the near-abstract style of draughtsmanship.

The art of the Spanish *Levante* belongs unequivocally to the Mediterranean, but is later in date than that of Lascaux or Altamira—perhaps even as late as the Mesolithic. And in any case, it concerns only a tiny sector of the enormous Mediterranean—which raises a problem in itself. Why, at the very moment when man-made art appears for the first time, does so little appear in the Mediterranean proper? Was life there lived differently, with other preoccupations? Was the truly miraculous aspect of the Mediterranean the development of language and speech in the eastern basin, as some have thought? But the origins of language are still mysterious: we are reduced to our imagination, or to later comparisons. The last tribe to be discovered in the Amazon basin, for example, not only does not practise the primitive farming of the other Indian tribes—it is a hunting culture like that of the early Stone Age—

Figure 1
Three pictures of hunters from the caves of the Spanish *Levante* (left to right: Cueva del Garroso, reproduction by M. Almagro; Els Secans, reproduction by Vallespi; Cueva Remigia della Gasulla, reproduction by Porcar).

Figure 2
Deerhunt, Cueva de los Caballos (Arana, Spain, reproduction by Hernandez Pacheco).

it also does not speak any known dialect. One observer who spent time among these people reported in 1969 that their onomatopoeic and grunting sounds, which had none of the features of an articulated language, seemed to express emotions and sensations, but not concepts. However that takes us into the realm of unverifiable hypotheses.

Is it conceivable that the rather advanced culture of the Solutré and Magdalene people in the west resulted from the advantages they derived over a long period from the herds of reindeer and other herbivores (saiga, horses, bison) which roamed the vast open spaces swept by howling winds south of the great glaciers? Humans were parasites on the abundant wildlife. They had only to attach themselves to one of these herds, following it in its seasonal migrations, to be supplied not only with food but with hides, for clothing and tents, and with horn, sinews and bones for making tools and weapons. Animals were already the servants of men. Thus liberated, these early people found themselves with more free time, which created new needs: they painted, carved and moulded objects, and dressed with greater care once the needle had been devised for sewing clothes. Alongside the caves, which were now adapted as dwelling places, they would eventually build huts with stone floors coloured with ochre, like those discovered at Arcy-sur-Cure in France.

The end of the last Ice Age and the retreat of the glaciers may have put an end to this time of comparative plenty and the ancient balance between man and nature which it represented. The melting of the glaciers led to much flooding, as new lakes, rivers and seas came into being: the English Channel and the northern Adriatic for instance. The rapid growth of the great forest mantle limited the area of grassland: reindeer and other herbivores moved north and the hunters had to resort to trapping, a much more hazardous matter, going after forest game such as roe deer, boar and other creatures. In short the triumph of birch, oak, willow and pine, which led to the shrinking of grazing land in northern Europe, also spelled the end of the magnificent art of the cave- and rock-paintings. An artistic pinnacle had passed, and possibly the climate is one explanation of this art "wrapped in a double mystery: where it came from and why it vanished."

The term "reindeer civilization" has often been used to draw attention to the benefits that the natural world first offered, then withdrew. But several prehistorians have strongly objected to the expression and the suggestion it carries of some kind of "decline" of the west in Mesolithic times.[7] They have rightly pointed out that during the Upper Paleolithic, the reindeer was by no means present everywhere. Near Nemours (Seine-et-Marne) the Magdalenians of the limestone plateau of Beauregard were eaters of horsemeat; an immense graveyard of horses has also been found at Solutré near Mâcon. In some of the caves in the Ariège, the favoured game seems to have been the Pyrenean goat. In Styria, humans ate the flesh of bears, and the remains of some fifty thousand animals have been discovered on a single site. And the forests brought some benefits too: the *Helix nemoralis*, the species of snail found in woodlands, was prolific and an important source of food if we are to judge by the impressive middens of snailshells. Water, both fresh and salt, was once more a resource at this time: fishing accompanied hunting.

What is more, Mesolithic technology certainly does not indicate any backward move. The bow and arrow was developed and many ingenious improvements were made to the microliths used for fishhooks and arrowheads, providing evidence of manual skill. And in the plains of northern Europe, from East Anglia to Russia, the many decorated objects, including attractive amber statuettes, artefacts made from wood, bone and horn, traces of dwellings, fishing nets, woven osiers and wooden canoes are all evidence of a lively culture known as Maglemosian, from the name of a Danish site.

This kind of argument rightly rehabilitates the hunters and fishermen of the Mesolithic Age in Europe. But that is not perhaps the most important point. The Mesolithic may not have meant an absolute change for the worse (debatable anyway for certain regions) but it may have brought change in the most important aspect of evolution: animal rearing and agriculture. The early domestication of animals, achieved in the Middle East in Neolithic times, and by the pastoral peoples of the deserts and the Asiatic steppes, was always a slow process: it developed out of the sustained relation between hunters and particular herds of animals to which they attached themselves. Such a symbiosis between a group of animals and a group of humans does not seem to have been possible in western Europe once the great herds of reindeer and other ice-age herbivores had disappeared. Although flocks of sheep and goats were to be found on the Mediterranean littoral in such places as Provence by the seventh millennium B.C., there had been a break in continuity, probably leading to a slowdown. In the Middle East on the other hand, there had been no disruption of the climate and here the flora and fauna lent themselves more readily to domestication. Here we find the beginnings of the great adventure of the eastern Mediterranean.

III

THE MEDITERRANEAN STRIKES BACK: THE FIRST AGRARIAN CIVILIZATION

In about 8000 B.C., just as the Franco-Cantabrian Magdalenian age was drawing to a close, genuine villages were already in existence at the other end of the Mediterranean. Their inhabitants were about to be "initiated into the secrets of making wheat germinate and animals bow to the yoke," as farming of crops and animals gradually replaced hunting and gathering. With this change came fixed human settlements, as villages were no longer camp-sites but were built on top of their own middens, forming those artificial hillocks with which archaeologists are so familiar: the *tells* of Asia, the *magoulas* of Thessaly, the *tumbas* of Macedonia, the *höyüks* of Turkey. Should we call this a revolution (the only one deserving of the name before the industrial revolution of our own times, originating in eighteenth-century England)? Gordon Childe was the first historian to speak of the "Neolithic revolution" without which *Homo sapiens*, for all his intelligence, would have remained a scattered and therefore defenceless species, like his predecessors.

The expression has inspired much controversy. Perhaps this arises from a simple misunderstanding over vocabulary. A revolution implies a break, a new spirit which relegates an archaic life to the past. It is true that a new kind of humanity, a new landscape, new social system and new economy did appear in a few limited parts of the globe during the Neolithic era. In this respect, yes, it was indeed a revolution. But I need hardly add that the word "revolution" also smacks of a truly *historical* vocabulary, denoting something rapid, sudden and dramatic. The "Neolithic revolution," like all truly prehistorical processes, took place very slowly at every stage, from its beginnings through to its settled phase and its expansion. The stages must be counted in thousands not hundreds of years. It would also be mistaken to think of it as a miraculous formula, discovered once and for all in the Middle East and then transmitted by degrees all over the world. It is possible that the formula, whether fully worked out or not, was arrived at in various parts of the globe independently. There may have been, as Emile Werth deduced from the diversity of wild grasses and animal species, several autonomous centres of invention from which the culture spread.

A further ambiguity is introduced if this particular revolution is seen as the birth of Civilization with a capital C. Civilization, another phenomenon which took immeasurable time to develop, can truly be said to begin with the first group of human beings, however limited their resources, from the mere fact that there was a group and that it had something to pass on. Civilization becomes established or confirmed with the appearance of beliefs, the first elementary attitudes towards death and the natural world. If it is to expand and influence others, civilization requires the existence of two things: first some kind of agriculture which attaches societies, villages, and above all towns and cities, to a particular site; and secondly writing, the cement holding together any coherent society. In short, civilization was not "born" at any particular time and place.

That said, it seems that in a European and Mediterranean context, the first steps towards an agricultural civilization were taken in the Middle East, in a few privileged and isolated spots within a vast area of inertia and indifference. Those privileged spots will be our present concern.

The question of origins remains to be decided by archaeological studies which will certainly deserve the label revolutionary. What is known already, and what will be known in future, depends on a series of excavations aiming to go as deep as possible, sometimes as much as twenty metres down, to the virgin subsoil. It will not be possible to locate any crucial turning points until we are able to reconstitute the entire sequence of layers, and read off all the stages in the slow process of change, eventually charting the sequence with as precise a chronology as possible. The first evidence of pestle and mortar, of flint knives with long bone handles, of sickles, silos, grain pits, the remains of animals, wild or domestic—all these are vital elements in the story requiring careful examination. The remains of a sickle, for instance, cannot necessarily tell us whether wild cereals were being systematically harvested or whether they were already being cultivated. Traces of the cereals themselves, when their species can be identified, are more instructive on this point. Mistakes and confusions are always possible: remains rather hastily identified as those of a dog on a site in Jericho turned out after further analysis to be those of a wolf—and this might be an important detail when one is looking for the beginnings of domestication of animals.

Nevertheless, a co-operative research network based on systematic carbon dating has made it possible to establish sequences of dates which seem either to concur or to differ in a logical fashion. Broadly speaking, the Mesolithic era is seen as dating from about 10,000 B.C., the Proto-Neolithic (without pottery) from about 9000, and the Neolithic proper (with pottery) from the seventh millennium—with local variations needless to say. The most significant discovery by far remains that of an early Neolithic era with no pottery—although pottery had long been considered, along with polished stone, as being the key structural sign of a Neolithic site. But is that so surprising? There is no necessary connection between pottery and elementary agriculture among certain primitive peoples still to be found in the twentieth century. In central Brazil, there are tribes which do not have ceramics at all, whereas they all "practise a kind of agriculture based on slash-and-burn methods, at which some groups have become very accomplished" (Claude Lévi-Strauss).

The other discovery, even more important, is that the earliest civilizations—those which combined cultivated plants, domestic animals, houses grouped in villages and towns, some form of art, and organized cults with recognized holy places—did indeed begin in the Middle East, but not (as was thought until very recently) exclusively in the great river valleys of Egypt and Mesopotamia. At the time of writing [1970] there are about twenty points on the map marking the key excavations of the last two or three decades. These are where the new evidence is to be found. They are certainly not yet complete, but already seem to point in a certain direction.

Three zones stand out as advanced: the valleys and west-facing slopes of the Zagros range near Mesopotamia; the wide southern border of Anatolia; and the zone broadly corresponding to Syria, Palestine and Lebanon. These regions are all at fairly high altitudes, well watered (over 200 mm of rainfall a year even today) and situated within that broad arc running along the northern edge of the Syrian desert known as the "Fertile Crescent." The fertility is the result of the relief, which halts and captures the rains of the winter depressions, as the mountains turn into a series of water-towers for the regions down below. The springs, streams and torrents pouring down from the hills explain the presence, so near the Syrian desert, of the woodland and vegetation which would have provided Neolithic cultures with plants for cultivation. But further excavation will be needed to cover the entire zone of early farming cultures.

Let us imagine that the Fertile Crescent is represented by a semicircle, roughly between the Dead Sea (or the Red Sea for that matter) and the Persian Gulf. Then imagine a tangent going off westwards from the highest point of the semicircle. Our brush stroke would have to be broad enough to take in all of southern Anatolia, between Çatal Höyük and Hacilar to the north and the sites of Kizilkaya and Beldibi to the south, almost on the Mediterranean. Neolithic development was particularly precocious and striking in this Anatolian offshoot—long considered, mistakenly, to be the barbaric and backward frontier of the Fertile Crescent. In about 5000 B.C., no doubt as a result of some foreign invasion, this early Anatolian civilization vanished, leaving no trace on the cultural development of the Middle East. On the other hand, during the sixth millennium B.C., a Neolithic culture established in Greece showed marked affinities with that of Hacilar (similar implements, similar pottery). The Anatolian influence seems undeniable, although we cannot work out how it was transmitted.

All these local identifications add up to a pattern. The zones where villages first appeared correspond to the original habitat of flocks of wild sheep, goats, cattle and pigs. They also correspond to the habitat of several wild grasses, found at between 600 m and 900 m altitude: emmer from the Balkans to Iran; barley from Anatolia to Persia, and from Transcaucasia to Palestine and Arabia; and spelt, which was to be found in all these localities. Peas, lentils and vetch were also available. Having since time immemorial gathered grain from the hills, women now began to plant it; and the hunters gradually moved towards the domestication and farming of livestock.

To get the authentic feel of these early stages of human culture, so crucial for future development but still at a rudimentary stage and not leading to any major civilization in this area, there is no substitute for concrete details from archaeological digs. Each of them corresponds to a culture, or rather a sequence of experiences, never identical. Three examples, briefly presented here, take us to Jarmo in the Zagros mountains; to Jericho on the lower slopes of Mount Carmel; and to Çatal Höyük in Anatolia. The problem is finding any connection between these different yet parallel histories, fitting them into a common chronology.

Jarmo lies on the edge of a deep wadi, the Adhaïm, one of several tributaries of the Tigris flowing down from the mountains to join its middle reaches. Here archaeologists have dug down to the non-ceramic Neolithic level (the seventh millennium B.C.). There are no fewer than eleven different levels below the first traces of pottery. All of them relate to a quite small village (twenty to twenty-five hearths, possibly 150 inhabitants). The earliest huts were built of sun-dried clay with a reed thatch; then the first fireplaces appeared, with ovens and chimneys. Hides, woven osiers lined with pitch, and stone jars were all used as receptacles. The remains of emmer, a grass still very close to the wild variety, and of spelt, two kinds of barley, peas and lentils unambiguously point to an already well-developed agriculture. Handmills, sickles, crushing tools and plenty of implements fashioned from flint and obsidian imported from Anatolia were found alongside crude earth-mother goddesses modelled from unbaked clay. The dead were buried outside the village. By the time pottery started to appear in about 6000 B.C., the houses already had stone foundations. But the only animals to be domesticated were the goat and possibly the dog. Most of the meat eaten by this community was still provided by hunting wild boar, or wild sheep and cattle.

The second example takes us to Jericho and the important excavations of 1954. We still do not know the whole story about this exceptional site which upset a number of older theories. No one expected to find a town[8] with over two thousand inhabitants at the dawn of prehistory. Yet this settlement existed at a very early date. The oldest level, thought to be identified as a site of sanctuary, has been carbon dated to about 9500 B.C. At this time, the village of "Jericho" and all those which succeeded it on this site in the course of the ninth millennium, were indistinguishable from all the other Palestinian sites belonging to the so-called Natufian culture, Eynan for instance, on the shores of Lake Huleh. This strange culture of unknown origin, established in caves and on levelled terraces, then in authentic villages with circular huts, has provided rich stone-age remains and interesting sculptures, the oldest in the Middle East. It seems to have been moving towards the Neolithic, with its heavy consumption of cereals (although there were no domestic animals), its pestles and mortars and its grain pits, etc. But it apparently stagnated or eventually quite disappeared from most of these early sites. The Jordan valley and Jericho in particular are exceptional in having retained its legacy.

By the eighth millennium, the cultivation of cereal crops was probably established. Was this the reason for Jericho's sudden remarkable expansion? After all, at this point on the shores of the Dead Sea, 200 metres below normal sea level, the conditions for successfully growing crops with the aid of irrigation were no better than anywhere else in Palestine. And yet the settlement became a town, with well-built circular houses made of dried brick on stone foundations, some of them having several rooms. Impressive trenches and ramparts (including a very large tower) were constructed round the perimeter, and the town possessed water cisterns and grain silos, all clear signs of a coherent urban identity. The explanation may lie in Jericho's exploitation of the salt, sulphur and precious bitumen (pitch) to be found in the Dead Sea—in other words very early trading activity, since we already find obsidian from Anatolia making an appearance in the ancient village by the ninth millennium. It would later be joined by nephrite and other volcanic rocks also from Anatolia, turquoise from Sinai and cowrie shells from the Red Sea.

This kind of evidence prompts the belief that alongside the agricultural revolution, there must have been a revolution in communications, in those early days of "civilization." That too must go back much further than we used to think. These long-distance contacts may not all have been beneficial, however, since after twenty-two levels of building and a thousand years of an existence which was prosperous though not always secure, to judge by the extended ramparts, the town was abandoned at the beginning of the seventh millennium. It was almost immediately reoccupied, but now by a different population, who took over the whole Jordan valley at this time: the signs are that these people came from northern Syria or Anatolia. The Natufian culture entirely disappears at this point: the houses in the new town were rectangular and had plastered floors in the Syrian tradition. The economy remained Proto-Neolithic, as it was to be for the next ten to fifteen centuries, the only real innovation being the domestication of the goat and dog. The Neolithic era with pottery was finally established in Jericho in the sixth millennium, and was probably brought there by a semi-nomadic people, following a second desertion of the town indicated by a gap in the layers. Oddly enough, the arrival of pottery corresponded to a long period of cultural impoverishment in Jericho, Palestine and the Lebanon, which lasted until the fourth millennium.

Our third example, Çatal Höyük in Anatolia, provides even more food for thought, since excavation in 1962–4 revealed, lying adjacent to Proto-Neolithic traces, what may be the earliest example of a Neolithic culture with pottery in the whole of Asia Minor. Çatal Höyük is a real town[9] of which unfortunately only one district has been prospected, the so-called "priests' quarter," half a hectare of a fifteen-hectare site. Twelve levels have been identified between 6500 and 5650 B.C. The earliest dwellings were single-storey rectangular houses made of dried brick, with a hole in the roof to let out smoke and small high "windows" to let in light. The way in was through an opening in the flat roof, reached by a ladder (houses of this type are still to be found today in Anatolia and even Armenia). There were no doors and no real streets. Sometimes there was an inner courtyard, shared by several houses, with tiny windows opening on to it. Alternatively, if dwellings were built all the way up the side of the *tell*, adjoining houses could have windows opening on to the neighbour's roof. To get from one house to another, people used short ladders laid across the roofs. Figure 4 on p. 44 explains this odd way of moving about more clearly than a description in words. The town thus presented to the outside world a series of blank adjoining walls, making it easy to defend, with windows serving as loopholes for archers.

The presumption that the inhabitants of this large settlement came from the nearby mountains (where primitive plants were to be found) suggests that they had an interesting previous history, about which unfortunately nothing is known. This is the more regrettable since it would have provided us with knowledge about the transition from the previous Mesolithic stage to the Neolithic "revolution."

In Çatal Höyük, agriculture had indeed reached a high degree of organization: the fields around the town were farmed, perhaps collectively, to bear wheat (three varieties), unbearded barley, lentils, peas, vetch, as well as pistachio, almond and cherry trees. Oil was pressed and beer was probably brewed. Sheep and possibly cattle were domesticated,[10] while other beasts were regularly hunted: wild cattle, deer, onager, roe deer, boar—and especially leopard. But what must be remembered is that the most important source of income for the town was trade.

Lying near two active volcanoes, Çatal Höyük operated a virtual monopoly on the trade in obsidian with western Anatolia, Cyprus and the Levant. In exchange, it received high-quality flint from Syria, many shells from the Mediterranean, and all kinds of stone: alabaster, marble, black limestone, and from the nearby mountains ochre, cinnabar, native copper and even copper ore. This material provided supplies for the town's already advanced craftsmanship: represented, for example, by a ritual dagger with a flint blade and chased bone handle, decorated with the coils of a snake, dating from the beginning of the sixth millennium. But even before this date, all the little objects which were placed alongside the bodies of the dead, the countless javelins, lances and arrowheads, the mirrors of polished obsidian, the necklaces of finely pierced beads carved from brownstone, blue apatite or shell, the pendants made of obsidian or copper, the metal beads (copper and lead), the vessels made of wood, bone and horn, the textiles of finely woven fabric, probably wool—all of these strongly indicate the existence of specialized craftworking. Finally, the pottery on this site, still crude in the seventh millennium, progressively becomes finer, first red or dark-coloured earthenware, then smooth, yellowish and mottled in different colours. In the final stages, which excavation has not yet discovered on this site, but which we know

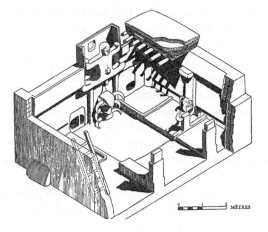

Figure 3
Çatal Höyük—inside a sanctuary: showing the goddess giving birth to a bull, the seats arranged around, the bull's horns and the ladder giving access to the upper terrace (drawing after J. Mellaart).

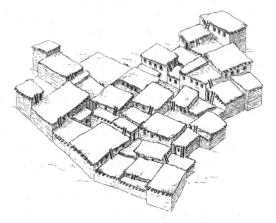

Figure 4
A district in Çatal Höyük: small groups of adjoining houses are clustered round several sanctuaries. On the outer side, the walls form a continuous barrier, protecting the village against marauders. The almost total absence of doors suggests that people moved between the houses via the terraces rather than at ground level (drawing by Laure Nollet).

about from Hacilar, painted pottery is found, red on a cream base or white on red (mid-sixth millennium).

But it is its sacred art which makes Çatal Höyük especially interesting. At the various levels of the different sanctuaries, a particularly rich collection of artefacts has been found: many sculptures made of stone, alabaster, marble or terracotta; some reliefs and paintings executed with a brush on a smooth plaster surface, the first known paintings done on a man-made wall. The fertility goddess, the essential divinity of Neolithic cults, appears here in many versions: as a young girl, as a pregnant woman, reminiscent of the Paleolithic Venuses, or sometimes giving birth to a bull. The bull is the male god, generally represented by a bull's head alone, or by rows of horns, only rarely in anthropomorphic shape.

Paleolithic religion still surfaces in places, with all its ancient imagery: mural frescoes and relief friezes representing animals: bulls, cattle, deer, boar, leopards (the goddess's sacred beasts). There are patterns made with handprints, painted or indented, as in the cave art of France and Spain, covering an entire panel in one sanctuary, alongside images of women's breasts and bulls' heads; and there are hunting scenes with dancers clad in leopard skins, and funeral rites in which priests disguised as vultures are officiating. In this culture, the bodies of the dead were indeed exposed for birds of prey to pick the bones clean. Their skeletons were then wrapped in their clothing and buried, with their worldly goods, in the house in which they had lived, under one of the raised platforms found in every dwelling, large stone benches on which people sat, worked and even slept, as in ancient houses in China. Women were always buried under the principal platform in the house, in the place of honour, a sign that this was a society where mothers, priestesses and goddesses reigned.

IV
CONCLUSION

The innovations of the Neolithic era took place, as far as we know, at pinpoints on the map, distant from one another, but with zones of influence around them. Can we say that these points added up to a kind of powder trail which caught alight and sent the flame further afield? The image certainly does not fit the slow propagation of agriculture and livestock farming. "Neolithicization" took only small steps from its eastern centres, and did not take hold everywhere: whole regions of the Mediterranean and Europe were left behind. Even in the Middle East, it would take another twenty or thirty centuries before the great civilizations of Mesopotamia and Egypt emerged.

But what I find fascinating about these early microcosms, particularly Çatal Höyük, is that their evolution was already reaching the stage of an urban culture. Despite what has been said about them, these were not merely large villages, the product of agriculture, livestock herding and the sedentarization of nomadic people. We can see in them the beginnings of a division of labour. Long-distance trade, in my view the key factor, was already present, not to mention the social organization necessary for any highly ritualized religion: each sanctuary in Çatal Höyük was at the centre of its own district. It is true that these towns did not last: at some point these ventures received some kind of mortal blow. But they had made a start, prefiguring the future. From that time on, the die was cast. Çatal Höyük and Hacilar would simply disappear; Jericho would decline into obscurity; Jarmo lasted only a few centuries and was in any case never much more than a hamlet. But the head start gained by the seas, the countries and the peoples of the Middle East had already become a fixture for millennia to come. This represents a geographical and spatial feat, the most lasting of victories. Local setbacks notwithstanding, it was here that civilization would first spring to life and here that its first outstanding examples would be located. From now on the Mediterranean would look towards these enlightened areas, and that orientation would be very long-lasting.

So we find that our sea was from the very dawn of its protohistory a witness to those imbalances productive of change which would set the rhythm of its entire life. They consisted both of north-south contrasts, as already described, and of east-west contrasts which very soon took the form of differences in level, leading eventually to marked conflicts between civilizations.

CHAPTER THREE

A Twofold Birth

The Neolithic revolution as here defined—the appearance of fields, cultivated plants, domestic animals, pottery, weaving, villages and eventually towns—extended over a large part of the Mediterranean area between the fifth and the third millennia B.C. It was of capital importance for the destiny of the sea that this early series of changes, leading to the great civilizations of the fourth and third millennia, should have taken place on or near its shores. The transformations were accompanied by a revolution in transport, both on land and on sea. Some time between the far-off tenth millennium (a very approximate date) and the second, coasts and rivers were gradually explored by shipping.

So it was that increasingly complex and well-organized societies developed, while the number of boats sailing on the sea also increased. From this double history, which is perhaps a single one after all, the historical Mediterranean derived its first identity.

I

MESOPOTAMIA AND EGYPT: THE BEGINNINGS

The first miracles took place not on the shores of the sea itself but along certain freshwater courses. The domestication of the Nile, the Tigris and the Euphrates lay behind the creation of Egypt and Mesopotamia: economic, cultural and already political giants dating from even earlier than the third millennium. Yet the areas in question were very small: Upper Egypt covered only about 12,000 square kilometres, Lower Egypt 11,000; Mesopotamia, if measured by its fertile gardens, represented about 20–25,000 square kilometres of irrigable land. On these modest territories there assembled an unprecedented concentration of peoples and resources. For centuries to come, the Middle East and the busy seas bordering on it would be centred on the Egypt-Mesopotamia axis, the whole forming a fragile entity but one gradually gaining in coherence.

Civilization in its first really *large-scale* forms came into being at roughly the same time in Mesopotamia and Egypt, in the fourth millennium. By about a thousand years later (hardly any time at all in this context of very slow change) civilizations had appeared on the distant banks of the Indus, and probably in China as well. The phenomenon did not happen everywhere at exactly the same moment in world history: it was not as if civilization was somehow "in the air" for all to experience. Rather, history started more or less from scratch, in one place after another.

These civilizations grew up on the banks of rivers which had to be tamed by the use of artificial irrigation, so that full use could be made of their alluvial mud which was easy to till and provided ever-renewable fertility. The results matched the effort: they produced both an unparalleled advantage in global terms and the visible subjection of individuals to the collective good. Such a disciplined society could not have been put in place without the networks of towns, made possible by the agricultural surpluses from the nearby countryside. Yet these towns had at first been inward-looking. Their self-centred preoccupations had operated only over a short radius. They were like aggressive wasps which had to be tamed and brought under control before they could be incorporated into a busy beehive. The operation succeeded by and large in Egypt, but had little or no success in Mesopotamia. This became a distinctive trait of their respective histories.

In order for the unequal dialogue between town and country to become established, certain things had to be in position: advanced economic links; some form of division of labour; social obedience based on strict religious beliefs, and a royal dynasty based on divine right. All of these—religion, a dynastic ruler, towns, irrigation channels, plus the skill of writing, without which no orders could be sent over distances and no accounts committed to memory—had to be created *ex nihilo*.

The rest followed in sequence. These urban societies had certain immediate needs: salt, wood for building, stone (even the most basic). Then, like any society which is developing towards a more sophisticated stage, new needs sprang up and quickly became necessities: gold, silver, copper, tin (essential for casting bronze), oil, wine, precious stones, ivory, rare woods. As it grew richer, a society would send abroad for these goods. In short, the range of commodities to be traded increased considerably, opening up to outside influence economic circuits which would otherwise have been self-contained. Road traffic became organized: caravans of pack-asses soon appeared, to be followed by wheeled vehicles (the heavy four-wheeled cart was not easy to manoeuvre, but was present in Mesopotamia by the fourth millennium), and cargo vessels, powered by sails or oars.

Specialists are virtually unanimous that Mesopotamia was the first to develop. Before Egypt, the first place on earth to develop the plough, the wheel, writing and later money was the "river island" between the Tigris and the Euphrates. At some later point, on the eve of the third millennium, Egypt borrowed from its distant rival a number of things: the cylindrical seal, the brick wall with redans and niches, a series of artistic themes, especially heraldic monsters, significant words such as *mr* (= house); possibly the keyword *ma'at* (= justice, truth); and perhaps the shape of its boats, in the view of scholars in the past: we are not quite so sure today. But these examples, inconclusive in themselves, do not in fact resolve the debate. There have been civilizations which borrowed more than others, but they were not on that account inferior or less precocious. A stone vase with indented carvings dating from the end of the fourth millennium, discovered by Keith Seele, and a vase of the same period in the British Museum, depict boats on the Nile of the same ancient type as those on the cylindrical seals of Mesopotamia: they have the same shape and possibly a more advanced design of sail. One specialist has rightly pointed out that if Egypt was in direct contact with Mesopotamia in the fourth and third millennia, it would have been odd if it did *not* borrow the wheel and cart we know to have existed in Sumer—but which Egypt did not in fact adopt until the second millennium when the Hyksos invaded the Nile Delta using chariots and horses. After studying the sequence of cultural and trading relations in the Middle East, the same expert concludes that the two civilizations probably never had any serious contacts except through intermediaries, such as the link-towns on the Syrian-Lebanese coast.

All the same, the development of the Nile Valley civilization in about 3000 B.C. shows every sign of being a "sudden mutation." While it may not have been the result of "a massive invasion of Egypt by Asiatic peoples," some writers do attribute it to "the infiltration of small groups of immigrants including . . . artisans," that is to some kind of "catalytic influence on the emerging kingdom of the Nile," at a time when political unity was being achieved with the first pharaohs. This may be the case. Another hypothesis, that the incomers were Mesopotamians who "came round the Arab peninsula by sea," is not impossible. Yet if Asiatic influence was so strong and decisive, it is surely surprising that Egyptian culture should from the start have been marked by its own special and original style, one which it would never subsequently abandon. From earliest times, it was "monolithic, singular . . . and intolerant of any dialogue." In the Narmer Palette, one of the most characteristic examples of an artefact showing a typically Mesopotamian motif (two fantastic beasts with long interlocking necks), the subject is the only thing that is Mesopotamian, since both form and handling display features and conventions which were to distinguish Egyptian art for three millennia. Menes-Narmer's outstretched arm, victoriously threatening his prostrate enemy, prefigures exactly the gesture of Tutmosis III, fifteen hundred years later, in the temple to Ammon at Karnak.

Although it is therefore doubtful whether Egyptian civilization can be traced to Mesopotamian origins, it is likely that the latter came first. But why should one civilization appear earlier than the other? And why at that time and in that place? The simple answer may be to look at the related geographical situations of Mesopotamia and of the narrow zone in which the first Neolithic advances were made.

There was clearly more than one "Mesopotamia." The famous artificial irrigation and its miracles were actually located in Lower Mesopotamia and only after the fifth millennium. Northern Mesopotamia was a dry zone looking towards the Euphrates and becoming progressively better watered to the east, thanks to the streams and springs of the Armenian mountains and the proximity of the Zagros. A land of hills and low plateaux, it corresponded in part to what we have earlier described as the Fertile Crescent. We know that agriculture and animal husbandry spread from the very ancient original sites to extend to the entire zone between northern Syria and the Iranian plateau, thus taking in a swathe of northern Mesopotamia. The people here had no need to travel to find the earliest rudiments of civilization: they were already on the spot.

It was in the north therefore that the earliest Mesopotamian cultures developed. They are known after their very fine painted ceramics: Hassuna (about 6000 B.C.); followed by Samarra (about 5500) and Halaf (5000). Viewed from close up, the development is very complex, with a variety of origins: the Halaf culture, for example, did not derive from the two previous groups, and in some areas was overlaid on the still existing Samarra. But in each case one can clearly recognize a trading area, given concrete shape by the spread of the characteristic ceramics. We find Hassuna and Samarra pottery confined to northern Iraq, while the Halaf zone is much wider, lying between the Euphrates and the Great Zab, a tributary of the Tigris. It was on the Iranian side, at Arpachiya in particular, that the art of Halaf ceramics developed in its most perfect form, and it was no doubt on the Syrian side, where it would have encountered echoes of Samarra and a strong local tradition of metal-working, that the Halaf culture developed the use of copper.

These successive cultures both echo and explain one another. The same is not true of the colonization of southern Mesopotamia. The earliest traces of this have been found at the southern site of Eridu, dating from about the fifth millennium; later traces appear at El Obeid and Uruk. The unprecedented scale of the irrigation schemes here must have mobilized many labourers, no doubt the surplus populations of the various Mesopotamian settlements, towns and villages from which pioneers emigrated. One particularly important immigration was that of the Sumerians, who gave the name of Sumer to the lower valley with its irrigation. We know little or nothing, alas, about these hardy and intelligent people, who laid the solid foundations of the civilization which famously grew up between the Tigris and Euphrates. Even their language, and their script, although the latter has been deciphered, do not reveal the secret of their origin. It was thought at one time that they came from Turkestan, or even the Indus. They may simply have been farmers from eastern Iran, from the region later to become Persepolis. Their early pottery suggests the influence of northern Mesopotamia, Samarra or Halaf. But this southern culture very quickly developed along its own lines, thanks to a new type of agriculture, which brought about a revolution in their way of life.

The Sumerians had settled on uncultivated and inhospitable land. The soil was certainly rich, composed of river mud which would be easy to till and to plant, and capable of providing fabulous yields (eighty grains harvested for every one sown, according to the Bible), but it had first to be reclaimed from stagnant waters, from huge reedbeds inhabited only by fish, waterfowl and wild beasts. The climate was torrid and the rainfall scanty, yet the floodwaters from the rivers were as catastrophic as the dry season. These rivers ran through a bed raised up by their own alluvial deposits, high above the plain, behind natural levees of their own creation, yet not strong enough to contain their regularly tumultuous floodwaters, caused by the melting of the Armenian snows. When that happened, the water spilled over the plain, turning every depression into a marsh. To avoid their crops being swept away, the earliest settlers had to strengthen the natural dykes, build channels to drain away excess water into pools later used as reservoirs to water plants parched by the summer drought. This all required not only unremitting labour, repeated year after year under the blazing sun, but also many technical miracles, the digging of raised-up canals for example with downhill sluices, or the cutting of irrigation channels far from the original river bank. Some divine assistance may have been called for: Enki, the fish-god of Eridu, is said to have revealed to humans the secrets of mastery over the waters.

Once the waters had been domesticated, Lower Mesopotamia did indeed become "the garden of Eden," where waves of immigrants came to settle, where there was an abundance of cereals, fruit trees and sesame (the essential source of oil in the Middle East for ages to come), and of course that marvel among trees, the date-palm.

The centre of gravity of Mesopotamia moved south as a result. While civilization had originally come from the north, now it would be located entirely in the south, and all those fragile early centres would be wiped out, swept away by the sheer weight of the massive civilization of the lower valley, triumphant and naturally expansionist.

Egypt too found that its mighty river was not an easy ally. If it did not exactly have to be conquered, it did need engineering work: the chief problem was to increase the area of arable land which was washed over then uncovered in the natural floodplain of the Nile. The situation was not the same as that on the Euphrates: Egypt and Mesopotamia would never be identically placed.

The most obvious reason is that Egypt was from the start surrounded by deserts, with arid wastes cutting it off on all sides. It was the increasing dryness of the climate which had created Egypt, by intensifying the encroachment of the Saharan sands from the seventh and sixth millennia onwards. Populations of mixed origin (brachycephalic, dolichocephalic, Negro, Mediterranean, and some related peoples of Cro-Magnon descent) fled there from the south, the east and the west, sometimes leading to confrontations. These refugees were moving closer to the vital water supply. This was the origin of the independent cantons and districts of Egypt, the future *nomes*.

It took time before the waters were brought under control. The Nile might have been reduced in volume by the increasing drought, even losing some of its tributaries, but it remained a monstrous natural phenomenon, a powerful body of water. Like the Mesopotamian rivers, it had built up its bed, creating on either side undulating banks of soft mud, over which it flooded every year, leaving pools and marshes behind it as it retreated. Water seeped into every hollow and lay stagnant. Lake Fayum, before it was "improved," was a huge swamp, covered in water plants. The super-rich zone of the Nile Delta, constantly accumulating further territory, was a labyrinth of lagoons, of low-lying amphibious islands and marshy swamps. It was a paradise for wild beasts and throughout Egyptian history it remained a refuge for human fugitives. The magnificent bas-reliefs decorating the tombs of Saqqarah (about 2500 B.C.) show hunters gliding in flat-bottomed boats among a medley of creatures: fish, crocodiles, hippopotami, and every kind of waterfowl: ibis, herons, ducks, kingfishers. Men and beasts alike could slip through the high clumps of papyrus, their forests of huge ribbed stems forming the regular background to hunting scenes in the Delta. On their great umbrella-tops, birds built their nests. A thousand years later, exactly the same scenery appears on the brightly coloured frescoes of the eighteenth dynasty: the same hunters, the same impenetrable thickets, the same light boats built of rushes bound together in thick bundles, the same flying birds, the same threatening hippopotami lurking in the depths of the marshes. Beyond these images we can glimpse the wildlife of early Egypt, its inhospitality to man.

But unlike the valleys of the Tigris or Euphrates, the regular flooding of the Nile between the summer solstice and the autumn equinox allowed for a predictable farming calendar. The flood brought everything that was needed, water and black Nile mud, but it was confined by natural features to the valley bed, since the river was enclosed on both sides by the hills of the desert, the Arabian chain to the east and the Libyan relief to the west. So in Egypt, floodwaters did not have to be checked and brought under control, merely channelled.

Prodigious feats of labour were nevertheless called for, to fill in the marshy hollows, to strengthen the banks, or to set up levees (embankments) running across the valley between the two deserts. The double strip of farmland on either side was thus divided into a series of basins, held in by levees.

When the floods came, the embankments were breached, then closed again once the basins were covered with rich muddy water to about a metre or two in depth. They would remain submerged for at least a month before the water would drain away by the force of gravity, from basin to basin. So, apart from the great labour of building the embankments (which should not be underestimated) a regular pattern was in place: the river brought water and fertility and prepared the way for crops. The earliest "machines" for artificial irrigation appeared rather late in Egypt: the *shaduf*, possibly an import from Mesopotamia where it was to be found in the third millennium; the *noria* which came with the Persians in the sixth century B.C.; and the Archimedes screw, imported by the Greeks in about 200 B.C. Egypt had been able to manage without these techniques for a long time: the embankments of the Nile had done the work unaided.

Surviving texts from Mesopotamia tell of much more complex activities. Here irrigation was far more artificial than on the banks of the Nile. The water level was under constant surveillance and one sluice or another was always having to be "opened" or "diverted," sending surplus water to the marshes or basins; the flow of irrigation had to be directed first one way then another, and there was a constant battle against the reeds, grass and mud which blocked the rivulets; sometimes the land had to be ploughed to enable the water to penetrate the earth ("getting out the oxen to water the earth"). In the surviving letters giving orders or describing the work accomplished, there are many vivid images. We may perhaps conclude with Maurice Vieyra: "Egypt was a gift from the Nile. Mesopotamia was made by human hands" (1961).

The victory over water was accompanied by other achievements and advances. Let us start with the most basic.

The invention of the potter's wheel in Lower Mesopotamia in the first half of the fourth millennium is one such. The first turned pots seem curiously devoid of any concern for beauty: they are very simple, in plain colours, beige or light yellow. Only after two or three centuries did they start to be decorated with red or purple glaze, still using plain colours. This was the style known to us as Uruk. In about 3400, and on the same sites, it began to replace the simple but delicate ancient ceramics of Eridu and El Obeid, or the inventive and beautiful pottery of nearby Susiana. Then this undistinguished and not particularly attractive pottery spread to the whole of Mesopotamia, where the great tradition of painted ceramics seems to have died out entirely.

This was perhaps only logical. Uruk was already an enormous city for the time (possibly 20,000 inhabitants); it was in touch with other large towns along the river and once it had acquired the wheel, it was able to turn out industrial pottery in large quantities, probably using less experienced labour than before. This undecorated pottery was exported in all directions in bulk, both in north and south Mesopotamia. Products varied only in shape. This was the first appearance of the "functional" pot. During the latter half of the fourth millennium, then, inventiveness, imagination and taste were to be found surviving among the potters of neighbouring Iran, sometimes in surprisingly poor villages, rather than in the great cities of Mesopotamia, which were at the cutting edge of progress. Every time one finds any local production in Mesopotamia where the potters have retained some skill in painting, it always happens to be in the regions in direct contact with Iran. Such for instance is the red and black pottery of the Jemdet Nasr period (*c.* 3200), related to the "scarlet ceramics" of the Diyala valley and also found on Iranian sites or in Mesopotamian towns such as Mussian near the Diyala (*c.* 2800). The same can be said of the "Ninevite V" style which spread in about 3000 through the region that would later be called Assyria, at one end of the passes leading to Azerbaijan.

In Egypt, amusingly enough, stone and clay seem to have been in competition with each other. Throughout the fourth millennium and beyond, hand-made pottery had become progressively refined in its firing procedures, colours and designs. At the same time, vessels made of polished stone, which called for hours of work, became a rare luxury, although the technology of flint tools had by then reached a magnificent level of precision and accuracy (witness the perfect regularity of the Jebel el-Arak blade, cut according to the undulation technique). But with the last pre-dynastic age, at about the time when Mesopotamia began regularly employing the potter's wheel, the Egyptians invented a stone-drill, worked by a handle. This made it possible to hollow out a block of stone with far less effort, and it is after this that we find the great age of stone cups and vases in Egypt, made of various materials each more beautiful than the last. Concurrently, from about 3200, the style of ceramics declines in quality, design and glaze, and shapes become utilitarian. The wheel, which was not in general use until 2600, although it had been invented earlier, led to increased output of pottery, but did not restore it to its past grandeur. Specialized and stereotyped designs were dictated by the vessel's destination. It was not usually decorated. In the coloured display pieces which have been found, the paint is generally fragile, having been applied after firing, and would easily have been removed by water. What is known as

Egyptian porcelain, so famous during the Middle Empire and exported over-seas, was actually vitrified enamel, baked in a kiln on a base made of stone or agglomerated stone dust and usually in a mould. The poor quality of pottery in Egypt helps explain the great vogue there of imported Cretan and Myce-naean ceramics from the fifteenth century B.C.

Other more important kinds of progress affected crops and animals. It is impossible to work out how much was contributed by the first hill-farmers and how much by the pioneers of the large crop farms in the plains. What we can be sure of is the steady improvement of cereal species, fruit-trees, olives, vines and date-palms. More breeds of animals were domesticated. In Meso-potamia, domestic animals, whether inherited from the Neolithic era or acquired more recently, included dogs, sheep, goats, pigs, oxen, onagers and later asses (which were not native). Latecomers were horses and camels, both imported, the first from the northern steppes, the second from Arabia, hence their names of "ass of the north" and "ass of the south."

The Egyptians had domesticated or captured the same or similar species, as well as other examples of African fauna. They had even experimented, sometimes rather unwisely, with such birds and beasts as pelicans, leopards, herons, cranes, antelopes, hyenas and gazelles. Other initiatives were of more permanent value. They successfully domesticated cats, Nile geese—flocks of which are depicted on the bas-reliefs of the third millennium—pigeons, and chickens, which appear only in about 1500 B.C. The Annals of Tutmosis III refer to this extraordinary bird which could lay eggs at any time of year.

Even more significant in Mesopotamia than the training of asses as beasts of burden in the third millennium, was the feat of harnessing oxen to carts and ploughs. The early plough, a kind of hoe dragged along by a team of ani-mals, can be identified on Mesopotamian seals of the fourth millennium, but it is not impossible that wooden ploughs with metal or even flint plough-shares existed even earlier, perhaps in the Fertile Crescent. In Egypt, where the plough appeared in the fourth millennium, grain was sown broadcast, then buried by ploughing or the hoofs of animals. In Mesopotamia in the sec-ond millennium, a sort of mould-board was fixed on to the plough handle. The grain fell into the open furrow and was covered by a rear-fitted harrow.

Should one call the arrival of the plough a revolution? It is tempting to do so. It certainly led to the spread and acceleration of agriculture even on fairly poor soil, and improved possibilities of cultivating the same land with short fallow periods. Longer fallow periods, which led to the growth of trees and shrubs, entailed the practice of slash-and-burn. But this method could not destroy the grass growing on short-term fallow land: for that a plough was needed. This progress was followed by an increase in the number of mouths to feed—unless it was the other way round and an increase in population called the technology into being.

There was another consequence. Until now, women had been in charge of the fields and gardens where cereals were grown: everything had depended on their tilling the soil and tending the crop. Men had been first hunters, then herdsmen. But now men took over the plough, which they alone were allowed to use. At a stroke, it might seem that the society would move from being matriarchal to patriarchal: that there would be a shift away from the reign of the all-powerful mother-goddesses and immemorial fertility cults presided over by priestesses to be found in Neolithic communities, and towards the male gods and priests who were predominant in Sumer and Babylon. At least, if we could be sure of this, it would be a good example of economic determinism! But the Earth Mother retained an important role, even after the appearance of the plough, and would continue to reign for a long time to come, especially in the Aegean religions in Crete and later in Greece. No doubt in this domain developments were too long-term and too complicated to be summed up in any formula. The domestication of large animals like asses and oxen, followed by horses and camels, took centuries. Metal-working, a noble craft reserved for men, was also to tip the balance towards male domination of society and its beliefs, "from a queen resembling the Earth Mother to a king resembling Jupiter" as Jean Przyluski put it. But here again, it was the result of centuries of social change. In the Babylonian myths, the sun god Marduk has to kill the terrible she-dragon Tiamat in order to create heaven and earth from her body. But in Sumer, the goddess Inanna was still queen of fertility, the deity to whom the fruits of the earth were offered (cf. the Warka vase).

Weaving

In the case of weaving, was it routine or progress that had the upper hand? Both, probably. Weaving cloth is a very ancient craft. We find it at Çatal Höyük or Jarmo in the sixth millennium B.C. and it probably goes even further back. The technology is similar to that of basket-work, which was already in existence in the Paleolithic. We may therefore suppose that from then on, whenever suitable raw materials were available, weaving will have been practised.

So it is not surprising that in Anatolia and the Fertile Crescent, woven woollen fabrics are found in tombs contemporary with the domestication of sheep and goats; or that in Egypt, linen weaving goes back at least as far as the sixth millennium, before the first dynasties. Cotton can be ruled out: it was first used by the ancient civilizations on the Indus, reaching Mesopotamia only in the first millennium, in the age of Sennacherib: it is found in Egypt only in the form of imported woven calico, in bright colours. Goat hair was used very little, except for making bags or bridles. Wool and linen had always been the two essential textiles. Egypt virtually confined itself to linen, Mesopotamia employed both and their respective merits were debated there.

Spinning and weaving probably developed their maximum potential fairly early on. A fragment of Egyptian linen dating from about 3000 B.C. has 64 threads for the warp and 48 for the woof over a square centimetre: this could hardly be bettered. The technology does not seem to change at all, whatever the age of the iconographical documents that have survived. To spin either wool or linen basically meant starting from a mass of raw material, and pulling out of this bundle, which was placed on the ground or in a receptacle of some kind, the threads to be twisted by the spindle. About twenty centuries separate women of the Diyala valley with their distaffs, as depicted on a vase, and a woman of Susa, sitting on a stool, doing the same task: the gesture is identical in both cases. Egyptian women always did their spinning standing up, or sometimes perched on a wooden platform, so as to increase the distance separating the raw flax from the spinner's fingers, thus giving more play to the distaff.

The new feature, in these early days of Egypt and Mesopotamia, was the sudden increase in textile production. Even along the Nile, where few clothes were worn, cloth production increased as costume became a sign of social status. From the days of the New Kingdom the simple male loin-cloth—traditional garb which gods and pharaohs were always depicted wearing in Egyptian art—was worn only by men of lower status. Richer men wore several such loin-cloths and tunics on top of each other, often pleated. Women were no longer merely clad in the long tunic of the past, but covered it with more flowing robes of fine transparent linen in many colours. (Until then, both sexes had worn only white linen.) Immense lengths of woven fabric were required for the preparation of mummies. And Egyptian linen was famous overseas, being widely exported. This foreign trade was a royal monopoly.

In Mesopotamia too, textiles, especially woollens, were one of the staples of the export trade from the third millennium. At Ur of the Chaldees, workshops were set up in the temples which were also the power centres of the time. The royal palace would later become the centre for organizing this active craft. Nothing more clearly tells us the extent to which weaving, a modest activity almost always carried out by women or wretched prisoners of war, in fact implied the organization of the whole economy and society.

The essential role played by wood in the Egyptian and Mesopotamian economy is hardly surprising. Most obviously, it was simply used every day as an all-purpose material, as in the rest of the world, including Europe, until the nineteenth century and beyond. But the problem was that the alluvial soil of both areas, despite all its advantages, could not produce this essential material. One Assyriologist says that the useful tree species in Mesopotamia can be counted on the fingers of one hand. What use were willows, or the fibrous trunk of the palm-tree? In Egypt, only the sycamore and acacia yielded hard wood. Later on, new species were established under the New Kingdom: pine, yew, lemon, beech, but these could never fully compensate for the lack of indigenous trees. For rafters, doors, pillars, furniture, ships, craft tools, looms, sarcophagi and sculpture, the residents of Egypt and Mesopotamia had always had to rely on imported wood.

Both civilizations knew and envied the forests of cedar and other resinous trees in the Amanus Mountains and Lebanon. Mesopotamian legend had already baptized "the cedar mountain" the "home of the gods." "There the shade was cool and refreshing" for Gilgamesh, the fabulous hero, and the great treetrunks slid into the rivers "like giant serpents" when Gudea, the priest-king of Lagash, felled them with his great axe to build the temples of his city. An Egyptian traveller fourteen centuries before Christ looked up in amazement at the sky above the forests of Lebanon, "all dark because there grew there so many cypresses, oaks and cedars." These forests explain the flotillas of sailing boats between Byblos and the Nile Delta, or plying up the Syrian coast to northern ports, towing behind them rafts of timber which would then be transported overland, heedless of cost, to the cities of Mesopotamia.

Wood was therefore the reason for the first proper links between Egypt and Syria, for the expeditions to Byblos sent by the Pharaoh Sahura and the "entrepreneurs" of Elephantine. Sargon waged a war over timber from the Mediterranean. This may seem unusual prominence to give a material usually passed over in silence in historical narratives. But there was no choice when such an everyday necessity was in such short supply. Egypt, where we find so many images of craftsmen wielding adze, hammer and pegs before the days of copper nails, had to import all its wood. Timber forced a breach in Egypt's economic isolation, and through this breach, many other things would flood in. A comparable example is northern China, another zone of muddy terrain, as barren as the moon, and obliged to look to the south or far south for timber. The same causes sometimes produce the same effects.

With the use of metals, a significant barrier was crossed. In theory the Stone Age was now left behind. In practice, however, nothing changed overnight.

From earliest times, metals such as locally occurring copper and even iron from meteorites had been worked like stone, using hammer and chisel. But the birth of metallurgy meant the use of a furnace and successful smelting. This began in the fifth millennium B.C. with copper smelting, attested in Iran and Cilicia, and probably carried out in the Amuq plains and north towards Diyarbakir, "the land of copper." Its success must have depended in part on the quality of the ores, which in these areas are often mixed with arsenic. Pure molten copper is not easy to cast in moulds. Copper smelting was transformed the day tin began to be systematically added to it—again by trial and error, by sprinking cassiterite (tin oxide) mixed with charcoal on the molten copper. The excellent alloy that resulted—bronze—appeared in Mesopotamia in about 2800, and in Egypt in about 2000 B.C.

Costly and rare, bronze, which has given its name to a whole era of human history, long remained a luxury. Only a few tools, ornaments, and the weapons of the powerful would be made of metal. Most ordinary mortals were still in the Stone Age. In Sumer, wool was still plucked from sheep's backs rather than sheared. The Egyptians long used stone knives, as did the advanced cities on the Indus, where the blades which have been found are made of black flint.

Specialized smiths very soon emerged for the different processes of metalworking, including gold and silver. Some handled ores, others the metal once it had been refined by hammering, crushing and repeated smelting. In Mesopotamia, pottery furnaces with blast pipes have been found: the bellows would be used to activate the combustion of charcoal mixed with the ore. Moulds for the molten metal, some made of limestone, have also been discovered.

The earliest copper and bronze smiths were undoubtedly working in a luxury trade, with its own rules, methods and traditions, its independent or itinerant workers who, like those of sub-Saharan Africa today, went round selling their own wares, or made them to order. Wandering craftsmen of this kind are thought to be responsible for the strange metal objects found on the shores of the Black Sea, in the Nahal Mishmar cave, dating from about 3000 B.C.:[1] copper weapons, sceptres, crowns, copper clubs of complicated design but technically perfect and certainly in advance of anything to be found in Mesopotamia at the time. Here the copper had a strong admixture of arsenic. Gordon Childe described metallurgy as the "first international science" of those far-off centuries. This would explain the curious resemblances found in some cases between copper and bronze objects enormous distances apart.

Another "international" aspect of metallurgy was that the raw materials, in the form of ore or crude metal, had to be fetched from distant sources. The Mesopotamians went in search of copper in Cappadocia or in the Taurus mountains, or procured it in the islands of Bahrain (dispatch points for metal and mineral ores from Oman). Tin came from Iran, silver from the Taurus. The pursuit of metal, like that of wood, thus obliged the cities of Mesopotamia to engage in the long-distance trade which was essential for the creation of a diversified society with its artisans and carriers and already equipped with a merchant class, complete with financial backers. The Egyptians had to go to Sinai for copper and to Nubia for gold. But being further away than Mesopotamia from both the creative centres and the travelling smiths of the early days of metallurgy, Egypt was slow to adopt their technology. Magnificent examples of goldsmithing existed under the Old Kingdom, it is true, as beautiful in their way as the cups and goblets of Ur with their fine pure lines. But bronze smelting did not become established in Egypt, if our dating is correct, until the end of the third millennium.

Writing is basically a technology, a way of committing things to memory and communicating them, enabling people to send orders and to carry out administration at a distance. Empires and organized societies extending over space are the children of writing, which appeared everywhere at the same time as these political units, and by a similar process.

The early pictogram, a rather clumsy form of proto-writing, was a mere mnemonic device: an outline vaguely reminiscent of the object it referred to. Several meanings were possible. "When we find the head of an ox, does it refer to the animal itself, or to one of its products? Perhaps it signifies a horn, or something that could be made from horn?" The meaning was clear only to those using it at the time. For the pictogram does not allude precisely to a single given word, distinguished once and for all from other words. Among certain peoples, even today, this kind of writing still exists. The second stage is the ideogram, a stylized shape which designates a single object but does so regularly. The final stage is the phonogram, which translates and expresses the sounds of a language, its phonemes.

But this is too schematic a description. In practice, the ideogram was not completely eliminated by the phonogram, the appearance of which signified greater precision in writing, rather than a system replacing what had gone before. So in Egyptian, the word for hoe, *mer*, was represented by three stylized strokes, but they also designated the sound *mere*, which could mean both canal and the verb to love. "In the first case, when it is used to mean hoe, it is still an ideogram, in the second, it has become a phonogram."

In Sumer at the end of the third millennium, when there first appeared what we now call cuneiform script—produced by the impression made on soft clay tablets by the scribe's stylus, a sharpened reed—this script combined ideograms and phonograms: it had become capable of transcribing all the sounds in Sumerian, and despite difficulties which would persist until the revolutionary invention of the alphabet towards the end of the second millennium B.C., cuneiform script was used to transcribe the phonemes of many other languages (Akkadian, Elamite, Cassite and Hittite).

By a somewhat similar process, Egypt moved from hieroglyphic to hieratic and then to demotic script, the last named being the most cursive and simplified. But at this point in our narrative, it is the oldest form of writing that interests us. The name hieroglyphics, sacred writing, was coined by the Greeks who, on first seeing these signs on temple walls, thought they must have religious significance. Sculpted in relief or by incision, encrusted in decorative glass, engraved on precious objects by a goldsmith, painted on the wall of a tomb or on a modest papyrus roll, hieroglyphics, although instantly recognizable, have to be interpreted with some latitude.

A Twofold Birth

The palette of Narmer, the pharaoh who has been identified with the legendary Menes (*c.* 3200) is the earliest written Egyptian document we possess. The reader may like to try reading in the top left-hand corner the pictogram of the victory of Horus (the falcon-headed god, but also the pharaoh himself) over a chained man who doubly represents northern Egypt: he is bearded, unlike the clean-shaven Egyptians of the Upper Nile, and the water plants around him signify the marshy north. It is a puzzle which can be translated as "The god Horus has conquered the northern enemy" or "the god Horus has conquered five thousand enemies in the north," since five lotus flowers could also represent the figure five thousand!

An important technical point is that a flexible form of paper, made from the cortex of the papyrus reed, was in use in Egypt from the time of the first dynasties. This made it possible to use the calamus reed as a pen and to write quickly, using black or red ink. The ingenious invention has had rather annoying consequences for us though: whereas the heavy tablets of Mesopotamian clay stacked in the palace "archives" have been found in large numbers, the fragile papyrus rolls have only rarely survived. For every few metres preserved in museums today, literally kilometres have disappeared—virtually all the public records.

More important than these technical details is the crucial role played by writing in these developing societies. It became established as a means of controlling the society. In Sumer, most of the archaic tablets are simply inventories and accounts, lists of food rations distributed, with a note of the recipients. Linear B, the Mycenae-Cretan script which was finally deciphered in 1953, is equally disappointing, since it refers to similar subject matter: so far it has revealed hardly anything but palace accounts. But it was at this basic level that writing first became fixed and showed what it could do, having been invented by zealous servants of state or prince. Other functions and applications would come in due course.

Numbers appear in the earliest written languages. The Egyptian system of numbering in hieroglyphics is a simple idea. It worked on a decimal basis, and the only figures used were for one, ten, a hundred and a thousand: thus "a lotus flower means a thousand, an index means 10,000, a tadpole means 100,000, a god with raised arms a million." Numbers to be added together were simply juxtaposed. So the figure for 10,000 needed only one sign—but 9999 would have required thirty-six: nine times the sign for 1000, nine times the sign for a hundred, nine times the sign for ten and nine times the sign for one. Hieratic numbering later simplified the system by avoiding repetition of

Figure 5
The Narmer Palette. From Hierakonpolis, it describes the victory of Horus. Schist, 64 cm high, Cairo Museum (drawings by Laure Nollet).

numerals. But Egyptian arithmetic and the system used there for fractions remained primitive compared to that employed by those wizards at calculation, the Babylonians.

At first sight, it is true, the Babylonian number system, inherited from the Sumerian, looks unduly complicated: being on the base of 60, it uses fifty-nine different symbols for the first fifty-nine figures. But for numbers higher than sixty, the position of the figure in the writing system changes value. Every figure thus has two values, its own and its positional value, as in the case of modern numerals. The Babylonian system for fractions moreover, already in use at the time of Hammurabi (1792–1750 B.C.), was extremely well devised and easy to use.

These early writing and number systems took years of apprenticeship to master, so the art of writing and calculating was restricted to a privileged and talented elite. At Ugarit, on the Syrian coast, a city whose importance and activity will be described later, a scribe had to know Sumerian (more or less a dead language by then); Akkadian, which in the second millennium was the language for international relations and legal documents; and a third script, as soon as the alphabetical cuneiform script of Ugarit itself began to be used. This was a body of science which had to be transmitted from master to pupil. One of the classic exercises consisted of copying, and probably translating into several languages, the "scribes' prayer": "To the young pupil sitting before thee, be not indifferent in thy greatness. In the art of writing, all secrets reveal unto him. Numbering, counting, every solution reveal unto him. Secret writing, reveal to him therefore." This prayer dates from quite late on (thirteenth century B.C.), but is nevertheless revealing. One could not become a "technocrat," a scribe or a literate person, without rigorous training. It was the price to be paid for enormous privileges. Egypt and Mesopotamia had their own mandarin class.

Cities played a crucial though ambiguous role in the new civilization. They were created by population increase, but they also generated it. They were created by trade, but they generated that too; they were tools in the hands of great political powers, but they also operated on their own account. The basic conditions of their existence seem always to have been the same: they all had a dependent hinterland, a temple, a palace, an artisan class (weavers, blacksmiths, goldsmiths), scribes, carriers, merchants. Once a wall had been built around the settlement, it was fixed perhaps for centuries, distinguishing the town from the surrounding countryside and making it in some sense superior. All these basic conditions accompanied the rise of a city but did not always determine its fortunes.

The destiny of a given town or city depended on a double balance of activity and exchange: the balance it created by its own efforts for the greater good of its little world; and the balance which might be imposed upon it by the economic and political forces of a greater world beyond. In Egypt, the towns do not seem to have had autonomous careers, except in the pre-dynastic era—and in those days any development was very modest. Who now remembers Hierakonpolis, the city of the falcon-god, or the strange city of Heliopolis, which specialized in inventing great myths, explanations of the Egyptian religion? Very soon, the all-powerful authority of the pharaohs was to exert its rule over the Egyptian cities, for their benefit, since the general level of prosperity thereby increased. Possibly there was something there which we cannot quite understand today, a kind of arrested development of urban life on the banks of the Nile. It is as if the old towns clung on with difficulty to sites which were all equally inappropriate, and as if the large capitals drew towards them all the urban potential of the country and exhausted it.

At any rate, when, for reasons external to Egypt, the Old Kingdom fell apart, it is striking to note that the country fragmented into *nomes*, or rural districts, becoming "feudalized" as historians often say, and that in this fragmentation, the leading role was played not by cities but by princes, temples and priests.

Mesopotamia provides no examples of this semi-silence, this urban decay—far from it. Sumer consisted of a galaxy of bustling cities in a small space; they grew up densely and had close communications—of necessity, since roads, whether local or long-distance, had to remain open to all. But all these cities—Ur, Uruk, Lagash, Eridu, Kish, Mari, or Nippur, a holy city like Heliopolis in Egypt—competed for power, promoting their various tutelary gods. And each of them manifested that urban patriotism with which Uruk is credited in the epic of Gilgamesh, the legendary founder of the city: "Look upon it even today: the outer wall bearing the tower, see how it gleams with copper; and the inner wall has no parallel. Touch the threshold, it is ancient . . . Climb on the city wall of Uruk and walk upon it . . . See how well it is built: are its bricks not fine and fairly baked?"

The Mesopotamian world always seemed to centre on a city, which might be built and rebuilt in the course of a stormy history. At the worst moments—which were never feudal—there was always an urban flame ready to rise from the ashes. Why should this be? Firstly, because Mesopotamia was less unified than Egypt, far more varied in composition, any attempt to construct a single political unit had always ended in failure (Sargon's empire did not appear until 2335 and lasted less than 150 years). Situated at the meeting point of every route, Mesopotamia was necessarily more open to the outside world, more dynamic than any other region. Its "bourgeois merchants" were to take the first known steps in history down the road marked "capitalism." I am inclined to think that it was copper, bought in the Bahrain islands, which provided the first impetus for the Sumerian cities. It launched them into the adventure of long-distance trade which, in every age, has been a revolutionary force.

In Egypt there was just the one river, and only one thing that mattered: the annual flood. Everything that happened on or around the Nile, from the first cataract at Aswan down to the sea, had an impact on the entire life of the country. Despite what has been suggested then, and despite differences visible to individuals (for someone from Lower Egypt, the Elephantine island was another world), the Egyptian people was essentially a single people, or very nearly so, from Upper to Lower Egypt. The *nomes* might have led independent lives at first, but regrouping took place very soon. The landscape, the people, the local gods, the towns, all resembled each other. The Delta became unified as Lower Egypt—the kingdom of the Bee and the Uraeus (the cobra); its prince wore a red tiara. Upper Egypt too, the narrow Nile valley, became established as a political unit—the kingdom of the Lily and the Vulture, its sovereign distinguished by a white cap. Eventually, Menes-Harmer, the master of the Upper Nile, brought the two together in about 3200, and wore as a sign of unity a double crown, red and white. Was he the first pharaoh? The title comes from the Egyptian *per aa* or Great House, the palace towards which all people turn. Only much later was it used to denote the ruler himself, some fourteen or fifteen centuries after Narmer's reign. But we might note that the confusion between house, palace and sovereign is significant.

Narmer's Palette [see Figure 5] shows from the beginning a pharaoh cloaked in the extraordinary dignity of a living god. His attitudes, his representative nature, his tall stature towering above other men—all these aspects would remain the same thereafter, at least in formal terms. The divine right of the monarch was in fact Egypt's "political theory" as S. Morenz has suggested. Upon it was founded the order of a society with an intensely religious consciousness. This right, rooted in religion, and this miraculous form of royalty came from the depths of Egypt's pre-dynastic and prehistoric past, from a magical and wild universe in which the gods were frightening and dangerous beings. The pharaoh became a god himself through his coronation, acquiring the strength of the crowns in the most realistic fashion, by eating them. In similar fashion, he acquired divine substance. In the Texts of the Pyramids is found the "famous hymn to the cannibal pharaoh who feeds on the gods, eating the big ones for breakfast, the middle-sized ones for dinner and the small ones for supper, breaking their backbones and tearing out their hearts, eating alive all those he meets on his way." In other words, the pharaoh is the greatest of all gods, or at least their equal, the master of men and objects, the master too of the waters of the Nile, of the land and even of the growing harvest. "I was someone who made the barley grow" were the words later put into the mouth of a dead pharaoh. This concept of a living god was to remain formally unassailable. Ramses II, in the twelfth century B.C. could still cry out, "Listen . . . for I am Râ, lord of heaven, come to earth."

But we should not over-simplify an institution which despite its longevity had been subtly transformed over the millennia. At first the pharaoh was Horus himself, the falcon-god, then he became his earthly incarnation, and the statue of Chephren is very significant in this context. When, finally, he became the *son* of Râ, of the lord of the gods, from the fourth dynasty onwards, did he perhaps lose some of his original grandeur? In the first place he was no longer the equal of the gods, but the son of a divine father. In the second, he was responsible before his father, as any son is, and on earth to carry out his father's commandments. Ramses III, the last great man to rule Egypt, told Amon: "I did not disobey the command." In short, Morenz thinks that we can distinguish "a progressive diminution of the divinity of the throne: . . . from identity to incarnation to filiality."

The pharaoh was nevertheless responsible for universal order. The word *ma'at* which meant rectitude, truth, justice, took on the meaning of the natural order of the world. The living god was the guarantor of that order and when he gave up his earthly life it was to be born into another existence, where he would continue with his beneficial task. The great pyramids of the fourth dynasty were built with religious fervour by a people who thought that by so doing they would preserve this active beneficence. The Egyptologist Cyril Aldred even concluded, paraphrasing a famous aphorism, that "Ancient

Egypt was a gift from the pharaoh." The sovereign provided the strength and cohesion of a civilization which often worked with a unity of spirit.

Political unity meant that Egypt was reduced to obedience. But the Nile valley machinery operated so much better under this order that its superiority seemed to have been demonstrated, to the advantage of the Living God. When an internally inspired cultural revolution brought down the grandiose construction of the Old Kingdom during the first intermediate period (between 2185 and 2040), it was ultimately realized that the best course of action would be to rebuild what had been destroyed.

So it was that Egypt accepted discipline as unavoidable. But what kind of Egypt was it? A mass of ordinary people, whose everyday toil can be seen on the bas-reliefs on the tombs of Saqqarah, and in the clay statuettes and paintings of the eighteenth dynasty: peasants in their fields, sowing, reaping, loading sheaves of corn on to the backs of asses, hauling up a millstone, carrying grain to the granary, binding flax, driving a herd across a ford, harvesting papyrus, drawing in a net, unloading a boat; craftsmen working with wood and metal; slaves brewing beer, grinding corn, or kneading dough with their feet, harvesting and trampling grapes. The hieroglyphs which accompany these images are full of familiar terms: "Haul away!" or "Come on, lads, faster," while a flute player provides music in time to the movements of the workers. Archives which have survived from the village of Deir-el-Medineh give a detailed account of the workmen on the site of the necropolis of Thebes (nineteenth dynasty), the tools they were provided with and the excuses for absence: "A scorpion bit him"; "Was drinking in company with X" (G. Posener). Was the drinker punished? One scene from the *mastaba* of Amenhotep is explicit: peasants who had not paid their dues were bastinadoed. The reason might change but the punishment was usually the same. This was the reality of Egypt: a people in a state of constant anxiety, whose lives were short and lived entirely under the sign of obedience, as strict as China under the mandarins.

Around the pharaoh were the vizier and princes of the blood. Mandated by him throughout all Egypt were the scribes, a privileged mandarin class, well aware of their status. At the bottom of the heap came the countless numbers of peasant slaves. In fact slave status did not become legally established until the New Kingdom when there was a plentiful supply of prisoners of war.

But even before it was official, slavery had surely existed since time immemorial. Every year, when the flooded valley disappeared under the waters of the Nile, the peasant had a moment of respite—and this was the moment when he was called on to labour for the royal household, to build the colossal pyramids. This was one form of slavery. Another was the tax system—which was the issue every time (very rarely) that a complaint is recorded. The excuses dating from about 1500 B.C. seem timeless in fact: there has been no harvest, "because there were too many rats, the locusts came, herds ate the crop, sparrows have devastated the fields, and the hippos ate the rest." The tax men did not give up: "they told the peasant: give us the grain—even when there was none. Then they beat the peasant savagely, tied him up and threw him down a well." The account is too literary to be true, but too circumstantial to be entirely false.

This was an over-obedient society, no doubt. But this was surely the fate of those early civilizations which Alfred Weber described as "blueprints." The gods were simply too present. Through their priests, they explained the origin of the world, revealed themselves in the celestial bodies or in sacred animals, told humans what to do—in short, "they wrote history." The many gods jostled for position, and changed with dynasties, cities or clergies. From among their names—Isis, Osiris, Horus, Bes, Hathor, Thoth, Ptah, Seth, Amon Râ and many more—every town, indeed every individual could choose a protective deity. With their appearance, mythology entered human existence: the many adventures of these gods, with their human dimensions, brought them closer to ordinary mortals.

J. M. Keynes, the economist's economist, joked about ancient Egypt that it represented human and economic perfection since any surplus production, agricultural or urban, was systematically consumed by putting up huge and "useless" pyramids. So the Egyptian economy ran no risk of "overheating"—but only on condition that it was self-contained. The Egypt of the Old Kingdom had little contact with the outside world except that it sent expeditions to Libya, Sinai or Nubia in search of precious or rare stones, gold, slaves and black mercenaries—and that it sent a few boats to Byblos to fetch oil and wood from Lebanon. Everything was to change when Egypt was forcibly drawn into the international scene in the second millennium B.C., and had to defend its own gates. Then the army began to consume what had earlier fuelled the peaceful building programme of the pyramids.

Lords of earthly life, the gods could dispense eternal life. For a long while, only the pharaoh could enjoy the precious survival which was achieved by a multitude of precautions: the embalming of the body, the many funeral rites, the tomb, the statues, frescoes, and images of his servants in case he needed assistance in the afterlife. It was during the Middle Kingdom that the wider immortality of the human soul's "double" was held to be acquired, at first only by the high and mighty, and then by all Egyptians who could make the ultimate journey to the kingdom of the dead by undergoing the trials of purification and the last judgment. Records survive of Sinouhe, an Egyptian born twenty centuries before Christ, and a traveller against his will, who lived in Syria. He made a fortune there, married the daughter of a local chief, and described the delights of this land of wine and fruit and abundant herds. But he came home at last, troubled by homesickness but even more by the fear of being buried one day "with a mere sheepskin for a shroud," and thus forgoing eternal life.

Mesopotamia was a place of constant turmoil: the powers that presided at its birth forgot to protect it from its neighbours, whether those of the surrounding mountains "which both guarded and menaced" it to the east and north, or those of the burning Syrian desert, to the west and south. The land between the two rivers had a history interrupted by many episodes, often dramatic ones. It was in Eden, in Mesopotamia, that the book of Genesis located the earthly paradise. Nomads from the uninhabited desert, mountain peoples and hungry travellers across the high plateaux were constantly tempted by the fields, gardens and cities of Mesopotamia. This blessed region, absorbed in its labours, was a fruit that everyone wanted to seize or share. The destiny of Egypt by contrast seems to have been a sheltered one, developing smoothly—though that is no doubt a simplification. To one specialist, Mesopotamian civilization seems like a tree forever putting out new branches or vigorous shoots from its very trunk. But every fresh flowering was bought at a high cost—war, exodus, destruction of cities, pillage and upheaval.

Nevertheless, a single civilization survived through all these vicissitudes. And all the regions surrounding the "land between the rivers" were so many offshoots of this civilization which acted as an unchallenged centre of influence. At the centre of a brillant and variable constellation, Mesopotamia was always the star, through all the storms. Every invasion ended with the newcomers being absorbed into local life, so that Semitic dynasties from the desert might succeed Sumerians, or vice versa, at the whim of history. Such changes were in the end marked only by cultural differences—some of them quite striking, it is true.

So Mesopotamia had a singular destiny. But the outside world, mountain or desert, was not solely responsible. The house was itself divided. Exaggerating only a little, we might compare it to Renaissance Italy. Sumer, like Italy, flourished under a plurality of powers, with fierce rivalries between cities. These cities—Uruk, Ur, Eridu, Kish, Larsa, Isin, Mari, Adab, Lagash—had taken the place of tribes and primitive societies. Each one had its particular divinities and its priest-kings (something very different from a king identified with a god). They fought each other unremittingly and hegemony passed from one to another: from Kish to Ur, then to Uruk, Lagash and Adab. The first serious unification took place under the Akkadian Empire, created by Semitic peoples. This state had a brilliant flowering with Sargon the Elder, but only a short life (2340–2230). Ur then took the lead for a while, before passing the torch to Isin, Larsa and eventually Babylon.

Did Mesopotamia suffer from some kind of political weakness, making it impossible to invent stable royal institutions, prince, king or monarchy? That is probably not the point. Let us say rather that the cities, enriched by agriculture and trade from the early Sumerian period onwards, became so prosperous that they were propelled forward by their original impetus, carrying all before them. The political instability of the region probably did not as a rule touch them deeply. It did not necessarily affect foreign trade which carried on operating across the whole area, from north to south and east to west. A change in dynasty could be accepted as long as tranquillity returned, and so long as each city, along with the labourers in the surrounding countryside and the workshops in town, was once more in control of its own sphere of influence and trading links.

So some forms of obedience on the Egyptian model were possible, particularly since early Mesopotamia was an even more god-fearing place than Egypt: its gods were dominant even if they were seen to be quarrelling amongst themselves, with some waxing and others waning, depending on human fortunes. Enlil had reigned over Ur; then, when Babylon triumphed, its own god Marduk imposed his superiority over all others. Later again, Assyria took its name from Assur, a god who also came originally from the old Sumerian pantheon of the third millennium. To have the superiority of its gods proclaimed was one way for a city to assert its authority. But such a triumph did not mean dispossessing the other gods of their particular functions:

thus Inanna (the future Ishtar of the Babylonians) represented fertility, Enlil controlled the destiny and the order of the universe, Anu was the redoubtable god of the heavens, Enki the wise and kindly bringer of springs and life-giving water.

These numerous and ever-present gods ruled everything and were never forgotten in the rhythm of everyday life. With their staring hypnotic eyes, they frightened and tormented human beings, without leaving them even the hope of the longed-for eternal life, as they did in Egypt. Even the hero Gilgamesh despaired at the thought of his own death. As owners of the city and all its lands, of all the fruits it brought forth, the gods left it to the priests to distribute plots of land to humans and to decide how much of the harvest should be brought to the temples. First the priests, and later the kings of city-states and early empires, were seen as the gods' representatives on earth. They were charged with carrying out the divine will and interpreting it through omens and oracles. These auguries were the mystery of the temple, and the sovereign was often a prisoner of his role. Like his subjects, he lived in fear of failing to understand the messages of the gods. The latter, according to the Mesopotamian world view, desired order and prosperity on earth, as a condition of their own happiness. It was natural therefore that the digging of canals, the ordering of trade, the great craft workshops and the administrative reforms, such as those of Hammurabi, always referred to a god as the original inspiration, for the greater glory of the community and the glory of the sovereign.

The entire social structure was thus attached to a religious infrastructure. Without divine commands, without the expert knowledge of the priestly interpreter, who could decipher these messages? Without the sovereign who desired to obey the orders from high, how could life go on? The obedience which was the rule in the first major human societies, Egypt and Mesopotamia, was therefore not simply the product of blind fear, but corresponded to a certain social coherence, one might even say an awareness of the obligations of collective living. Was everything for the best in the best of all possible worlds? We may doubt that in the light of our own sensibilities, but then these are not competent to judge such distant societies.

II

BOATS ON THE RIVERS, SHIPS ON THE SEA

Even before the network of maritime links throughout the Mediterranean had taken shape, its balance was tilting towards its eastern reaches. The

Mediterranean system was after all created to fulfil the demands and the potential of two great social units: Egypt, which had limited but direct access to the sea itself, and Mesopotamia, which used the active intermediary of the Syrian seaboard to obtain access to the "Upper Sea." Regular shipping was only ever established in the service of the powerful, and operated either through Syria, gateway to the valley of the Euphrates, or through the many inconvenient but active ports in the Nile Delta. Egyptian gold and Babylonian silver were the lifeblood of Mediterranean trade, which reached significant levels in the second millennium B.C.

But to inaugurate shipping links meant finding vessels and mariners to sail them, neither of which appeared by magic. The shipping that was so well established by the second millennium presupposed other less successful shipping initiatives, well before the glorious days of the pharaohs. This early chapter in the Mediterraean's life-story remains obscure, however. Few documents have survived. Underwater archaeology has located a few sunken ships. But the sea is less ready to yield up its secrets than dry land, where they are more easily preserved for us to discover.

We do know something of the boats which in very early times plied up and down the rivers—the Nile, the Euphrates, the Tigris and even the Indus—but next to nothing about the ships that sailed on the Mediterranean, the Indian Ocean and the Red Sea. Was river navigation an ancient skill and seafaring learned more recently? That seems a bit too simple to be true. But river boats were undoubtedly circulating at the heart of the oldest civilizations in the world: they figure in the earliest iconography of Mesopotamia and Egypt. Seafaring remained marginal to these early civilizations, and although it too must have begun at the dawn of history, its origins are lost in silence. The future, however, was to belong to seagoing vessels.

River craft sailed on the Euphrates and even on the Tigris, despite its dangerous whirlpools, from very early times. In the beginning, inflated animal hides must have been used, although we find no formal evidence of them before the Assyrian monuments of the eleventh century B.C., which show soldiers riding astride these blown-up skins on their way to attack a city; others are fleeing the enemy on the same strange steeds; sometimes several skins were lashed together to make a raft. These were the Babylonian *kalakkus* capable of carrying very heavy loads downstream with the current (as the Arabian *keleks* still do today, using hundreds of inflated hides). Once they reached their destination, the wood and rigging of the rafts was sold, and the skins deflated and sent back by pack-animal.

The most ancient Sumerian cylindrical seals (late fourth millennium B.C.) show boats being used for ritual processions. They have no masts but both ends are hoisted high out of the water by taut ropes, and they are made of reeds lashed together or plaited, as indeed are the boats still to be seen on the Euphrates, consisting of a basketwork base coated in pitch or covered with leather. In about 3000 B.C., canoe-shaped boats were used to hunt wild buffalo in the marshes: a silver model of one of them, discovered in the royal burial ground at Ur, shows seven rowing benches and six pairs of oars.

Sailing downstream with the current, these boats were simply steered by long poles, but going upstream they had to be propelled by oars, or hauled from the bank. Sails must have developed quite early on: trading links with Bahrain and no doubt with the Indian coast, via the Persian Gulf, suggest that sails and seagoing ships were already in existence. These links are known to have been operating by the third millennium B.C. At this stage, it is true that they were far from having the density of the traffic on the river. Mesopotamia was obliged by its very nature to depend on internal exchange: the many towns in the lower reaches of the plain needed the stone, timber, pitch, copper, wine and livestock that Upper Mesopotamia produced or imported from neighbouring regions. These floated downstream, while back up the river by boat or pack animal, went grain, dates, even reeds for building houses, and eventually manufactured articles.

Texts from the second millennium describe this activity: the boatbuilders in riverside yards, the voyages, the variety of traffic, the lawsuits that followed accidents. A governor from the time of Hammurabi urges one of his subordinates to hasten the building of a boat: "Deliver [to the boatbuilder] the grain and dates he will request from you for the reed-weavers and other unskilled workers." To another boatbuilder in the same yard at Larsa he writes: "assemble whatever boards and beams are needed to build a barge." So at this period, both timber and reeds were being used to make boats. The owner of a boat generally did not sail it himself but hired it out to a boatman. The Code of Hammurabi contains clauses referring to what happens if a negligent boatman lets the craft fall into disrepair: he becomes liable for the damage. If he allows the boat and its cargo to sink, he is sentenced to reimburse the owner in full—unless he has had the presence of mind (and the material means) to refloat the wreck, in which case he will "only repay half the money." We see here surely the kind of relation between employer and employee which already foreshadows a capitalist society.

All the evidence points to the great importance of river traffic in Egypt: many written or pictorial documents; over eighty words for types of boat, large and small and fitted in various ways; and the very religion of the Egyptian people, which is full of nautical terms and metaphors. The gods and pharaohs all had their boats, and the journey of the dead towards their judgment is imagined as a voyage on the familiar river.

Boats had been sailing on the Nile since the pre-dynastic period. We can see what they looked like from artefacts: a pot in the British Museum, a stone vase dating from about the same period (3500–3200) in the Chicago Museum, or the ivory handle of the marvellous knife of Djebel-el-Arak: these depict ships with square-rigged sails, and high, almost vertical bows and stern, the shape typical of the Mesopotamian reed boats. In Egypt, a more familiar sight was the long flat punt, made of bundles of papyrus carefully bound together. The two ends were slightly elevated, and its low draught enabled it to circulate in the shallow waters of the marches or over sandbanks in the river. This is the boat depicted in hunting or fishing scenes, and invariably it is a boat of this kind which appears on the walls of Egyptian tombs, ferrying the dead on their last voyage.

The same design, developed and enlarged, was used for the Egyptian merchantmen or warships which travelled on both river or sea. Progress consisted of replacing the papyrus with timber; but timber, at least of good ship-building quality, was in short supply in Egypt itself. Beside cedar imported from Lebanon, sycamore and acacia wood from the region near present-day Khartoum was used. The treetrunks were sawn up into short thick planks, which were then solidly assembled, using mortice and tenon and even swallowtail joints, or merely leather straps. Such boats were flat-bottomed, and their entire design was reminiscent of the papyrus model. They had no keel, the hull was strengthened by the transoms, and the curved ends were maintained simply by a thick cable running fore and aft which could be tightened as required. A two-footed mast, located forward in the early versions, was replaced by a central mast, carrying a quadrangular sail.

The sail had made its appearance by the fourth millennium. Boats were also rowed or hauled upstream, but since the wind blows from the north almost all year round in Egypt, this inevitably led to the increased use of sails going upstream. The Egyptian language used two different hieroglyphs to describe journeys on the Nile: the sign showing a boat with a billowing sail meant the voyage south; the sign for a boat with a furled sail referred to the trip north, which could be accomplished simply by going with the current.

It would be fascinating to know what kind of ships first ventured out on to the open sea, braving its dangers. Alas, we do not. We can speculate for hours on end, but will never reach any firm conclusion, since the very few items of evidence that exist are difficult to interpret.

The first sea crossings must have developed very early, between the tenth and the seventh millennia. But the evidence is flimsy. There is nothing serious to connect the enigmatic drawings engraved on cave walls near Santander, on the Atlantic coast, and near Malaga, on the Mediterranean. Do these vessels date from Paleolithic times? The Abbé Breuil thought so, but without further proof, it is rather a rash assumption. Nor does any formal evidence support the hypotheses made by certain geographers that maritime shipping originated on the Red Sea and on the coast of Asia Minor, or in the large islands neighbouring the Aegean. The fact that Crete and Cyprus were apparently already inhabited in the early Neolithic era, roughly between the seventh and sixth millennia, would tend to support this notion. These first inhabitants could only have arrived by sea. So rafts or primitive vessels, if not genuine boats, may have existed as early as the seventh millennium, and probably earlier. It is not impossible that traces of habitation going back to the Mesolithic or even Paleolithic eras will one day be found on one of the islands that has never been linked to the mainland—Cyprus for instance, where not all the caves have yet been explored.[2] If so, our problem will have to be reformulated.

My personal view, though with little to back this up, is that attempts to sail out on the open sea go back a very long way. There was after all no insuperable obstacle. Primitive societies in various places have overcome the dangers of the sea: one has only to think of the rafts made by American Indians, or even the reed boats, the *caballitos* or little horses, in which fishermen still set out to sea on the coast of Peru. Besides, in the case of the Mediterranean, the early development of coastal shipping seems to be the only explanation for the spread of certain commodities.

Thus the spread around the Mediterranean coasts of so-called cardial pottery (the design was impressed on damp clay with a shell, the cardium) could have been achieved via short-haul voyages, perhaps from the gulf of Alexandretta, inshore from Cyprus. From there, rafts could have been sailed to Greece, Italy, Provence, Spain, Sicily, Malta, or even the shores of North Africa—since on all these seaboards pottery fragments showing the same impressions are to be found. It was originally thought that they dated from the third millennium, but recent excavations have pushed the date much further back. But how far? In Thessaly they are thought to date from the end of the sixth millennium. In the western Mediterranean, the date is still a matter of debate—possibly the fifth or fourth.[3] What is known for certain is that this pottery everywhere corresponds to the spread of early Neolithic agriculture.

It was by sea too that the two waves of settlers came to pre-ceramic Greece, from Asia Minor, bringing with them the secrets of primitive farming (though the first of these waves may possibly have come overland, if the Aegean landmass had not yet been submerged at that time).

A firmer and less hazardous chronology can only be established by jumping many centuries and dating developments on the great clock—so to speak—of Egypt.

Egyptian ships were sailing both to Byblos and the Red Sea from an early date—exactly when we cannot say. But cooking oil from Syria was already arriving in pre-dynastic Egypt, carried in pots of non-Egyptian origin. And by about 2600 B.C., we know that Egypt already had plentiful contacts with Byblos, through which it gained access to the cedars of Lebanon, pitch from the Dead Sea, gold from the Taurus mountains, and the oil and wine of Syria. The boats which ceaselessly plied to and fro on these trips were known in the middle of the third millennium as the "Byblos boats"; but while Egypt certainly financed them, and while their design was Egyptian, we do not know whether they were in fact built in Byblos or in Egypt, nor whether their crews came from one or other place, or both.

These must have been large-scale shipping ventures, as is proved by the number of boats shown being assembled at Saqqarah for the expedition led by King Sahura. Even more conclusive is the huge organization apparently centred, oddly enough, on Elephantine Island, at the first falls on the Nile. In the age of the pyramids, in the twenty-fifth century B.C., the royal "civil servants" of Elephantine (whom we may think of as entrepreneurs and even venture to describe as capitalists, to judge by the extravagance of their tombs), controlled shipments of granite down the Nile to the capital, Memphis. They also controlled the quarries in the desert, the transport of these great blocks of stone to the river, the roads from Coptos to Koseir on the Red Sea, the turquoise mines of Sinai and, lastly, the maritime links with the Punt via the Red Sea, as well as with Syria. There was thus a curious set of connections between the overland routes, the sea passages and the river craft on the Nile, between the granite of Upper Egypt and the squared cedar trunks coming from Byblos. The glimpses we have of them leave us wondering whether we should imagine active seaports in the Nile Delta as early as the twenty-fifth century B.C. Alas, everything is buried under mud today.

About a thousand years later, under the Eighteenth Dynasty, a Theban painter depicted boats built by Canaanites (as the peoples of the Syrian coast were called, the ancestors of the Phoenicians) landing goods from their country on to a quayside. The boats were unquestionably of Egyptian design, similar to, if a little rounder than, the ones which Sahura sent to Byblos, with their familiar raised ends. The boats which Queen Hacheptsut (Eighteenth Dynasty) launched for her maritime expedition of 1480 B.C. to the Punt, and possibly to Somalia, were longer and lay lower in the water, but had similar rigging. The mast was in the centre of the hull and carried a large square sail: two long paddles acted as a rudder. The beautiful model of a fully rigged sailing ship in Tutankhamun's tomb, a hundred years later, shows identical features in hull and mast to the Punt ships. Only the system for the rudder is different.

Typically, these Egyptian-Syrian vessels operated almost entirely under sail. Unlike the small boats on the Nile which used oars, these large sailing vessels used oars only when manoeuvring into and out of port.

But we should not exaggerate the maritime achievements of the Egyptians. At ease on the Nile, they were less enthusiastic about the open sea. Egypt lived a largely self-contained life, with its river and its alluvial plains. The distant world interested the Egyptians, but did not tempt them unduly—or rather, it was more likely to come to Egypt, drawn by its wealth. Why go far afield? External trade was often handled by foreigners who had settled at the mouths of the Nile: Canaanites, Cretans, Phoenicians and finally Greeks. After all, the "first Suez canal" was only dug in 610–595 under Necho. This would link the eastern branch of the Nile with Lake Tinset and the Bitter Lakes, and according to Herodotus two seagoing ships could pass alongside in it. It was undoubtedly a major achievement, but rather a late one: it was to be completed, or rather re-created, by Darius. Similarly, it was Alexander the Great who provided Egypt with its first properly equipped harbour, by building Alexandria. Yet as early as 2150, the Egyptians had not hesitated to open up canals through the hard granite of the first Nile falls at Aswan. The early date of such major works on the river provides a contrast with the later and more episodic interest the Egyptians showed for the sea.

It is doubtful whether Egyptian ships ever sailed on any of the Mediterranean sea crossings, except the convenient and familiar route from the Delta to Syria: this meant four to eight days at sea each way. The key progress in shipping came from other directions and can be glimpsed only as part of the composite history of the seas of the Levant: the Phoenician coast, the islands and shorelines of the Aegean, the large island of Crete, and the Greek mainland.

Here too, little is known for certain: there are many doubts and controversies. The only thing we can be sure of is that the sea was effectively conquered during the second millennium B.C., by crossings of the Aegean and the Levant seas. But the moment one tries to go into more detail about the circumstances, the chronology or the causes of this development and the technical conditions or kinds of ship concerned, the picture becomes very complicated. The images that have survived, which are the essential documents in this respect, have given rise to various mutually incompatible theories and hypotheses.

In 1933, Spyridon Marinatos, a meticulous and well-informed historian, compiled a catalogue of sixty-nine drawings of the ancient ships of the Aegean; in 1957, Diana Woolner listed and reproduced thirty-eight graffiti showing ships carved on a pillar in the great megalithic temple of Hal Tarxien in Malta. So we have about a hundred representations of vessels at our disposal—and yet the result is disappointing. The drawings are all too often schematic and inaccurate, and do not obey any rules of perspective. Any models that have survived, generally made of clay, are only very approximately shaped. There is nothing here like the accuracy of the Egyptian drawings. Apart from the Maltese graffiti, which were scratched on to stone with a metal tool, these pictures of boats are illustrations from the sides of vases or other utensils, from seals or cylinders, rings, or hieroglyphic tablets. Their dates are generally uncertain and are spread out across more than a thousand years.

Nevertheless, since naval design did not substantially change for centuries on end (and in any case new types of ship co-existed with old ones), it would not be out of order to assume that in a sense all these ships were sailing the sea at roughly the same period, whatever the actual dates of the vessels. They can be seen as the available pool of shipping, if you like, as if they could all have sailed to the Egyptian Delta, or to the quayside at Ugarit, in response to the appeal from the king of the Hittites for grain for his starving cities in 1200 B.C.

What questions should we ask of these images? Quite elementary ones. First of all, we ought to be able to tell bows from stern, so that we can see which way the boat was travelling. This can be worked out by the position of the oars, when there are any. Greek oarsmen, like their Mycenaean and Cretan predecessors, rowed with their backs to the direction of travel, unlike the Venetian gondolier for instance, who stands in the stern of the boat facing the way he is going. Another way to tell is from the width of the vessel, if it can be gauged, as it can in at least one model: in that case, the forward end, the bow, will be the wider, since the boat was always narrower at the stern (a rule which aeroplanes also respect because of air-currents: this is the "fish-shaped body" theory). And of course, when the vessel has a rudder, made of one or two moveable paddles, these naturally indicate the stern. The reader will notice that the poop of Aegean ships was often higher than the bows, but the rule was not absolute, and it is often difficult to tell which end is which.

There are other questions too: did the vessel have a deck, and if so was it a whole one or a half-deck? Did it have oars, benches, masts and sails? Ships in the Aegean, since they had plenty of oars, did not always carry sails as an extra means of locomotion. Where sails existed, they seem to have been square, carried on a yardarm. Sometimes two square sails were attached side by side to the same yard and mast. This kind of rigging was tending to disappear, but a late example is found in a ship from Pompeii.

The number of oars, usually accurately represented (up to a maximum of fifteen) enabled Marinatos to calculate the possible lengths of some boats (by estimating the distance between two oarsmen as 90 cm). He concluded that the maximum length was about 20 metres (allowing for the area without oars), in the case of the largest vessels with fifteen oars, but much less than that on average, since most boats had no more than five. So most of these vessels were quite small, long and light, with a single mast, propelled by oarsmen and using sails only as an extra aid.

But the important point to note is that from early times, from the middle Minoan period (before 2000 B.C.) there were also to be found alongside these ships others with no oars at all but a full deck, as is conclusively proved by a clay model dating from about 1500 B.C. These ships were much broader than the other kind and suggest the possibility of cargo vessels under sail, perhaps larger than other Cretan ships and thus a very early case of the traditional division in the Mediterranean between the rapid longships with their banks of oarsmen, used for war or piracy, and the rounded sailing vessels, carrying merchandise. I agree with Kirk that the alternation we find at different periods between artistic images of long and rounded ships does not necessarily point to a preference by the sailors of that time for one or the other, and may merely reflect changing artistic fashion. Both forms must have co-existed in the shipping of the Aegean: the longships generally had a low-lying bow with a kind of ram and a raised poop. The roundships had both bow and stern raised and curved, as can still be seen on some late pottery from Cyprus.

The origin of the ram is a key problem. When its development had reached completion in the first millennium B.C., the entire force of the warship, Phoenician or Greek, was concentrated on this dangerous weapon, prolonging the ship's keel forward into a sharp point. The ram seems to have been an Aegean refinement to the longship.

On the earliest models we know of, in the Cyclades (depicted on the "frying pan" pottery of Syros), the bow of the ship is prolonged in a curious shape strongly reminiscent of a battering ram. This projection is found in a series of drawings and clay models. Kirk, writing in 1949, was no doubt right that this was the ancestor of the battering ram, but also correctly surmised that it was not conceived of at this stage as an instrument of war. The initial function of this spar (which might project from either end of the boat) was to consolidate the ship's structure, in particular the bows, which were exposed to the shock of the waves and also suffered whenever the vessel was hauled up on a beach (hence the upward curve of the early versions.) The first straight ram was simply the extension of the keel, the backbone of the ship on which the whole structure of the Aegean vessel was based.

This was an original development. Egyptian boats and the Canaanite boats of the second millennium had no keel, no ram and no ribs. And while it is possible that the Cretan roundship, which appeared in the second millennium, was a copy of the Syrio-Egyptian kind of boat, it is clear that "the Aegeans made great progress when they added to this very practical design those essential elements of naval construction, the keel and ribs. Thus was created a stable and solid type of vessel, still found today" along the Greek coast. It was indeed the first transport ship truly adapted to sea-going.

It is no surprise to find that those born intermediaries of the Levant, the coastal traders of the Syrian coast, long accustomed to the Egyptian crossing, should rapidly have taken over the Aegean type of ship. They had seen it come into being, since Cretan vessels were frequenting the Syrian seaports long before they went to the Nile Delta. As the centuries went by, there would hardly be a type of vessel known in the Mediterranean which had not been adopted—and adapted—by the Phoenicians, the direct descendants of the Syrians of the second millennium.

The Aegean longship, with its oarsmen and keel, now fully developed, appears for the first time on a bas-relief in Karatepe, a zone of Phoenician influence in the former Hittite region, in about the eighth century B.C. Were the Phoenicians or perhaps the Mycenaeans responsible for its perfected design? Thanks to this design it became the classic longship of the Mediterranean, the kind depicted on a Spartan ivory as well as on so many geometric vases with black figures; the design, too, which Sidon chose to put on its coins in the fifth century B.C., as did the Greek island of Samos. This kind of ship would be further improved by the Greeks, who made a lighter version by taking out the decks. They were therefore able to extend its length to 30 or 35 metres and put up the number of oarsmen to fifty: this was the famous *pentecontor* on which the Athenian fleet relied, according to Thucydides, down to the battle of Salamis (480 B.C.). After that came the reign of the trireme with its three tiered banks of oarsmen.

It is a mistake, however (derived from a few Greek vases with faulty perspective), to credit the Greeks with the invention of the bireme. A perfectly unambiguous document proves otherwise. On the walls of the palace of Nineveh, the Phoenician fleet is shown fleeing the port of Tyre before the city was attacked by Sennacherib (700 B.C.): roundships with symmetrically raised ends are shown alongside longships with pointed bows. The lessons of the Aegean had evidently been fully assimilated by the Phoenicians, but with one innovation: all these ships had two banks of tiered oarsmen. This was the bireme, the importance of which may in any case have been exaggerated. According to Kirk, the Greeks borrowed the design from the Phoenicians later on, in the sixth century, but only for a short while, preferring the *pentecontor* which was safer at sea. The Phoenicians themselves used the bireme only in calm weather and close to shore.

At the same period, for the coastal convoys of timber mentioned earlier, the Phoenicians were using other boats of more mysterious origin, known to the Greeks as *hippoi* because their bows were decorated with a horse's head. It was on such a ship that King Assurbanipal went hunting on the Tigris, and this kind of boat may have been taken by the Phoenicians all over the Mediterranean if we can place credence on a Phoenician jewel found at Aliseda in Spain. According to Strabo, it was still in use in the Mediterranean at the end of the first century A.D., and only fifty years ago or so, fishermen on the coast near Cádiz used to carve a horse's head on the bows of their boats.

The graffiti in the third temple of Hal Tarxien in Malta have played little part so far in our account. That is because they are not easy to interpret. The sailors who scratched these ex-votos on a stone pillar, in a chapel which was probably abandoned some time after 1500 B.C.[4] were giving thanks after a dangerous voyage or a shipwreck to some mother-goddess, an early *stella maris*. The temple is near the large natural harbour on which the city of Valletta was much later founded, a port which provided a refuge every autumn as winter approached for ships which had been surprised at sea by bad weather.

Unfortunately these drawings are partly effaced and overlap with one another: each grateful sailor drew his boat at the height he could reach, like those who had come before him and those who would come after. And on limestone, any new scratch mark shows up as white, instantly obliterating any previous graffiti. As time passes, it merges with the rest.

Taken as a group, these forty-odd drawings do make sense: they prove that from the first half of the second millennium B.C., Malta was being reached by ships which, for once, we do not have to imagine. Whether or not they were tempest-tossed, ships were arriving at Malta and putting in there.

The ones which made the voyage in good weather and without incident are probably not represented in the ranks of the thank-offerings. But they must have existed too.

One could linger at length over the designs of these boats. Their key feature is diversity. I agree with Diana Woolner, who has made a study of the graffiti, that we have here a certain number of Aegean, Cretan, and Mycenaean ships, with raised bows and sterns. Like Woolner, I also recognize at least one boat of Egyptian type, perhaps more. But we should not therefore conclude that Egyptian vessels were actually reaching Malta. Even Eduard Meyer's hypothesis of some time ago, that the Egyptians reached Crete, is today seen as very doubtful: the Egyptian vases and sculptures found on Crete were probably carried there by Cretan ships, either directly from Egypt or from the Syrian coast. So it is even more unlikely that the Egyptians ventured as far as Malta. But during the first half of the second millennium, as we have already noted, Syrian ships had imitated Egyptian designs. We know that they were trading with Egypt and had an active trade in the Levant. They may also have begun, alongside the Aegean ships, to explore the western basins of the sea. Once more we face the thorny problem of relations between east and west Mediterranean.[5] If the Aegeans and the Syrians were putting in at Malta at the beginning or middle of the second millennium, they were surely not stopping short there. Was the island not the centre of a trading system, notably in obsidian from Pantelleria and the Lipari islands, a stone which is also found in southern Italy, as far up as Lucera? Mycenaean pottery has also been found both in the Lipari islands and in Italy.

The landfall made by so many ships at Malta does not invalidate these archaeological clues; quite the contrary. And it also fits the general hypotheses which have been suggested by that extremely curious phenomenon, the megaliths.

III

CAN THE SPREAD OF MEGALITHS EXPLAIN THE EARLY HISTORY OF THE MEDITERRANEAN?

I do not propose to tackle the difficult topic of megaliths simply for the pleasure of presenting a few images from a strange world which has remained mysterious. My concern is with the sea itself, unknowable and untamed. The reader has seen that the quest for the earliest ships does not really enable us to grasp much about the early periods of the sea, and that the current of evidence carries us ceaselessly onward towards later eras much easier to understand. Will the megaliths be able to take us further back in time?

Unfortunately, any dispassionate attempt to trace the history of megaliths leaves one with the impression of a vanished dream, a problem that may never be solved. This is the more regrettable since this widespread phenomenon concerns the entire Mediterranean area, with similarities between one place and another that suggest some unified movement. But the data at our disposal are far from clear.

Are we even talking about a single problem? To regard megaliths, those large and sometimes enormous blocks of crudely hewn stone, as the symbol of a particular *culture* is not *a priori* problematic. But even then the symbol has to to be found in association with the same cultural elements.

As regards the stones themselves, we are all familiar with the terminology of French, or rather Breton, origin: menhirs are vertical standing stones, dolmens are walls made of several cut stones topped with horizontal slabs. The reader may have seen lines of standing stones or stone circles (cromlechs) made up of menhirs, and will almost certainly be familiar with pictures of Stonehenge near Salisbury in England, an impressive site, although now in ruins, dating from between 1700 and 1500 B.C.: it is made up of several concentric circles of bluestones and large boulders with slabs over each lintel, brought from quarries in the Welsh mountains many miles away. These stones, traditionally supposed to be of sacred nature, were always thought to have been linked to Celtic history and Druid rites. Only very recently have they been recognized as possibly belonging to a much more widespread culture, probably of Mediterranean origin.

Other signs of this culture are found in the multiple burial chambers, sometimes covered by cairns made of overlapping stones and sometimes accessible only via a long low tunnel. Readers familiar with classical archaeology will recall the Mycenae tombs (inaccurately described as Agamemnon's treasure): a circular tomb (*tholos*), reached by a corridor (*dromos*). These multiple tombs might of course vary in overall design.

The last and crucial series of signs are as follows:

1 Megalithic monuments are linked to the cult of earth-mother goddesses, represented in many forms, sometimes as schematic faces where the eyes have a special place, or as stone columns with only a notional face but two curved arms indicating body shape.

2 Megaliths are *usually* linked to copper and bronze-working, as the example of eastern Spain clearly shows.

3 These megaliths are also connected in the west to early kinds of farming, which often preceded them. There is therefore some link between settlement and the establishment of villages on one hand and on the other a new cult and the technology of metal-working, brought by immigrant populations (possibly travelling smiths) or spreading from several centres by mere imitation.[6]

This being so, one can foresee considerable difficulties of interpretation: uncertainty about chronology—but then that is normal in prehistory—and gaps in the picture, as certain elements may not be where one would expect them, or may appear in an unusual form.

And yet one general feature seems to be clear. Since thousands of megalithic monuments have already been found, a huge number of positions can be charted on the globe, from Thailand, India or Madagascar to northern Europe. Within this huge and chronologically incoherent area, if we concentrate on the European and Mediterranean sector, one conclusion seems inescapable: this phenomenon must have spread by means of sea crossings. The monuments are overwhelmingly found in coastal areas, and in particular on islands: Malta, Sardinia, the Balearics, Britain, Ireland, Zeeland (the Danish island where some 3500 monuments of this type have recently been inventoried), and the coasts of North Africa, Provence, Spain and Brittany. In Brittany, where they are plentiful, they may be the consequence, somewhere between the second and the first millennia B.C.,[7] of voyages undertaken to fetch gold from Ireland and tin from Cornwall, since Brittany was the indispensable waystation. In the Mediterranean, the zone in question reminds one of the more limited zone dating from two thousand years earlier, defined by cardial pottery.

This civilization of huge stones was therefore propagated by sea, and not, as was thought in the past, by conquerors on horseback. Since the sea is now recognized as the prime route, it is tempting to suggest that the Mediterranean played the role of initiator. This hypothesis has the support of a conference held in Paris in 1961. The suggestion is that once more the Middle

East, both on land and sea, was the origin of the phenomenon. Professor M. Stekelis's excavations, which have dated the menhirs of Palestine and Lebanon to between the fifth and sixth millennia B.C., provide us, at least until more data is available, with a plausible centre from which it might have spread.

If this indeed was the case, then the "cultural universe" of the megaliths moved from east to west. But it certainly did not do so in any regular fashion or from any single source. We shall be able to chart their spread, if spread there was, only when we have succeeded in dating all the megalithic monuments, region by region.[8]

The experts do not by any means agree for example on the date of the megalithic temples in Malta, or even on the date of the first human habitation of the island (which was probably reached via Sicily): the evidence consists only of a very few shards of cardial pottery. Some very ancient burial chambers have, however, been unearthed by excavation, containing a mixture of bones still coated in ochre and human blood. Later than these are the immense catacombs of Hal Saflieni, discovered in 1901, in which over seven thousand skeletons were found, their bones scattered apparently at random.

At some very early date—and this is peculiar to Malta, giving it a special place in megalithic history—genuine temples also appeared. About a dozen of them have been preserved, differing greatly from one another, and combining huge boulders with more ordinary building stones. Although their chronology is uncertain, excavations throughout the island have made it possible to classify these temples in relation to one another. The two oldest ones at Mgarr have a clover-leaf design, with three oval main chambers, a feature which is always found in later temples, despite the increasing architectural complexity which make them truly enormous monuments.

This is true for instance of the temples at Gantija, Hagiar Kim, and Mnaidra, and of the fantastic complex at Hal Tarxien, made up of several successive temples, not far from the present-day capital, Valletta.

The hypothesis advanced by J. D. Evans in 1959 seems quite plausible: that these temples were originally primitive tombs which later changed their usage, remaining dedicated to the cult of the dead, who had to be placated by propitiary rites and sacrifices. This would explain, among other things, the curious frieze in the Hal Tarxien temple, depicting rams, pigs and goats, potential victims. Here too we find the Earth Mother, represented by many carved images (not merely menhir-statues as elsewhere). The style varied greatly with the period, but in the final generation of temples (dating from the first half of the second millennium), the style of the sculpture and certain motifs such as the spiral make one think there may have been some direct Aegean influence.

This temple civilization in Malta was suddenly and totally destroyed in about 1500 B.C.,[9] by invaders who probably originated in southern Italy. The boat graffiti mentioned earlier cannot be later therefore than the middle of the second millennium. But the newcomers, who destroyed the island's first civilization and used the ruins of the Hal Tarxien temples for their own ends, had one special feature: they brought with them copper weapons. This advantage no doubt made up for their inferior numbers compared to the builders of the megalithic temples. Of those builders, nothing else remained, neither their pottery—which was replaced by a much cruder variety—nor their art. Their successors appear themselves to have belonged to some form of megalithic culture, however, and they in turn covered the island with small dolmen tombs, of fairly crude design, in which pottery characteristic of the occupation has been found.

Malta may perhaps have played a key role in the megalithic chain. I say "perhaps" advisedly. This has often been suggested, but we should not allow ourselves to be carried away by the size and grandiose strangeness of the Maltese stones. After all, it is equally possible that southern Italy (Bari, Otranto, Tarentum) and Sicily, where huge mass tombs cut into the rock have left plentiful traces, associated with bronze-age artefacts, may have played just as influential a role in this primitive culture, if not more so. The small sea-girt island of Malta, producing a fantastic set of stone monuments, yet having no knowledge of metals, seems too special a case to have played the role of cultural transmitter in the spread of megaliths, as some people have hypothesized.

Sardinia, equally strange and special, is also worth pausing to consider. This is a very curious island, long uninhabited, like its neighbour Corsica. Being larger and even more isolated from the mainland than the latter, it has been perhaps the most conservative region of the whole Mediterranean—at every stage in its history. As in Malta, there was both a deviation from and a development of the usual megalithic pattern.

Collective tombs were present from the very first human occupation of the island, which was probably not before 2250 B.C.[10] They include the mysterious tombs of Li Muri, with their raised stones and their refined stone artefacts; somewhat later, it seems, came the tombs cut into the rock, which correspond to the first identifiable culture on the island, known as the Ozierian. Everything about these tombs seems to point to a link with eastern culture—the bulls' heads carved on the rocky walls, the idols of Cycladic type, the spiral designs at Pimenteli, which are a symbol of fertility widespread in the eastern Mediterranean from Sumer to Troy, Mycenae and Syria. But there is some western influence too, particularly from southern France, and certain imported artefacts argue for contact with both Sicily and the British Isles, possibly Ireland.

Of later date, but almost contemporary with each other,[11] are the tombs with dolmens, which would later develop into the great mass burial chambers known as the "tombs of the giants," and the first villages with *nuraghi*, towers, very characteristic of the island, and similar to the Corsican *torri*. About 6500 of these towers, more or less well-preserved, have been recorded on the island, and the list is probably not complete. Their name, which may come from a pre-Indo-European dialect, may mean a heap or a hollow. Originally they seem to have been watchtowers for defensive purposes, built on a platform and on the cairn principle, thus creating inside a kind of *tholos*, a vaulted chamber, on a more or less steep slope. They went on being built until Roman times (238 B.C.) and even later, The *nuraghi* thus spanned a thousand years of existence, during which time they were gradually embellished with various refinements, like the temples in Malta, a protective outside rampart for instance, or supplementary towers. With the Carthaginian invasion in the sixth century B.C., they had to be defended against engines of war: numerous projectiles have been found at the foot of the *nuraghi*. The huge complex at Barumini, where recent excavations have identified at least two successive periods, was the result of these progressive improvements and refinements.

These complexes, built of massive boulders, sheltered defenders, families, tribes and their chief, and sometimes armaments. As for their religious life, about which little is known, it centred first on the tombs of the giants, then on sanctuaries located near wells or fortified temples. These sites are reminiscent of those on Malta, but they are not identical, and we should note that they are in fact of much later date. Yet they come from the same stock of formal possibilities.

Unlike Malta, Sardinia had early knowledge of metals. Artefacts, probably imported, including copper which analysis shows to have come from Spain, the south of France, and Ireland, have been found in the Ozieri tombs. After this, local workings rapidly came to occupy an important place in this mining island, as we shall see later. One would like to know the date at which the foundries connected to the fortified temples and the *nuraghi* were built.

The Balearic islands, or at least Minorca and Majorca (Ibiza was uninhabited until the Carthaginians arrived in 636 B.C.), would give rise to observations comparable to those one might make concerning the whole Mediterranean "from Cyprus to Mycenae, by way of Crete and the Aegean islands," Malta and above all Sardinia. The tombs and towers in these two islands have not yet been systematically excavated. There are about a thousand towers, both round and square, locally called *talayots*. Do they date only from the first millennium, as seems possible? At any rate, they had time to develop, culminating in groups of towers and houses, surrounded by thick walls. The village of Capocorp Vell for example, near Lluchmayor, is about two hundred metres long and forty across; it has a wall three metres thick, and includes seven *talayots*, three round ones and four square. The cultural and historical meaning of this megalithic architecture has yet to be deciphered.

In Spain itself, the spread of megaliths was even more curious. From Almería to the Ebro and even to the Llobregat, the Mediterranean coast is absolutely free of any trace of this kind of construction. The region seems to have been penetrated from the south, through a narrow gap near the famous archaeological site of Los Millares (mid-second millennium).[12] After having come in via this entrance, the newcomers moved westwards, towards the Atlantic coast and Portugal. If the archaeologists are right, these people were invaders, since their skeletons, found in large numbers in the necropolises, seem to indicate a different racial group from that already established in Spain and North Africa.

These invaders were newcomers then, and they were familiar with metallurgy. The objects in the tombs reveal the combined use of copper and stone, daggers made of metal or flint, pikes and some remarkable arrowheads. Above all, and this is particularly noteworthy, the newcomers headed for the mining areas of Almería, Jaen, the Sierra Morena and the Lower Guadalquivir. These were the only inland regions they colonized, otherwise settling only in coastal zones. Was it mining or seafaring that made their fortune? Both, probably. Evidence of their prosperity at any rate lies in the existence of towns without any equivalent in the west at the time. On what is now the *despoblado* (uninhabited site) of Los Millares in Almeria province, we must imagine a genuine city with walls and flanking towers, an aqueduct bringing water from three kilometres away, and many rich necropolises. The practice of burying princes or chieftains surrounded by their entire families points to a "patriarchal and aristocratic society."

These collective burial sites help locate the invaders in the great megalithic movement: eastern influence seems clearer here than elsewhere.[13] In the Los Millares tombs, a corridor leads into a round or oval chamber made of great slabs of upright stones, welded together with clay, and topped by a false dome, as in certain *tholoi* in the Aegean from the first half of the second millennium. Sometimes a group of *baitlos* (sacred stones) painted red is found at the mouth of the corridor, very like those of Byblos. Other tombs, enormous in size, as at Antequera or Lacara near Merida, use more of the heavy raised stones of the dolmen type. Some of the tombs are underground, cut into the rock (as in Sicily and very frequently in the Aegean) and they always follow the pattern of the corridor and the cairned chamber. Martin Almagro Basch has unhesitatingly related this architecture and its associated pottery, weapons or stylized idols, to the Cyclades culture dating from about 2000 B.C. to the end of the Mycenaean period. Once more we find links between a megalithic culture and Aegean or Syrian influence, emanating therefore from areas already in close contact with each other in the seas of the cosmopolitan Levant of the second millennium.

The megalith problem, which we have not explored beyond the Mediterranean area, remains obscure, complex and controversial. Is the whole quest a wild goose chase, as one archaeologist maintains? All hypotheses remain possible, and the specialists often come up with contradictory ones, although they are almost always suggestive. What if we were one day to find firm evidence that the dolmens and menhirs of Brittany go back to the fourth millennium and are the oldest of all the groups in the west?[14] One theory however does not seem convincing: in order to refute the idea of an eastern origin, and thus of any kind of unity in the whole megalithic culture, one school of thought points out that the chronology we currently use provides no clear evidence of an east-west progression. It has therefore chosen to conclude that "the very simple ideas and technology" underlying the megalithic monuments must have sprung up spontaneously "in many regions" in Europe and the Mediterranean, without any obvious connection between them. But was it such a simple and straightforward matter, in terms of technology, to transport the great boulders of Stonehenge from a quarry some hundred and fifty miles away? Was it "natural" to build these huge collective tombs (which G. Bailloud has rightly identified as the essential feature of a culture including "the dolmens, the hypogees and the *tholoi*"), and is it really plausible to assume that it appeared everywhere more or less spontaneously?

The spread of a cultural phenomenon which included but was not confined to the megaliths does not of course signify total coherence or absolute uniformity. This would hardly be likely, since the process was spread over one or two millennia, and in environments geographically and humanly very different. Nevertheless a certain world view of forms and rituals did manifest itself, probably spreading by sea, rather than by large-scale population movement, and that does pose the enigma of the origins of those who created these monuments. Were they missionaries of a kind, founding a religion? The expanding temples on Malta and the funerary cults seem to point unavoidably to religious life. But in those days, what people did *not* build its life around its religion? Were they adventurers, setting out from the east in search of new tin or copper mines? I would be inclined to favour this theory, in spite of the early Maltese civilization which had no metal. The fact that ambulant metal-workers and smiths are well known in the history of the Middle East tends to strengthen me in this belief. We know that they travelled large distances, from the early third millennium. In about 2500, in the great cities of the Middle East, metal craftworking was usually in the hands of guilds of foreigners, who guarded their secrets jealously and did not mingle with the urban community. A little before 2000, it seems that there was a serious crisis in the countries which had been longest in possession of bronze, from Asia Minor to Iran. Was it caused by social movements, natural disasters, or simply by the working-out of local mines? At any rate, it resulted in many groups of metal-workers moving south. They took with them identical technology and artefacts: large-headed pins (known as mace-shaped), torques (a kind of open necklet), bracelets of the same shape, bi-conic beads or beads in the shape of stoned olives, daggers with triangular blades. These "torque-wearers" as C. Schaeffer called them, possibly because of two silver statues from Ugarit, each of which wears a golden torque, can thus be traced from Ugarit to Byblos, Palestine, Egypt, Cyprus, Crete, and central Europe via the Adriatic.[15] Was it contact between the Syrian or Cretan sailors and the "torque-wearers" which explained the first voyages towards the western mines, those of Sardinia, Spain and central Europe?

If the same people were also those who exported the megaliths, our problems would be solved. But that would perhaps be too good to be true. What is clear is that some kind of shipping route was established, and as always in these cases, a number of influences were at work. It also seems clear that this revival of the mines and western metallurgy was a sort of preface to the Phoenician voyages of the first millennium. These, far from being a blind leap into the unknown, seem to have become linked directly to the exploitation of mines in Spain and Sardinia, and no doubt also to the tradition left behind by the early invaders, who had sent out colonial expeditions long before the Phoenicians.

CHAPTER FOUR

Centuries of Unity: The Seas of the Levant 2500–1200 B.C.

In attempting an overview of the Middle East in the fifteen or so centuries between 2500 and 1200–1000 B.C., the period roughly corresponding to the Bronze Age, we are obliged to take the long view and recognize that there will be large gaps in our knowledge. Our acquaintance with this age has progressed in leaps and bounds in the last few decades, but even so, when the time-span is so great, many black holes remain. It is a daunting task to sketch an overall picture, when so much still lies in shadow, and when any fresh evidence may set off a kind of chain reaction, undermining a series of explanations previously thought valid. What must it have felt like in 1915, when the scholar Bedrich Hrozny (1879–1922) first deciphered the cuneiform script of the Hittite archive of Bogazköy? He was convinced (hence his success) that the Hittite language must have been Indo-European. A similar sensation was caused when the press announced on 3 September 1969 that the language of the civilization of the Indus had been deciphered: it was said to be Dravidian, and thus related to present-day dialects in the Deccan.[1]

Such events can destabilize an entire sequence of explanations: what we thought last year may no longer be valid today. We always have the exciting feeling that we are on the point of discovering what really did happen—then we may be sent back to square one. The fantastic images from the Cretan palaces still exist, but we no longer see them through the eyes of an Arthur Evans or a Gustave Glotz: we do not call these figures "the Parisienne" or "the Prince with the fleur-de-lys."

I
EVER ONWARD AND UPWARD?

The Bronze Age began in the Middle East in the middle of the third millennium and ended in the twelfth century B.C., with the turmoil brought by the so-called "Peoples of the Sea." The story of the Bronze Age could easily be written in dramatic form: it is replete with invasions, wars, pillage, political disasters and long-lasting economic collapses, "the first clashes between peoples." But all these rival empires and aggressive cities, all the barbarians from mountains or desert who overcame by force or cunning peoples more advanced than themselves, were caught up in a general tide of creative progress which washed over everything, a civilization which spread regardless of frontiers. In this way a certain unity was created among the countries and seas of the Levant. The history of the Bronze Age can therefore be written not only as a saga of drama and violence, but as a story of more benign contacts: commercial, diplomatic (even at this time), and above all cultural.

Might this expanding cultural universe have been capable of taking over the entire Mediterranean? It seemed to be heading that way shortly before the invasions of the Peoples of the Sea. These invasions proved a disaster for the whole area, not only for the destruction they wrought, but because Greece and the Aegean were now cut off and isolated from the Middle East, eventually becoming foreign to it. This schism, which was never to be healed, contained in embryo the future great cultural divide between East and West.[2]

Bronze metallurgy itself played an important role in this constructive expansion of trade, especially once metal-working reached the densely settled societies of Egypt and Mesopotamia.

As with the earliest types of farming, innovation in metal-working (and the same was later true of iron) did not originate in the most privileged areas. The smelting of copper and its alloys developed from the fourth millennium B.C. in the northern sector of the Fertile Crescent: western Iran, the Caucasus, Armenia and Asia Minor. The excavations which have revealed the sites of palaces in Troy II, Alishar, Alaça Höyük and Kültepe, and the treasures of Astrabad, Tepe Hissar or Maïkop in Transcaucasia, unequivocally mark out a broad zone where bronze was in use. Nowhere else in the Middle East, even in

Egypt or Mesopotamia, has there been discovered such profusion of rich metals as in the tombs of Alaça, dating from *c.* 2300: everything is there—gold, silver, copper, bronze and even iron—at the time a more rare and precious metal than the others.

Bronze made its very first *appearance* in Mesopotamia in about 2800, and did not reach Egypt until about 2000. More significant for developing trade was its generalized *use*, which is harder to date with precision—say about 2000 to 1500, with Mesopotamia starting early and Egypt lagging behind. In the tomb of King Tutankhamun (*c.* 1350 B.C.) there are more copper objects than bronze.

This gradual extension, a sort of second career for bronze, was linked to waves of emigration by the metal-workers of Asia Minor already mentioned. They were to be found at Ugarit, where they remained for two hundred years or so, until about 1700 B.C.; in Byblos, an important metal-working centre in about 2000, where they developed very fine techniques of "damascene," the art of chasing gold thread on to copper, silver or niello; and their traces are also found in Cyprus, Palestine, Egypt and central Europe. Richer regions were the beneficiaries of this important diaspora. With bronze, it became possible to manufacture that impressive armoury of offensive and defensive weapons without which there would have been no state, no prince who commanded respect. It became the foundation of a material civilization—just as iron and steel are still the basis of our own civilization. Copper and tin mines would therefore become coveted objects, jealously guarded. Comparatively rare, but scattered across the known world, they usually had to be exploited from a distance. To capture trade in these precious metals, rich regions had a built-in advantage, using their trading networks which had long been organized around the so-called "palace economy."

For it was indeed the princes who, having started by controlling the daily life of their subjects under the system of barter, later drew into the palace coffers any resources which could be mobilized—dues paid in kind, taxes, unpaid labour, customs duties. It was in the palace workshops that craft production intended for foreign export was organized. This "royal palace" system would expand further, feeding off the new developments in trade. The palace was not only the most important economic centre in the region, it was often the only one, with the prince himself being the leading producer, financier and customer. It was for his benefit, and for that of the small group of people attendant on his person, that trade was organized and developed. Religious temples too, with their landed estates, peasants and craftsmen, were "palaces" in an economic sense. Sometimes they had even preceded the princes in this respect. In the second millennium B.C., such economic concentration can be found not only in Egypt and Mesopotamia, but in the Hittite Empire, or in Crete—where the fabulous palace cellars with their giant amphorae of oil or wine (70,000 litres in stock according to Evans's calculations) speak for themselves, as visitors to Knossos can attest. The palace at Ugarit was regularly extended to match the city's fortunes and those of its rulers, and the development of its "administration." King Solomon too had his "palace economy."

So without a palace there could be no state—and where there was a palace there was always a state. The system was only viable because it was based on the ruthless exploitation of masses of peasants and craftsmen. If the economy expanded, the people's dependence could only increase. Before long every region had marked out its own jealously guarded supply zones, from which it derived both luxury goods and military strength. Centred on these zones, a form of private capitalism was soon seeking to expand beyond the palace economy in the narrow sense. Copper from Anatolia, Arabia (via Bahrain) or Cyprus, and tin from Iran or possibly already from Tuscany, Spain and England, were circulating in the form of crude, half-finished (or even finished) products. Primitive furnaces, dug in the ground, have been found in Sinai, where copper ore was treated before being dispatched to the Nile. When in 1960 underwater archaeologists discovered a wreck dating from 1200 B.C. off Gelidonya on the Turkish coast, its cargo was found to consist of forty copper ingots in the shape of "oxhides," bearing the mark of the Cypriot copperfounders.

The network went on expanding, taking in Malta, Iran, Turkestan, and the Indus; it stretched from the north which produced copper, tin and amber, to Nubia in the south, a colonial territory mercilessly exploited by the Egyptians. Overland caravans and shipping convoys connected with each other. Ships and boats were already venturing into the seas of northern Europe, perhaps already hoisting the leather sails the Venetii were using when Caesar defeated them in a hard-fought naval battle. The north-south land routes must have been even busier across the narrow European continent, obeying the call of the Mediterranean. The same drawing power affected the Red Sea, where a Theban tomb painting (sixteenth century B.C.) depicts the local coasting trade: native producers are taking their goods to an Egyptian port, possibly Koseir at the far end of the route running from Coptos on the Nile to the Red Sea. What I find particularly striking is that these round boats, probably made of osiers, and built to a design still found in Arab countries today, have a triangular sail, carefully rendered by the painter. Now the triangular sail is characteristic of the Indian Ocean. Two thousand years later, Islamic sailors were the first to introduce to the Mediterranean this exotic shape of sail (so well adapted to its waters that it came to be considered typically Mediterranean, as compared to the Atlantic, and was known as the "Latin" or lateen rig). So the Theban painting suggests links with that other zone of sea travel, from the Persian Gulf to the Indies, governed by the monsoon.

This traffic on land, river or sea benefited from favourable circumstances. I am not suggesting that there were no pirates on the high seas or brigands on land routes. But these long-distance connections implied a degree of complicity between one city or state and another. In Mesopotamia, goods were passed efficiently from city to city, like the ball in a good rugby match. The great caravans of black donkeys, for example, which travelled north from Assur to Kanesh (present-day Kültepe) carrying tin and fabrics bought in southern Mesopotamia, and bringing back copper from Anatolia on the return trip, were never intercepted or harassed on their regular routes. A Babylonian document from this time (early in the second millennium B.C.), mentions "royal travel permits," which no doubt had to be paid for, and the itineraries were well-organized with overnight halts and "refreshment-providers at the crossroads." Even so, the journey was tough going and dangerous enough for the Mesopotamians to invoke the protection of Shamash, the sun-god, before leaving: "O Thou, helper of the traveller whose road is harsh, and comforter of him who crosses the sea, fearing the waves."

Mesopotamia lay at the crossroads of many routes: it bordered on Iran and the Indian Ocean, stretched up as far as Asia Minor, and could make contact with Cappadocia through the good offices of Assyrian merchants. But the most vigorous arteries of trade ran to Syria, beyond powerful Mari, aggressive Carchemish and Aleppo, towards the Orontes valley, and down to the sea and the great port of Ugarit (modern Ras Shamra). An early version of Genoa or even Venice, Ugarit was the gateway to the "upper sea of the setting sun," as the Mesopotamians called the Mediterranean, as opposed to the "lower sea," the Persian Gulf.

Without necessarily seeing Mesopotamia in the ages of Sargon and Hammurabi as an illustration of the theory of "poles of growth," one is forced to recognize the region's obvious precociousness, revealed very early by the rise of an economy that used currency. This was not money-as-symbol in the sense we know it today. But a monetary economy is one in which a single commodity—say, a precious metal—tends to be used as a measure for all others and to be substituted for them in trading. It was the mighty Persian Empire which much later on generalized the Lydian invention of money in the modern sense, using stamped coins which it dispatched all over the Middle East, including Mesopotamia and Egypt (the latter being rather resistant to them, as it happens).

The earliest form of currency used for payment by the Sumerians was a measure of barley. So in Mesopotamia money had its origins in crop cultivation, rather than in livestock, which was the unit used in Rome (*pecunia*), in Greece (*bous*) and in India (*rupia*). Barley as currency continued to be used for ordinary transactions, since metal, when it made its first appearance (first copper, then silver, in weighted amounts), was a sort of money of account, a scale of reference. Barley continued to be the "real" money. A contract, after stipulating the price in silver, would indicate in an appendix what the current exchange rate was between silver and barley. For foreign trade, however, the currency which acted as a stimulus and became widely adopted was, of course, metallic.

Silver, as soon as it appeared and began to be used as real currency for some transactions, tended, in fact, to prevail over other forms of payment. This explains one decision of the code of Hammurabi: if the proprietress of a tavern will not accept grain as the price for drink, but receives silver and therefore "makes the price of the drink fall below the price of grain, the said proprietress will be seized and flung into the water." This unexpected detail indicates the ambiguous nature of a semi-monetary economy. Perhaps as one expert suggests, barter was retained when it was possible to pay in kind in heavy goods—near rivers or by the sea—or when palaces had been built, since they could store goods in quantity. The monetary economy would have prevailed, on the other hand, among "capitalists" who did not have enormous storehouses to draw on, and whose "travelling salesmen" travelled the roads, with their "agents carrying their capital," as suggested in the invocation to Shamash quoted above.

The rapid appearance alongside palace officials of authentic merchants, some of them travelling wholesalers, others providers of funds (the latter definitely the more important), was an unmistakable sign of Mesopotamia's economic precociousness. In every city these merchants made up a community apart, the *karum*. To judge by the *karum* of Kanesh, which we know about from its plentiful correspondence, they had at their disposal warehouses and the facilities of a trade association which acted as a sort of chamber of commerce. They were competent to handle silver for payments, and were familiar with notes of hand, bills of exchange and compensatory payments—which proves that the instruments of capitalism emerge spontaneously whenever circumstances favour them. In Babylon, there were even banking houses, so we are not surprised to find a monetary economy in Ugarit, the outlet on the coast for the Mesopotamian hinterland: it was an active port (150 vessels are mentioned as being there) and not far from the Taurus silver mines. The city's merchants, importers and exporters, some of them foreign in origin, paid for their purchases of wool, slaves and even land in silver *sicles*.

Did the choice of silver, as a less cumbersome form of payment than copper or bronze, promote Mesopotamia's foreign trade? One would think so. But silver itself had to be purchased. In return for imported raw materials and foodstuffs—silver, timber, copper, tin, precious and semi-precious stones, oil and wine—Mesopotamia could offer only barley, dates, hides, woollen fabrics, engraved cylinders and other craft goods. It also acted as an intermediary, taking a commission for its services. The rule seemed to be to buy as much as possible from the south and east, where silver was highly valued (so southern Mesopotamia preferred to buy copper from Bahrain rather than from Anatolia) and to sell luxury goods and textiles to the north and west, the suppliers of silver. Perhaps the Mesopotamian economy did not operate entirely on the standard rule for advanced countries—buying raw materials and making a profit by selling them on, either in original condition or as manufactured products. It could be that Mesopotamia was already benefiting from the rule which prevailed so long in the Mediterranean, whereby the use of silver, an over-valued commodity in the Far East, was an advantage in itself, a beneficial "multiplier" of trade, at least for return goods. In that case, the choice of silver currency in Mesopotamia, close to the currents of trade with India, would carry extra significance. But the explanation is based on rather slight evidence.

To explain everything in terms of silver would be an exaggeration. And to explain everything by the contrast between Egypt and Mesopotamia would be equally so. Yet that contrast is striking and economists register astonishment and even exasperation when confronted with the spectacle of life in Egypt: fantastically well-ordered and intelligent, yet obstinately archaic. Just as the potter's wheel took a long time to enter everyday life, so too did bronze. First introduced in about 2000 B.C., it was not in common use until 1500, after an interval of five hundred years during which it was hardly used at all. Similarly, Egypt only ever had one money of account, the shat (7.6 grammes) of copper or bronze, dating from the fourth dynasty. In about 1400 B.C. this was replaced by the qite (9.1 grammes). This should not be regarded as a strengthening of the currency: money remained of marginal significance in Egypt, barter being the rule until the Persian or indeed the Greek conquests.

And yet Egypt, like Mesopotamia, had to engage in the foreign trade necessary for its survival and its luxuries. It exported manufactured products: linen cloth renowned for its fineness, porcelain, multi-coloured glass, furniture, jewels and amulets. But it was not as committed to this long-distance trade as Mesopotamia, since except for timber, Egypt could obtain either at home or on its doorstep almost all the raw materials it needed: copper from Sinai (ingots from Syria and Cyprus were not imported until the middle of the second millennium B.C.); various types of stone for building, to be found along the banks of the Nile—granite, sandstone, schist, limestone or basalt; many precious and semi-precious stones from the eastern desert; coral from the Red Sea; ivory, ebony and especially gold from Nubia (the name itself means "land of gold"). Gold was obtained by primitive panning methods, carried out by labourers who were treated as slaves. Production was plentiful. Under Tutmosis III (1502–1450 B.C.) Nubia sent the pharaoh two or three hundred kilos of gold in a single year. This is a fabulous figure, if one thinks that Spanish America, from the first voyages of discovery until 1650, was delivering on average hardly more than a ton a year. There was some truth then in the repeated claims in the diplomatic correspondence of Amarna (Amenophis III, 1413–1377, and Amenophis IV, 1377–1358 B.C.) that in Egypt gold was as common as sand. Pusratta, the emperor of Mittani, a contemporary of Amenophis IV, preferred to say "like dust between the toes." Silver on the other hand was in short supply, so the gold-silver ratio under the Middle Kingdom was only 1 : 2 or even 1 : 1.

By possessing gold, Egypt was unconsciously but effectively in a strong position. Was this an encouragement to stagnate? Whereas Mesopotamia was obliged to make constant efforts, to remain active and alert and to launch into foreign trade, Egypt suggests to us, *mutatis mutandis*, China in the eighteenth century A.D.: self-confident and supremely self-centred.

The Mediterranean economy described above had its highs and lows and experienced a number of crises. It was admittedly prosperous for centuries on end: evidence for this lies in its expansion, or in the creation of mighty states and huge palaces, whose interest is not confined to art history. It is even possible that the move beyond the palace economy, traceable in the regions of "cuneiform script," was both proof and result of economic expansion greater than elsewhere. All the same, ups and downs occurred. We are fairly sure that routes were sometimes blocked, that prices fluctuated, and that the size of the population rose and fell (at least in Egypt and Crete), and we also know that there were political accidents or upheavals which could not help but bring economic catastrophe in their wake.

All this being so, and since I have rather provocatively brought the word "*conjoncture*" (trend) into the debate, can we find a genuine use for it? Some kind of overall pattern must have existed of course, but we can do little more than imagine what it was like, on the basis of some sketchy evidence and hypotheses which are no more than plausible.

1 I would imagine that this world, with its criss-cross trading links, and allowing both for inertia and abrupt change, must nevertheless have had some kind of overall rhythm, though that would of course have concerned only the higher forms of trade.

2 The only indicators we have, and they are very imperfect, concern Mesopotamia and Egypt. The former was active, and carried much weight, but was, so to speak, lacking in direction, or rather disrupted by excessive political change; the latter by contrast was a huge but passive economy: all trade routes seemed to lead there but it was often manipulated from outside, as in later times Cantonese China would be by European capitalism.

The evidence from Egypt is the clearest and the most uninterrupted, but not necessarily the best. Let us start with it, however, because it is the easiest to interpret.

The long periods of political collapse are unambiguously signalled in Egypt by the term "intermediary periods." The first of these, between the Old and the Middle Kingdoms, ran from about 2280 to 2050. The second, between the Middle and the New Kingdoms, ran from 1785 to 1590. It was during this very long interval that the well-attested episode of the Hyksos took place. These "foreigners" were a pastoral people who settled in the eastern part of the Delta, where they built their capital, Avaris. Their rulers played the role of pharaoh so well that they became the titular holders of the Fourteenth and Fifteenth Dynasties. The third and last intermediary period, which did not ever really end, ran from the eleventh century B.C. until the seventh and beyond. The Saite period (663–523) was only a short-lived interlude. All in all then, we can see Egypt as on a rising curve until 2280 B.C., then a downward one until 2050; rising again from 2050 to 1785, before a downturn from 1785 to 1590; it then witnessed a very pronounced upturn in the age of glorious victories of the New Kingdom before it declined into the endless morass which affected the whole of the Middle East after the convulsions of the twelfth century B.C.

Of these three long periods of breakdown in Egyptian history, the first—a sort of cultural revolt, emerging from the depths of the country's interior, accompanied by an Asiatic invasion and a total breakdown of trade with Byblos on the one hand and the gold-producing countries on the other—was much more pronounced than the second. The Hyksos episode did not produce quite such extensive collapse: the incomers appropriated the economic activity of Lower Egypt without destroying it. Little is known about this activity but we do know that the Delta under Hyksos domination maintained its former links with Syria, Crete, the Levant coast and even with the Hittites. The final and third breakdown, however, spelled the end of an era.

The periods of rising prosperity correspond to the many hundreds of years of success of the three successive Kingdoms. Let us take the example of the Middle Kingdom (2040–1786): order had been restored in the Nile valley, the regime of monarchs and interdependent temples had been suppressed, the country had once more recovered its cruising rhythm and a certain prosperity. It was then that the pharaohs created a standing army—a bottomless pit of expenditure; not only that but burial tombs, ever more numerous, were no longer confined to the royal dynasties, yet they became more richly equipped than ever: frescoes, statues and precious objects accompanied the dead, while wooden statuettes provided them with the army of servants without which no grandee could live in this world or the next and be happy. Luxury in all its forms entered Egyptian life: the luxury of clothes, jewels and perfumes; of festivals at which young women in rich finery sat listening to musicians, attentive slaves offered guests lotus flowers and bunches of grapes or a costly perfume cone, to be set like a white diadem on their dark tresses.

That said, if one compares the threefold Egyptian pattern with the ups and downs of Mesopotamia (see Table 1), it is by no means a perfect match, and that ought to reassure us, since the indicator being followed here is essentially political; it cannot be applied with any precision to economic change. What is more, the secular trends do not fit the different regions at exactly the same time. So we are faced with only very broad correspondences, for which the imperfect chronologies at our disposal can legitimately be used.

Let us call the three Egyptian crises A, B, and C; and the three Mesopotamian crises which ought to correspond to them A(i), B(i) and C(i). The correlation between A and A(i) is satisfactory: the Akkadian Empire, founded in about 2340, came to an end in about 2230, and the Old Kingdom in Egypt collapsed in about 2280; the Middle Kingdom emerged in 2050 and the third dynasty of Ur in about 2100. So A = A(i), or near enough. For B and B(i) there is an even more clear correlation: the disorder on the Nile began again in about 1785, lasting until about 1590; in Mesopotamia, we can suggest the dates of 1750 (the death of Hammurabi) and 1595. The third dynasty of Ur lasted only a century perhaps, but it was followed by the Larsa dynasty and the powerful state of Mari, and then by the Babylonian dynasty, with the Amorite Hammurabi who conquered both Larsa and Mari and re-unified Mesopotamia. This complicated history once more corresponds to rivalries between cities, but at no time seems to have affected a thriving trade, which is known to us through abundant written records. The fragmentation which followed the death of Hammurabi, on the other hand, corresponded to a social explosion, hitherto contained: private property and interests now came into conflict with the organization of the state. Hammurabi's code had been an attempt at compromise, seeking to satisfy aspirations while channelling them, and preserving a strong state. But the attempt was a failure and the famous code remained a dead letter. Restoration of order came only with the Kassite dynasty in 1595. We may conclude then that B = B(i). And C = C(i), beyond a doubt, since the twelfth-century crisis was widespread, sparing no region either in the Middle East or in Greece, now under Mycenaean control.

These six periods—three ages of decline and three ages of comparative good health—allow us to locate certain events. If we call the "euphoric" periods (a), (b) and (c), we will note that the Hittite Empire, formed in about

1600 and lasting until 1200, coincided with a long upward movement (c), which also benefited the Babylon of the Kassites (not as prosperous as all that, however), the New Egyptian Kingdom, and its ally the Mittani state which was occupying northern Mesopotamia. In Crete this corresponds to the so-called second palace period; finally, the fourteenth century saw the rise of Assyria. Working backwards, the (b) period coincided on one hand with the Middle Kingdom, and on the other with the two or three striking attempts at Mesopotamian unification, coming to grief after the death of Hammurabi; it also corresponds to the first palace period in Crete. The (a) period is probably the most remarkable of all: this was the age of the Akkadian successes and the first prosperity arising from mining metals, across a wide band covering the whole of Asia Minor from Iran and the Caucasus to the Aegean and beyond. Egypt experienced these changes in fortune less dramatically, since prosperity had long been established there. But Egypt was such a large presence that everything seemed to start or finish there.

The parallels to be observed between the economic fortunes of Egypt and Mesopotamia are the more interesting since, apart from a few caravans of pack-animals travelling between Sinai and the Euphrates, these two great civilizations had little direct contact. But impulses were communicated between the two via the great turntable formed by the Syria-Lebanon region. Whenever the economic climate favoured its powerful neighbours, this intermediary region took advantage of the general wave of prosperity and active trade which invigorated the whole of the Middle East. Gradually this whole area of the Mediterranean therefore became a unified economic zone, throughout which all kinds of exchange were possible: artefacts, techniques, fashions, taste, and of course people. Art bore witness to the cosmopolitan culture which W. S. Smith's fine book (1965) dates from about 2000 B.C. He distinguishes two main periods of cultural contact: the twentieth to nineteenth centuries and 1500–1200 (very broadly corresponding to the second and third periods of economic prosperity).

This unified civilization affected only half the Mediterranean, but it was already going beyond the Middle East in the strict sense. There could be no better vantage-point from which to observe both the gradual unification and the extension of this civilization than the island of Crete. Crete was a newcomer, entering the game for a few centuries only, but to dazzling effect.

Table 1 Chronological table showing comparative fortunes of Egypt and Mesopotamia

EGYPT	MESOPOTAMIA
c. 2700 B.C.	*c.* 2700 B.C.
Old Kingdom (Third to Fourth Dynasty); Cheops, Chephren and Mykerinos (Fourth Dynasty); establishment of power of pharaohs.	Sumerian power in southern Mesopotamia; foundation of the dynasties of Uruk, Ur, and Lagash (*c.* 1490); foundation of Akkadian Empire by Sargon the Elder (*c.* 2340).
c. 2280 B.C.	*c.* 2230 B.C.
First intermediary period (Seventh to Ninth Dynasty); various royal families; decadence of the central power; hegemony of the nomarchs.	Decline of Akkadian Empire (2230) weakened by raids of the Guti, who occupied Babylon.
c. 2050 B.C.	*c.* 2100 B.C.
Middle Kingdom (Twelfth Dynasty); Ammenemes I founds a new dynasty (*c.* 2000); the country is brought under control; administrative reform of Sesostris II (*c.* 1950).	Sumerian renaissance; third Ur dynasty; Mari and Larsa states conquered by Hammurabi who creates the first Amorite dynasty in Babylon and unifies Mesopotamia.
c. 1785 B.C.	*c.* 1750 B.C.
Second intermediary period (Thirteenth to Seventeenth Dynasty); the Hyksos invade the Delta and make Avaris their capital (*c.* 1750); political and social disturbances.	Death of Hammurabi; Babylon captured by the Hittites and end of the first dynasty of Babylon; Kassite raids in Mesopotamia from 1740.
c. 1590 B.C.	*c.* 1594 B.C.
New Kingdom (Eighteenth to Twentieth Dynasty); Amenophis unifies the kingdom (*c.* 1590); Ramses II begins reign of 67 years (*c.* 1300); policy of conquest and alliances.	Kassite dynasty established in Babylon for treaty of alliance with Egypt; expansion of Syrian cities and Hittite Empire (apogee from 1380 on); further alliance with Egypt.
c. eleventh century B.C.	*c.* eleventh century B.C.
Third intermediary period (1070); weakness and decline of the Egyptian kingdom.	General crisis in Middle East. Babylon destroyed by Assyrians (1087); end of Hittite Empire.

II
CRETE: A NEW PLAYER IN THE COSMOPOLITAN CIVILIZATION OF THE MEDITERRANEAN

Pre-Hellenic Crete, known to us as Minoan from the name of its legendary kings (the term Minos was used like that of pharaoh) offers a fascinating and enigmatic spectacle. We are told on good authority that no prehistoric society is better known than Crete; yet it is what we do *not* know about it that perplexes us, since our curiosity has been so whetted by what we do know.

Since 1953, when Michael Ventris first deciphered Linear B, the third and final form of script used on the island, the problem has changed in character but has become no easier to solve. Some people have even argued, seriously or otherwise, that it has actually become more obscure. We certainly have a choice of narratives about Crete. Archaeologists have suggested two or three versions and the day someone deciphers Linear A, another will no doubt emerge. All we know for the present is that the earliest Cretan language is not an Indo-European language.[3]

Ancient Crete was an island marooned in a desert of salt water in the southern Aegean. Large and mountainous, it was bisected by plains (the Messara plain in central Crete is sizeable: 40 km long, 6 to 12 across), and bristling with limestone mountains which acted as water-towers, culminating in Mount Ida, almost 2500 metres high. So one finds here in microcosm the familiar Mediterranean contrast between sea-level and mountain tops. Yet although the Cretan highlands seem to have been cut off from the foreign influences which caused such upheavals lower down, they apparently posed no particular threat in prehistoric times to the plains, cities and palaces of the lowlands. Transhumance of flocks was practised, but it seems to have been uneventful and provoked little comment. In short, ancient Crete was nothing like its later incarnation as Candia, under Venetian rule, when the mountains contained a wild, dangerous and menacing population. Should we deduce that Minoan Crete, existing so peacefully within its own limits, was actually under-populated for a long time in relation to its potential?

The strongest and most unexpected contrast is one which became established between the north- and south-facing coasts of the island: the former looking to the nearby coasts and islands of the Aegean, the latter looking out towards distant Africa, Cyrenaica and above all Egypt. The former is like many other Mediterranean seaboards, the latter a kind of climatic curiosity, with something tropical about it, reminiscent of the Spanish coast around Malaga. Swallows come there to winter, as they do in Egypt.

An island is always a self-contained world. In Crete there were scarcely any native animals, apart from mountain goats, badgers, wild cats and ferrets which were kept as domestic pets to control the mice. There were no foxes, wolves, eagles or owls, few harmful creatures at all if we except scorpions, vipers and a poisonous spider unknown on the mainland. The Greeks were later to say that "the island of Zeus" had been protected from natural scourges by the king of the gods or by Herakles. The real reason was the protection provided by many miles of sea. And this isolation did indeed offer advantages to Crete in the early days. Other islands, almost as large, like Rhodes, or even larger, like Cyprus, were just as well situated for sea-routes and better connected to the mainland. Yet Crete was the one which stood out.

Crete had played only very a modest role, however, in the very first Aegean or quasi-Aegean civilization: the Cyclades and Troy, south of the Hellespont, were the stars in this galaxy. Like the rest of the Aegean, Crete had seen its earliest settlers and its first forms of agriculture arrive from Asia Minor, in about the seventh millennium. Several waves of later immigrants had introduced pottery and eventually, in the course of the third millennium, metal-working reached the island. Yet if we can believe the archaeologists, whose diagnosis is based on pottery, in the early days Crete lagged well behind regions like Argos and Thessaly, which were more closely linked to Anatolia. It even lagged behind the island of Syros, which is known for the pots familiarly described by archaeologists as "frying-pans": flat-bottomed receptacles, no doubt for ritual use, decorated with white reliefs in the form of spirals, triangles, stars, suns, boats and fish. The first Helladic civilization, like that in Anatolia, had as its symbol the omnipresent earth-mother goddess, represented in the Neolithic Age by naturalistic statuettes like those of the Asian mainland; and later in the early Bronze Age, by the strange so-called Cycladic idols, which may be less ethnically Aegean than has been suggested. The "violin-shaped" figurines for example, which seem to have been carved out of marble or clay slabs, are found not only in Troy, at practically all levels from I to VI, and in Crete, but also in Thessaly; on the Asiatic side of the Bosphorus; and at Tel Eilat Ghassul (north of the Dead Sea). Similar little silhouettes, cut out from gold leaf, have been found in certain tombs in Alaça

Höyük. From Crete, these artefacts travelled westwards—to Sardinia, where they inspired many of the local statuettes made of stone or marble (early second millennium), and in the sixteenth century B.C. to Malta, where we find stylized equivalents in the shape of violins, or flat discs. In Spain, in the megalithic tombs of Purchena and Los Millares, they are one of the many signs of eastern Mediterranean influence.

The eastern edge of the Aegean, and the coast of Asia Minor with ports at the mouths of the valleys running down from the plateau, served as staging-posts in the cultural current which for several millennia flowed from Anatolia towards the Aegean and Greece. The brilliant career of Troy, on the slopes of Mount Hissarlik, not far from the Hellespont, which began in about 3000 B.C., is the story of one such staging-post. Nine successive cities were discovered by Schliemann (in 1870) on the site which until then had been thought legendary. The oldest of all, Troy I, was a very small settlement, but already undeniably a town, with walls and a princely palace on the safest site inside the fortress. Hand-thrown pots were made there, grey and black, incised and encrusted with white, and so were many stone implements (an unsurprising survival of the past). But the presence of copper reveals that an early form of metallurgy was not unknown. The inevitable Earth Mother turns up here too of course. Troy II, on a larger site, lasted only two hundred years, 2500–2300, and disappeared in a fire—as, about a thousand years later, did Troy VII, the city of Priam and Hector, after a long siege by a Greek army. But during those two centuries, Troy II played an important role in the spread of metallurgy throughout the Aegean. Excavations have discovered a mass of precious objects there, made of gold, silver, lead, electrum, even iron, daggers with silver and bronze blades and handles of carved rock-crystal, and sophisticated goldsmith's work, using techniques of filigrane, cloisonné and beading. All these precious things show signs of having been buried hastily, possibly just before a moment of great danger. There are the remains too of turned pots alongside hand-made ceramics.

In that second half of the third millennium, Troy was evidently in touch with Mesopotamia (as we know from the cylinders and seals of Jemdet Nasr), with the Anatolian plateau, Thessaly, Macedonia, the Aegean, Egypt and even with the Baltic, via the Danube (since amber of Nordic origin has been identified by chemical analysis). The variety of materials in use, semi-precious stones in particular, indicates that these were not just fleeting contacts.

It would be rash to generalize, to judge the early civilization of the

Aegean from one, perhaps exceptional example. But it serves to alert us to what may be the case: by now sufficient traces of authentic cities and even palaces have been discovered on the Greek mainland and islands to suggest that an active civilization, nourished by early sea-borne trading, had spread through the whole of the Aegean by the third millennium.

This civilization was dramatically snuffed out by the Indo-European invasions around the twenty-fourth century B.C. The Troad, Anatolia, the Greek mainland, and many islands in the Aegean were invaded by peoples far less advanced than they were—probably the ancestors of the Mycenaeans in Greece, and of the Hittites and Louwites of Anatolia. All the Aegean cities and their palaces went up in flames. Troy, Haghios Kosmas (near Athens), Lernos and Tiryns in Argos, Poliochni on the island of Lemnos. The general economic and cultural level of the Aegean fell drastically. Thessaly reverted to barbarism. All the lights went out—except in Crete. Less accessible, saved by its remote location, the island was not invaded. This was probably its first stroke of luck.

Before the decline of the first Aegean civilization, Crete's prosperity had already emerged in about 2500, but in an oddly limited form, as if an advanced economy had carved two islands out of one big one: on one hand a small fragment in the east, between Zakro and the gulf of Mirabello, centred on the site of Vasiliki and the off-shore island of Mochlos; on the other hand, the central plain of Messara, vast but enclosed and set apart by its natural wealth, evident to us from its collective burial sites, with their *tholoi*. Unlike the rest of the Aegean, which in the third millennium was receiving almost everything from the west coast of Anatolia, Crete had contacts with Syria and, directly or indirectly, with Egypt. Was it for this reason that, even before 2000, this former poor relation of the Neolithic Aegean was developing an active, outward-looking and original civilization, reformulating for its own use its diverse borrowings from elsewhere?

There were no real cities yet, or palaces, in this forerunner of ancient Minoan civilization. But the tombs on the east coast have yielded some rich finds: pitchers with spouts in the Anatolian style (as in the rest of the Aegean); stylized marble statues of goddesses; tools and weapons made first of pure copper, then of bronze; gold jewels already showing distinctive features; original kinds of pottery, including "teapots" with long spouts, apparently imitations of metal originals; and above all, many stone vases of obvious Egyptian inspiration (some even imported), which have caused much debate among the experts. It is now thought that Crete did not have direct links with the Nile in the early third millennium, the date when these vases occur in Egypt itself, but rather indirect links via Byblos. But was this a straightforward import trade, or did Crete allow entry to refugees from the Nile, who had travelled by way of Syria? And if so, when? At the time of the distant conquest of the Delta by Narmer? Or from the first intermediary period, in the twenty-third century, which witnessed so much looting of very ancient Egyptian tombs? Such theories might account for the penile sheaths which male Cretan costume included from a very early time (and which are thought to be characteristic of the Delta as much as of Libya); they might also explain the many pottery seals found in the Messara plain (at Hagia Triada), dating from the very early Minoan period, pre-2200, and directly imitated from seals of the first intermediary period in Egypt—themselves Asiatic in inspiration. Other specialists simply think that the Cretans who went to Byblos travelled on to Egypt with the local traders.

By the end of the third millennium, at any rate, Crete was already poised for take-off. But at the beginning of the twentieth century B.C., and as if by chance, there was a remarkably sudden burst of expansion: cities and palaces rose and flourished; wheels and wheeled traffic arrived in the island; the potter's wheel was adopted there in about 2000 and, miraculously, this did not harm the quality of the pre-existing pottery, on the contrary. The boom was so remarkable that it has again been suggested that it could be explained by some "migration": peoples from the Syrian or Palestinian coast might have taken refuge in Crete, fleeing from Lugalzaggisi, the Mesopotamian ruler of the third Ur dynasty, who at this time opened up the way to the "upper sea of the setting sun."[4] The legend of Europa being carried off by Zeus from the Phoenician coast and taken to Crete across the sea might contain a grain of truth.

But does one need to invoke any migration to explain what can be quite adequately accounted for by the renewed vitality of trade and "international" relations in the early second millennium? From the time of the ancient Minoan civilization, before 2000 B.C., the Cretans had adopted a hieroglyphic form of script, and this feature alone indicates how detached they were from the Aegean world and its illiterate barbaric invaders. Cretan sailors were certainly familiar with the route to the Syrian coast. Cut off from the

Aegean world, Crete looked towards Cyprus, Ugarit and Byblos; and through these places, it made contact with Egypt and Mesopotamia, without which any serious development would have been unthinkable. Crete was from then on enmeshed in a context of eastern civilization.

The great cities and palaces are those at Knossos, Phaistos, Mallia and Zakro, a site excavated in 1946. Unless there are more marvels waiting to be discovered on the site of former Kydonia to the west (as tradition hints that there might be), the list of large urban and palace complexes is complete. There were also a few more modest palaces or noblemen's villas. Indeed there was scarcely a cultivated plain or active town which did not have its local palace and prince: these include Arkhanes, just a few kilometres away from Knossos, where bronze-age walls can still be seen incorporated into the walls of present-day houses; Monastiraki which controls the fertile valley of Amari; Kanli Kastelli or Gournia, with its "houses piled round the little palace and its courtyard, just as medieval towns clustered around their church or château."

If these sites are plotted on a map, the pattern is revealing. Unless new finds do turn up, there is absolutely nothing in the west of the island. Yet it was just as fertile as the east and certainly better watered. This must prove that Crete was influenced from outside, and from the eastern side of the compass only. In similar fashion, western Argos and peninsular Greece west of Mount Pindus and Mount Parnassus long remained areas inhabited by primitive peoples (according to Spyridon Marinatos).

Plotting the rise of these centres over time is also instructive. There were, broadly speaking, two generations of palaces: the first from 2000 to 1700; the second, from 1700 to 1400. Fire, earthquake, foreign invasion or social revolution—every kind of explanation has been put forward for the many vicissitudes of the Cretan palaces. What is certain is that they were destroyed and rebuilt on the same site more than once, and that the period of the second palaces corresponds both to economic prosperity and to the spread of the high art of Crete.

What is also certain is that the number of palaces corresponds to a large number of city-states. The Minos was not a pharaoh. Knossos probably never exerted tight political control over the rest of the island until the Mycenaean conquest, if then. Its political and possibly religious hegemony was exercised over what we may imagine as a loose federation of city-states, each with its own prince, on the model of the early Sumerian cities, or rather the pocket rulers of the towns of Syria. The whole enterprise was a peaceful one—hardly any Cretan cities had ramparts.

Moreover, alongside every palace there was a city, built at the same time if not earlier. Just a few steps from the outer esplanade at Knossos, one is in an urban settlement which may have had as many as 60,000 or 100,000 inhabitants. This city of artisans, shopkeepers and sailors did not necessarily obey its masters in deed and word. It is logical to suppose, as H. van Effenterre did in a brilliant article, that there was a class of merchants with their own private commercial interests, outside the strict control of the palace economy. The island's dispersed overseas trade, and the many merchant "colonies" it had founded in Syrian or Aegean towns must have encouraged this economic independence. It is also not impossible that these notables played some political role in a patrician system of rule within the city; or that the people, meeting in a public square, may have had its say in some form of agora; or that the king might have played the role of an arbiter—like the Minos of legend—as a religious leader rather than head of state. If we agree with van Effenterre about this, then Minoan Crete might have been an early version of the future Greek city-state. The hypothesis is a seductive one, although the arguments put forward to support it—the existence of an elders' council chamber at Mallia and of a public room near the palace—could equally well apply to certain Babylonian cities, where we know that the merchants were organized and masters of their own affairs, but without playing a political role.

The last point of which we can be certain is that these luxurious palaces were the ceremonial setting for a divinity as much as for the man who, here as elsewhere, probably derived his authority entirely from his title and function as priest-king. Was the so-called Throne Room at Knossos, with its gypsum seats and its fresco of griffins, later restored by Evans, a public reception room for the Minos, or a sanctuary reserved for the earth-mother goddess? All the Cretan palaces contain a multitude of religious artefacts: tables for libations (as at Mallia), statuettes representing the goddess, rhytons, double axes (*labrys*), consecration horns, shields in the shape of a figure eight, or the strange "sacred knots" made of pottery or ivory, representing a knotted scarf with a golden fringe.

So the palaces were at once temples, stately residences, and huge warehouses in which much of the economic life of the island was concentrated.

The beginnings of Cretan urbanization had corresponded to a general improvement of the economy at the start of the second millennium B.C. The second age of palaces, an even more thriving period, corresponded to increased demand in the Egyptian New Kingdom, just then embarking on its grand and dramatic foreign policy, by expelling the Hyksos and intervening in Asia. The new wind of cosmopolitanism blowing through the Middle East was responsible almost unaided for Crete's material wealth. This dependence on the outside world explains why Crete continued to prosper materially until about 1200, when it was hit by a wave of catastrophes. Certainly the earlier Mycenaean conquest (about 1400?) and the destruction which accompanied it had not dented Cretan prosperity. Those newcomers had found a place for themselves in the former pattern of economic activity in Crete without apparent disruption.

During the first half of the second millennium, Crete adapted to this prosperous external trade which was gradually turning it into the centre of a huge network. It began to develop into a naval power of the first rank. But can one really speak of a "thalassocracy" or of a "Cretan sea-borne empire"? As we have already noted, Crete was not a powerful political machine. Its sailors no doubt had their ports of call: Thera (Santorini), Melos, the obsidian island, Cythera, which could be seen on a clear day from the west coast of the island, and was a look-out point on the route to the Peloponnese and points west— all of these had been occupied by Cretan mariners and even settlers. Cretan merchants had settled at Miletus on the coast of Asia Minor, in Rhodes, Cyprus, Ugarit and probably, like the Syrians themselves, in the ports of the Nile Delta. Minoan ships had sailed to Malta, Sicily and southern Italy.[5] But these contacts, defence posts and facilities, usually on a friendly footing, did not add up to an empire.

They did, on the other hand, carve out a sphere of cultural influence: Cretan art and design invaded the whole of the Aegean. On Melos, the palace of Phylakopi, for instance, rebuilt in the seventeenth century B.C., with its columns and its fresco of flying fish, was cast in the image of Knossos. They also indicated that Cretan trade had conquered the sea, with all the consequences and profits that entailed. Finding enough men to man the oars and sailing vessels of Crete had only been possible by recruiting sailors from throughout the Cyclades and as far away as Caria in Asia Minor. The folk memory of Carian pirates first being pursued by the Cretans and then becoming effective policemen of the sea in their service probably has some truth in it. This kind of thing would happen many more times in the history of the Mediterranean, where there were so few sailors that a fleet of any size simply had to rely on foreign recruits. This was to be as true of Athens in the age of Pericles, Istanbul under the Turks, or Renaissance Venice, as it had been of Minoan Crete.

With these developments, the trading activity which had hitherto concentrated on the eastern tip of the island would soon establish its main axis further west, based on the road between Knossos and Phaistos, the former on the north coast, the latter on the south. It is not surprising that these should have been the two largest palaces on the island (Knossos represented 20,000 square metres of buildings, probably up to three storeys high). They stood at either end of a north-south road joining the two coasts of the island, an excellent example of an isthmus route, that is a short overland road between two shipping centres. This vital road was naturally well maintained: it was paved, ran across a viaduct at the southern end, and was used by pack animals— probably more often than by the sedan chairs or heavy four-wheeled vehicles of which models survive. The wheel first appeared in Crete in about 2000 or 1900 B.C., probably imitated from Syria or Mesopotamia.

The road joining Knossos and Phaistos suggests that there was increased activity on the southern shores of the island. This could have been associated either with coastal shipping on east-west routes to Rhodes, Cyprus and Syria; or, more plausibly, with direct crossings to the African coast, Cyrenaica or Egypt. General histories have argued for too long that navigation on the high seas out of sight of land, in particular the Rhodes-Egypt crossing, cannot have been undertaken until about the third century B.C., in the Hellenistic period. It must surely be accepted now that this major feat—and it certainly was one—had been accomplished earlier. The modest sailing ships of Minos had been the bold pioneers. A late piece of evidence, but all the same earlier than the Hellenistic period, unequivocally supports this view. Odysseus, arriving home in Ithaca disguised as a Cretan merchant, is described as saying: "I proposed to go on a voyage to Egypt. I equipped nine ships and men flocked to them. For six days, these brave people feasted with me. On the seventh we set sail, and from the plains of Crete a fair and full north wind took us straight there, as if on the current of a river. We had only to sit and let the wind and our pilots take us. In five days we had reached the fine river Egyptos." We might note that this feat would not be surpassed even many centuries later, in the days of Barbarossa and the Turks. The north wind was the secret responsible for these performances. One had to have the courage to trust to it—but the rewards made it worth while: Egypt was a land of gold and treasure.

It is striking all the same to note that most of the Cretan seaports are on the north coast, between Knossos and the gulf of Mirabello. Crete's function was essentially that of a staging post between Europe, Asia and Africa. To the north, the island faced countries which had become more backward than itself—peninsular Greece and Argos with which it had maintained contact since the Achaean invasion—while to the west lay the even more primitive regions of southern Italy and Sicily. How far did its sailors venture towards these distant places? We do not know with any certainty. And once more we are faced with the obscure and controversial question of the first sea voyages from east to west.

Like all seafaring peoples, the Cretans often acted as carriers for others, delivering in foreign ports merchandise which they had not manufactured themselves. But their own import-export trade was nevertheless considerable. Their fine painted pottery has been found in Melos, Aegina, Lernos, Mycenae, Cyprus, Syria and Egypt. They also exported fabrics (their bright colours were sought after in Egypt, the land of white linen), jewels and bronze weapons: the latter have been found in Cyprus where the Cretans went to buy copper, although their own island had a few deposits of it. Their obsidian came from Melos and Yali, and Egypt provided them with many semi-precious stones and amethysts, used for engraved seals.

These trades indicate that there was a large population of craftsmen. A city like Gournia appears to have been a weaving centre. The "industrial" boom was such that Crete may actually have been exporting skilled labour, to Egypt for instance (from the nineteenth century B.C. and much later to Amarna) and no doubt to Mycenae as well. But even at the height of its prosperity, Crete also depended on the labour of its foresters, peasants, shepherds and fishermen. It exported wood, especially cypress, along with olive oil and wine. Yet it seems to have imported wheat—a sign of a developed economy where everything was interlinked.

Nevertheless Crete had its share of dramatic incidents, and always following a familiar pattern: palaces were destroyed, rebuilt, then destroyed and rebuilt again, until they finally disappeared. The experts rarely agree about the dates and causes of these catastrophes. But they could only be of two kinds: either the gods (or nature) were responsible, or they were provoked by men and the violence of war. The two events which have given rise to most controversy are one natural disaster, the volcanic eruption of the island of Thera, and one man-made cataclysm: the conquest of the island by the Mycenaeans.

The explosion of the island of Thera (Santorini), which was first identified by S. Marinatos in 1939, has since then fascinated so many archaeologists, vulcanologists and underwater explorers that we can more or less reconstruct what may have been "the greatest natural catclysm in history." Santorini, which still seems to be active (the last eruption was in 1925–6), is a sort of Vesuvius, today three-quarters under water. With its "walls of lava and ash, alternately black, red and green, on which are perched the dazzling white villages, it is the strangest landscape in the whole archipelago."

It was in about 1500 B.C. that a volcano which had apparently been extinct for thousands of years started to become active again. A series of violent earthquakes, traces of which can be detected in the ruins at Knossos and Phaistos, had heralded an eruption or eruptions which buried the Cretan or Cretan-influenced villages on Santorini itself under several metres of lava. The inhabitants apparently had time to flee. But all this was a mere prelude. In about 1470 or 1450 B.C., the island literally exploded—like Krakatoa, in the Straits of Sunda in A.D. 1883.

The scale of that more recent disaster enables us to imagine the violence of the explosion of Thera—apparently four times more destructive, if one measures the amount of the cone of the volcano which was destroyed. But the scenario seems to have been similar: several years of earthquakes, followed by a series of eruptions and finally a massive explosion, creating a fantastic cloud of burning ash, accompanied by a tidal wave. In the case of Krakatoa, the sixty-foot-high waves destroyed three hundred towns and villages, tossing a ship and several railway engines over the rooftops. At Thera, in the Aegean, where the relatively shallow sea was under enormous pressure, the tidal wave must have been even more fantastic, the waves higher and certainly much faster-moving.

Crete, 120 kilometres from Thera, was not only hit head-on by this massive upheaval of the sea, but also shaken by earthquakes, showered with ash and overwhelmed by toxic gases. The whole of the eastern end of the island and even the centre were devastated. A single palace survived at Knossos, damaged but not destroyed. The cities of Phaistos, Mallia, Haghia Triada and

Zakro were all destroyed along with their palaces; as were Gournia, Palaikastro, Pseira and Mochlos. The vegetation was annihilated; ash at least ten centimetres thick lay over everything like a blanket and made any cultivation or rebuilding impossible for years. There was a wave of emigration to the western end of the island and probably to the Mycenaean mainland too, as appears from excavations.

Driven by a north wind, the toxic clouds reached as far as Syria and the Nile Delta. The biblical book of Exodus speaks of a terrifying darkness for three days, during which the Jews held captive by the pharaoh took the opportunity to escape. Some people have tried to match this up to the Santorini eruption. Is that too fanciful? Perhaps. Chronologically, it is hard to reconcile the two. But in 1945, I saw with my own eyes the black clouds arising from the terrible bombing of Hamburg: a hundred kilometres away, we literally experienced darkness at noon. The Krakatoa explosion plunged places two hundred kilometres away into total darkness. Nature is even more powerful, alas, than mankind.

The explosion of Santorini, so long unknown, seems now to be taking on prime importance as a historical explanation. It has been suggested, in an intelligent little book by Rhys Carpenter (1966) and a well-documented study by J. V. Luce, *The End of Atlantis* (1969), that this may have been the real-life event which formed the basis for the famous legend of Atlantis to be found in Plato—referring to a great island, home to a powerful civilization, which vanished under the sea "in a day and a night." Both authors refer the reader to the beginning of the *Timaeus* and the *Critias*. Atlantis, according to the account of the Saite high priest and the Egyptian "temple archives," was situated far to the west, at the limit of the known world. Plato therefore naturally placed it beyond the Straits of Gibraltar, in the middle of the ocean, but for the Egyptians of the eighteenth dynasty, the "western limit of the known world" would have been Crete. So was the destruction of Atlantis possibly a combination of two events, telescoped together in traditional folklore: the end of the Minoan ascendancy and the eruption of Thera?

This hypothesis suggests that the two key events mentioned above, the explosion of Thera and the Mycenaean conquest, occurred within a short time of each other. If that is true, the Mycenaeans would have arrived in Crete shortly after the cataclysm.

The Achaeans or early Greeks, Indo-European invaders who were the ancestors of the Mycenaeans, had in fact arrived in Greece towards the end of the third millennium B.C. They had mostly settled round the edge of the Aegean, among the pre-existing populations whom they subjugated, destroying their cities and their culture. In Lemnos, for instance, the layer of remains immediately following the burning of the town contains traces of a completely new culture: the shape of the houses, the modes of burial and types of pottery all change. It would not therefore be surprising if the newcomers also imposed their language on the area. But perhaps, after all, the Aegean civilization they overthrew on the Greek mainland was a still-fragile graft, established only along the coast and in a few inland sites, in a territory which was not yet fully settled.

These first people of the Aegean (the Pelasgians of Greek tradition) had nevertheless left lasting traces. Linguistic analysis offers unequivocal evidence in this respect. The newcomers may have retained their own language, but they also borrowed a great deal from those they conquered. The Greek language thus inherited a considerable number of local borrowings. Place names and personal names tell us this quite forcefully: the names of cities as famous as Corinth, Tiryns or Athens, the very name of Mount Parnassus, above the oracle at Delphi, in the very heart of Hellenic civilization, the "navel of the world"—are not Greek in origin. Neither—sad to say!—are the names of Homeric heroes such as Achilles and Ulysses/Odysseus, or the Cretan names of the arbiters of the underworld, Minos and Rhadamanthus, or of the queen of those dark regions, Persephone. Even more significant is the non-Greek origin of many words connected with agriculture: the names for wheat, vines, figs, olives, lilies, roses, jasmine or marjoram. Lastly, terms to do with the sea are borrowed too: the art of navigation was a gift more precious even than the vine and the olive-tree from the non-Greek peoples of the Hellenic region to their Indo-European invaders. The latter were strangers to the sea: neither *thalassa* nor *pontus* are Greek words!

But the lessons were quickly learned. In Argos the newcomers were introduced to the network of established links, in particular with Crete. The island, just then on the crest of a wave of prosperity, was a beacon for the Cyclades and the nearest mainland coasts. In the eighteenth century B.C., potters on both mainland and islands, possibly émigré Cretans themselves, began to imitate Cretan models, in the so-called Camares style: seals, jewels, and decorative Minoan motifs were exported and copied. In the fifteenth century, a uniform culture of Minoan inspiration, linked to the Middle East, spread throughout the southern Aegean, so that it is often impossible to tell whether an object found at Phylakopi, say, on Melos, or at Aegina, Mycenae or Pylos was imported from Crete or produced locally.

Mycenae is the most striking example of this process. Since the city asserted itself over the other cities of Argos, the term Mycenaean has become the standard name for the whole civilization. In fact, that civilization really took off during the period of the new palaces in Crete: witness to its splendour are the princely tombs in Mycenae which have been found intact: they date broadly from the sixteenth century B.C. (with a few somewhat older ones and others from the early fifteenth). It is curious to find in them, alongside the preponderant Cretan influence, very clear traces of Egyptian influence too. It is true that between 1550 and 1470–1450, the Mycenaeans and Cretans seem to have engaged in friendly exchange as well as trading side by side, not only in the Aeolian islands, where their pottery has been found in close proximity, but also in Rhodes, where the Mycenaeans appear to have intermingled with the Cretan colony, and even in Egypt, where documents mention Keftiu (Crete) and "the Islands in the Middle of the Great Green," a term thought to refer to all the non-Cretan Aegean islands, plus the Peloponnese.

This parallel rise of Cretan and Mycenaean trade in the sixteenth and fifteenth centuries is sufficient to explain the wealth of the tombs at Mycenae, the abundance of gold objects (the gold came from Egypt) and in particular the amazing gold masks covering the faces of the dead: this was a non-Cretan custom, probably imported, like the gold, from the banks of the Nile. Another hypothesis is that Cretan sailors might have acted as transporters for a mercenary force of Mycenaeans, called in by the pharaoh Amosis in about 1580 B.C., to get rid of the Hyksos from the Delta. These mercenaries may have been identical with the Haunebu, the heavily armed soldiers whose lances, helmets, shields and long swords would have made short work of the Asian intruders. They might have gone home laden with Egyptian gold. But there is no scientific evidence to support this romantic legend.

True or not as this may be, the Mycenaeans undoubtedly followed in the footsteps of the Cretans. Both their civilization and their economy cannibalized the centuries-old model which they found in Crete and which they destroyed, almost unintentionally. Mycenaean expansion, if I am not mistaken, followed the upward trend of trade: it was a success related to the economic climate. And since that expansion was rapid, the area of the sea covered by Mycenaean shipping and influence first duplicated then went beyond the area of Cretan sway. They reached Rhodes and Cyprus, elbowing their predecessors aside, before moving on to the coast of Asia Minor, Syria, Palestine and Egypt, where their pottery was landed in great quantities at Amarna. They also travelled westwards: "Fragments of Mycenaean pottery are to be found almost everywhere in Italy." The signs all point to a rapid and energetic expansion, perhaps using force, as was the case in the straits leading to the coast below Ilium: the Trojan war, dated about 1250 B.C., was in the Mycenaean period. Their ventures beyond Troy into the Black Sea (Pontus Euxinus) may also have used force.

There can be no doubt that the civilization of Mycenae, of Tiryns, Pylos, Argos, Thebes and Athens, was flourishing. In the fourteenth and thirteenth centuries, huge palaces were built on the Cretan model, with the same columns and identical styles of fresco. The open central courtyard of the Cretan version was however replaced by the *megaron*, a large room with a hearth in the centre surrounded by four columns: it had no chimney and the smoke went out through a hole in the roof. The *megaron*, we might note, was a feature introduced from Asia Minor.

But it is not my intention to linger long over Mycenae and Tiryns, or to describe the features of this warlike society, with its kings of Indo-European type and its warriors who went to their tombs accompanied by sumptuous armour. What interests us about the Mycenaeans is the Cretan civilization which they took over, and which therefore became embedded in what would become the Greek civilization of later centuries. Mycenae provided the intermediary stage, an imperfect one as it happened, since it came to a dramatic end, but the only possible one, since in about 1400 or a little later, the final destruction of Knossos meant that the entire Cretan and Creto-Mycenaean legacy was to be found in Argos.

Returning to Knossos then, the city was undeniably captured by the Mycenaeans—but when? There is some evidence for a date of 1460–1450, in particular the Egyptian painting on the tomb of Rekmire in Thebes, where Cretan men bearing offerings to Rekmire have been "re-clothed." The painter has eliminated the classical costume with penile sheaths—traces of them can still be glimpsed—and has replaced them with a Mycenaean-style loin-cloth, ending in a point. In another tomb dating from several decades later, "the men of Keftiu and the islands of the Great Green" are still wearing loincloths. Was this just a change in fashion? Or was it a kind of recognition by Rekmire, the minister who received foreigners at Thebes on behalf of the pharaoh, that there had been a change of dynasty in Crete? From about 1400 at any rate, all mention of Keftiu disappears from the Egyptian inscriptions.

Other signs are that the repairs to the palace of Knossos, after the explosion of Thera, mark the appearance of tablets written in Linear B, similar to those in Pylos, Thebes and Mycenae. And lastly there is a clear change of style, both in pottery and burials, between the R(ecent) M(inoan) IB (which enables us to date the major volcanic episodes on the island) and the so-called "palace style," RMII, which appears at Knossos and Knossos alone. It is logical to conclude, in the light of recent work on the Thera catastrophe, that the Mycenaeans were able to take advantage of the desolation produced in Crete to occupy Knossos, the only palace left standing at the heart of Cretan power. After all, the island had witnessed the destruction not only of many towns with great loss of life, but of several ports and settlements in the Aegean islands which were equally badly affected. There was a vacuum to be filled. The Cretan diaspora, probably in all directions, which followed these disasters, contributed in large measure to the rising star of Mycenae. Crete eventually attained comparative prosperity once more, but would never thereafter be more than a Mycenaean province.

But who then was responsible for the final destruction of the palace at Knossos which the Mycenaeans had occupied? Here all the uncertainties return, including uncertainty about the date. One explanation is that the oppressed Cretans rose up against the new masters of Knossos and sacked the palace, in about 1400 B.C. This has often been suggested but the evidence seems to be contradictory. For example, the fact that the Greek language on the tablets in Knossos is more developed, and therefore in theory later in date than that on the tablets in Pylos, is a problem. Other scholars think we ought to revise our ideas radically about the date of the destruction of Knossos, either putting it in the mid sixteenth century B.C. and attributing it to enemies, possibly simply neighbouring towns, against whom the Mycenaean cities built enormous ramparts—or else putting it much later, in the latter half of the thirteenth century, in which case Knossos simply shared the fate of the other Mycenaean cities and palaces. But that is another story, to which we shall return later.

In the end, what was to have greatest significance in the overall destiny of the Mediterranean was Cretan civilization itself. The problem is that to use the term "civilization" begs many questions—and we have very few of the answers. Only fragmentary images of everyday Cretan life have survived—a handful of "snapshots" which a novelist could turn into a narrative only by using a great deal of imagination. As for Cretan institutions, I have already referred in passing to the gist of what is known: very little. We know there were priest-kings, palaces, cities, communities of artisans, and seafarers. But the organization of this society remains far more mysterious than that of Babylonia or Egypt. The absence of any written documents is a daunting obstacle (the decipherment of the Linear B tablets did not remedy this, since they consisted almost entirely of inventories, and in any case dated from a late period). The only avenues open to us are religion and art.

We know enough about Cretan religion to be able to glimpse something of it, but not enough to be certain of anything, nor in particular to grasp its structure, which might have helped reveal the secrets of the island's social organization. Once we reach the period when the gods of Olympus occupied Crete—when Zeus, escaping his terrible child-eating father Cronos, took refuge in the sacred cave on Mount Ida—then we find ourselves faced with a familiar mythology: the gods referred to in Linear B are all Achaean. But what about the earlier period? A mythology in which divinities are lent human form needs images of several gods engaging in collective exploits. But in ancient Minoan Crete, there is absolutely no sign of them. Religious significance was clearly attached to many objects found in the palaces which were the high places of the official religion (there are no temples in the modern, Mesopotamian or Egyptian sense of the word in Cretan cities), or in the sanctuaries on mountain tops, in caves or sacred groves: trees, columns, the two-headed axe, the horns of bulls and ritually knotted scarves all had some religious importance. Some animals were sacred: the snake and the dove, symbols of earth and heaven. But only one divinity appears to be in evidence: the omnipresent goddess-mother, who sends us back to the earliest human mentalities, and the dawn of religion. She is directly descended from the fleshy goddesses of the early Neolithic Age in Crete: these figures, holding up their breasts with their hands, were patently fertility symbols, that is dispensers of bounty. After all, what could the Cretan people possibly wish for, since they were not divided regionally among different hostile tribes and did not have local gods in rivalry with one another, except that the goddess of nature should protect their fields and flocks, the land and sea, the animals and the people she had created, and that she should cure them from bodily ills? These do indeed seem to be the attributes of the miraculous statue of the so-called goddess "of the Poppies."

On this account, the term monotheism has been applied to Crete, perhaps correctly. Why should one make distinctions between the goddess with the snakes, the goddess with the flowers and the goddess with the doves? But monotheism is normally connected to new and forward-looking religions, whereas nothing could be more ancient than the Earth Mother, queen of Nature. The usual process was that she evolved into a divine couple, a god and goddess (the god always rather less impressive), or into a trinity providing them with a child. The sixth millennium b.c. in Çatal Höyük was "monotheistic" by this reckoning, as were the stone-age hunters who revered the "Venus" of the Gravettian era. I am inclined to suggest that the Aegean, which received all its culture from Neolithic Asia Minor rather than from the densely settled civilizations of Egypt and Mesopotamia, remained faithful to the fertility goddess of the early farmers, instead of adopting the pantheon of gods to be found in more advanced civilizations, and from which the male gods were for the first time displacing the female goddesses.

The impression persists, however, that in religion, as in art, the Cretans took over and thoroughly transformed whatever cultural borrowings came from elsewhere. The priestess-vultures in the lugubrious ceremonial depicted on the walls of Çatal Höyük are a far cry from the whirling young women represented on so many Cretan frescoes or jewels—dainty ballerinas dancing with swirling skirts. This is a quite different approach to life and death, a sort of escape from the religious dread which was natural among primitive peoples. If we survey everything we know about the ritual life of the Cretans: the flocking of the faithful to the cave on Mount Ida or the cave of Erleithya near Amnissos; the crowds of believers thronging into the central courtyard of the palace to attend a ceremony; the bullfights in which there was no killing, but a spectacular and dangerous display of acrobatics; the massive processions at harvest time, as depicted on a fine vase of black steatite, where all the participants are shown open-mouthed, laughing or singing; or even the enigmatic sarcophagus of Haghia Triada, which shows a dead man standing in front of his tomb and attentively receiving the last offerings of the living: in all these representations, there is no sign of people living in dread of their gods, their priests, or the fear of death. On one fresco in Knossos, women in light-coloured dresses, yellow, blue and white, dance bare-breasted in front of a large crowd seated under blue olive trees. Another picture, in an only partly surviving and unidentified fresco, shows what may be a bullfight in the palace courtyard. Seated in the place of honour are more women, ladies of the court or priestesses perhaps, and behind them hundreds of heads crowded together. The colours are bright: red, blue, yellow, ochre and white. It is clear that some ritual is being performed in both ceremonies, yet the atmosphere is one of a joyful popular festival, a society in which men and women meet each other freely. One has only to compare these scenes with the fresco at Mari known as the "investiture" fresco (eighteenth century B.C.)—in which the king Zimri Lim solemnly receives sacred emblems from Ishtar, goddess of war, in the presence of other divinities, animals and hieratic beasts—to be convinced that these are two separate worlds deeply divided by their religious attitudes and their conception of life.

Cretan art confirms this impression. It is certainly the most original in the eastern Mediterranean, and the one that speaks to us most directly in its fantasy, its appetite for life, its pursuit of happiness, and the liberties it takes with form and colour in the interests of expressiveness. During the great age of Cretan art—the second palace period—before the Mycenaean age which froze all this free expression, naturalism triumphed. Plants and animals were painted everywhere, on walls and vases: here a spike of grass, there a bunch of crocuses or irises, a spray of lilies against the ochre background of a vase, or the Pompeian red of a wall-painting; reeds arranged in a continuous almost abstract design, a branch of flowering olive, an octopus with tangled arms, dolphins and starfish, a blue flying fish, a circle of huge dragonflies—all these were used as themes, but they are not treated with the botanical accuracy of, say, Dürer's flower and herb paintings. They are the unreal decor of a fantasy world, where a blue monkey picks crocuses, a blue bird perches on red, yellow or blue rocks, striped with quartz, as wild roses flower all round; a wild cat lurks in the ivy in wait for an unsuspecting bird; a green horse pulls a chariot in which two young goddesses sit smiling. Frescoes and pottery all lent themselves to this inventive fantasy. It is remarkable to find the same plant or marine motifs handled in a thousand different ways on so many vases turned out by the potter's wheel and exported by the hundred—as if the artists wanted to relive the pleasure of creation every time.

The one area where the Cretans seem to have been ill at ease was sculpture, perhaps because it leaves less to the imagination. Their ceramic statuettes are often conventional and stiff. Some of their beautiful objects are nevertheless unforgettable: the lithe form of an acrobat, made of ivory, caught in mid-leap; several heads of bulls; a dark brown leopard carved in schist decorating an ornamental axe in Mallia. Even more remarkable are the reliefs carved on stone vases and rhytons, the countless seals made of gold, amethyst, rock crystal, agate, cornelian and ivory; and the extraordinary jewels.

Cretan art does indeed seem hard to explain: it contains borrowings of every kind, and at the same time displays all-round originality. Perhaps this is something common to island cultures. Cyprus with its extraordinary pottery from the first millennium B.C., and Sardinia with its strange little bronzes from the same time, also raise the question of the uniqueness of islands. They are extreme micro-universes, wide open to the outside world, vulnerable to invasions of people, technology and even fashion—yet in the intervals between such episodes they may be quite cut off, and their trade more sporadic and less regular than elsewhere. Every foreign borrowing develops in an island as if in a laboratory, exaggerating features which become very different from the original model. This is true of other things besides art of course.

Yet Crete in the second millennium B.C., along with the rest of the Aegean under its influence, was an integral part of the Middle East in a way that Greece never would be, not even in the so-called Oriental period or in the heady days of Hellenistic influence in the east. All the Middle Eastern civilizations of this period, despite some clashes, stood on an equal footing, with open access from one to another. There was no imbalance: trade went in both directions, with mutual exchange. Across the whole area covered by these trading links, there existed a curious kind of community, a vast cultural superstructure, connecting the various regions. W. S. Smith is right to see this as the essential feature of the Bronze Age. The operative unit was the Middle Eastern region as a whole, rather than any single sector, not even Crete at the height of its brilliance or Egypt in the Eighteenth Dynasty. And indeed, if one were to look for the most dynamic element in this cultural blossoming, one would probably choose the Ugarit–Byblos axis in Syria. As a long-established hub of communications, it lay at the heart of this unified area, this confluence of contacts: from Knossos to Susa and from Mycenae to Elephantine, the history of Middle Eastern civilization in its fully developed state is therefore really a single story.

For such freedom of communication to exist, a number of conditions had to be fulfilled: above all, as noted earlier, a favourable economic climate, the presence of communities that were both prosperous and acquisitive, and an efficient network of international exchange. Lastly, encouraged by the favourable context, there was a new spirit of curiosity, quickly verging on an obsession with everything that was foreign: it influenced fashion and technology, art, architecture and even the first steps towards diplomacy. An international context was beginning to appear and, in this perspective, detailed archaeological research to determine the origins and the incidence of a given style of ornament, type of pottery, architectural detail or technique of fresco painting or goldsmithing, becomes quite fascinating—especially if one is not too obsessed with that perennial question, always the same in these studies of influence: "which came first?" In relation to the overall history of the Mediterranean, this question is not very important. What really matters is that an extraordinary capacity for comparatively *rapid* cultural diffusion had emerged in a world where shipping was still an adventure.

Take Mallia for instance, on the north coast of Crete, one of the oldest palaces on the island, restored from time to time, but never completely rebuilt like Knossos or Phaistos. It is the only one which can give us an approximate idea of the first Cretan palaces dating from early in the second millennium. When excavations carried out at Mari on the Euphrates uncovered the marvellous Mesopotamian palace of Zimri Lim, extending over several acres, with a labyrinth of buildings around the great open courtyard, it was natural to think that this famous edifice—which people came from miles around to visit during the reign of Hammurabi (eighteenth century B.C.)—had served as a model for the Cretan palaces. It is older than they are and the overall plan, as revealed by aerial photographs, looks very similar to that of Mallia. The same functional demands are after all likely to produce the same kind of architecture. And we also know, from tablets preserved at Mari, that Cretan merchants who had a colony in Ugarit were engaged in active trade with the powerful city of Mari, which had trade links as far south as the Persian Gulf. If there could be commercial contacts, why not cultural ones? But then in 1954–9, excavations by a British team in Beyce Sultan on the Meander in Anatolia, turned up another palace, also built round a central courtyard. This one was smaller, and less of a "labyrinth," but had several features in common with the palace at Mallia: colonnades and pillars which are entirely absent from Mari. This complicates the picture of cultural cross-fertilization, since the taste for columns may be from Egypt, and we know that there were links between Egypt and Anatolia. Yet in Mallia, a curious hypostyle room unequivocally points to direct Egyptian influence. Well, why not? After all, an Egyptian statue, probably dating from the nineteenth century B.C., has been found in Knossos, and a Minoan vase has been found at Abydos in Egypt among Egyptian objects from the same period. I have no intention of joining in this debate among specialists, and will simply conclude that Mesopotamia, Crete, Anatolia, Syria and Egypt all shared certain architectural features during the second millennium B.C. Even the bathhouses with tiled walls and drains, which were once thought to be a Cretan invention, have been found at Mari.

And that is not all. The Cretan frescoes which only appear rather late on, in the second palace period (sixteenth century B.C.), look as if they could have been inspired by the frescoes which the last king of Mari had had painted for the Zimri Lim palace, before the conquest of the city by Hammurabi in 1760. The techniques of moistening are the same, and the colours are very similar, no doubt because they were obtained by crushing the same stones, lapis lazuli for instance for the brilliant blues which were still beloved of the Etruscans centuries later. The themes are similar too: sacrificial processions, ritual scenes. But the religious inspiration, as already noted, is very different: in Mari a hieratic and entirely Mesopotamian spirit inspires the "investiture" scene. Yet on the same panel, the Semitic fantasy which had already enlivened the severity of the Sumerian decoration, in the time of Akkad, is given full rein: it shows two trees, one a date-palm being climbed by two men (probably for the ceremony of fertilizing the flowers), the other a make-believe tree—its tall trunk is crowned with a bouquet of flowers like Egyptian papyrus. Between them flies a blue bird. That blue bird alone, flying between the two green trees, seems to be a link joining Mari and Crete.

But yet again, the current could have flowed either way. Around the great picture of the king's investiture at Mari runs a border of regular spirals. It is usually assumed that the spiral, the image of the waves in a stormy sea, is an Aegean design, although some pre-dynastic pottery provides early examples of this motif. But does it matter what was the origin of a fairly common design feature? It is more interesting to chart the progress of the spiral, which turns up all over the place in the Aegean in the third millennium: it is found on the "frying pans" of Syros, on handsome stone jars in Crete, and on jewels in Troy II (Priam's treasure, as Schliemann called it). From about 2000 it turns up simultaneously in the Mari frescoes, on the ceilings of Egyptian tombs and palaces, and decorating the fantastic animals of the fine polychrome pottery known as "Cappadocian," made at Kanesh (Kültepe) at a time when the pre-Hittite town was home to a colony of Assyrian merchants. The spiral is found on Egyptian seals and jewellery from the Twelfth Dynasty, on ceramics in Crete and other islands in the Aegean, on Cyprus porcelain, on the tombs with *tholoi* in Boeotia, and even in the spiral curls in the beard of a god (or prince) at Mari—something which might seem quite natural of course, but their perfect geometrical regularity is surprising. The god of war on the doors of the Hittite palace of Bogasköy (sixteenth century B.C.) even has a sort of loin-cloth covered in spirals.

This detail, insignificant in itself, is a timely reminder that cultural exchanges could proceed by numerous modest and unexpected paths. Thus, arguing from the evidence of printed or embroidered fabrics, from figures on vases and cylinders, Egyptian scarab amulets, or from travellers' tales (even apocryphal), W. S. Smith *imagined* that the Cretans travelling to Byblos as early as the twentieth century B.C. must have gone on to Egypt, in the wake of the Canaanite merchants of the town, and thus could have visited the Middle Kingdom tombs carved in the rock—after all, the tombs had always been open to public view. So Egyptian painting might have contributed as much as Mari painting did to the art of the Cretan fresco. But the opposite is even more convincing: Minoan naturalism could certainly have provoked the curiosity of artists on the Nile, leading them to imitate it, and it also influenced Syria, especially the north. This is a good example of cultural transmission.

But it poses a difficult question about chronology. It was particularly in the sixteenth and then the fifteenth century that the Cretan palaces were decorated with frescoes, but it was only in the fourteenth century, after Crete had been overcome by the Mycenaeans, that Egypt saw the flowering of the so-called Amarna style, which is too close to the Minoan for there to be any doubt that it was connected. And it was in the fourteenth century too that in Mittani in Syria seals were produced decorated with the familiar lithe and long-haired silhouettes of young Cretans and the bull-fighting motifs which are also found at Kahun in Egypt.

There are two possible explanations, and they are not mutually exclusive. The first is the presence of migrant labour: skilled Cretan craftsmen might certainly have chosen, after the capture of their homeland, to flee to northern Syria, which they knew well, or to the prosperous and sophisticated Egypt of the Eighteenth Dynasty, where there was a ready demand for skilled labour. The other explanation, subtly developed by W. S. Smith, has the advantage of providing a more detailed story of how the Cretan style found ways and means of infiltrating the resistant traditions of the formal Egyptian style by the sixteenth century.

In Egypt as in Mesopotamia (think of the handsome vase of Warka or the "standard frieze" at Ur of the Chaldees), there was a very ancient practice of representing a scene or decorating a painted vase in superimposed strips (like a strip cartoon). The onagers in Ur, harnessed to a chariot of war, appear in the frieze on three levels: but rather like a sequence of stills from a film, it is really always the same onager (a kind of donkey), his gentle trot gradually turning into an all-out gallop. Similarly in Egyptian reliefs, the corn is cut, loaded on to the back of donkeys, carried to silos and unloaded: the characters follow each other through the horizontal strips which regularly divide up the wall, with no big picture displaying each element within an overall composition. The actors in the scene are linked conceptually, not spatially. Movement is therefore sacrificed. The background or the landscape disappears, and is evoked only symbolically: an ear of corn or a flower positioned over a bull denotes a cornfield or a meadow on a Mesopotamian vase; in Egypt, a few lotus blossoms, a fishing scene and some explanatory hieroglyphs are enough to indicate an estate in the Delta, the property of the departed. In the eastern Mediterranean, only the Aegean artists *compose* pictures in the sense we would understand the term: the flowers or scrolls, often asymmetrical, on a vase from Camares; the Cretan dancers or Mycenaean warriors randomly placed on the oval setting of a gold ring, or the blue bird of Knossos in a rocky landscape: all these freely occupy the space re-created by the artist.

Egypt went on being broadly faithful to its traditional strip-cartoon compositions until Roman times, that is for about three millennia. But there were a few interruptions which therefore take on some significance. At the end of the sixteenth century B.C., in the time of Tutmosis I, a period when foreign fashions were very popular, Egyptian art was tempted by a new sense of *movement*. This was the first temptation. Animals in flight from a hunter—undoubtedly inspired by the "flying gallop" dear to the Cretans and Mycenaeans—occupy the whole space of a picture, this time without any horizontal divisions. Or sometimes the dividing lines start to undulate or move apart to depict a hill or a feature of relief. Cretan influence can be detected too in a more impressionistic use of colour: a drawing is obscured by a patch of colour, lines become blurred, a penchant for curves makes a skirt swirl or a banner flap in the wind.

In the last decades of the century—in the time of Amenophis III, who collected plants during his Syrian campaigns and had them carved on the walls of his tomb at Karnak and painted on the walls of his palace—another decorative feature from the Aegean caught the fancy of the Egyptians, the art of flower painting. During the reign of Amenophis's son Akhenaten, who sidelined all the ancient gods and worshipped only one, the sun god, the tradition of tomb painting changed radically along with everything else. The prince built from scratch a new capital city, Tell el-Amarna. In this revolutionary climate, the new style triumphed: it combined movement—birds on the wing, lions or greyhounds chasing a gazelle—with plants, flowers, insects, fish, all handled with the freedom and naturalism of the Cretans. The "green room" in the northern palace at Amarna, with its painted thickets of papyrus, was nothing like the countless marshland scenes which were previously a favourite subject of Egyptian painters. The new style invaded not only painting but porcelain, painted and carved furniture, and caskets. It was copied elsewhere: a porcelain rhyton found in Cyprus might have been manufactured in Amarna, give or take a few details.

Is it so surprising then that the eclectic art par excellence, in an age of eclecticism, should have been the Syrian art of Byblos and Ugarit? Its luxury products—ivories, bowls made of gold or chased silver, jewels, multicoloured pottery—were made for export to foreign places. This was the beginning of an "international art," conscious of differences in style and playing on them, shamelessly borrowing from every kind of source simultaneously. It was produced for a foreign clientele who had to be charmed into buying.

One could easily prolong this review of the cultural exchanges and influences of the second millennium, especially if one wanted to do justice to the spread of plants, of vines and olives in particular, or of technologies like glassblowing, pottery and enamelling; or even to the spread of medical remedies, if we are to judge by the Egyptian doctor who is depicted in a Theban painting at the bedside of a Syrian prince.

But in those far-off times, the essential language of civilization was clearly that of religion. Mesopotamian and Hittite mythology, the poems of Ugarit would yield many examples of strange hybrids. Gods and myths travelled throughout the Middle East, along with the most everyday cultural goods. The example of the Hittite pantheon, in which three or four religious traditions came together, is perhaps too good to be true. We might look instead at the curious poem in which the messengers of the gods of Ugarit fly to Crete to bring back the god of the Cretan artisans, their patron saint so to speak, Kothar Wa-Khasis: he is then commanded to build the Palace of Baal. It would also be easy, but perhaps a little repetitive, to trace the travels from place to place, through all their metamorphoses and name-changes, of the gods of the weather, thunder and the heavens.

The new and exceptional character of the cultural awakening of the second millennium B.C. can best be grasped from the example of Egypt: here was the most structured religion, and the least open to the outside, of any in the Middle East. As a national religion, it excluded all non-Egyptians, and the exclusion was often formally set down. In the temples of Khnum, the ram-headed god who dispensed the waters of the Nile, an inscription reads: "Do not permit any Asian to enter the temple, be he old or young." The Egyptians were the only legitimate believers, and indeed the only legitimate inhabitants of the world. It is true that in Nubia and certain cities in Syria which the Egyptians more or less controlled, Egyptian temples were built where some local divinities were admitted into the Egyptian pantheon, with the addition of symbols like the horns of Hathor or the winged disc. But that was just another way of dominating and controlling colonial subjects. Still, Baal and Astarte, who were introduced in this way into the ranks of Egyptian gods, did gather a certain following independently of any political stratagems or calculations. Some borrowing did occur, and the secret door of religious exchange was at least partly opened.

The process becomes clearer during the religious and cultural crisis which started to appear from about the Eighteenth Dynasty and came to a head under the reign of Amenophis IV, the strangest pharaoh in history, whom we met briefly earlier. The sun god had revealed himself to the pharaoh, who proceeded to proclaim the omnipotence of this single god, represented in simple and symbolic fashion by an image of the sun as a disc with rays ending in outstretched hands. This god's name was Aten and the pharaoh took the name of Akhenaten, meaning "he who has been approved by Aten." There followed a religious war between Akhenaten and the stifling powers of the priests of Amun, who had been enriched by gifts from previous conquering pharaohs. The pharaoh was forced to leave Thebes, the capital where the spurned god Amun still reigned, and to create a new capital city, built hastily in Aten's honour—the city we now know by the name of the nearby village of Tell el-Amarna. Fragile and lively, it flourished for a mere twenty years.

But for our purposes, the interesting thing is not this revealing episode in itself, nor the unsuccessful attempt to introduce the worship of a single deity, something that was already in the air before the reforming pharaoh and which, despite some immediate reaction against him, would continue to trouble the hearts of the faithful thereafter. The interesting point for us is that the Egyptian religion should have shown that it could open up to a certain universalism, that it was for once willing to take notice of the foreigners who had hitherto been so undesirable. Akhenaten's "Hymn to the Sun" actually credits the god with the creation of many different races: "The tongues of men are different when they speak, and their character is different too, as is their skin. Thus hast thou made thy people different." But these foreigners, provided they are guided by the Book of the Dead, will be saved like the Egyptians, and will have access to the afterworld—although by their smell, the gods will know that they do not come from the holy land of Egypt.

In other words, the sun shines on all mankind alike: all people can live in peace under Aten and his associate on earth. It is true that the problems Egypt faced at the time, treachery and military defeat in Syria and religious conflict at home, were too serious for these declarations not to correspond to some underlying political intentions. If the sun god was accepted by all, he might consolidate and save the empire. But these ideas were held within an undeniable spiritual context, and cosmopolitanism had already infiltrated the old house of Egypt for several generations before the mystical reign of Akhenaten brought it briefly into the centre of the Egyptian religion.

III

ACCIDENTS, DEVELOPMENTS AND DISASTERS

If we were now to review the picture painted above and insert all the events that took place over the same period, they would cast a dark shadow over the whole scene. During the endless Bronze Age, the Middle East witnessed all kinds of hardships, upheavals, dangerous developments and catastrophes. Its history is extremely complicated, but can be reduced to a number of quite clear patterns, a kind of geography of human migration.

Geography can be a marvellous explanatory tool, so long as we avoid loading it with elementary determinism. It clarifies questions and formulates them, but it cannot resolve them. Men and their history complicate the picture and confuse the issue.

Let us simplify by saying that in the earliest times, the Middle East could be divided into five or six types of region, depending on whether they attracted and retained populations or, alternatively, dispatched emigrants elsewhere. These population shifts, which could easily lead to catastrophe, are at the heart of the dark picture we shall have to paint.

In the first place there were the regions attractive to settlers, cyclonic zones so to speak, which drew in the different currents. These were areas which had a long history of sedentarization, and already possessed fairly settled towns and villages, and stable patterns of cultivation and grazing. The most populous of these—Mesopotamia and Egypt—were the most attractive, but they were also well able to defend themselves. The less populous areas, which covered much wider areas than these privileged regions, were more open to migration or indeed invasion. They yielded to incomers, without necessarily noticing what was happening: Asia Minor in the broad sense and archaic Greece were both examples of such regions.

As opposed to these sought-after regions were those where there was strong population pressure and a constant overflow of people. It was not that demographic density was greater there than elsewhere; on the contrary, it was inferior to what could be found on the banks of the Nile or the Euphrates. But these regions were over-populated in relation to their resources—hence the disequilibrium which gave them an unsettled history. They were situated in the mountains, deserts and steppes and on many sea-coasts. Seagoing people of the Mediterranean might be farmers and cultivators as well, but the narrow coastal zones, usually hemmed in by the nearby mountains, were not as a rule self-sufficient. They were also dependent on the sea.

The dramatic events of the Bronze Age were thus the result of the different zones into which the Mediterranean was divided. Human populations were as much victims of the natural forces all round them as of their own customs, desires and rulers.

For all that, the classic Mediterranean stereotypes—hill-dwellers coming down from the high valleys, or seafarers setting sail from their native land never to return—do not appear so frequently, or in such a straightforward way, in the Middle East, a continental landmass not very open to the sea and where the mountains are somewhat peripheral. Structurally the Middle East continues the great platform of ancient rocks making up the Sahara, interrupted briefly by the Red Sea then continuing on into Iran. Fragments of this platform had collapsed to form the Red Sea and the Dead Sea, while others had been raised: the mountain ridges of Libya and Arabia on either side of the Nile, and the mountains of Lebanon and the Anti-Lebanon: But the real mountains are to the north, beyond the double line of the Taurus and Zagros. They form part of Asia Minor and part of Iran, linking up with the mountains of Armenia and, further north, with the mighty Caucasus.

So the threat from the mountain-dwellers was confined to the north of our region. It did not therefore take on that immediate and familiar character it had in Italy and Greece, where mountain people simply had to travel downhill to find themselves in the cities and cultivated fields of the plains. Emigration from the mountains to the Middle East was often a long journey, punctuated by halts: the populations which came from the Caucasus stayed for years or centuries in Armenia, then settled down again in the Zagros or Iran before reaching their journey's end in Mesopotamia, Syria, or Asia Minor, where the plateaux and the high and low plains were still desirable lands to take over. These emigrants from the mountains are known to us as a rule at their point of arrival, where recorded history illuminates their presence. But what was their history before that?

The Gutu, for example, seem to have originated in the Zagros, that is the mountain barrier to the east of the Mediterranean. But for all we know, they may have come from further east. Their rapid rise was favoured by the internal upheavals of the Akkadian Empire. They then occupied Babylon in 2160, setting up a government there which the troubled times rendered immediately ineffective. By 2116 or so they had been driven out again. So their triumph had been short-lived.

The Hurrians, whose language bears no relation to any other known language apart from Urartian, may have come from Armenia towards the end of the second millennium B.C. They were probably artisans, bringing with them metal-working techniques, as well as equestrian harness and the light war-chariot. Whoever they were, they scattered throughout the cities of Mesopotamia, Syria, Cappadocia and Cilicia. They settled in large numbers in Carchemish and Ugarit, cities where industry was implanted early, and they took part, but as foot-soldiers so to speak, in the construction of the state of Mittani under the leadership of Aryan chiefs, between the sixteenth and fourteenth centuries B.C.

If we take another famous example, the Kassites, their origins too are uncertain. They may have come from Iran, Armenia or the far-off Caucasus, or perhaps from all three. They are first detectable in the Zagros, the launchpad for their final emigration. Their language, another non-Indo-European one, might have provided some clues, if these immigrants had not so quickly abandoned it: they adopted Akkadian as soon as they arrived in Mesopotamia in the second millennium. They had at first attempted to enter it as conquerors in 1740 B.C., as the old dynasty was collapsing after the death of Hammurabi, but without success. In 1708, a second attempt also failed. But the Kassites had a destiny rather like that of the Germanic tribes vis-à-vis Rome in later times. They began the peaceful penetration of Mesopotamia as mercenaries or even labourers. It was an accidental event from outside (a Hittite chariot attack, taking Babylon by surprise) which opened up the gates of power to them on the rebound in 1594. A Kassite dynasty took over and reigned until 1160, which is something of a record in length, but the conquerors had themselves been absorbed by the local culture and language well before their victory. In the absence of any other achievements, they did succeed in changing sartorial fashion: it was from them that there came the long tunic with short sleeves which was to be the classic garment later worn by the Assyrians. The history of the Kassites then is that of a poverty-stricken people who had several strokes of good fortune: they knocked at the gates of Mesopotamia when they were not securely closed; they took power thanks to the exploits of others; and they reigned when the general situation was in a prosperous phase.

Seagoing peoples do not provide such striking examples of aggressive migration. Did they shrink from taking on a political role? Trade merely requires the absence of war and the co-operation of others. Cretans and Mycenaeans had settled in the Cyclades, at several points in Asia Minor, and in Rhodes and Cyprus. The Syrians had several small trading colonies in Egypt, which were certainly prosperous, and may even have begun to prospect in the western sea. These settlements are not negligible when viewed in detail, but cannot compare with the great waves of colonization of the western Mediterranean which were to follow during the first millennium B.C.

And yet, to warn us against making hasty judgements, it was the Peoples of the Sea (a name given them by the Egyptians) who were to play a leading role in the decisive crisis of the twelfth century. Their disturbances were the signal, if not the single cause, of the approaching catastrophe which brought the splendours of the Bronze Age to a close.[6] And if they created panic everywhere, was that not primarily because no one was expecting them? An entire population crossing the sea was something astonishing, unheard of! Similarly, the Arab invasions in the seventh century A.D. were a total surprise: no one had anticipated an attack or a threat from that direction, from the desert which had for so many centuries seemed empty.

The desert is not the same thing as the steppe, but a steppe that sees its scanty grasslands disappear can quickly turn into a desert—and the reverse is sometimes true. The Syrian desert was a complete desert, on the borders of Lower Mesopotamia, isolating and protecting it to some extent, but also affecting it by its perpetual drought. But it was prolonged by steppes towards northern Mesopotamia, where non-irrigated agriculture remained the rule. Today, this border steppe is "desolate and uncultivable; it greens over after the short rainy season and a thousand flowers bloom: a precarious grazing area, this is the Arabian *badiya.*" Naturally, it was an ideal way into Mesopotamia for the desert nomads, who sometimes came as peaceful visitors and hirers of grazing lands.

But the contrast between steppe and desert is not an essential one as regards population movements. Nor is that other contrast, clear-cut though it is, between hot and cold deserts: Iran, warm, yet cooled by the altitude of its plateaux and mountains, provides a transitional link between the two kinds. The important thing is that all these deserts of the Ancient World formed a continuous mass to be crossed, rather like linked seas, from the Atlantic to China: they ran from the Sahara to Arabia, to the Syrian desert, to Turkestan—linked, awkwardly but nevertheless the link is there, by the Dzungarian gate, to the deserts of Takla-Makan, the Gobi Desert and beyond it the steppes of northern Mongolia and southern Manchuria. The Dzungarian gate was also roughly the dividing line between Caucasians and Mongolians. But everywhere in this great tract cutting across the Ancient World, human populations faced the same imperatives: the scarcity of water and grass, the constant need for massive migration. In the end, sooner or later, they all devised the same difficult and ingenious responses, the same techniques of nomadism.

Nomadic life cannot be assumed to have been perfected at the dawn of human history—although people often mistakenly think so. Large-scale nomadism, using fast-moving animals like the horse and the dromedary (and later the camel, from Bactria in Turkey), only emerged at a late date. It had taken a long time and many successive adaptations to reach this equilibrium, which was first achieved in the hot Syrian and Arabian deserts; and it happened even later in the Sahara, the last of the family of great deserts to be mastered.

An elementary form of nomadism, almost older than agriculture, had nevertheless grown up from the early days of the domestication of animals. Men and dogs drove flocks of smaller livestock: sheep and goats. But it was the settled farmers who domesticated larger beasts, the ox and later the horse, creating a mixed economy of which the second type of nomadism was a mere by-product. Grazing in the steppes, where there were plenty of wide-open spaces, represented a way out for settled populations, whenever poor harvests, drought, or the existence of too many mouths to feed made village life difficult. Whole communities thus found themselves driven into an unbalanced and incomplete economy, and caught thereafter in a web of obligations. They had to use different grazing grounds at different seasons. In order to follow the herds, their houses became temporary shelters, tents or carts loaded with women, children and belongings. Their life remained precarious: it only took another drought, a lost battle for grazing grounds, a surplus of population, or a lack of success when trading at the markets on the fringes of settled communities, to generate panic, leading to migration and the invasion of cultivated areas.

Before the twentieth century B.C., the steppes and deserts from Hungary to the Black and Caspian Seas and to Bactria (Turkestan) were occupied by Indo-European peoples. They were semi-sedentary, and knew how to grow wheat and barley, but their numbers or the exhaustion of their arable land regularly turned them into pastoral people, wandering far and wide. We do not know much about these Indo-Europeans, who were probably divided into several different populations. But studies carried out by prehistorians— of the so-called Tripolye civilization near Kiev in 3500–1900; of the Usatovo civilization near Odessa (*c.* 1800) and of Afanasievo (3000–1700) and Andronova (after 1700)—provide unequivocal evidence that all the economies which have left any traces were mixed, being both agricultural and pastoral and therefore still connected to village settlements. Herds of livestock were, however, becoming a major feature: sheep, goats and cattle (though not pigs) and later camels and horses.

The use of horses was obviously a decisive factor, but they did not become available overnight. Large herds of wild horses were in existence in the Paleolithic, reaching even into western Europe. They may have been domesticated for the first time in southern Russia, before being tamed elsewhere. But when the chariot first appeared in the fourth millennium, it was pulled by teams of oxen. The harnessed horse made its appearance only in the second millennium, probably by way of the Hurrians, a people originating in Armenia who had settled in northern Mesopotamia. It was here, on the edge of the great plains, that the light two-wheeled chariot was probably invented: it was harnessed to one or two horses and its complicated construction would have required an expert workforce: this was to revolutionize the conduct of war for centuries to come. The suggestion that it originated in this area on the borders of present-day Iran and Armenia is plausible. Between Lakes Van, Sevan and Urmia was an area characterized by forests and metal-working. Excavations by Soviet teams have established that there were many two-wheeled vehicles in the region, and later on four-wheeled ones, at dates as early as—or even earlier than—in Mesopotamia. These vehicles had solid wheels: spokes were a later invention.

The light chariot spread rapidly across the steppes and had a long career in the Middle East, where this costly and aristocratic instrument of warfare was a status symbol. Egypt, as ever lagging behind, did not adopt it until the second half of the sixteenth century; it appeared in Crete a little earlier than in Egypt and probably it had arrived even sooner in Mycenae (in the first quarter of the century). At the battle of Qadesh in the thirteenth century, several thousand Hittite chariots were pitted against those of the Egyptians.

One final step had still to be taken, the use of riders on horseback, who are glimpsed as early as the fourteenth century. But it was only in about the tenth century that this strange cultural phenomenon, so inexplicably late in developing, became established on the confines of the Caucasus and Iran. When it did, it completely changed the basis of social and economic life in the steppes: a herdsman on horseback could watch over huge flocks of animals. The soldier on horseback did not have to be a wealthy patrician like the charioteer of the past. Migrations of population from east to west were hastened, heralding the dramatic events to come. The first signs were the disturbances provoked by the Cimmerians, the semi-nomadic, semi-settled people north of the Black Sea, who had encamped in what was later southern Russia (now Ukraine). They were driven out in the eighth century following violent attacks by the Scythians, who seem to me, as they have to other writers, to have been the first "truly" nomadic people.

So in the Bronze Age, down to 1200 B.C., we are still far from the time of the great nomadic invasions. The Indo-European migrations of the period did not take place without violence of course, but they lacked the powerful weapon of cavalry. These were invaders who triumphed by dint of audacity and warlike determination, whether in the west of Europe, in Iran or India (fifteenth century) or in Greece and the Middle East. Their invasions were often, in fact, long-term infiltration across sparsely populated regions. The newcomers mingled with the resident populations and sometimes even joined forces with them to march on. This is perhaps how one should view the raid by the Hyksos on the Nile Delta, which they controlled for about a century. They were probably Indo-Europeans but seem to have been associated with other peoples too: the new weapons of horse and chariot helped them accomplish their famously rapid victory.

As for the theory that the Indo-European invaders were rich incomers who dominated a vanquished peasant population, like most generalizations it seems to be only very broadly applicable. The Hittites who settled in Asia Minor after the Luvians, their brothers in arms, arrived there early enough to have adopted the ancient cuneiform script. Their written language, which is well-attested, would soon only have twenty per cent of Indo-European words, the rest being borrowed from peoples on the spot who were non-Indo-European. The same thing happened to the Hittites as to the Achaeans in Greece: they became sucked into a cultural inheritance which was originally not their own and which outclassed them.

Just as the Greeks had to become Greek, so the Hittites, on arrival in Asia Minor, turned into Hittites. They probably embarked upon their historical destiny before the beginning of the second millennium. It was about then that they arrived, possibly from the shores of the Caspian, or from Thrace, and settled in the high mountainous regions of Anatolia, freezing in winter, baking hot in summer. Sturdy and vigorous people, these Indo-Europeans who mingled with the local population were recognizable by their light-coloured hair, blond or auburn, and their characteristic "Greek" profile, which so struck the Egyptians, those connoisseurs of ethnic types. They were undoubtedly a farming people from the continental interior, and for a long time deliberately avoided the sea, establishing their capital Hattusha (Bogasköy) inland in the valley of the Kizil Irmak, known to the Greeks as the Halys. It was here that their good fortune took root.

Thereafter, their energetic population, their rulers' ambition, their thriving metal production and the massive use of chariots enabled them to extend their domination to limits which cannot be accurately charted in retrospect, particularly since their empire was based on a kind of feudal system, granting estates, manors, principalities and so on—a source of weakness which was to have serious consequences. For a brief moment in 1595 B.C. they surprised themselves by capturing Babylon, but were so disconcerted by their extraordinary victory that they abandoned it immediately. But they pressed on through Carchemish, Aleppo and Ugarit, sometimes by force, sometimes peacefully, towards the sea and the Fertile Crescent. This long period of expansion provided them with strength and fuelled their ambitions. Mesopotamia to the south, divided between Babylonia and Assyria, could hardly hold them up for long; they also overcame the Mittanians on the key sites on the bend in the Euphrates, and stood up to the formidable power of Egypt. The battle of Qadesh in 1285 B.C., a sort of monstrous stand-off between the Hittites and Egyptians, marked the end of these exhausting wars. Each side could claim victory and would not budge thereafter.

There followed a period of prudence, leading to the signature in 1280 of the oldest peace treaty of which the text has survived. It was the result of lengthy diplomatic negotiations and exchanges of messages. These tablets, written in Akkadian, the international lingua franca of the time, have been found in Amarna, Bogasköy and Ugarit. A postal service was maintained by the larger states from Anatolia to Egypt. An entire book could be written about this early version of diplomacy, about the exchanges of doctors, sculptors and craftsmen, about the policy of dynastic marriages between princely families so typical of the fourteenth and thirteenth centuries, and the Babylonian, Mittanian or Hittite princesses who became the guarantees for alliances and reconciliations of varying sincerity. These contacts between Egypt and the outside world were in fact linked to Egypt's determination to expand towards Syria, beginning in military terms in the sixteenth century with the Syrian campaigns waged by the pharaohs of the Eighteenth Dynasty. The aim was to get rid of the Hyksos, who had been driven out of the Delta but were now entrenched in the Palestinian cities. Victorious and determined to remain so, Egypt was to exert a sort of protectorate, always needing reinforcement, over Mittani and the city-states of the Syrian coast.

When Hittites and Egyptians confronted each other in these territories which were foreign to both sides, it was therefore a matter of imperial rivalry, but within a context of self-conscious international relations which had never previously existed. Wars and diplomacy succeeded each other until a semblance of balance of power finally became established, shortly before the catastrophic twelfth century B.C.

Hittite civilization was itself a good example of the cosmopolitanism of the second millennium. Everything seems to have been borrowed from elsewhere. The very name Hatti was borrowed from the local Anatolian population, as were traditional Hittite building techniques, their red glazed pottery with multi-coloured decoration, their libation vases in the shape of animals, their shoes with turned-up pointed toes, their gods with conical headdresses and so on. From the Mesopotamians they borrowed many items of the legal code, cuneiform script and the practice of representing people on horizontal friezes. From the international style of the sixteenth century B.C. they borrowed the Aegean spiral, the drawings of galloping animals and plants using spiral motifs. From Egypt, via Ugarit no doubt, they borrowed certain details such as the representation of the sun as a winged disc, which is found in connection with images of the king in the sanctuary at Yazilikaya and elsewhere. Lastly, the Hittite pantheon with its "thousand gods" accepted all the local deities without missing a beat. Greatest of all were the god of weather and storms, possibly to be identified with Adad, the Mesopotamian god of thunder, and Reshef or Baal, the Syrian god. The latter usually appears riding a bull in Hittite sculptures. At his side was the great sun goddess, none other than the indestructible stone-age Earth Mother of Anatolia, whom the Hittites had decked out with some of the attributes of the Hurrian goddess Hepat.

The fascination here lies in being able to look back many centuries to discover the first Indo-European people to be recorded from the inside, thanks to the ample documentation found at Bogasköy (so ample indeed that it will take a long time to record and translate it all) and thanks too to the examples of Hittite art, still recognizable despite all the borrowings, and very expressive in spite of its conventions.

Is it fanciful of me to think of the Hittites as a straightforward and brave people, down to earth, life-loving, fond of dancing and music, and kind to children and animals? Several engaging sculptures show the young prince playing as he stands up in the queen's lap, or bringing her samples of his writing exercises. This was a still-naïve people, basking in the glow of nearby civilizations and gradually constructing its own imperial conventions. But the Hittite king never claimed to be a living god as the pharaohs did. Although ruling over a people of warriors, he was nevertheless one of those who chose to use diplomatic channels rather than make war to achieve their ends. Observers have noticed among the Hittites the absence of that warlike ruthlessness so typical of the age, even in Egypt, and which would later become truly terrifying under the Assyrians. There is one last significant feature worth mentioning: the attitude towards the status of women—rather surprisingly among this soldier-tribe—seems to have been as liberal as in Crete.

In the second millennium B.C., the Syrian desert and the more archaic Arabian desert had not yet been disturbed by the aggressive way of life of the Beduin. The horse and dromedary were both present from early on, but neither was being used to full capacity. According to the experts, the domestication of the dromedary may even have taken place as far back as the third millennium, possibly in eastern Arabia, nearer the Gulf. But they do not detect it being used as a major pack animal for caravans until about 1300 B.C. (and this important step used to be dated even later, in the tenth century B.C.).

Until then, caravans consisted of donkeys with their drivers, the *hapiru* of the Mesopotamian texts. This word—if it really does mean donkey-master and not simply man of the desert, Beduin, as was once thought—would provide valuable and precise evidence: it first appears in the twenty-third century B.C., then disappears in the thirteenth. An Egyptian painting from about 1890 B.C. shows the Semites of the "Asiatic" desert, wearing long multi-coloured robes as they travel to Beni Hassan in Egypt with their donkeys, bringing gifts for prince Knumhotep: kohl (eye make-up) and desert gazelles. Did they take the route which is thought to have linked Mesopotamia and Egypt and which might explain the prosperity in very ancient times of a settled population in Sinai and the Negev, something which seems odd at first sight? The ultimate development of sea-borne trade would have spelled the end of this ancient overland route across the stony surface of the desert. Dromedaries would have been able to use the tracks nearer the sea, where the sand was too deep for the small hooves of donkeys.

But why was the valuable dromedary not used earlier? Possibly because of the problem of harness: it was not until the ninth century B.C. that a new type of saddle for the dromedary appeared. "About the time that the first horse-back riders appeared somewhere in the northern Arabian desert, the dromedary drivers gradually acquired the new elements of the revolutionary saddle perched up on the beast's hump." Previously they had ridden with a cushion on the crupper. The new saddle was improved by a complicated system of girths in the eighth and seventh centuries and then by the high pommels which came into general use in the third and second centuries B.C. (see Xavier de Planhol). Only then did the southern deserts witness the "second wave" of nomadism, which came into historical focus many hundreds of years later (in the seventh and eighth centuries A.D.) with the wave of Arab conquests. We might note once again how very long these processes took.

So the Syrian desert bordering Mesopotamia remained undisturbed for a long time. What normally happened was that the nomad came cap in hand, needing to rent grazing land, to sell livestock, or to hire himself out as a carrier or heavy labourer. This is the unchanging story, recorded in the documents of Mari. Large-scale invasion, capable of taking the form of a "conquest," could happen only if the settled population allowed it; if, for example, they needed labour to work their land or help in fighting a neighbouring city, or if internal dissension had undermined the authority of their leaders. In short, between these two worlds, which operated like communicating vessels, one rather full, the other rather empty, compensatory movements hardly ever took a violent form.

The peoples of the Syrian desert were Semites, divided among many small tribes. They were moving north into Syria and Mesopotamia as early as the third millennium. The first people to settle there—known conventionally and probably inaccurately as the Akkadians—moved into the areas round the rivers near Assur, Kish and Mari. Fortune favoured them: under Sargon they founded the so-called Empire of Akkad (2340–2200). The second Semitic wave consisted of Canaanites and Amorites who decisively occupied the Syrian-Palestinian area, the former to the south around Byblos, the latter to the north and east around Ugarit, Mari, etc. Small groups of Amorites also infiltrated the cities of Mesopotamia, eventually seizing power after having contributed to the destruction of the third dynasty of Ur: Hammurabi was an Amorite. But by this period the Amorites had, like the Akkadians before them, become assimilated into the thriving civilization of Mesopotamia, though it is true that in Akkad, Mari or Byblos, some art works show Semitic influence.

Over the course of the centuries, many other Semitic tribes were to cross the frontier leading to zones of stable settlement, among them the Haneans, the Benjaminites and the Suteans. The invasion of the Aramaeans was on a larger scale, becoming noticeable by the thirteenth and twelfth centuries as they eventually forced their way through the frontiers of the Middle

Euphrates, despite the fortifications put up on the bend of the river by Tiglath Pileser I (1117–1077 B.C.). The role they played in the Fertile Crescent and Mesopotamia is well known: their language replaced Akkadian there as a lingua franca. It is a curious feature of these Semitic migrations that while they adopted virtually wholesale the culture, technology and art of Mesopotamia, they preserved their languages (Akkadian, Aramaic) and even imposed them on others, first in the zone they occupied in Mesopotamia, then, thanks no doubt to the spread of their civilization from Mesopotamia to the rest of the Middle East, as international languages. The Hittites, the pharaohs, Ugarit and Cyprus all used Akkadian for their diplomatic correspondence, long after the dynasty of Akkad had disappeared.

It was the upheavals caused by the twelfth-century crisis which ensured the success of the Aramaeans. Similarly it was in the midst of these disturbances that the Hebrews settled, apparently before 1230 B.C., in the semi-populated mountains of Palestine: the Canaanites and Philistines stopped them reaching the plains. Bringing up the rear came the Arabs, noted for the first time in Babylonian records in the ninth century B.C. It would be some time before their deeds reached centre stage in history.

The story is a repetitious one, as we see. It reflects a basic set of human relations which remained unchanged across the centuries. If nomads frequently came swooping down to seize the wealth of Mesopotamia (wide open to invasion, unfortunately for its inhabitants), Mesopotamia in turn was nourished by the mass of hungry humanity outside its gates: desert and mountain were basically reservoirs of exploited people who in their turn exploited others.

The twelfth century B.C. brought such catastrophes that the preceding centuries seem benign by comparison. Cataclysmic changes had not spared them, it is true, but there was generally some compensation: the fragile Cretan palaces were rebuilt; and when destroyed again, they were rebuilt again; Egypt was invaded and attacked both from outside and from within, but recovered under first the Middle and then the New Kingdom; Mesopotamia had to contend with more numerous and even more serious difficulties, but nevertheless emerged and survived. And through everything, progress continued its forward march. But after the upheavals of the twelfth century, only the most robust of political units survived, if at all, and then in a piteous condition. The experience was devastating and universal. So an age of history was brought to a close, as things generally are in history: sometimes very abruptly, with a bang, and sometimes hardly noticed, with a whimper.

At first sight, the dramatic historical events are the first to capture our attention. But what a strange history this is! Nothing about it is immediately comprehensible, and on reflection the picture becomes even less clear. The collapse of the Hittite Empire in about 1200 happened quietly, with less disturbance than a sandcastle softly subsiding. And we cannot work out who was responsible. About thirty years earlier, in about 1230, the Mycenaean palaces were almost all destroyed, and many cities on the Greek mainland and islands were abandoned. Here again, there is no obvious culprit: those who used to be held responsible, the Dorians, the last Indo-European invaders of ancient Greece, did not arrive until the end of the twelfth century, some hundred years later at least, or so archaeology now tells us. Indeed, as one serious historian has asked, somewhat tongue in cheek, was there ever a Dorian invasion at all?[7] As for the Peoples of the Sea, the key figures in these apocalyptic times, we glimpse them only on the two occasions when the Egyptians crushed them in battle. We may not be surprised to find that they survived these bloody defeats. But who were they exactly? They remain a puzzle to historians: when confronted by a dramatic disaster which knocked out several civilizations, and by the almost total shipwreck of the *Bronze Age itself,* they would like some clear explanations—but these are hard to come by.

There are four separate groups of events to deal with:

1   The Hittite Empire (the Hatti) collapses in about 1200.

2   The Mycenaean palaces are destroyed and burned in about 1230.[8]

3   The people whom the Egyptian documents variously describe as the Peoples of the North, the Peoples of the Islands, or the Peoples of the Sea, head for Egypt and are defeated twice in 1180 and 1225 approximately (dates of which we can be reasonably sure).

4   A long period of drought strikes the Mediterranean at the end of the second millennium B.C. Was this last player, the climate, the most important of all?

Let us consider each question in turn.

The collapse of the Hittite Empire, according to documents discovered at Ugarit (Ras Shamra), took place not at the end of the thirteenth century but at the beginning of the twelfth. There is a slight discrepancy. Claude A. Schaeffer, who was in charge of the excavations at Ras Sharma, wrestled with the explanation for the apparently silent death of this warlike empire. There are a few certainties, but they are negative ones: the Peoples of the Sea followed the coastline, crossed Asia Minor via the west and south, attacked the vassal states who were allies or tributaries of the Hittites, ending up at Cyprus, Cilicia, Carchemish and Ugarit. But there is no trace of them to be found in the Anatolian interior, notably at the excavations at Bogasköy. A further detail is that the Hittite king, before succumbing in this mysterious way, had defeated the Peoples of the Sea, with the aid of boats from Ugarit, in a naval battle off Cyprus. But that does not rule out the possibility that afterwards, by cutting the Hittite kingdom off from the sea and its vassals, the invaders may have dealt it a mortal blow. Neither were the Phrygians from Thrace (another negative finding) directly responsible for the fall of the Hatti. Like the Dorians in Greece, they arrived on the plateaux of Anatolia *after* the almost simultaneous destruction of the great Hittite cities.

Moving on then, there are at least two hypotheses. Claude Schaeffer does not accept that some invader deliberately burnt down all the public and private buildings of Hattusha (Bogasköy), Kanesh (Kültepe) and Alaça Höyük. "Is it likely," he writes, "that a conqueror of the capital city and the other contemporary urban centres of Hittite Anatolia would have derived any advantage from consigning to the flames not only the palaces and fortifications but all the private dwellings in towns which he intended to occupy?" The letters found in Ugarit and Bogasköy seem to him to prove that the Hittite Empire collapsed essentially from within, from some central inadequacy, after being weakened by Assyrian attacks, by revolts and defections by its vassals and allies (starting with Ugarit, whose loyalty by the last years of the empire was in some doubt), and lastly by serious drought and famine. The last king, Suppiluliuma II, asked Ugarit to provide a large ship equipped to transport grain to Cilicia from the valley of the Orontes—"it is a matter of life and death," he wrote—plus "all the available boats in the country" to transport the king, his family, his court and his army. So by this stage Suppiluliuma had probably already abandoned the capital. Why? Probably, according to Schaeffer, because of repeated famines caused by drought and the devastation of his kingdom by violent seismic shocks: evidence of such shocks throughout the second millennium has come from excavations in Turkey. The Anatolian region of Turkey is an unstable zone with frequent earthquakes, and these could also cause fires to break out. At the time when the Hittite cities were being destroyed and consumed by fire, the archaeological level contemporary with Ugarit was itself, according to Schaeffer, disrupted by some extremely violent earthquakes. Other specialists, however, hold to the theory that there was some form of human intervention, a "foreign" invasion, which might perhaps have joined up with the human tide formed by the Peoples of the Sea on the move in the south.

The end of Mycenaean civilization is equally mysterious. In the thirteenth century B.C. it was still very healthy. It was based on a densely settled population, large cities, a wide-ranging network of outposts and flourishing trading relations. The only worrying sign was that all the cities on the Greek mainland were reinforcing their defences and building huge walls around them. On the Acropolis in Athens—which was once a Mycenaean town—the Pelargicon wall dates back to these defensive works, dictated either by prudence or by fear. In the citadels of both Athens and Mycenae, wells dug to a gigantic depth have been found, going right down to underground springs: the besieged city-dwellers would thus be able to drink water drawn from under the feet of their enemies. A huge wall was also built across the Corinth Isthmus, a sort of miniature Great Wall of China (some of it still remains in the south-east part of the isthmus). All this is revealing: the Mycenaean cities felt themselves to be under threat. They were certainly rivals amongst themselves (tradition tells of a war between Argos and Thebes), but some common danger seems to have been looming over them.

We know that in about 1230 the palaces were destroyed for good, in Mycenae, Pylos and Tiryns, where the skeletons of the defenders have been found under the walls under a mass of burned debris. We know that entire regions were abandoned. So what became of the Mycenaeans? Per Alin (in 1962) tried to trace them across the Greek mainland, by following a trail of pottery in the IIIC style, which became established just after the fall of the palaces. So one might conclude that many Mycenaeans took refuge in the mountains of the north coast of the Peloponnese (which kept the name of Achaea) and that they continued to occupy Attica, whose population and prosperity seem actually to have increased after the destruction of the palaces; that a very few of them remained in Euboea and Boeotia; and that they almost universally deserted the centre of Mycenaean civilization, Argos, southern Messenia, Laconia. Several islands in the southern Aegean were also completely abandoned. In Crete, the local people took to the mountains. These were former Minoans, since their descendants in the classical period were still speaking a non-Greek language in the east of the island and are known as "Aeteo-Cretans," in other words "true Cretans." Other islands however, such as Cephalonia on the west coast, or Rhodes, Kos, Kalmos and Cyprus (which seems to have been occupied by the Mycenaeans after an armed attack), all of them former trading centres, received larger contingents of Mycenaeans. They seem to have settled in Cilicia under the name of Dananiyim (Danaoi).

Who was behind these flights and emigrations? Who destroyed the great Mycenaean palaces? Who can it have been if not the Dorians?

There are two possible theories about this as well. The first suggests that there was an Indo-European invasion before that of the Dorians: the invaders might have been those "Greek" peasant populations who had been living for some time on the north-eastern and north-western frontiers of the Mycenaean world, in Macedonia, from where the Mycenaeans imported their pottery, or in Epirus where tombs unlike those at Mycenae (and of a type that later spread through Greece in the Dorian period) had existed since the thirteenth century B.C. Bronze armour of Mycenaean origin has been found there. In that case, as Sinclair Hood has remarked, the Mycenaeans would have been defeated with their own weapons (just as the Germanic tribes defeated the Romans using Roman weapons). For we know now that neither this first wave of invaders (if it existed), nor the Dorian wave, possessed iron weapons—as was once believed. The "black metal" did appear in the Aegean towards the end of the thirteenth century, but it came in from the East, via Anatolia. Nor did the newcomers bring the practice of cremating the dead, which also came from Asia Minor.

If there really was a pre-Dorian invasion, that would solve at a stroke all the problems relating to the destruction of the Mycenaean centres. But we can only guess at this, for want of a better explanation, and it raises in turn other problems which even supporters of the theory such as Vincent Desborough (*The Last Mycenaeans and Their Successors*, 1964) cannot resolve. Firstly, this warlike raid has left no traces anywhere: in many instances there was no damage, and in any case, there is no trail of unusual objects such as would indicate the passage of foreigners. It is impossible to chart the itinerary of the invaders—something which would help us discover their origin. And there is no sign of them at their destination either: where on earth can they have settled? Most of the Mycenaean sites were simply abandoned and lay deserted for a long time, without being destroyed by human hands. The palaces were pulled down, but the towns remained standing. They were, however, deserted and the population left them for some new destination, as we noted earlier, for reasons which remain totally mysterious. Can we really believe there was an invasion, when Desborough himself concludes: "We have no evidence of any settlement. The natural and logical answer is that the invaders did not settle in any of the zones they conquered, but moved on." Rhys Carpenter simply concludes that "there were no invaders." His hypothesis is that some natural, possibly climatic, calamity must have occurred. I am inclined to agree with him, having noted myself long ago the extraordinary historical consequences which may follow a change in the climate in an area like the Mediterranean, in an age when agricultural life still dominated the entire economy.

The climate or the "return of the Heraclidae." We might bear in mind a remark reported in Plato's *Timaeus,* supposedly made by an Egyptian priest in conversation with Solon: the climate inclines periodically either towards rain or towards drought, bringing with it "at wide spaced and regular intervals" a kind of "sickness" in which either water or fire destroys everything. On this particular occasion, "the deviation of the bodies turning in the heavens" had unleashed the chain of disasters associated with drought. This language is not so far removed from that of today's meteorologists, who think that there are oscillations in the climate, and that there are movements extending over several centuries, possibly related to sunspots or the circulation of the atmosphere.

Every summer in the Aegean, the system of Aetesian winds becomes established. These blow from north-northwest towards Egypt and the African coast. If the sea-crossing from Crete or Rhodes to Egypt was so easy, it was thanks to this wind which blew uninterruptedly for months on end: an absolutely dry wind, blowing out of a clear sky, but raising crests of foam on the waves, and sufficiently strong, if you are island-hopping on a windy day, to slow down the little Greek ferries of our own century. It is the apparent move northwards of the sun in summer which causes the development of this relentless and well-established system of winds. It brings drought with it and affects the Middle East, including Greece and the islands, between March and September. In autumn, the dry winds usually make way for rain from the ocean, carried on the west wind.

Rhys Carpenter's theory is that the last decades of the thirteenth century B.C. saw a persistent phase of drought in the Mediterranean reach a peak. This considerably extended the duration of the Aetesian winds and the zone over which they blew.

Let us follow Carpenter's hypothesis, though of course there is no evidence for it. But if it is correct, the Hittites, Mycenaeans and Peoples of the Sea were all victims not of some human aggression but of a drought lasting year after year, extending the summer months, drying up the crops, as the volcanic fall-out of Thera had once done. The cities of Mycenae perished in this long-drawn-out crisis because they were in a particularly dry zone, as was the plateau of Anatolia. They were simply abandoned. If the palaces were sacked and burned that was because they held stores of foodstuffs levied from the toil of the peasants, whom hunger drove to revolt and pillage. And it so happens that the grain store in the palace of Mycenae was the first building to be destroyed.

What lends credence to this hypothesis is the geographical spread of the abandoned areas and the zones chosen as a refuge by the Mycenaean population. In a time of drought, any precipitation coming in from the Atlantic only benefits west-facing coasts and hills: the windward mountains of western Greece; the northern zones, which mostly escape the curse of the hot dry winds; regions like Attica in the east, at the natural mouth of the Gulf of Corinth which (according to navigational charts) attracts "stormy depressions from May to July or in September and October"; plus a few islands unprotected from the incoming rain: Rhodes and Cyprus. Crete, where the mountains run east-west, is less well placed. Plains cut off from the west by high mountains, or islands in the Aegean in the lee of the great Greek peninsula, would be particularly drought-prone. And these regions were in fact all abandoned. Where did the emigrants from Mycenae settle? In Achaea on the edge of the Gulf of Corinth; in northern Messenia and Epirus in western Greece; in favoured Attica, and the islands of Cephalonia in the west, Rhodes and Cyprus in the east, Thessaly and Macedonia in the north. In other words, the geography of rainfall fits the geography of Mycenaean dispersal.

In this light, what we refer to as the Dorian invasion, and what Greek legend describes as the return of the Heraclidae escorted by the Dorians, may take on a new meaning. The Heraclidae, sons and descendants of Herakles, were probably Mycenaeans from Argos. Tradition has it that they left the Peloponnese after defeat in war and on orders from the oracle at Delphi, and voluntarily went into exile to Epirus, the Pindus mountains, Thessalonia and Macedonia. They returned about a hundred years later, accompanied by Dorian shepherds and soldiers under their orders. Finding their homeland virtually uninhabited, they had little difficulty resettling there. It was equally easy for the Mycenaean inhabitants of Attica, who had never left, to defend their lands against a Dorian invasion. Did these migrations lead to the diffusion of Mycenaean epics, including the story of the Trojan war? It is certainly possible: the oral tradition which led to the writings of Homer took shape at about this time.

What can be stated with certainty, from the archaeological evidence, is that this return of the northerners spread a form of art known as "geometric": recent excavations indicate that this originated in Thessaly rather than Attica. A hundred years of exile had turned the former Mycenaeans into authentic Dorian peasants and they brought back with them this rustic form of pottery. A more serious effect of their exile was that they seem to have forgotten the art of writing in the interval. But they had not forgotten their origins. The kings of Sparta knew they were not Dorians but Heraclidae—and centuries later the dynasty of kings of Macedonia, including Alexander the Great, claimed to be descended from Herakles.

The intractable problem of the Peoples of the Sea would—if this version of the Mycenaean drama is correct—become a lot clearer.

This was a long-drawn-out episode, since the Egyptian records in 1225 B.C. describe these Peoples of the Sea as being allied to the Libyans, their worrying neighbours who were invading the western delta of the Nile. Among them were Lycians, and some ethnic groups which may correspond (according to the names given them by the Egyptians) to the future Sardinians and Etruscans, as well as Achaeans and Mycenaeans. Were the latter the people whom the Egyptian texts describe as "of great stature, with tall white bodies, fair hair and blue eyes"? The battle was a tough but decisive one. Thousands of prisoners remained in the hands of Egyptians, and the bloody booty of the war included heaps of the severed hands and genitals of their slaughtered enemies. This drama occurred very shortly after the destruction of the Mycenaean palaces; it happened in Egypt, a country well known to the seafarers of Argos; and the incomers were allied to the Libyans, a people who, if there had been serious drought, would automatically have migrated towards the Nile. We might therefore imagine that some Mycenaean seafarers, having been suddenly deprived of their usual trades, turned pirate.

A few decades later, danger loomed again for Egypt, just as it was emerging from a long crisis of authority and thus of military might: the profession of soldier which by its hardships turned a man into "an old worm-eaten block of wood" had become a despised occupation. The new pharaoh, Ramses III, enrolled Libyan mercenaries branded with red-hot iron, and sailors pressganged from the Syrian coast. These were prudent precautions, since the raid launched by the mixed Peoples of the Sea, whom the last Ugarit documents (1200 B.C.) show as based in Cyprus and Cilicia, would reach Carchemish and unfurl southwards, destroying Ugarit on the way. Sailing ships from the "islands of the Great Green Sea" (an expression which probably covered the whole of the Aegean, including the mainland coasts) accompanied these overland convoys which followed the shoreline, men, women and children and all their wordly goods travelling in ox-carts. In 1180, Egypt inflicted two bloody defeats on these people, one at sea, probably just off the Delta, and the other on land, in Syria, probably in the Hala plain north of Tripoli.

Although the Egyptian victory was uncontested, it did not settle the problem for good. It seems that Ramses III eventually had to allow "some of the Peoples of the Sea to settle as colonists and mercenaries in the Delta." As for the Philistines, with or without the pharaoh's consent, they settled in the land to which they would give their name—Palestine—which they had to defend against the Hebrews. So according to the traditional accounts, the terrible Peoples of the Sea vanish at a stroke into the oubliettes of history. The cities of Syria which had not been occupied were saved by Egypt and later recovered their prosperity—except for Ugarit. But Egypt, although victorious, had lost for good its Asian empire.

Who were these desperate people? They were certainly a mixture of ethnic groups, as they had been on the occasion of the invasion of the Delta. Among them were the "Dananiyim" of Cilicia, alongside the Ahijjiva and Purasati—in other words Achaeans and Philistines, the latter possibly from the north, although the biblical account, curiously, has them coming from Crete. It seems abundantly clear that some Mycenaeans were still playing a part in this migration, but this time it was those who had been settled rather precariously for about twenty years in Cilicia and Cyprus. We may imagine that they were accompanied by other groups, either driven on by the drought which had ruined their fields or expelled from good agricultural land by a stronger enemy. The Hittites disappear from our view along with the tablets of Bogasköy and Ugarit. But we later find a neo-Hittite civilization installed, as it happens, not on the plateau but to the south of the Taurus and the Anti-Taurus and in the plains of northern Syria, at the foot of the mountains which provided water, in regions which had once been vassals of the empire. Did the vassals simply have to move over to make room for emigrants from the plateau, or were they expelled and forced to join the populations on the move? The Peoples of the Sea were very probably a mixture of various groups driven on to the road by famine. An Egyptian inscription seems to offer a fitting account of the origins of this explosion: "The islands shook, and vomited forth their nations all at once."

One final image complicates the picture: the reliefs at Medinet Habu depict the ships of the Peoples of the Sea during the naval battle with Ramses III. These are sailing-ships, without oars, having both ends raised up at right angles, one of them decorated with an animal's head. From which Mediterranean region did these boats come? Of the images known to us so far, the only ones that are anything like them are the Phoenician *hippoi* which we find several centuries later hauling rafts of timber behind them along the Syrian coast; or the boats which King Assurbanipal used for hunting; or the boats which brought tribute from Tyre, depicted on the bronze gates of Balawat, and the image of a ship on a Phoenician jewel found in Spain. In other words the only parallels come from a single region: Syria. And therefore they may also have links with Cyprus and Cilicia.

The events of the twelfth century were followed by a long dark age. Light seems to dawn again, to some extent, only three or four hundred years later. So the chief problem is not the twelfth century, dramatic though it was, so much as this dark age which seems to have followed and which seems concealed in the thickest of shadows.

The move back into the past seems to have been most marked in Greece. Along with writing, that jewel amongst achievements, all the luxury arts vanished too: jewellery, mural paintings, engraved precious stones and seals, sculpted ivory and so on. Only pottery turned on the wheel seems to survive, with the last relic of the Mycenaean style vanishing during the eleventh century to be replaced by the first proto-geometrical ceramics.

At the same time, all links with the Middle East seem to have been severed after the Dorian invasion and would only be restored much later when Greece and the Aegean in the full flush of expansion began to trade once more with the Syrian ports and Egypt, establishing outposts on the coast of Asia Minor. But this Middle East, which fascinated the Greeks when they first saw it, leaving a powerful influence on the artistic period known as "orientalist," had itself only recently and imperfectly recovered its former prosperity and health.

There are no doubt some deep-seated explanations for this general relapse, and not only those we might connect with climatic change. Above all, one must certainly reckon with the fragile nature of the early forms of long-distance trade, dependent upon luxury goods which served the needs and wants of a very narrow circle, a thin upper layer of society. The dazzling civilizations we have glimpsed may have been no deeper than a layer of gold leaf. The palace economy had already entered on a slow, internally generated decline, well before the catastrophic twelfth century. War was too expensive, and so was long-distance trade. The under-privileged were restless and the privileged had little sense of *noblesse oblige*. The Hatti Empire fought endlessly against the feudal regime which was undermining it. Egypt had the greatest difficulty maintaining its political and economic protectorates in Asia. After its victory over the Peoples of the Sea, it was to lose all of them. A serious decline in Egyptian royal power followed, marked as always by countless tomb-robbings, revolts by the *fellahin*, anarchy, and administrative impotence. In Mesopotamia too, things were falling apart, except in the pugnacious state of Assyria. If we are looking for medium-term explanations, we find a recession lasting several centuries and doing so because it corresponded to a particularly stubborn structural crisis.

We should not be too hasty to call this crisis the "crisis of the Bronze Age." F. M. Heichelheim suggested long ago that the end of the Bronze Age meant that in the Middle East—the most advanced part of humanity on the globe—a transformation of the basis, the infrastructures of life came about. Iron-smelting, which may first have been accomplished by the metalsmiths of Cilicia and northern Syria, may have already been spreading before the twelfth century B.C. The disturbances provoked by the Peoples of the Sea, which contributed to destabilize, open up and bring new elements to local communitites, probably helped it spread even further. And in the long term, iron permitted the widespread use and "democratization" of weapons, bringing to an end the centuries when bronze had been available only to the privileged. Any people, however poor or however inexperienced in battle, now had iron at its disposal. Iron ore was available everywhere. There followed, still according to Heichelheim, a chain of linked mutations. The new invention undermined the great centralized states of the past, with their extravagant palaces, their mercenary armies and their downtrodden masses. Iron was a kind of liberator.

This may well be true. But a unilateral explanation is always dangerous and this one has the disadvantage of anticipating on events. Iron displaced bronze only slowly, just as bronze before it had taken a long time to oust cut and polished stone, even in the decisive domain of weapons. The most advanced peoples took centuries to digest the new invention—as we shall see. When the mutation was entirely accomplished, the entire world moved forward. But this would be a completely different world, and some ancient wounds and cracks never quite healed. As W. S. Smith remarks, the "close understanding" which had linked the Aegean and the eastern world "would never again be recovered." There are some rifts which time cannot heal.

CHAPTER FIVE

All Change: The Twelfth to the Eighth Centuries B.C.

After the great upheaval of the twelfth century, the Middle East took a long time to recover. Some light appeared on the horizon in the tenth century but real improvement did not come until the long upward movement in economic fortunes which became established in the eighth century or possibly a little earlier.

Nevertheless, after the traumatic episode of the Peoples of the Sea, life went on somehow. A rich cultural heritage had been saved. Egypt remained Egypt, despite internal strife, low living standards and devastating foreign invasions. Mesopotamia remained Mesopotamia, despite all its disturbances; the coast of Canaan, or as we should now call it Phoenicia, continued to play its role of intermediary. But now, a sign of the times, the intermediary was no longer a subordinate: at least it began to take some liberties towards its former masters. When in about 1100 B.C. Uenamun, the envoy of the priests of Amun, travelled to Byblos, he received a rather dusty answer and found it hard to obtain the timber he needed to build the sacred boat for the god.

So the world went on turning, and logically enough new patterns and a new world-map emerged in these centuries with no apparent history. When in the eighth century B.C. everything moves into the light, when human existence becomes easier and more readable to us, the new world picture was nothing like the one that had been shattered in the age of the Peoples of the Sea.

The map of the Middle East had become extremely complicated. The simultaneous decline of Egypt and Mesopotamia and the collapse of the Hittite Empire had brought into being a multitude of small warring states, which occupied the forefront of history with their minor but noisy squabbles.

In Asia Minor, Urardhu, centred in Armenia, received part of the legacy of the Hurrians, the talented artisans mentioned earlier. This was a mountain state, energetic and aggressive. It made good use of its metal-working (as revealed by Russian excavations at Karmir Blur). The area under its domination had its centre of gravity near Lake Van and ran broadly from the high valleys of the Tigris and Euphrates to the Caucasus. Phrygia had taken root, at about the time of the Dorian invasion, on the plateaux of Anatolia where the Hittite Empire had first built then lost its dominion (the Phrygian capital Gordium has been brought to life before our eyes by the American excavations begun in 1950). Westwards, Lydia occupied the parallel valleys of the Hermos and the Meander and was expanding towards the Aegean, where in about 1000 a string of early Greek cities appeared on the coast: their decisive moment would come later. To the south, some neo-Hittite states still survived. Then out of the desert came the Aramaic states, the chief of them centred on Damascus: we should not underestimate them since they controlled the caravan routes leading to Asia, which were the overland counterparts to the Phoenicians' active sea crossings. Further south again was a Jewish state, whose brief days of splendour ended in about 930, when it split into two kingdoms, Judah to the south, Israel to the north.

The Jews had had to win their rather poor territories one by one from the Semitic Canaanites, whose traditions, culture and language they appropriated. They underwent the same process as the Hittites and Greeks: they were absorbed by what they took over. A further disadvantage for them was that despite having a seaboard, they had difficulty reaching navigable stretches of the coast since they were hemmed in both by their enemies the Philistines and by the Phoenicians who were their friends or indeed allies. It was Phoenicians from Tyre who had built the temple and royal palace in Jerusalem in the age of Solomon (c. 970–930), and Phoenician boats which had sailed on behalf of the Jewish king to Ophir (in southern Arabia or India?), taking the long route via Esion Gaber on the Gulf of Akaba and down the Red Sea. In the same city of Esion Gaber and also in the reign of Solomon, Phoenician artisans had built large metal-working furnaces for smelting copper and iron, the most advanced in the ancient world, according to W. F. Albright. These were the good times for the Jewish state. Nobody could then have foreseen either the hard times ahead or the fabulous future of the spiritual message of Israel, as it slowly matured through the vicissitudes of history.

Although its territory, hemmed in by the Hebrews and Philistines to the south, and the neo-Hittites to the north, represented only part of the ancient land of Canaan, Phoenicia¹ was nevertheless the first power in the Middle East to recover a degree of prosperity. It was a sort of "sheltered sector," like Holland in the general recession of the seventeenth century A.D. All this took place despite certain upheavals whose nature remains obscure: the former supremacy of Byblos fell away, as first Sidon then Tyre gained prominence, with Tyre becoming the leading city after about 1000 B.C. The Phoenician coastline began to revive, thanks to the bounty of the sea. The Jewish state by contrast had built its prosperity around the crossroads of overland routes, between the Euphrates, the Mediterranean and the Red Sea, a good bet in peacetime but dangerous in time of war. And war was becoming endemic in the Middle East.

In this relentless and soon terrifying series of wars, the tiny state of Assyria was the principal actor. To start with, it was no more than "a small triangle," a limited area and a poorly guarded one, in the high valley of the Tigris, wedged between Mesopotamia with its irrigation and its cities to the south, the harsh mountains to the north, and the desert with its Aramaic marauders to the west. Assyria was a house open to the winds, its people forced to live in fear and insecurity. It could achieve peace of mind only by threatening others and intimidating them in turn. Without holding any brief for the Assyrians, I should record that their cruelty was a response to cruelty from their neighbours, particularly the Aramaeans. In order to survive, Assyria had to stamp out those it conquered, crippling them with taxes or deporting entire populations, bringing them into its own territory where, in days to come, their large numbers would make them a permanent threat. The friezes on the palace at Nineveh graphically recount the whole sad story.

But in the process, Assyria became rich: gigantic palaces rose from the ground. War had become an industry, a way of obtaining the wealth which previously had reached the Babylonian cities via trade. From the end of the tenth century to the end of the seventh, the Assyrians would live off plunder and tribute exacted from Urardhu, Damascus, Tyre, Sidon and the kingdoms of Judah and Israel. They even committed the sacrilege of destroying Babylon, abolishing the cult of Marduk and sacking the temples. Then it was Egypt's turn. In 671 B.C., Lower Egypt was occupied and a few years later, Thebes was sacked in indescribable fashion. When in 630 the great prince Assurbanipal, a man of learning as it happened, died in his sumptuous palace in Nineveh (its gardens were as magnificent as its library), the empire was at its zenith. But a few years later it collapsed in the face of a widespread assault by its enemies and subordinates. In 612, the Medes and Babylonians formed an alliance and stormed Nineveh to the general satisfaction of all the peoples in the area. The Assyrian cities were themselves destroyed and the survivors carried off into captivity. They became the builders of the palaces for the king of Persia, palaces which recall vanished Assyria in every respect.

For all the valour of the Assyrian army, ever ready under its priest-kings and its warlords to wage a holy war against all its neighbours at once, and for all the efficacy of its troops under their harsh commanders, with their powerful siege-engines and cavalry armed with pikes and arrows, Assyria would never have achieved these bloody triumphs if Egypt and Babylon had not both gradually been declining to the rank of second-rate powers, mere pieces in the "Balkan" jigsaw that the Middle East had now become. Babylon at this time was not unlike Constantinople in the fifteenth century A.D., the only living outpost of a Byzantine Empire at its last gasp. In ancient Mesopotamia, everything was falling apart, even the admirable system of irrigation canals, which were now worn out and allowing the calamitous infiltration of salt water. Egypt was even worse off. The future belonged from now on to "users of iron." But Egypt, which had received iron in the past from the Hittites, was embarking on the Iron Age without owning any. The land of the pharaohs would from now on, as an Assyrian general ironically reminded the people of Jerusalem, be "a broken reed . . . whereon if a man lean, it will go into his hand and pierce it" (Isaiah 36.6). Thebes was looted to death and never recovered.

So the Middle East was doomed to experience a vicious round of constant alerts and internal warfare. To this was added another calamity, the dramatic appearance of the horsemen of the northern steppes.

Between the Caucasus, the Ukraine, the loess plateaux of Podolia, and the immense forests of central Russia, changes were coming to completion which were to affect lands further south, throughout the Middle East. Nomadic life, which had first developed centuries earlier, was coming to maturity here. Its essential revolutionary element was horseback travel; now everything would echo to the hoofbeats of a galloping horse. Away to the south, the old seats of civilization and countries which were regaining civilized status were more vulnerable than ever to the incursions of the nomads.

The first signs of the hurricane came, as we noted earlier, with the Cimmerian invasion at the end of the ninth century. The Cimmerians were probably half-sedentary, half-nomadic peasants, who had been driven south from their previous home in southern Russia by natural forces, or rather by pressure from Scythian attackers on horseback. Of their former territory the Cimmerians retained only the Kuban peninsula and part of the Crimea, and this only for a time. Fleeing with their carts and chariots, they crossed the centre and the west of the Caucasus. Their pursuers, according to Herodotus, took the wrong turn, crossed the Caucasus on the eastern side and emerged in Media, which they sacked.

The Cimmerian invasion quickly exhausted itself in repeated raids on Urardhu, Assyria, Anatolia, the kingdom of Phrygia (which was destroyed), and Cilicia. In Lydia, the looters took Sardis, but were unable to capture the citadel; they inflicted damage on several Greek cities on the Aegean before finally becoming completely absorbed into the populations of Asia.

The Scythians, whom they had drawn south quite unintentionally, represented danger of a quite different order—skilled horsemen, and the first "real" nomads known to history. Their violent adventure, which lasted some thirty years (twenty-eight, according to Herodotus), resembles the familiar image of the Huns galloping across Europe in the fifth century A.D. The only difference was that the Scythians were white Indo-Europeans, whereas Attila's hordes were predominantly olive-skinned. Skin colour is hardly significant—the phenomenon was basically the same. The Scythian raids, devoted to pillage, were carried out at great speed and over long distances by gangs of determined young men. Sometimes they were joined by adventurers from outside the "royal" tribes. This was a "democratic" system of sorts, based on the fact that the new fighting machine—the horse—was available to all, whereas previously the war chariot had been the prerogative of the rich and powerful. This social change added to the incredible power of the explosion. The sacking of Media by the Scythians already represented a formidable leap forward over the Caucasus and Armenia, but they penetrated much further, into Anatolia and even Assyria, with excursions as far afield as Syria and Palestine. Psammeticus kept them out of Egypt only by bribing their chiefs with gold! And the permanent threat they posed was driven back northwards only by the eventual victories of the Medes. At this point the Scythians made their way back home to their old stamping-ground, the immense steppes of southern Russia.

It was here that Herodotus, with his insatiable curiosity, was able to observe them on the spot. He studied them with the same care and the same astonishment that he had bestowed on the strange customs of Egypt. He describes at length the great plains where these half-civilized people led their nomadic lives: this was a land of extraordinary rivers, where prodigious falls of snow in winter filled the air with flying "feathers," where rivers and even seas froze over so that they could be crossed on foot. Everything surprised and delighted him, the manners, the soothsayers, the horse sacrifices, the scalps or skins of conquered enemies carried as trophies, the burial rites, and above all the life of the tribes in their tents, on their carts, a life of endless wandering governed by the movement of their herds.

But the modern historian will not find in these long descriptions any mention of what for us constitutes the chief glory of the Scythians. While Herodotus writes of the masses of gold, of jewels, belts and ornaments on reins and harnesses, he says nothing about the beauty of an art which reached its maturity once they had returned to the southern Russian steppes. It was a remarkable art of animal representation, an ornate, barbaric art, whose style was to be adopted towards the end of the first millennium B.C. by all the nomadic horse-borne tribes, as far afield as the distant borders of China. It is a strange and satisfying synthesis, drawing at once on the cultures of the forested steppes of the north, on that of Karasuk towards China, and on Caucasian, Anatolian, Assyrian and Iranian influences picked up during voyages or more prolonged sojourns in the Middle East. Some Greek influence gradually made itself felt as well, becoming stronger when the Scythians, driven back by the Medes, returned to their territory on the Black Sea. Scythian motifs and Greek mythological figures—Pegasus or the Gorgons—sit side by side on the golden ornaments of tombs in the Crimea, for instance. Here the Scythians came into direct contact with the Greeks. And in due course this was where Athens was to recruit its picturesque police force, the Scythian archers who on meeting days marshalled latecomers towards the Pnyx.

Eventually, the area settled down. But it would be wrong to underestimate these intrusions of the peoples of the steppes—or indeed their subsequent invasions of Europe and Asia—on the grounds that they were fairly rapidly wiped off the surface of the civilized world. These violent incursions had more than merely marginal significance.

In the first place, they penetrated deeply into the countries of the Middle East, and these were too closely linked for a shock received by one not to be passed on down the line, from Anatolia to the banks of the Nile. The balance of power in the Middle East worked in the invaders' favour: the Cimmerians were supported by Egypt, while the Scythians, if we are to believe Herodotus, were relatively loyal allies of the implacable Assyrians, even if they pillaged them from time to time. In other words, the nomads increased the military capacity of the various powers, dragging the Middle East ever deeper into this game in which there could be no winners.

More importantly, the Scythians subjugated the Medes, and the latter lived for years under their rule and learned from them. The Median cavalry, which was the ancestor of the great cavalry of Persia, was no doubt inspired in part by these revolutionary warriors on horseback. And without that exceptional cavalry, there would have been no Persian Empire, no unification of the Middle East, no "Pax Persica," perhaps no temptation for Alexander the Great. . . . As long as the Middle East was absorbed in its endless quarrels, throughout the long and monotonous tragedy of the "Assyrian centuries," it had been to all intents and purposes absent from world history, which was being played out in the distant western reaches of the Mediterranean. Once the Persian conquests had taken place, at the end of the sixth century, so much power had accumulated in the east that the Mediterranean world suddenly tipped towards it again. It was this pendulum swing which tied the destiny of Greece to the east—to the great regret of the present writer!

The west was not created *ex nihilo* by colonization from the east. During the millennia and centuries which preceded their meeting, immense changes had taken place. The west had become a major historical force, a central player in the destiny of the Mediterranean.

"West" is an imprecise term. Let us take it to mean central Europe, from the Alps to the Baltic and the North Sea, the Italian peninsula (rather than the surrounding islands), the territory that would become Gaul, the Iberian peninsula, and North Africa in the narrow sense of the term, from the Gulf of Gabès to the Atlantic.

But this part of North Africa was to acquire an ambiguous status: geographically western, it quite soon became culturally oriental, for the great migrations which affected the west during the first millennium, while encompassing the Mediterranean from Asia Minor to Iberia, did not reach as far as the "Maghreb." They crossed the great rivers, Danube or Rhine, and the mountains, Balkans, Alps or Pyrenees, but stopped short at the "flowing Ocean," at Gibraltar. Was this because the Phoenicians were present very early on—if not with trading posts, at least with commercial contacts—from the bay of Cádiz to present-day Tunisia? At the height of their colonial prosperity at any rate, the Phoenicians were alone in their access to the immense resources of Africa, a sparsely populated primitive land where wild beasts abounded—and they exploited their monopoly shamelessly. The African peoples, still partly nomadic and strangers to progress, were easily tricked. Carthage profited in the same way, and over a long period of time, from the native peoples surrounding it, and from those equally primitive tribes who brought gold dust across the Sahara, whether to the present-day Rio de Oro on the Atlantic or to the shores of southern Tunisia.

Such trade implies a civilization capable of mastering the immensity of the Sahara. But we do have evidence of such a civilization from Neolithic times: take, for example, the widespread use of specialized stone tools, whose distribution coincides significantly with that of the rock paintings showing horse-drawn carts. The latter must have derived from the Libyan mercenaries who served in the Egyptian army under the New Kingdom, in the the sixteenth century B.C. (when Egypt had just adopted the horse-drawn chariots of the Hyksos). Thus there were already routes leading from Egypt to Morocco in the west and to the Niger in the south. At certain points along them, traders from civilized countries could obtain gold on the cheap, thanks to the profitable and unfair barter which Herodotus describes so vividly.

Leaving North Africa on one side, what we mean by "the west" is above all central and western Europe, that entity which Emmanuel de Martonne liked to describe as a funnel narrowing from east to west: Europe, that little "promontory of Asia," is still very wide at the Russian "isthmus," grows narrower at the German "isthmus," and narrower still at the French "isthmus." The steppe has always driven its surplus population westward: landless peasants, fugitives, shepherds with their families and their flocks. To the south, the funnel has a series of apertures, a wide one leading to the Balkan peninsula, then two narrow gaps leading to those partially isolated worlds, Italy south of the Alps and Iberia south of the Pyrenees.

A number of obstacles thus faced the peoples moving west: the increasing narrowness of the European peninsula, the barriers of mountain and river, the dense forests, not to mention the peasant populations already occupying the land. But the journey from east to west, on the Caucasus-Atlantic axis, was shortened by the invention of revolutionary forms of transport (cart, chariot and horse), hence the sequence of invasions which over the centuries hesitated between the Middle East and the European west, but always ended up on the shores of the Mediterranean.

These population movements were stop-and-start affairs, as temporary halts became the next points of departure. Staging-posts of this kind were provided by Bactria (Turkestan), the plains of the Black Sea, the foothills of the Caucasus, Thracia, the plain of Hungary and the Illyrian coast. In the first millennium, the formidable area of central Europe, still a wild country of immense forests among spreading rivers, rather like the Siberian forests of today, was a sort of holding bay for the west. As early as Neolithic times, sizeable peasant populations had settled there on the easily cultivated loess strips, clear of trees. These clayey deposits, following the rim of the former glaciers, form a continuous corridor from Russia to central France. Clearings were also opened in the forests, using stone or metal axes or fire. Thus Neolithic farmers occupied this area with their villages, plants, domestic animals, primitive ploughs and draught oxen. Even more significantly, the mineral wealth of the region favoured the early development of metallurgy, which had already begun when travelling metal-workers (the "torque-wearers") arrived in central Europe from the east, via the Adriatic and the Balkans, early in the second millennium. With a skilled labour force, abundant ore, and fuel galore in the forests, everything was thus set for this part of Europe to be radically transformed by the use of metals—copper, lead, gold, and before long iron.

For all these reasons, population accumulated between the Rhine, the Danube, the Baltic and the North Sea. The history of the west did not all originate in this region, but it was fed by this human reserve army always on the point of bursting out of its confines, a "pressure cooker in constant danger of exploding," as it has been put, and one which did explode on two or three occasions. The image is not an absurd one, so long as it is not taken to imply something rapid and sudden. The Indo-European invasions lasted centuries; their history was often played out in slow motion.

The end of the Bronze Age (twelfth century) saw a major new development in this prehistory of central Europe: the arrival of new Indo-European populations. Several peoples were involved: they differed from one another, but over the centuries came to intermingle, exchanging material objects and even languages. From the beginning they shared one common feature by which they are known to archaeologists: they all cremated their dead. This was not something absolutely new—cremation had already been practised by some Europeans—but the novelty lay in the scale of the phenomenon, which marked a clear break with preceding civilizations. Throughout the area "urn fields" have been discovered, great cemeteries of "flat tombs" in which urns containing the ashes of the dead are buried side by side.

The existing populations, those who buried their dead, first resisted this influx, then gave ground, and abandoned vast areas to the new peoples. Having occupied central Europe, some urn people—probably the Umbrians and the Villanovans—moved into Italy, driving back the Ligurians (to use an outdated word designating earlier invaders, probably of pre-Indo-European origin); they next occupied eastern France, advancing to the Rhône valley, and carrying on across the Pyrenees into Catalonia and the region of Valencia. They reached as far as the coasts of the British Isles in the north. All these newcomers, practising cremation, were probably Indo-Europeans, who mingled with the Neolithic peasants they found *in situ*—and these encounters prepared the way for the ultimate disappearance of urn burial.

This must have been a period of turbulence in Europe. It still belonged to the Bronze Age, but the ninth century saw the appearance of iron, which was to hasten the course of events. The word "hasten" needs some clarification, however. The first Iron Age corresponds to the so-called Hallstatt civilization (named after a resort in the Tyrol); but although iron was used then, it was not of central significance. It became widely used only after the sixth century, in the second Iron Age, the so-called La Tène civilization (named after a resort north of Neuchâtel), which lasted until the Roman conquest. And it was in the La Tène period that the real explosion took place with the tumultuous waves of Celtic invasions.

The two maps in Appendix II showing the expansion of the urn-burial peoples and the movements of the Celts give an oversimplified view of the problem, presenting as definitive solutions which still remain uncertain, but they do have the merit of indicating correctly and clearly the two enormous flows of blood which complemented and overlapped with one another. Europe, from Bohemia to Gaul, became a powerful heart, and its heartbeats sent pulses racing in the distant Mediterranean, land of sunshine and vines, so different in nature and in history from the north. A dialogue began, and it was to prove of crucial importance.

The first exchanges in this conversation had of course taken place long before the La Tène or even the Hallstatt period. When the Achaeans had arrived in the Balkan peninsula at the beginning of the second millennium, the great machine for multiplying and spreading people was already in place. But in the first millennium everything began to happen more quickly. The civilizations of the Mediterranean discovered the biological potency of their turbulent and alarming neighbours. Using different names—Celts, Gauls, Galatians—they described these strange people, tall, fair-haired, blue-eyed, courageous and given to boasting. They came in waves—we no longer imagine them as Henri Hubert did, arriving "in small groups, slipping side by side across the great continental spaces." As André Varagnac puts it, "the pre-Celtic and Celtic invasions took the form of vast population movements, as described by Caesar in his account of the migration of the Helvetii at the beginning of the Gallic Wars."

It was their demographic weight which made the Celtic invasions so important. When they arrived, these peoples were a turbulent force; they had to be domesticated, by warfare if necessary. In our history books they appear as the losers, the vanquished. But these masses of peasants and skilled craftsmen put down lasting roots. It seems wrong therefore to speak of the great defeat of the Celts who, having "civilized Europe as the Greeks had civilized the Mediterranean," were supposedly swept away by the Romans. What do words such as defeat and victory mean when applied to living masses who settle down permanently and are still recognizable today? Any civilization at full strength can only survive thanks to a continuous supply of people. These biological necessities made themselves felt in Mesopotamia and Egypt, as in Rome; they give a deeper meaning to the sound and fury of the "invasions."

But while the Celts possessed a highly developed material civilization, they remained backward in their social organization. In the Hallstatt era, monarchical governments had led to a concentration of wealth in large fortified houses, a sort of palace civilization. The La Tène period was marked by greater "democracy," or more accurately by the appearance of turbulent aristocratic republics. In the Celtic world, powerful tribes lived side by side, making it hard for towns to develop. Polybius, describing the Boyans of Cisalpine Gaul, portrays them scattered through the countryside *ateikhistoi*, without towns; when there were towns, they lacked walls. In such circumstances, it was perhaps inevitable that these elementary cells should be swallowed up by those higher organisms, the urban civilizations, of the Mediterranean.

———

General history has yet to explain the origins of these immense population movements. The Celts may have been fleeing from overpopulated regions north of the Alps, where from the year 1000 B.C. the climate was becoming more or less that of today. The increasing cold reduced the habitable area and perhaps drove out some of the urn people of the Hallstatt period. What seems even more certain is that these were chain reactions, beginning in the east. The Cimmerians who settled in southern Russia in the ninth century were descendants of the semi-nomadic Indo-Europeans who had established themselves there towards the second millennium, driving out the peasant population of the Tripolye culture. Then the Scythian horsemen, who reached the Carpathians in the ninth century, defeated the Cimmerians, "something which corresponds remarkably closely to the beginnings of the first iron-based culture," i.e. the Hallstatt period. Several hundred years later, at the beginning of the sixth century B.C., it was again the Scythians who returned en masse to "Scythia," the Black Sea steppe, a movement which coincided with the La Tène culture, the migrations of several Germanic peoples, and the arrival of the Celts in Gaul, complete with their chariots of war; in the Champagne region, Gaulish chiefs had themselves buried with their chariots, like their distant equivalents in Armenia. This battle vehicle, although soon falling into disuse, kept going long enough for Julius Caesar to have the surprise of coming face to face with chariots of war in England.

To conclude, then, the earliest of the successive waves of Indo-Europeans, those human explosions we call invasions, took place towards the year 2000, originating in the Black Sea region, between the Caucasus and Hungary; the second group, between 1500 and 1000, began in Hungary and Bohemia; and the final sequence after 600, the Celtic invasions, affected the lands beyond the Rhine and Gaul. The centre of the explosion thus gradually moved westward. But perhaps these were all chapters in a single story.[2]

We have so far been able to sketch out a picture of these dark centuries (twelfth to eighth centuries) without saying a great deal about iron-working. The carburization of iron (the manufacture of hardened iron by an admixture of carbon), had begun in the Caucasus or rather in Cilicia, and was long a monopoly of the Hittite Empire. If the Peoples of the Sea, in particular the

Philistines, owned iron tools and weapons, this may have been through their links with the Hittites or Cilicia. It is thus possible, as has often been claimed, that the break-up of the Hittite Empire contributed to the worldwide diffusion of ironsmiths and their mysterious craft, often seen as the work of the devil. After all many peoples had a blacksmith god in their pantheon, often a distinctly sinister character. But iron-working depended on unfamiliar processes which inevitably took time to spread and be mastered. The transition between the old order, the Bronze Age, and the new Iron Age, lasted a very long time.

In Mesopotamia, where things normally moved faster than elsewhere, the collapse of the price of iron, which is proof of its widespread use, only really began in the tenth century. In Egypt, widespread use of the new metal dates only from *c.* 600 B.C., if that. Central Europe, with its wealth of mines, remained ambivalent for a long period: until the sixth century, bronze remained the principal metal for tools and weapons.

This creeping progress of the iron "revolution" fits the general pattern of this period which ruled out any rapid change. What after all did it imply? The replacement of one metal by another. Almagro Basch (1960) was not entirely wrong in claiming that "iron did not represent such a radical change in the history of civilization as that introduced by the working of copper and its alloys." The slow advance of iron thus supports a sceptical approach to the materialist explanation which might at first sight have seemed quite plausible. No, iron did not mean an immediate democratization of warfare; and no, iron weapons did not appear overnight. Some crucial elements were very late to emerge, for example, the important invention of soldering. According to legend, it was invented in Cos on the Aegean. The first soldered object we know about is an iron head-rest, found in the tomb of Tutankhamun and dating from around 1350. But the process remained very unusual, to the point that a soldered iron tripod was kept until Roman times in the treasury of Delphi as a rare object. And we may recall that in Homeric times (the eighth century B.C.), the prize which Achilles offers at Patroclus' funeral games is an iron ball!

Similarly, iron did not immediately transform tool-making. No doubt it subsequently played a crucial role in improving agricultural yields. But when did this begin? It seems a piece of risky guesswork to present it as the cause of the fall in grain prices in Assyria between the eighth and seventh centuries. These prices depended on so many other factors: security, foreign imports, the seasons. . . . Rhys Carpenter would no doubt point out that the eighth century saw the return of a wetter climate!

The alphabet is another revolution that belongs to these obscure centuries. The whole of the Middle East had known writing systems in the Bronze Age: hieroglyphics in Egypt, cuneiform script in Asia during the preceding centuries, Linear A and Linear B in Crete, Linear B alone in "Minoan" Greece. These were all already simplified systems, but they remained difficult and called for expert hands. The scribes formed a literate caste, determined to defend its prerogatives and the prestige of its profession by insisting on its mysteries and difficulties. It is not entirely surprising that this costly luxury should have disappeared virtually overnight in the land that became Greece after the end of the Mycenaean period. A simpler technique might have been more readily accepted among the Indo-European barbarians.

It was in the end such a technique of wonderful, revolutionary simplicity that evolved some time before the end of the second millennium, to emerge into the full light of day with the linear alphabet we call Phoenician. The twenty-two symbols of this alphabet corresponded only to the consonants, which form as we know the essential structure of the Semitic languages. When the Greeks copied the Phoenician language in the eighth century, they needed signs corresponding to the vowels in order to provide an intelligible notation of their language. So they used for the vowels the symbols for a number of Semitic consonants which did not exist in Greek and, hey presto, a complete alphabet with both consonants and vowels. But it was the culminating point of a long history.

It was in Syria (broadly understood), and particularly in Ugarit and Byblos, that the revolutionary simplification had first been worked out centuries earlier. All manner of trades, languages and peoples had come together in these two busy cities throughout the second millennium. But the merchant, not possessing the costly services of a scribe with his stylus, needed a rapid means of transcribing his contracts, bills, accounts, and letters. So a complicated writing system, the grandiose creation of the state, gave way to an accelerated form of script, the logical creation of the merchants. The earliest of these experiments, the Ugaritic of the documents of Ras Shamra, uses *cuneiform* signs for its thirty-letter alphabet. This ABC (the oldest known to man) has been found on a tablet dating from the fourteenth century B.C.

A linear alphabet was developed at the same same time in Canaan, between the fifteenth and tenth centuries. Some experts believe that its origins lie in a form of writing used in the second millennium by the Semitic workers in the Egyptian turquoise mines on the Sinai peninsula. This was a half-hieroglyphic, half-alphabetical script, in that it employed the principle of acrophonia: the use of a consonant-plus-vowel symbol to represent the consonant alone, so that it is in effect a genuine alphabetical letter. The idea is like that of spelling out the name Robinson on the telephone by saying R for Richard, O for Obadiah; or the Abel, Baker, Charlie system. The Semitic peoples proceeded in the same way to choose names for their letters: the sign Beth—meaning house—becomes the letter B in the alphabet (B for Beth), whence in due course the Greek *beta*.

This very gradual process culminated in the Phoenician script which became widely used in the first millennium. It was simple, and could be rapidly written with a brush on a roll of leather, parchment or papyrus, or with a sharp point on a lead tablet or a wax-coated wooden board—a kind of "slate" which could easily be scraped clean and recoated with wax. The oldest example of the script is an inscription, probably from the tenth century, carved on a much older sarcophagus, that of Ahiram, king of Byblos. As early as the tenth century, Hebrew inscriptions were copying this script exactly. As for the Greeks, it was *possibly* in Al-Mina, a city originally founded at the mouth of the Orontes by the Greeks of Euboea, but which became Phoenician, that they learned to use the alphabet at the beginning of the eighth century. At the same time, as the inscription at Gordium shows, the neighbouring Phrygians also adopted an alphabet derived from the Phoenician.

A Greek cup found at Pithecussae on the island of Ischia near Naples, and dating from the late eighth century, carries an inscription in verse, and it was this Chalcidian alphabet (named after Chalcis, capital of Euboea) that was eventually adopted by the Etruscans. It is possible therefore that it was Cumae, a Euboean colony, that passed on the new writing to Italy. However, nothing is ever entirely simple in these gradual transfers, and an ivory tablet with twenty-six Phoenician letters has been discovered at Marsiliana d'Albegna in a rich Etruscan tomb dating from around 700 B.C. It closely resembles Phoenician tablets of the same type found at Nimrud in Assyria, and among the objects found nearby there is a little box (*pyxis*) and a comb sent by a merchant of Tyre. One can see in this a kind of invitation to use the alphabet for commercial correspondence, and in any case proof that the Phoenician alphabet was available to the Etruscans through direct contacts as well as in a Greek adaptation.

Nowhere, in fact, was the spread of the alphabet simple or rapid, any more than that of iron or bronze. Indeed, it was hardly any more rapid than the spread of agriculture, and certainly no faster than the gradual spread of money and a money economy. Yet who could fail to describe the invention of the first alphabet as truly "revolutionary"?

PART TWO

Figure 6
Phoenician warships with rams and roundships carrying freight. Drawing after a bas-relief in Sennacherib's palace (704–681 B.C.), Nineveh.

After the particularly obscure centuries between 1100 and 700, Mediterranean life emerges into the full glare of history and everything seems much simpler. The drama can be said to unfold in three great acts:

- The colonization of the western Mediterranean by peoples from the east (Phoenicians, Etruscans, Greeks), a move which provided the Inland Sea with dynamic unity for the first time.

- The rise of Greek civilization, founded on sea-power but eventually coming to grief after the over-ambitious war of conquest against the Achaemenid Persians.

- The victorious destiny of Rome, whose empire became coterminous with the Mediterranean.

These are three classic stories, so familiar that it will be difficult to retell them here, given the wealth of attested facts and the number of theories they have inspired. But we shall consider them from a very specific point of view, that of the sea. Broadly, we are faced with three great movements: first, the Mediterranean expanded westwards with the colonization of the western seas, then the balance swung back towards the east with the insane conquests of Alexander the Great, and finally Rome created a sort of equilibrium. But to control the whole of the Mediterranean world from east to west for centuries on end was an arduous task, and even Rome could not maintain its power for ever.

This very simple view of things is not without its problems. The history of the ancient world may be separated from us by two millennia or more, but it continues to arouse strong feelings. In the previous chapters we have already encountered partisans of Mesopotamia and of Egypt, admirers of Crete and Greece, advocates of the west and passionate defenders of the east. Ideally, of course, I would like to strike a balance: to avoid both uncritical praise of the Etruscans and over-adulation of the Greeks; to avoid joining the chorus of historians who criticize the Phoenicians and condemn the Carthaginians for their child sacrifices to the gods; to resist being endlessly dazzled by the Greeks (though heaven knows there is reason enough!) or tempted into repeating Hegel's charge that Rome was the "prose of history"— as if prose had no beauty. In short, I ought not to lean to one side or the other, but to keep an open mind. But is this always possible, or even desirable? These contradictory passions are the flame that keeps history alive, both the history that is told to us and the history we try to create in turn. And as we do so, how can we avoid feelings of pain or enthusiasm, even if these are a sin against the sacrosanct rules of impartiality?

CHAPTER SIX

Colonization: The Discovery of the Mediterranean "Far West" in the Tenth to Sixth Centuries B.C.

Colonization is an ambiguous word. It is one thing to cast anchor in a creek and do a little trading before sailing off again, quite another to settle permanently. The word colonization will here refer to the latter activity, which may have come long after the former.

In broad terms, from the tenth century to the sixth, if we leave aside the occupation of the Black Sea (essentially by the Ionian Greeks), it was the central and western Mediterranean which were colonized. This "Far West," hard to reach and harder still to take possession of, was fought over by Phoenicians, Etruscans and Greeks. All of them came bearing a superior civilization from the east. (The Etruscans are a special case, in fact, since we know little about their origins or the chronological and geographical development of their contacts with the east.)

There is no mystery about the Phoenicians or the Greeks. The former came from the coastal regions of the Levant, the latter from the Aegean and from a maritime city of central Greece, Corinth;[1] both had behind them an advanced civilization. This conforms to the usual pattern of colonization, whereby the weak are dominated and instructed by the strong. Strength in this instance meant civilization, the intense activity of the cities, techniques of navigation and metal-working, the practice of trading and the power of the markets. To set out from the Middle East at this time was like setting out from all-powerful Europe many centuries later, after the voyages of discovery of the fifteenth and sixteenth centuries A.D. The colonizers of antiquity, when they set up their trading posts and their towns on distant shores, did not, admittedly, have to confront advanced civilizations comparable to those of the Aztecs, the Mayas, the Incas and the Great Mogul Empire.

But like modern Europe, the Orient of antiquity exported to distant places not only its strengths, but also its inner divisions, its conflicts of interest and its inveterate hatreds. These god-given lands, where the colonizer and the merchant could impose their will without too much difficulty, and where towns sprang up overnight, would eventually be divided up between rival masters, who brought war in their train.

I

THE FIRST IN THE FIELD: PROBABLY THE PHOENICIANS

Scholarship has not yet provided all the answers in this area but if I were putting money on the first ships to arrive in the west, my choice would be: Phoenicians, Etruscans, Greeks, in that order. But we use the language of betting only when we have no real evidence. In any case, the order refers mainly to the earliest voyages, the first attempts at bartering along the coasts, the really pioneering ventures. The serious settlements and first towns appeared more or less simultaneously. They began in the eighth century, at the time when economic activity was taking off again, and they may have coincided with the spread of the ribbed hull, the high-sided ship better able to weather storms at sea. This opened up a whole vast area in the western Mediterranean—and opened it to all comers.

Half a century ago, our current favourite would not have seemed a likely winner. Everything that was said in the Phoenicians' favour (by the admirable writers Victor Bérard or Eduard Meyer) was immediately ruled out as "Phoenicia-mania" or "Herodotomania." The Greeks were flavour of the month. Recent as they are, these days are now gone—though perhaps not for good.

For some specialists, two or three small pieces of evidence have been enough to undermine the case of the "Grecomaniacs" and the reluctance of the archaeologists who until quite recently had found no tangible trace of a Phoenician presence in the western Mediterranean before the seventh century B.C. Naturally, these three traces of evidence are *controversial*. First there was the discovery in the Museum of Cyprus in 1939 of a damaged inscription, unnoticed until then, which can be dated to the ninth century B.C. The script on it provided a neat explanation of a strange Phoenician inscription discovered long ago (in 1773) in Sardinia, near Pula (Nora in antiquity) and now in the museum of Cagliari. Its archaic character had been recognized by R. Dussaud in 1924. But according to W. F. Albright (1941) the script is identical with that on the Cyprus inscription, and must therefore belong to the same period. Since then, two similar fragments of inscriptions have been found in Sardinia, dating presumably from the first half of the ninth century.

Putting up monumental inscriptions is not of course the first priority of sailors on voyages of discovery. It is therefore *possible* that the first visit of the Phoenicians to Sardinia could go back to the tenth century or even earlier, since it would be normal for colonial settlements or even seasonal trading posts to be preceded by a long period of sailing from harbour to harbour, with the ship acting as a kind of mobile trading post. If we take this view, we might even return to the traditional dates, probably too early though, given for the "foundation" of the Phoenician colonies: Gades (Cádiz) in *c.* 1100 B.C.; Lixus in Morocco earlier still, if we are to believe Pliny; Utica a little later; and Carthage (which means *new town*) in 814–813. On the other hand, deep excavations have found no foreign influence before the sixth century at Lixus or before the seventh at Mogador. Some traces apparently belonging to the period of the earliest voyages (tenth century) have been discovered in Spain by the archaeologist B. Nazar (1957), and Pierre Cintas (1949) has noted on Salammbô beach near Carthage some very fragmentary indications of a *visit* there by sailors from Cyprus at the beginning of the second millennium.

In a word, there is as yet no definite proof for the explanatory hypotheses of Sabatino Moscati (1966), which are based essentially on the fact that after the arrival of the Peoples of the Sea, the only power to survive miraculously intact was that of Phoenicia. Three centuries—the eleventh, the tenth, and the ninth—separate the fall of Mycenae from the first beginnings of Greek expansion westward. "It is natural," writes Moscati, "that Phoenician expansion should have filled this historical gap." And indeed, nothing prevents us from *imagining* that during this eclipse of Greek seafaring the Phoenicians had a clear field to exploit the distant—and empty—sea, launching simple maritime expeditions of a kind very common in history; and then that to counter Greek competition from the eighth century on, they were obliged to consolidate their presence at key points of this vast network. Thus a purely commercial presence may have preceded genuine colonization.

This hypothetical account has to answer a number of common-sense objections. What about the so-called logical sequence of a gradual westward expansion of Phoenician discoveries and settlement, by successive moves along the North African coast? In that case, Utica and Carthage would have to be older than Gades and Lixus—which would bring us back to the shorter time-span. But it is quite conceivable, contrary to this theory, that the Phoenicians preferred to use the open sea routes and settle first in the west, close to the silver of Spain and the Atlantic trade; only later would they have felt the need to strengthen their intermediate staging-posts. This makes a long time-span more probable, the essential thing after all being to find out what happened in the earliest, most distant stages. Only the archaeologists can decide the question, so only time will tell!

Before trying to unravel this long thread, let us return to Phoenicia itself, a very long thin strip running between the mountains and the sea. From Acco in the south to Arados in the north, its width varied from about seven miles to hardly more than thirty miles. It was in fact a string of small ports, set among little valleys, steep hillsides and tiny off-shore islands. Communication between the towns was difficult on land, but excellent by sea.

Each of these ports saw itself as an autonomous world. Having sited themselves on easily defended headlands or islands, they turned their backs on their mountainous hinterland. Tyre, which is now connected to the mainland by alluvial deposits, was originally built on a narrow island. This gave the city what it most needed: defences which defied all attackers except in the end Alexander the Great; two harbours, a natural one to the north linking the city to Sidon, an artificial one to the south for trade with Egypt; and finally, located in the sea itself, a bubbling spring of fresh drinking water which could easily be tapped separately from the surrounding salt water. Everything else had to be brought in by sea. Thereafter, the Phoenicians constantly strove to recreate this ideal urban geography in their colonial settlements, situating them where possible on islands or promontories.

On the strip of coast dominated by the mountains of Lebanon, these strange urban excrescences were an ancient Canaanite legacy. The people whom the Greeks called *Phoenikes*, the Red People (no doubt because of their famous purple cloth), and whom we call Phoenicians, were directly descended from the Semitic Canaanites, who had long been settled on the Syrian–Palestinian coast. The original Phoenicia was part of Canaan, the part which survived the onslaught of the Peoples of the Sea.

All its towns thus had their roots in the distant past. Byblos was trading with the Nile Delta before the beginning of the third millennium. Egypt still exerted much influence there at the beginning of the following millennium, but it was as yet that of an important customer, admired and even copied, rather than of a political master. In the seventeenth century B.C., the Canaanite cities managed even to escape the threat of the Hyksos. *Indirectly*, though, it was the Hyksos who put their freedom in jeopardy. From 1580 on, the Egyptian New Kingdom, while driving the invaders out of the Delta, felt the need to guarantee its security by creating strongholds in Asia. After the battle of Megiddo (1525), Egypt took control of the cities of Canaan. Quite soon, it is true, this control became more nominal than real. Although the army of Ramses III helped to defend the Canaanite ports against the onslaught of the Peoples of the Sea, Egypt did not maintain much authority there beyond 1200. Canaan was once again free. This was the time when Sidon enjoyed a certain supremacy over the other cities of the coast before being ousted around 1000 by Tyre, the proud city described by Ezekiel. Meanwhile Byblos had become a second-rank town. Amid the general economic recession, though, Phoenicia remained a "sheltered sector."

These Canaanites, though favoured by fortune, now had only a much reduced territory. To the south, the Philistines had taken the southern littoral from them, but without really competing with them, since as iron-workers and farmers the Philistines tended to establish their towns inland. To the north, the Syro-Hittites and the Aramaeans kept them away from the coast of northern Syria and the strategic mouth of the Orontes. Even so, Phoenician influence was strongly felt in this area, at Al-Mina for example, or further north at Karatepe, where Phoenician was spoken. To the east, the Hebrews had seized the hinterland of Canaan, but the maritime cities were not greatly concerned by the loss of this poor land, much of it occupied by a semi-nomadic population. When Solomon offered several Galilean towns to Hiram, king of Tyre, as a reward for his loyal services, the king went to inspect them and turned the offer down, preferring to ask Solomon for an annual supply of grain and oil.

So this was a tiny but independent country, forced by the proximity of the mountains, by its neighbours, and by its own way of life to make do with a poor, barely existent territory, a few cornfields, some beautifully cultivated orchards, the occasional forest and a little grazing land. The over-populated cities had to buy from abroad the food they lacked, to compensate for their disadvantages.

Industry was thus indispensable to the Phoenician cities. They all contained an active body of artisans, weavers, ironworkers, goldsmiths and shipbuilders. These skilled workers were often called on by foreign states, as engineers are in our own industrial age.

The "industries" of Phoenicia excelled in everything. Their woollen cloths were famous, as were their dyes, extracted from the shells of the *Murex trunculus* or the *Murex brandaris*, with shades ranging from pink to purple or violet. This essential industry was kept well away from the towns, since the flesh of the molluscs had to be allowed to decompose at length in the open air, producing disgusting smells. Enormous piles of murex shells marked the presence of numerous dyers' workshops, both in Phoenicia itself and in its western colonies. The weavers, the most highly skilled of all craftsmen, produced precious carpets, using a technique still employed two millennia later in the Gobelins tapestry works in France, as well as the multicoloured fabrics which are often mentioned in Homer. These are the colourful clothes worn by the "Asiatics" who are seen being trampled underfoot by the victorious Tutankhamun in paintings on wooden caskets, or by the prisoners of Ramses III depicted on the enamelled tiles of the temple of Medinet Habu.

Other traditional arts were extensively developed by the Phoenicians with a view to the export market. Large numbers of intricately carved ivory plaques inlaid with gold and coloured stones have been found at Nimrud (Assyria), Samaria, Khorsabad and Arslan Tash, but also at Samos in Greece and in Etruria. Most of these ivories, which date for the most part from the ninth to the seventh century, have been attributed, following the work of R. D. Barnett, to the Phoenician workshops at Hamat on the Orontes. Some may come from Syrian centres further north, and a few reflect a local Assyrian or even Iranian style (Ziwiye), but these people were inspired by the work of Phoenicians who had been brought in voluntarily or involuntarily.[2] The style derives directly from the "international style" of the Bronze Age, with a mixture of disparate influences from Egypt, Mesopotamia, Syria, the Hittite Empire, Assyria and elsewhere.

We find the same continuity of style in the silver or gold cups which have been found in Assyria, Cyprus, Greece, and Crete, or in Italy in countless Etruscan tombs. Their archaeological context dates them from the seventh century, but they could easily be mistaken for work of the second millennium with their repoussé technique and their varied motifs taken from the stock images of the oriental peoples. This was a Phoenician speciality; Homer speaks of "craters [bowls] from Sidon," when one of these precious objects is presented to Menelaus or given as a prize at the funeral games after the death of Patroclus.

But there was one new element in the productions of the Phoenician craftsmen: glass—seen in the countless baroque globules, amulets, pendants and beads, the glass phials and little multicoloured vases, all of them sold by the thousand all around the Mediterranean. This did not call for any new technical invention. The production of glass—which was originally simply the potter's glaze without its earthenware base, in other words *opaque* glass— had developed independently and simultaneously in Egypt and Mesopotamia before the second millennium. The techniques were similar, even if the raw materials and colouring agents differed. Glass-blowing remained unknown until Graeco-Roman times, but glass was sometimes moulded or even hollowed out from a solid mass. More normally, a nucleus of clayey sand, compressed in a mould of fine cloth and mounted on a copper rod, was plunged into the liquid glass to cover it with a layer of glaze. Before it hardened, little pieces of coloured glass were inserted into it (the charming patterns of lines and festoons which one sees on so many Egyptian or Phoenician vases), then the whole surface was smoothed, usually by rolling it on a table, and handles and ornaments were attached. Once it had cooled, it only remained to remove the core of sand and the cloth surrounding it.

The Phoenicians and Cypriots imitated the Egyptian glass-workers at first. But from the seventh century on, the Phoenician and later the Punic cities created a homegrown glass industry, developing among other things transparent glass (which in Egypt made its appearance rather late, from the time of Tutankhamun).

On the other hand, being the sensible traders they were, the Phoenicians never tried to compete with Egypt in the field of ceramics, where the Egyptians were themselves engaged in the industrial production of trinkets. They contented themselves with selling, alongside their own glassware, the innumerable amulets (of cat- or crocodile-headed goddesses, figures of the god Bes or eyes) and scarabs which Egypt had long been exporting to the Aegean and which are found in great numbers in the earliest tombs of Carthage.[3]

Similarly, although they had had settlements in Cyprus since at least the tenth century, they did not try to compete with the local speciality: extraordinary painted pottery, a Mycenaean legacy transmuted by oriental fantasy. Nor, unlike the Etruscans, did they imitate Greek pottery, even though they sold it all over the Mediterranean. They remained faithful to their own ceramic tradition, with its polished iridescent red pots from the Lebanese coast. This was imitated by the towns of Israel in the tenth century in the elegant crimson pitchers and cups known as "Samarian ware." The most widespread Phoenician vessel—the pear-shaped pitcher which is found in both Carthage and Phoenicia—was copied in other materials: glass, bronze, silver, and even ivory. But the art of painted pottery was never adopted by the Phoenicians.

Industry would have been nothing without trade. The Phoenician ports, crowded with ships, were obliged to engage in large-scale commercial activity, stretching from the Red Sea and the Indian Ocean to Gibraltar and the Atlantic. The whole of the Mediterranean was caught up in this far-reaching network.

Broadly speaking, there were three routes from the east to the western Mediterranean. The first kept close to the northern coasts, going by Greece and the Greek islands as far as Corcyra (Corfu). From there, with a favourable wind, a light sailing vessel could cross the Strait of Otranto in less than a day, and then follow the Italian coastline to the Straits of Messina. This narrow passage was the final destination of the earliest Greek travellers, and no doubt of the ships of Crete and Mycenae. In due course the Tyrrhenian Sea was to be the crossroads by which the Greek sailing ships reached the west, though not without difficulty.

The southern route followed the African shoreline from Egypt to Libya and what we now call North Africa, an endless coastal navigation leading finally to the Pillars of Hercules and the Straits of Gibraltar. On this lengthy route, the Phoenicians had ports of call in friendly countries, for instance in the Nile Delta, and trading posts, such as those on the coast of Cyrenaica or the Maghreb. They always chose sites either on inshore islands—Nora in Sardinia, Cádiz opposite the mouth of the Guadalquivir, Motya in Sicily, Utica at the mouth of the Bagradas (Medjerda), Mogador in Morocco—or on easily defended isthmuses. Carthage, on the hill of Byrsa between its two lagoons, was compared by Appian to a ship at anchor.

The third, shorter, route went straight across the middle of the sea, by way of a chain of islands: Cyprus, Crete, Malta, Sicily, Sardinia, the Balearics. Two millennia later, at the time of Philip II and Don John of Austria, this was still the "straight and rapid" route, the one followed by Spanish ships from

Sicily to the Balearics or the Balearics to Sicily; further east, from Sicily to Crete, Cyprus and Syria, it was the central axis of the famous Levant trade. Sailing on the direct route obviously meant abandoning coastal navigation for the high seas.

Did the ships of the Phoenicians take this central sea passage, far from the coasts? Probably they did, since there are clear indications that the Phoenicians, and later the Carthaginians, at least called, and possibly stayed, at all the islands along this route. Moreover, the Phoenicians had earned the reputation of outstanding seamen: "Thy wise men, O Tyrus, that were in thee, were thy pilots . . . thy rowers have brought thee *into great waters*" (Ezekiel 27; my italics). According to Strabo and Aratos, the Phoenicians taught the Greeks a sure method of telling the north by the Little Bear (rather than the Charioteer and the Great Bear). They sailed even by night, venturing far from the coast and outdoing all other mariners of the time, who only sailed by day. In addition, they had drawn up marine charts and made tables of distances and winds; the detailed account of the voyage of Hanno down the African coast was publicly displayed in a temple.[4]

It is probable that of the two coastal routes the northerly one was the safer for sailing boats and for oarsmen (to judge by the practice of the Turks in the sixteenth century A.D., when they controlled both routes). The land provided shelter from northerly winds. But the southern route too was possible and in its western sector often preferable. In the west, the northern route had to cross the wide seas between Italy and Spain; the Phocaeans and later the Marseillais only overcame this very real difficulty by using larger ships. As for the central route, it offered speed (relatively speaking), space, and liberty: the large expanses of water between the islands gave ships the protection of an empty sea and safety from pursuers. No wonder then that the Phoenicians and the Carthaginians were so determined to hold on to the islands from Cyprus to the Balearics, including invaluable Sicily, and to keep control of the "Sicily-Balearic bridge." Once Rome had captured Sicily, that was the end of Carthage's naval supremacy.

The prosperity of Phoenicia thus depended on long sea voyages. A passage in the Bible indicates, if our interpretation of it is correct, that a given ship, fitted out by King Solomon and sailing with the Phoenician fleet, could go to Tartessos in far-off Spain and back in three years. This was about the time taken for a return journey between Seville and Spanish America in the sixteenth century A.D.

Both the voyage to Tartessos and that to America implied the existence of cities with rich capital resources, capable of waiting years for a return, and profits proportional to the immense investment of time. In both cases, it was silver (plus tin arriving from the north in Andalusia) which allowed the miracle to take place. A great deal of Spanish silver must have been circulating, because in Egypt the gold : silver exchange rate went from 1 : 2 to 1 : 13! There must indeed have been a glut of silver on the Egyptian market, as there was in Europe in the sixteenth century with the arrival of silver from America. From Spain, the "conquest" of the mines seems to have moved to Sardinia,[5] which was also colonized early on, and where silver mines were the first to be worked; the copper mines of the Barbagia region were established only in about the eighth century, and the copper they produced was mostly consumed on the island. Diodorus of Sicily, for his part, has no hesitation in attributing the power of the Phoenicians to the trade in the silver they extracted from Spain and Sardinia.

The miracle of the Phoenician voyages, the first systematic use of the sea, was at first sight due to human skill and courage. But perhaps there was something else. The Phoenicians possessed abundant supplies of bitumen, if only that of the nearby Dead Sea, which had been in use from time immemorial. Pierre Cintas writes: "I am inclined to believe that their success at sea was largely due to the use of bitumen for caulking their vessels." Leaks and inadequate watertightness were indeed the enemies of early navigation. In those far-off days, ships were invariably pulled up out of the water, either on to the sand for the night, or in port, where the hull could be exposed to the air for checking and careening. Bitumen, a kind of natural tar, was certainly used for this purpose by the Phoenician sailors.

Indeed the architects in Carthage used it too. The clay walls of the tall houses were often tarred on the outside, and Pliny speaks of their "pitch-covered roofs." Therein lies the explanation for the terrible fire of 146 B.C. The Romans would never have been able to burn the city down to ground level had it not been for the highly inflammable bitumen, which is still being found by archaeologists in "little plaques" in the layer of ashes covering Punic Carthage.

Communications between Tyre and Cádiz in the Far West of the Mediterranean depended on a fragile thread—fragile because of its great length. For many years the system survived thanks to the presence of Carthage as a halfway house. It collapsed only in the seventh century, for a number of different reasons.

Firstly, the Phoenicians no longer had the Mediterranean to themselves as in the early days,[6] but faced competition from the Etruscans (which was manageable) and then the Greeks. Secondly, Phoenicia was under attack from the Assyrians, who took Cyprus in 709. Arados, Byblos, Sidon and Tyre resisted for a long time, but events took a dramatic turn when the Assyrians occupied Egypt in 671. Thereafter, the "kings" of the Phoenician cities were obliged to manoeuvre, submitting, scheming and launching vain attempts at revolt. "Yakimlu, king of Arados in the middle of the sea [Arados was indeed on an island] had not submitted to my royal ancestors," says a text of Assurbanipal, "but I made him wear my yoke. He himself brought his daughter to Nineveh with a rich dowry to be my concubine, and he kissed my feet"; he also paid a tribute of "wool dyed purple and violet, fish, and birds." The "Baal of Tyre" had similarly to hand over one of his daughters and even his son, whom Assurbanipal returned to him. In 574, almost forty years after the fall of the Assyrian Empire, when everyone might have been able to breathe freely again, the Babylonian Nebuchadnezzar in turn conquered Tyre.

These wars, and further upheavals in cities where the kings were giving way to suffetes (magistrates), causing disruption to trade, did not immediately wipe Phoenicia and its ships from the world map. But they impelled Carthage to become a power in its own right, all the more so because it did not have to free itself from the bonds of colonial power in the modern sense of the word. What linked it to the mother country was the common worship of Melkart in Tyre, and business connections between groups. These links slackened of their own accord without Carthage or its ruling aristocracy of merchants having to struggle for independence. The centre of Phoenician life now shifted to Carthage, which was better situated than Tyre, at the exact meeting point of the two Mediterraneans and out of reach of foreign aggression. Phoenician civilization continued there, at once the same and different, rather like modern European civilization in America.

The differences were accentuated by distance, by the inevitable gap between two sets of cultural practices, and not least by the mixed origins of the town. Pierre Cintas went so far as to say that Carthage was founded by various peoples "from the sea" as much as by the Phoenicians themselves. Perhaps this is to give too much weight to the evidence from two early

Carthaginian cemeteries dating from the seventh century; one, at Darmesch to the north-east of the city, was reserved for those who buried their dead (Phoenicians), while the other, on the hill of Juno, was for those who practised cremation (were they Greeks?). Cintas concludes that at the time of the first permanent colonial settlements, there was a mix of different peoples emigrating westward. Unfortunately this all remains unclear. And in any case the Phoenicians were the majority; they set the tone and it was their language that was spoken.

Nevertheless, being a new city which had sprouted like an American town, Carthage was also a melting pot. It was "American" too, even more so, in its materialistic, down-to-earth, fast-moving civilization, preferring the sturdy to the refined. This was a powerful city, attracting sailors, craftsmen and mercenaries from far afield. Accepting many different cultures, it was by nature cosmopolitan. For seven centuries, it made its hard-felt mark on Mediterranean Africa, but at the same time it probably absorbed into its veins all kinds of African blood. The colonizing power was in its turn colonized, and this was what destroyed it in the long run, since it was the treachery of the Numidians and their cavalry which destroyed Carthage on the battlefield of Zama (202). But more of that later.

The thing that most of all distinguished Carthage from Phoenicia was its relation to a dense hinterland which it could not ignore.

Of course Carthage lived on the sea and from the sea as adventurously as the sailors of Tyre. The Tyrians, setting off from the Red Sea in about 600, very probably circumnavigated Africa on the orders of the pharaoh Necho. Similarly, Carthaginian ships in search of tin set off in about 450 B.C. under the leadership of Himilco, and sailed north up the Atlantic coasts of Europe as far as the British Isles (the Cassiterides). A quarter of a century later, Hanno was exploring southwards in search of gold dust, following the Atlantic coasts of Africa as far as present-day Gabon and Cameroon.

The new city could thus have followed the Phoenician example, turning its back on the desolate continent behind it, had it not been for the fact that its trading route was along the North African coast, dotted with obligatory ports of call. These ports of call gave birth to villages, and then to large towns (for instance, on the coast of what is now Algeria: Collo, Djidjelli, Algiers, Cherchell, Guraya, Ténès) which all gradually turned towards their hinterland to increase their prosperity. In due course, the economic downturn of the fifth century obliged Carthage itself to look to North Africa and to install on the plains surrounding it an efficient form of agriculture, to which we shall return.

There was thus an increasing symbiosis with the life of the native peoples. This part of North Africa, which had barely emerged from the Stone Age when the Phoenicians arrived, received almost everything from its new masters: fruit-trees (the olive, vine, fig, almond and pomegranate, all of whose fruits were exported to Italy), techniques of agriculture and wine-making and many craft processes. Carthage was its tutor, and the lessons went in deep. Many centuries later, in the time of Saint Augustine, when the Roman Empire was collapsing, the African peasants, Augustine's compatriots, were still speaking Punic and calling themselves Canaanites: "Unde interrogati rustici nostri quid sint, punice respondentes: Chanani. . . ." E.-F. Gautier, a great historian now undervalued or rather misunderstood, claimed that this "orientalizing" Punic influence had left an indelible mark on the divided continent of North Africa and Spain, so that when the Arabs invaded in the seventh and eighth centuries A.D., this age-old complicity worked in their favour. Specialists have attacked this bold theory, pointing out that there is no immediate evidence based on events of the time. This is true, of course, but the history of civilizations is full of time-bombs. The light of distant stars sometimes arrives on our planet long after they have died.

This explanation is all the more attractive because Carthage, a genuine fragment of the Orient, was not contaminated by Indo-European influences. Its position preserved it from any invasion from the north. If people and cultures circulated, it was from east to west, by sea or westwards from the Nile by routes over the Sahara. Logically then, we find the Carthaginians dressed in oriental garb: long tunics with wide sleeves, long travelling cloaks, skull caps on their heads. E.-F. Gautier sees in these the prototypes of the fez, the gandoura and the burnous of today. On Punic steles, one finds the image of a right hand extended with open palm in a gesture of benediction (another eastern trait), something very like the "hand of Fatma," a popular amulet often reproduced over house doorways in modern-day North Africa. Similarly, many aspects of everyday life in ancient Carthage are reminiscent of the life led today on the same spot. Excavations of the rustic tombs of poor people from the Punic period at Smirat in 1941 revealed a way of living much like that of the peasants of today: "A room, a few storage vessels, an amphora for water, and a mat to sleep on" (G. and C. Picard).

———

Situated at the meeting place of the western and eastern Mediterranean, it was easy for Carthage to take advantage of the immense difference in their economic and cultural levels. The west was barbarian and under-developed. Carthage could obtain everything cheaply there, including metals: tin from the Cassiterides and north-western Spain; lead, copper and above all silver from Andalusia and Sardinia; gold dust from sub-Saharan Africa, brought north by caravans (of horses, not dromedaries at this period); and finally slaves, wherever they could be captured, at times even on the high seas.

All these dealings were transacted by barter. The Carthaginian merchants brought from the east their own manufactured products and those of others, or else spices and drugs which had come from the Indies by the Red Sea, and exchanged them for ingots of silver which they could sell back in the east. This is why actual money was late to appear in Carthage, not until the fifth century in Punic Sicily and the fourth century in Carthage proper, in order to pay the mercenaries. Should we share Sabatino Moscati's surprise at this (1966)? No, because it was not a simple matter of ignorance. Tyre and Sidon had their own currencies. The only possible explanation is that Carthage had no need for money. The same thing was to happen, *mutatis mutandis*, in China, which, for all its inventiveness in this domain (money, even paper money, was known there very early on), was very slow to make use of it. Like Carthage, China was surrounded by economies in their infancy (Japan, Indochina, the Malay Archipelago), easy to dominate and well used to barter.

This does not mean that the absence of money was not in the end a weakness, when Carthage found itself in competition with other economies. If there was a Greek "boom" beginning in the fifth century, with even Carthage buying the fancy goods produced by its rivals, a possible reason for this, though not the only one or the best, may lie in Greek monetary superiority. One is on safer ground in saying that backwardness in this field deprived Carthage of the advantages of banking and a credit system, which appeared very early in the Greek cities. Like ultra-rich Persia (though here coins marked with the head of Darius were in circulation), Carthage accumulated great quantities of precious metals, gold, silver, and even bronze, but without putting them to work.

In the same way, while some writers are rightly surprised at the undeveloped state of metallurgy in Carthage when the city controlled so many mines, can this really be attributed to the shortcomings of the labour force? All that was lacking was the will. But Carthage, absorbed in its extraordinary seafaring activity, chose here too the easy solutions offered by the undemanding routines of commercial life. In the struggles of history, early winners finish up by resting on their laurels and may lose everything if they persist in their old ways. So the arrival in the city of Greek merchandise in the fifth century seems to me to be attributable to the Carthaginian way of doing things rather than to any decisive commercial superiority on the part of the Greeks. From the beginning of the seventh century, Carthage had been importing Corinthian pottery, Etruscan *bucchero* vases and a variety of Egyptian manufactures. This was because Carthaginian trade was particularly active in Corinth, Etruria and Egypt. In the same way, in the sixteenth century A.D., it did no harm to Venice to import and then re-export manufactured goods from southern Germany. The Dutch did the same thing in the seventeenth century, carrying merchandise over the seven seas, buying here, selling there, and engaging in primitive barter whenever possible in the Malay Archipelago. Like them, the Carthaginians were carriers, intermediaries, buying with one hand and selling with the other.

Does this mean that the intermediary is inevitably in a position of weakness? Not necessarily, since Carthage was able to defend its essential assets, and in particular its "monopoly" on mining in Spain: it succeeded in keeping the Etruscans, the Greeks and then the Romans away from most of the profitable part of the Iberian peninsula. It managed also to defend its most important maritime ports of call, its luxury industries (woven fabrics as renowned as those of Phoenicia, as well as ivories and furniture) and its day-to-day trading activities, notably the wholesale grain trade and the thriving salt fish industry. To this end it set up fisheries and salt-pans in many different places, and in particular at Cádiz and a whole series of little harbours along the west coast of Spain and Portugal, facing the Atlantic Ocean with its rich fishing waters. When the Roman salting industry came here subsequently, all it had to do was take over the Phoenician legacy.

Nor was the power of Carthage affected by the fact that neither the art nor the life of the great city was able to escape the influence of Greek culture, which to a greater or lesser extent permeated the whole of the Mediterranean, both east and west. It was a long-standing Phoenician tradition to adopt the dominant style of the moment (earlier it had been Egyptian). The influence of Greek art was felt on the Phoenician coast as well as in Carthage, particularly in funerary steles and in architecture, and all the Carthaginian colonies followed suit, in Sicily, Sardinia, Spain, and on the African coast. The Greek impact on Spanish-Carthaginian sculpture, in the fourth century for instance, or even at the end of the fifth, shows clearly that one should distinguish between the *cultural* influence of Greece on the Punic world and its economic influence. Carthage was happy to import from Greece its town-planning, its characteristic houses with central courtyards, its ornamented vases, its cement and hydraulic concrete (see Chapter 8 for explanation), its sarcophagi, some of its gods (Demeter and Kore, around the year 396), but also its Pythagorean philosophy and some of its exponents. It was the example of Alexander the Great which inspired Hamilcar, the father of Hannibal, to embark on the conquest of Spain. Hannibal himself was imbued with Greek culture, and even his use of elephants covered with brightly coloured trappings, which terrorized the Roman soldiery, was borrowed from the Hellenistic world.

Carthage, living off the Mediterranean, was inevitably affected by its fluctuations, its shifting fortunes. The history of the city was shaped by the rhythms of Mediterranean life.

In the seventh and sixth centuries B.C., the Greeks were everywhere. In about 600, the Phocaeans founded Massalia (Marseille); they established themselves at Ampurias in Catalonia and perhaps also to the south of Mainake (Malaga). This represented a threat to the mining monopoly of the Phoenicians. But Carthage took things in hand, driving the Phocaeans out of Alalia in Corsica after a sea battle between the Greeks and the joint fleets of Etruria and Carthage (540–535). It was not the end of the struggle, but this time the Carthaginians came out on top.

In 525, Persia seized Egypt and consequently acquired the use of the powerful Phoenician navy which the pharaoh had fitted out. However, Darius was defeated at Marathon (490) and Xerxes at Salamis (480), and in the second of these battles at least, it was the Phoenician ships that were beaten. The same year, the Punic army and navy were crushed at Himera in Sicily, and a few years later the Greeks destroyed the navy of the Carthaginians' Etruscan allies at Cumae (474). This was the beginning of a dramatic period for the Carthaginians; a crisis that was at once political, religious and economic. The ruling Mago dynasty was removed from office and the aristocracy seized power. Tanit, the tutelary goddess of the city (like Pallas in Athens), became the chief deity. Carthage reacted vigorously to its economic difficulties: imports were reduced, an austerity programme was put in place, and relations

Cycladic ship

This flat ceramic vase, probably used ritually, is known as a "frying pan." Decorated with spirals, it shows a many-oared vessel of the kind used in the Aegean in the third millennium. The prow is shaped like a ram. Syros, third millennium B.C.

Egyptian ships

A ship carrying passengers and goods returning to port. The boat, heading north, features a rolled square sail. One of the ends of the boat is upturned. Limestone bas-relief from the mastaba of Ipi at Saqqara, Fifth Dynasty. (Cairo, National Museum)

Trading ship heading up the Nile, to the south. Painting from the tomb of Sennefer, called the Tomb of Vines. Necropolis of Cheik el Gournah, Valley of the Nobles. Western Thebes.

Two examples of the ship of the dead. In Egyptian tradition both ends are slightly upturned.

Sketch of the mural frescos from a tomb at Giza, from around 2400–2300 B.C.

Papyrus boat representing a ritual of the dead, portrayed on an ivory plaque from the Bernardini tomb in Praeneste (Palestrina), 7th century B.C. (Rome, Archaeological Museum, Villa Giulia)

Minoan ships

This fresco discovered at Thíra (Santorini), from around 1500 B.C., shows the ceremonial fleet, merchant ships, and small boats that plied the Aegean. The boats are arriving at and leaving a port city with stone houses. Several Minoan ceremonial ships are powered by rowers, who carry high-ranking passengers protected from the sun by a velum. (Athens, National Archaeological Museum)

A fisherman from the Greek Isles returning home with his catch. Detail from the frescos of Thíra (Santorini), around 1500 B.C. (Athens, National Archaeological Museum)

Hippopotamus hunt on the Nile. Saqqara, Mastaba of Ti, Old Kingdom, end of the Fifth Dynasty. Relief.

Assyrian ships

Cedar from the mountains of Lebanon and Amanus was transported either by floating and towing or by placing it on coastal boats. These boats went by the Greek name of *hippoi* because they were sometimes decorated with a horse head. Assyria, 7th century B.C., detail of a bas-relief from the north wall of the court of honor of the palace of Sargon, Khorsabad. (Paris, Musée du Louvre)

Longboat with a ramming prow, shown on a Phoenician coin of CA. 340 B.C. (Beirut, Archaeological Museum)

Boat with two rows of oarsmen, part of a Nineveh relief representing the escape of Luli, king of Tyr and Sidon, from the armies of the Assyrian Sennacherib, in the 8th century B.C. (London, British Museum)

Etruscan Ships

Fishing scene. A fisherman hauls in his net inside the boat; fish stir up the water; a flock of birds covers the sky. Tarquinia, Hunting and Fishing Tomb, c. 520 B.C.

A vessel showing warships (one Etruscan) facing off, c. 630–620 B.C. (Paris, Musée du Louvre)

Greek ships

One of the oldest Greek representations of a boat
with two rows of oarsmen, end of the 8th century
B.C.

This black-figure cup by Exechias shows Dionysus upon a square-
sailed ship, one of whose ends is upturned, c. 530 B.C. (Munich,
Staatliche Antikensammlungen)

A black-figure Attic *œnochoe* showing a small merchant ship powered by a sail and a single row of oarsmen, c. 510 B.C. (Meermanno Westreenianum Museum van de Boek)

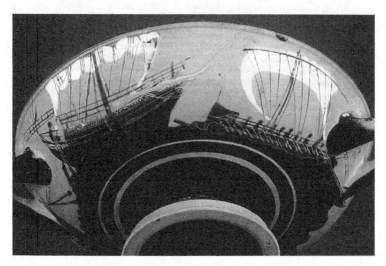

A merchant ship attacked by pirates. The rigging attaching the sail to the yard and the ram used to pierce the side of the enemy craft are easily distinguished. Black-figure Attic cup, c. 510 B.C. (London, British Museum)

Ships of the eastern Roman world

This Nile scene was made for a temple in Latium by Greek artists in the oriental style then popular in Rome. It shows river life and the Nile's many ports. Roman mosaic, end of the 2nd century B.C., from the sanctuary of Fortune, ancient Praeneste. (Palestrina, Prenestrino Barberiniano Museum)

This bas-relief of a merchant ship comes from Sidon (Saïda), 1st century A.D. (National Museum, Beirut)

Ships of the western Roman world

A merchant ship, for both river and sea travel, with a bowsprit mounted with a dolphin-eyed ram. Such ships transported wine to the Moselle in barrels, a Gallic invention that came to replace the older amphorae in the Mediterranean. (Neumagen Ship, 3rd century A.D., Rheinisches Landesmuseum Trier) with sub-Saharan Africa and the Cassiterides were strengthened. Above all, Carthage fell back on North Africa, taking over a vast surrounding area for livestock-raising and orchards. The native Libyan peoples who had been driven out of this land continued to produce barley and wheat.

The long century when Carthage was on the defensive allowed the city to gain new strength and take advantage of the weakness of Athens following the failure of the Athenian expedition against Syracuse (415–409). Immediately, Carthage began to wage war ferociously against the Sicilian Greeks, attacking their towns, capturing the inhabitants and thus acquiring a slave labour force which was to transform the economy of the city itself. The conquests of Alexander (334–323) brought new alarms; the very life of the city seemed in danger. But the almost immediate disintegration of Alexander's excessively large empire allowed Carthage to breathe again, since there was now less to fear from the divided empires of the east, which were too far away to do much damage. And indeed, was it possible for the east to do without the west? The Ptolemy who seized the eastern Mediterranean (including Phoenicia) after Alexander's downfall adopted the Phoenician system of measurement and quickly restored the favourable situation of Carthage.

In the end the danger that was to prove most fatal materialized nearer home, at Rome, the ultimate catastrophe coming in 146 B.C. It was a tragic ending. Who in his heart—and even the impartial historian has a heart!—can fail to grieve at the *delenda est Carthago* of Cato the Elder and the pitiless destruction ordered by Scipio Aemilianus? This was the final silencing of a very special voice.

Carthage did not die in the usual way. As a result, it is difficult for archaeologists to reconstitute much of the life and society of the city. All we have is indirect knowledge, made up of random fragments.

Thanks to Aristotle's curiosity, we know something of the Punic constitution. Originally ruled by kings, Carthage later adopted an aristocratic form of government. The principal families of the city provided two suffetes (etymologically, judges), chosen annually by popular suffrage, as well as the members of the Senate and of the committees who dealt with the actual tasks of government: a sort of Venice *avant la lettre* with a Council of 104 which was as much feared as the Venetian Council of Ten. How many generals were crucified on its orders!

It is hard today to imagine the city itself as it once was, on the hill of Byrsa (now the hill of Saint-Louis, plus the hill of Juno and the plateau of the Odeum), with its temples, the *tophet*, its narrow streets and tall many-storeyed houses, as in almost all Phoenician towns (Appian speaks of six-storey buildings between the forum and the acropolis of Byrsa), its water tanks and the freshwater spring known as the fountain of a thousand amphoras. The handsome vaulting over the fountain, although much altered by the Romans, is the only remaining piece of genuine Carthaginian architecture. Recent excavations have, however, uncovered, three or four metres below the Roman city (which was built on the ruins of Carthage), a part of the Punic city dating from the Hellenistic period. It is thus certain that at this time Carthage had straight and passable streets, linked by flights of steps, and a drainage system similar to that found in the towns of Sicily. The houses are simply identical groupings of a number of rooms.

On the beach of Salammbô there were two harbours, a rectangular one for merchant shipping, and linked to it a circular one where warships were often drawn up out of the water, under the vaults of the Arsenal. An island in the middle of the military harbour housed the headquarters of the admiral commanding the navy.

Enormous walls, double or even triple on the landward side, surrounded the city, with its fortress on the hill of Byrsa, and the crowded districts around the harbour. Halfway between the harbour and Byrsa was a public square, a kind of agora. Further north was the suburb of Megara with its gardens, orchards and aristocratic villas. From the top of the hill, one looked north to the salt-water lagoons of Sebkha er Riana and south to the lake of Tunis. The city had a huge population, perhaps as many as 100,000. Alongside the rich governing minority lived a plebeian mass of craftsmen, labourers, slaves, sailors and sometimes mercenary soldiers—all forming a distinctly volatile crowd. Carthage was often shaken by internal riots.

The city was surrounded by a finely kept countryside. The rich clearly took pleasure in well-cultivated land, beautiful gardens, the grafting of trees and the breeding of animals. A Carthaginian agronomist, Mago, fragments of whose work have reached us indirectly, gives scores of methods for planting vines so as to preserve them from excessive drought, for making fine wines, cultivating almond-trees, keeping pomegranates in clay for export, choosing the right qualites in breeds of oxen, etc., etc. He adds a piece of advice to rural landowners which is not without significance: "The man who buys land should sell his house, lest he find living in the city preferable to living in the country." It seems that the Carthaginians of the third century resembled the

Tuscans of the fifteenth and sixteenth centuries A.D. in their keenness to buy land out of town.

Extensive excavations at the site of Carthage have found nothing but thousands of bodies, buried or cremated, and the objects which went to the grave with them. There are hundreds, even thousands, of funerary *cippi* or steles monotonously listing the names of the gods; scholars have even attempted a mathematical calculation of the most worshipped gods according to their frequency and the order in which they are named!

This is not much help if we are trying to get to the heart of a religion whose strangeness horrified the Romans (the horror was often quite genuine) and whose mythology, theology, structure and vision of the world remain unknown to us. If we knew better the Phoenician religion, from which that of Carthage derives, we might be able to make sense of the few details we have. Unfortunately this is not the case, in spite of the unexpected light cast on the matter by certain Ugaritic texts, some writings in Canaanite, and what we find in the Bible.

Each Phoenician city had its own gods, though some of these were common to several cities. But it is difficult to be specific about the names of these gods. El, Baal, Adonis and Melkart are in a sense generic terms: El means God; Baal and Adonis mean Lord, and Melkart, king of the city. So Melkart, the "king of Tyre," can easily be called Baal Melkart. The gods are thus enveloped in vague names which do not correspond to any easily recognizable divine function.

Generally speaking, the Phoenician pantheon is dominated by three figures whose names vary from town to town: a god-king, a mother-goddess or fertility goddess, and a young god who every year must be born, die and be reborn, like vegetation as the seasons change. In Sidon, the trinity consisted of Baal, Astarte and Eshmun (assimilated by the Greeks to Asclepios—Aesculapius in Latin); at Byblos it was El, Baalat (a feminine version of Baal) and Adonis, whose myth we know via the Greeks. Adonis was also the name of the river which descended from Lebanon and ran close by the city; a sanctuary marked its source in the mountains. Every year, as the dust-laden winds reached it, its waters suddenly turned red like human blood; this was the signal for Byblos to go into mourning for Adonis. In Tyre, it seems that the functions of the young god who dies and is reborn were assumed by Melkart, the "Baal" of the city, and there was a festival to mark his resurrection.

Every city probably adapted myths explaining the world and its creation and the destiny of man to suit its own local gods. In the texts of Ugarit, for example, Moth figures at once as death, as the terrible heat of summer, and as the ripening corn. He must be put to death every year, so that nature and humanity may live. Different functions clearly gave birth to different gods: Baal Lebanon was the god of Lebanon; Baal Shamin the lord of heaven; Reshef the god of fire and lightning; Dagon the very ancient god of wheat; Chusor the god who invented iron, and so on.

This religion was rooted in the ancient world of the Semitic imagination, close to the earth, the mountains and the waters; its simple, cruel rituals were those which a nomadic people had long ago celebrated in the open air. Sacred woods and hills near to the cities served as sanctuaries, though of course there were indoor temples too. The altar was simple, with very little if anything in the way of anthropomorphic images; a pillar, column or raised stone might represent the deity. Silius Italicus has left us a description of a religious service still conducted in the ancient Phoenician manner in Gades during the Roman period: barefoot, shaven-headed priests, dressed in linen, officiated in a bare sanctuary devoid of sacred images, where a perpetual fire burned.

The religious life of Carthage was at first modelled more or less on that of Tyre. The dominant god was Baal Hamon; the mother-goddess, sister of Astarte or of the Ishtar of Mesopotamia, was soon to become Tanit, whose name, unknown elsewhere, remains a mystery; the young deity, god of the sun or of vegetation, was either Melkart, the Tyrian god, or Eshmun, the healer god, confused with both Apollo and Asclepios, as Melkart was to be confused with Heracles. Fierce competition between the two cults did not result in the elimination of either. Melkart was to be the favourite god of the great Barcidae family, in which the recurring names of Bomilcar and Hamilcar were related to that of the god. The temple of Eshmun on the acropolis of Byrsa, the most beautiful temple in Carthage, was to be the last bastion of the defenders of the city in 146.

Apart from these dominant gods there were dozens more, Phoenician, Egyptian or Greek. The pantheon of Carthage seems to have been as welcoming as that of Etruria, which is saying something. Later, during the period of difficulties and cultural assimilation, Baal Hamon could easily become Cronos or Saturn, and Tanit Hera or Juno.

The distinguishing feature of the religion of Carthage was the sensational growth of the cult of Tanit, which took on the appearance of a spiritual revolution. From the fifth century, the goddess came to dominate all other divinities, supplanting the old god, Baal Hamon. Carthage lived now under the "sign of Tanit," which like the goddess was almost entirely confined to the west.[7] It consisted of a disc on top of a triangle, with a horizontal line between the two. The whole sign readily suggests a human figure, especially when the horizontal line bends upward at each end like two raised arms. Other symbols associated with Tanit came from the east, in particular the "bottle" and the open hand, the crescent moon joining with the solar disc, which is perhaps a representation of Baal. These are all doubtless allusions to myths which remain a mystery to us.

But it is not so much these mysteries that create a problem as the obsessive weight of the Carthaginian religion, an enduring, terrifying and imperious religion springing from the depths of a prehistoric past. The human sacrifices of which the Romans often accused their enemies were only too real: the *tophet* of Salammbô has yielded up thousands of vessels containing the charred bones of children. When Carthage wanted to avert a danger, it sacrificed to its gods the sons of its most notable citizens. This is what happened when Agathocles, in the service of Syracuse, invaded the territory of the city. Certain distinguished citizens having committed the sacrilege of buying children as a substitute for their own, a sacrifice of two hundred children was ordered by way of expiation. Religious fervour increased the number to three hundred. Prisoners of war were sacrificed too, often in their thousands.

Does the blood of these victims sully the name of Carthage? In fact, all primitive religions have had similar practices. In this respect Carthage was following the Canaanites of Byblos or the Semites of Israel; was not Abraham on the point of sacrificing Isaac? The astonishing thing is that while the Carthaginian economy was so forward-looking, its religious life remained centuries behind, and even its "revolutions"—the cult of Tanit in the fifth century—did not free it in the least from this inhuman and fearsome piety. It is a striking contrast with the openness of the Greeks, who sought harmony between man and the natural world. In Carthage, an intense economic life, which a historian would not hesitate to describe as "capitalist," was not incompatible with a backward-looking religious mentality. What would Max Weber have thought?[8]

II
THE ETRUSCANS: AN UNSOLVED MYSTERY

The Etruscans, the original creators of Italy, were not colonizers in the normal sense of the word. Were they indeed colonizers at all? They pose a fascinating problem, which remains unanswered. In spite of the progress of knowledge we cannot be sure that the mystery will ever be cleared up.

The first mystery is the Etruscan language itself, a non-Indo-European language. It can be deciphered—since it uses the Greek alphabet—but it remains incomprehensible. Perhaps one day a bilingual inscription will be found that explains everything. But for this to happen, we should need an inscription with the right kind of text, for such a find has already been made and has proved of no help. On three strips of gold found in 1964 at Pyrgi, the port of the Etruscan city of Caere (present-day Cerveteri) three inscriptions were indeed discovered: one of them, in Punic, corresponded to one of the other two, which were in Etruscan. But the Punic text itself was hard to interpret. It concerned the dedication of a temple to Astarte by the king of Caere in around 500, proving yet again the close relations between the Carthaginians and the Etruscans, and the willingness of the latter to accept foreign gods, Astarte being in this case assimilated to Uni (Juno), one of the Etruscan deities. But as far as the language was concerned, the comparison of these two short inscriptions produced no definite results.

For the time being, Etruscan has to be deciphered on its own terms, by the juxtaposition of known fragments, using what is called the "combinatory" method—better described as "divinatory" according to Albert Grenier. Nevertheless, the vocabulary of Etruscan is growing year by year: *clan* (son), *sec* (daughter), *puia* (woman), *ati* (mother), *lupu, lupuce* (he died), *svalce* (he lived), *avil* (years). *Zil*, meaning "to govern," gives *zile* or *zilath* (magistrate); *purth*, the chief *zilath* of a city, corresponds to the Roman *praetor*; *lucumon* is the king of a city. . . . About 200 words have been recognized, but they do not yet explain a great deal. And even if the language were completely deciphered, it is not certain that the historian would be any better off.

Indeed, the Etruscan texts we possess (almost entirely funerary inscriptions) are too short, too devoid of what one might call serious historical content, for us to able to arrive at any reliable reconstruction of the early history of Tuscany. The only long text known so far is one in the museum of Zagreb; it is written on the twelve wrappings of an Egyptian mummy of the Graeco-Roman period found in Alexandria. There are 1500 words in all. It seems to be a religious calendar, but so far it has defied interpretation. The same is true of two inscriptions of over 100 words, known as the "Capua tile" and the "Perugia cippus." And in any case, even if all these texts could be interpreted, would they give us more than a few vague clues to rituals and beliefs?

Where did the Etruscans come from? When did they arrive in Italy? These two questions of time and place remain unanswered. Consequently, every historian rises to the challenge, turning advocate or even detective. It would no doubt be wiser to steer clear of such fruitless controversies, but wisdom is not such fun.

There are moreover three or four undisputed facts:

1 The language, religion and social life of the Etruscans *insistently* remind one of the east.

2 The incontrovertible evidence of the tomb furnishings shows no sign of the brilliant civilization of the Etruscans before the seventh century B.C.

3 Since the Greeks settled as early as 750 in the bay of Naples, it is difficult to envisage Etruscans arriving after them from the south, as they would surely have been stopped in their tracks by the Greeks.

4 There thus seem to be two chronological limits to the arrival of the Etruscans: the earliest as early as the twelfth century, the latest as late as the sixth.[9]

The problem in presenting the conflicting theories is that the discussion has been going on for so long that neither party is willing to do battle any longer. The two basic theories—the *eastern* and the *autochthonous*—are thus tending to converge, but still without providing any definite solution to the essential mystery.

No one today doubts seriously that the Etruscans were of eastern origin, as was claimed by all the Ancients except Diodorus of Sicily. In 1886, two sixth-century funerary inscriptions were found at Kaminia on the island of Lemnos to the south of the Dardanelles; they are written in a non-Greek language (the Athenians only having conquered the island in 510). According to Raymond Bloch, they show "word endings, word formations, and even terms" found in the Tuscan texts. If the language is not Etruscan, it is, as

Jacques Heurgon says, "at least the language most closely resembling Etruscan to have been found outside Italy"—in other words, a related language. In addition, objects resembling those in the tombs of Etruria have been unearthed in a necropolis of the eighth or seventh century not far from Kaminia. Etruscan jewellery, which is unusually beautiful and original, displays certain details comparable to Lydian jewels.

And finally, what we know of Etruscan religion suggests the east. Thus the Etruscans in Italy were always considered experts in divination, including the interpretation of portents and the art of reading the future in the entrails of sacrificial victims. A bronze model of a liver found in Piacenza in 1877 is a kind of teaching aid, with some forty divisions each corresponding to the different zones of the sky and the deities in control of them. Similar models made of terracotta have been discovered in excavations in Mesopotamia or the Hittite Empire. And there are other analogies, though less conclusive ones, since they might be explained by the influence of orientalizing art via the Mediterranean and Greece in the seventh century.

All this being so, why not simply go back to the well-known text of Herodotus (I, 94)? According to him, the Etruscans were emigrants from Lydia, who had been driven out of their country by persistent famine in the thirteenth century. This grain shortage in Asia Minor recalls the beginnings of the stormy episode of the Peoples of the Sea and the desperate complaints of the Hittite king in *c*. 1200. These emigrants, goes on Herodotus, "made their way down to Smyrna, where they built ships for themselves. They put on board all the equipment they might need and sailed away in search of land and livelihood. Their journey took them past a number of peoples, but eventually they reached the Ombricians [people of Umbria], where they founded settlements and still live to this day." This text gives such a strange description of what we take to have been the lamentable adventure of the Peoples of the Sea that one is tempted to complete it as follows: in the course of this interminable exodus, the Etruscans might even have attempted to enter the rich territory of Egypt. They could have been the *Tursha* whom the pharaoh claimed to have driven out of the Delta, together with other invaders. It seems straightforward enough to move from this name to the names *Tyrrhenes* or *Tyrsenes* given them by the Greeks, and *Tusci* or *Etrusci* given them by the Romans. But if they set off so early, how and when did they eventually arrive on the shores of the Tyrrhenian Sea to which they gave their name? Did they stop in other places? No one knows the answer.

Those who argue for an early date thus find themselves faced with a sizeable problem, since the Etruscans, having supposedly set off in the twelfth century, only reappear five centuries later with the first sumptuous tombs dating from around 650. Perhaps the starting date is impossible, then? Perhaps the Etruscans left Asia Minor as late as the seventh century, as A. Piganiol suggests, and were driven out, not by famine, but by the Cimmerians. That is possible, but does not *a priori* rule out an earlier exodus. Although Carthage was founded in the eighth century, refugees from Tyre had been arriving there over the previous two centuries. What is clear is that there was no sudden disruption of life in the Italian peninsula in the seventh century which might signify the abrupt arrival of an alien civilization already at the height of its powers and immediately capable of draining the plains and building the cities of Tuscany.

In any case, whatever the date of their migration, we can be sure that the oriental origin of the Etruscans connected the first "Tuscans" to an *ancient* eastern civilization, but that this mingled with an "Italic" civilization which was itself archaic in character. It seems to me impossible that the cultural influence of the east, however strong it was in the seventh century, could have been the sole source of the language, religion and customs which continued to make Etruria so distinctive a presence in Italy.

This is what has prompted a modified version of the so-called *autochthonous* theory. According to this view of things, the Etruscans came to Italy at a very ancient date, in the second millennium, as part of a conquering wave of oriental civilization. They were then conquered in their turn by the incoming Indo-European "urn people" of Villanova. Thus for centuries a very deep layer of Mediterranean civilization lay beneath the surface, submerged but not destroyed. At the end of the eighth century, this layer came to the surface again, kindled into life by Greek and Phoenician influence and by the general level of prosperity. Is this narrative any closer to reality than the one just outlined? I wouldn't bank on it. Not that such revivals are impossible, far from it—and this theory has the advantage of taking on board the oriental origin of the Etruscans, while situating their adventure firmly on the home ground of Italian soil, the only place where it can be properly explained and given its true meaning. For if they came by sea from the east in very ancient times, the Etruscans would at best have been a handful of pirates and adventurers (like the Vikings in the Middle Ages), who forced themselves on the residents as an aristocratic minority.

But here too there is a snag. Recent excavations have gone down beneath the Villanovan level to find an earlier culture known as the Apennine (it seems to have developed all along the mountainous axis of the Italian peninsula). And this new world is vast but undistinguished, with no suggestion of the wonders of the east.

In the end, there is no way of deciding one way or the other. All we can safely say is that an old civilization of oriental character suddenly appears in all its glory at the beginning of the seventh century. The metals of Tuscany—copper, tin, iron—allowed it to grow rich quickly. Even more importantly, it gained new splendour from the increasing proximity of the Greek cities. Etruria remained permanently "colonized" by this civilization, which it absorbed with unflagging enthusiasm. Even those achievements of Etruscan art which once seemed the most original (because we used to know very little about Greek painting beyond what was reported in the literature of the time), that is to say the tomb paintings, may be called into question. The discovery of the painted sarcophagus of Paestum known as the Tomb of the Diver, which seemed to herald a rich programme of excavations,[10] was the signal for fierce disputes about who came first, since this Greek painting is contemporary with the Etruscan frescoes. But if we accept that there was Greek influence in Etruria, that will raise once more the question of the relation between Greece and the east. The few fragments discovered in the east and analysed by Smith suggested to him the existence of an oriental tradition of wall-painting, going back almost uninterruptedly to the Assyrians. What if tomorrow the cities on the Tigris or Euphrates, or in Cyprus, had surprises like that of Paestum in store for us?

Etruria corresponds to Tuscany in the broad sense, from the Arno to the Tiber, from the Apennines to the Tyrrhenian Sea, whose very name recalls the Etruscans. This original Tuscany contained a part of what is today Umbria and Lazio [Latium]. To the west, bordering on the sea, it included low-lying stony plains, in parts marshy, the Sienese Maremma and the Pisan Maremma with their sandy watercourses and thorn-bushes; to the east, as one approached the blue line of the Apennines, their summits picked out in snow, was a land of hills and narrow plains. This was the essential *Etruria felix*, with its rich harvests and its orchards, still today the most beautiful rural landscape in the world. Pliny the Younger later built here his charming country residence of Tifernum Tiberinum.

Some twenty towns, relatively independent of one another, constituted the durable strength of Etruria. According to tradition, twelve of them formed a federation, the League of Twelve Peoples, the precise membership of which remains uncertain. The oldest, such as Caere and Tarquinia, with their narrow territories, lay to the south. These first towns were not far from the sea, but not actually on the coast; they were connected to harbours such as Pyrgi, which served as an outlet for Caere and even at one time for Rome. All were built on heights, "on the country's back," thus making them easy to defend (they were walled in the sixth and fifth centuries) and setting them above the miasmas of the plain, where there was probably malaria. The growth of the towns was accompanied by the draining of the surrounding plains and the exploitation of the mineral resources of the region. If Populonia was situated on the sea, this was the exception that proved the rule, the reason being that the crude iron of Elba was constantly being landed on the quays of this smoke-blackened industrial city.

Later, when Etruria declined, it was driven to depend more on its cereal-growing plains in the east, and its hillsides covered with vines and olives, where there remained a prosperous aristocracy of rural landowners. This movement eastward meant that Arezzo, with its agricultural and industrial wealth, became the centre of gravity of Etruria at the time of Scipio Africanus (its "lucumons" were ancestors of Maecenas). The other towns stagnated, including stubborn Tarquinia with its fields of flax and manufacturers of sailcloth.

Etruria, colonized by mysterious incomers, spread beyond its original limits and in turn colonized the surrounding regions, both to the south and to the north.[11]

From very early on, the Etruscans had reached the rich southern plain of Campania, where the Greeks had arrived before them. Etruscan Capua flourished alongside Greek Cumae. Like the Greek cities, Capua could only survive by defending itself against its highland neighbours, the Oscans and the Samnites, whose ever-present threat eventually triumphed over all the cities of the plain in the fifth century. Until this time, however, as successful excavations have shown, Capua enjoyed a period of great prosperity. Built on the broad plain, the city's grid-plan development, imitated no doubt from the Greeks, met no obstacle comparable to those encountered by the old Etruscan towns, hemmed in by mountains, or by early Rome, hampered by its seven hills.

Capua being a "bridge-head," it was necessary to have effective communications between this southern town and the "motherland" of Etruria. The best place to cross the Tiber was in Rome, opposite the Isola Tiberina, on the site of the old Sulpicius bridge. We know that Rome, despite the pious falsehoods of tradition, was dominated, re-created and reshaped by the Etruscans; this strenuous tutelage left an indelible mark on the city. In many aspects of their religion, institutions, games, town planning, and the external trappings of everyday life—the lictors marching in front of the consuls, the curule chair of these magistrates—in their food and in their music, the Romans were to remain permanently marked by Etruria.

Northwards, Etruria was expanding across the Apennines[12] as early as the eighth century, and this expansion had increased greatly by the sixth century. The mountains were a formidable obstacle. The splendid autostrada from Florence to Bologna allows us to admire the beauties of the landscape today and forget about the problems it posed! In antiquity, it was possible to cross the range only by way of the deep valleys cutting into it; there are many of them, it is true, but one has to make the crossing from one to another, for example from the Tiber or the Arno valleys to the valley of the Reno which runs down to Bologna, the Po delta and the Adriatic.

There was a time when specialists talked of an Etruscan Empire in the Po valley, a "League of Twelve Peoples" to match that in Etruria. Today they are more cautious: in Mantua, Milan or Atria (Adria) on the Adige, there is no evidence of any political control, or of anything more than mere economic or cultural exchanges. However that may be, Marzobotto (where excavations have uncovered an ancient city whose name remains unknown), Bologna (formerly Felsina), and Spina at the mouth of the Reno, were all strongly marked by the people and arts of Tuscany. Marzobotto was laid out on a grid plan and extended across 100 hectares on its *insulae* (165 metres long by 35, 40 and 68 wide), with canals and high pavements. In this huge space however, the houses, shops and workshops were not particularly impressive. Spina, dating from the fifth century, was a kind of Venice, today submerged under the water; one can still make out a rectilinear grand canal, with subsidiary canals, and a perfect grid plan. This was a Greek as well as an Etruscan town, which no doubt explains why in the fifth century, when less pottery from Attica was being imported to Etruria, more of it was reaching Spina. It was by this route too that Etruscan traders reached the Alps, to meet the amber and copper of central Europe.

Etruria was doubtless at the height of its power at the time when its navy, in association with that of Carthage, defeated the Phocaean fleet off Alalia in

Corsica (540–535). This effectively denied the Greeks access to the Tyrrhenian Sea, which became an "Etruscan lake." But this situation only lasted half a century.

In 474 Hieron of Syracuse won a decisive victory over the Etruscan fleet off Cumae. Almost immediately Capua was abandoned to its fate and forced to do a deal with the Oscans. The Etruscan presence in Rome came to an end soon afterwards. Traditionally this happened either in 507, with the revolution culminating in the proclamation of the republic, or in 504, with the end of the reoccupation of Rome by Porsenna, king of Clusium (Chiusi). These dates of 507 and 504 are questionable, however. The Roman revolution was surely similar to that of other Etruscan cities which had also got rid of their kings. It seems probable that Rome recovered its freedom a little later, when the Syracusans, after their great victory at Cumae, were devastating the Etruscan coasts and even the Adriatic ports.

Etruria may have been on a downhill slope, but these repeated blows did not destroy it. The gradual process of its disappearance took more than two hundred years. The Celts, who had been attacking its strongholds beyond the Apennines, took Felsina (Bologna) in 360. Then Rome, which was fighting all the peoples of Italy, engaged Etruria in a war of attrition punctuated by deceptive reconciliations—a kind of civil war. Veii was taken in 396, Volsinii in 265, Falerii in 240. This last date could perhaps be regarded as the final stage in this very complex process of annexation. The Etruscan cities still retained their magistratures, their claims, their aristocracies, their peasant populations chained to the soil like serfs, their harshly treated miners. But Roman civilization and the Latin language were taking a hold that would last for centuries.

What Rome created with some difficulty—the unity of the Italian peninsula, as a prelude to the conquest of the *Mare nostrum*—could also have been achieved by Etruria. In terms of political strategy, its misfortune was to have too many enemies at once and to be itself divided among towns all jealous of their independence—the annual assemblies of the Etruscan cities, at the *Fanum Voltumnae* on the territory of Volsinii, were religious gatherings, not the makings of a political body. Etruria suffered from the same weakness which caused the disasters of the Greek cities.

Like them, however, it did survive after a fashion: Tuscany has remained a world apart in Italy. Is it just an illusion that today, in the streets of Orvieto, Tarquinia or Florence, one seems to recognize in the men or women one meets the smiling faces and strong features of the Etruscan tombs? An art-loving friend of mine used to say of the Italians of the Renaissance: "They are Etruscans, not Tuscans," an idea borne out by the portrait of the Etruscan we find in Jacques Heurgon's description of Maecenas, a descendant of the "lucumons" of Arezzo, "minister of the interior for the emperor Augustus," protector of Horace and Virgil. His nonchalance and subtlety, his easy-going way of life, taste for the ornate, passion for music, scorn for vulgar distinctions, acute understanding of his fellow men and determination to reconcile them—one is tempted to see all Maecenas's attractive qualities, leaving aside a few darker elements, as a legacy of the ancient civilization of Tuscany which lay buried but not dead beneath the glory of Rome!

Perhaps we should feel less frustrated by the enigma of the Etruscans if we knew more about the religion central to their lives than the hints we find in later sources of doubtful reliability. It was a religion of the book, or rather of several books, but we do not possess these books. We have a few extracts from them, and some commentaries from Roman times, but nothing really to reveal the kind of "structure" which would organize it all into a coherent world-system.

With its origins in the archaic east, this Etruscan religion was very much alive. The pantheon was overcrowded (the forty-four squares on the bronze sculpture of a liver at Piacenza are not enough to contain all the gods) and it welcomed foreign deities almost indiscriminately—Italic, Greek and occasionally Phoenician.

The presence of the Italic gods with "deformed but recognizable" Latin names raises a number of problems. Uni comes from Juno, Nethuns from Neptune, Maris from Mars, Satre from Saturn, but it was no doubt Menrva, an Etruscan goddess, who gave her name to the Latin Minerva. And as the Greek gods flooded in, their personalities, mythologies, and spectacular, complicated romantic adventures became identified with those of the Etruscan gods. Tinia, the supreme god of Etruria, who is shown holding a sceptre and brandishing a thunderbolt, is inevitably seen as a copy or avatar of Zeus. Menrva is naturally born from the head of the king of the gods. The Etruscan Hermes has his own Etruscan name—Turms—but he wears "the chlamys, petasos and caduceus of Hermes." As for Herakles, he was simply transformed into a god, the god of war, travellers and sea-voyages, as well as the admired conqueror of Hades.

The specific features of the Etruscan religion are hidden behind this confusing medley of Greek and Italic names and these images which herald the pantheon of the Romans (Tinia, Uni and Menrva are the essential trinity, comparable to that of the Capitol). One would like to know more about Vertumnus, an important young god, who changed his costume with the seasons and according to Roman tradition abandoned the Etruscan cause for that of Rome. But where did he come from? There is in any case one sure sign which points to an oriental origin: unlike those of Greece and Rome, Etruscan religion was a revealed religion. Its sacred books transmitted the revelation uttered by the nymph Vegoia and by Tages, the child with an old man's wisdom, who emerged one day from a ploughman's furrow in Tarquinia.

But it was only late in the day that the orally transmitted *disciplina etrusca*, as the ancients called it, was given a fixed form in the books which so fascinated the Romans of Cicero's time: the *libri haruspicini*, on the art of examining the entrails of victims; the *libri fulgurales*, on the interpretation of thunder and lightning; and the *libri rituales*, *libri Acheruntici*, an Egyptian-type manual on the voyage of the dead. In a word, it offered a complete system of protective magic for divining (and thus not crossing) the redoubtable will of the gods; for foretelling the future by consulting the entrails of victims; and for interpreting portents, particularly lightning in its various forms, depending on where it appeared in the sky and whether it struck once or repeatedly, etc. The system gave rise to rules applying equally to the life of individuals and the existence of the state.

With all these things to worry about, the Etruscans were, according to the Ancients, the most cowed and religious of people. But that is only in comparison with Roman or Greek religion. Perhaps we should simply say that they did not escape the magic circles of oriental religion with its fears and formal rituals. Etruscan religion weighed heavily on the faithful, but does not seem to have set out any ethical system or promise of rewards—though there were punishments enough, as we shall shortly see. But was this not equally true of many oriental religions?

The Etruscan cities, with their mainly narrow streets and their great walls of stone blocks piled up without mortar, have almost entirely disappeared. But the many hundreds of tombs have their own strange story to tell.

The earliest, dating from the Villanovan period, were mere pits containing bi-conical (or house-shaped) urns with the ashes of the dead. But soon burial became general; first came lengthwise graves, and then, from the seventh century, chambered tombs for the rich, cut into the volcanic rock. Near the site of the ancient city of Caere, outside the city walls as was customary, there are three necropolises covering a total area of 350 hectares, so that the city of the dead was bigger than that of the living. And Caere was no exception. Many of these tombs have been robbed over time or their materials used for other things. Recently, in order to discover the best places to excavate, archaeologists have devised an ingenious method of prospecting: a periscope lowered into the tumulus allows one to see in advance whether a given tomb contains anything valuable, or perhaps some wall paintings. This is a wise use of inadequate resources, but the pace of work remains slow, alas.

From the eighth to the fifth century, these tombs are our best evidence for Etruria itself and for the complex movements of international art. The objects found in them give a condensed picture of the Mediterranean trade in artefacts: pottery vases and amulets from Egypt, silver gilt drinking vessels and glassware from Phoenicia, countless pieces of proto-Corinthian, Corinthian, Ionian, Attic, and Laconian pottery, perfume phials from many sources. And the general development of Mediterranean styles, from the orientalizing period to that of gradual Hellenization, from the smiling art of archaic Greece to the severe classical style, from black-figure vases to red-figure vases—all these perceptible changes in fashion can be traced in the innumerable objects found in Etruria: weapons, mirrors, tripods, bronze chests, so-called *bucchero* vases made of black clay to look like metal, imitations of Greek pottery, goldsmiths' work, sculpture, and architecture, especially that of the temples. The greatest period of Etruscan art, when it was at its most powerful and most original, runs from the early days in the seventh and sixth centuries to about 475. This was the period of the finest jewellery, oriental in style, of the greatest sculpture, the magnificent terracotta statues (late sixth century) which adorned the temple of Apollo at Veii, and of the most charming funerary painting.

"Charming" is indeed the word that comes to mind. A visit to the houses of the dead in Tarquinia is a joyful pilgrimage, as one goes from one to the next, constantly meeting the colours and sunshine of springtime in Tuscany. The Etruscans believed in a future life in a quite material sense. The dead person was going to live in the tomb itself, in one or more of these chambers adorned with benches, carved stone friezes, or, from the first half of the sixth century, fresco painting. The whole setting was designed to suggest a private house, to conjure up around the dead person the brightly coloured world of the living.

Let us take as an example the so-called Tomb of the Leopards in Tarquinia; it is not the most beautiful or the biggest, but it is one of the best preserved. A staircase leads to a square underground chamber. On the wall opposite the entrance, three couples are stretched out on couches eating and talking, with servants in attendance. On the side walls, servants and musicians walk towards the triclinium in a setting of flowering tree-branches. Above the diners, on the pediment, the two leopards after which the tomb is named stand face to face. The charm of the ensemble does not depend on the artistic quality of the original. The draughtsmanship is in fact somewhat crude, the gestures clumsy and the hands rather graceless, particularly if one compares them with the astonishingly delicate and confident depiction of dancers in the contemporary Tomb of the Triclinium, or with the extraordinary movement of a half-naked couple dancing a wild dance in the so-called Tomb of the Lionesses, constructed some fifty years earlier. Even so, as one looks at the crudely applied colours, violently contrasting blues, reds, greens, and blacks, the suggestion of a theatrical scene played out between the diners and a servant brandishing an empty jug, the blonde, fair-skinned women, the young men with their dark hair, the whole thing is full of joy, spontaneity and life.

There is nothing conventional about the themes. They vary from tomb to tomb. The dead are surrounded by what gave them pleasure in life: grand banquets, which suggest funeral rites no doubt, but also the revels of the living; music, athletics, attentive servants, wild dancing; a fine ship in harbour, a naked diver plunging from a red and blue reef into the midst of a multi-coloured flock of birds, riders on horseback, extremely beautiful and delicate horses with the slim legs of racers, and backgrounds full of plants, animals and fish. All this is done with great freedom of colour and composition. It would be interesting to imagine how the Egyptians would have treated the theme of the paintings in the Etruscan "hunting and fishing" tomb: the sea is alive with fish, a fisherman is hauling his net in to his boat, overhead flies a cloud of birds as a hunter aims at them with his sling. The same subject could be found in Egypt, but this is another world, full of joy and a sense of humour, of the ridiculous even, which one also finds in certain Etruscan sculptures verging on caricature. In all the ancient tombs of Etruria, the descent to the underworld is a hymn to life, however much the Etruscans may have feared the gods whom they saw as tormenting them.

Everything changed mysteriously in the fourth century, or maybe even a little earlier. The style suddenly became dignified, sometimes pompous, borrowing themes from Greek classical mythology, though sometimes with lovely details such as the famous portrait of Velia in the Tomb of the Ogre. At the same time, the charming scenes from daily life disappeared, to be replaced by demons who are not the most cheerful figures in the Etruscan pantheon. There is Tuchulcha, for instance, with the beak of a bird of prey, long ears, and two menacing snakes rearing up over his head; or Charun (who is Greek in name only), an even more sinister figure with a horrible bluish face and rotting skin, a hooked nose, horse's ears, and a mallet which he wields with monstrous joy to batter the mortal whose last hour has come. These malevolent beings belonged to the ancient stock of Etruscan popular beliefs, but this was the first time they had appeared on the walls of tombs. They tormented the dead person during the frightening transit from life to death, a very unpleasant stage before his final arrival at the peace and perpetual delights of the underworld—an underworld represented here for the first time in the Greek manner, with Hades and Persephone presiding over the banquets of the afterlife.

These sombre images became more frequent in the fourth century, as the Etruscans lost their material well-being, and night fell over Tuscany.

III
COLONIZATION BY THE GREEKS

Greek expansion presents the same problems and ambiguities as Phoenician colonization or the history of the Etruscans. Our knowledge here is greater, but as to the chronology and motivation of the Greek colonizers there are many more grey areas than about the founding of Carthage, and our questions often remain unanswered. An excess of information means an excess of different opinions, and the early history of Greece is all too rich in both.

Not long ago this history seemed relatively simple. Cities in fairly close proximity to one another created a network of towns from the Crimea to Spain, all linked to their mother cities. Barring a few exceptions, each new foundation was the result of a deliberate voyage, generally undertaken on the advice of the Delphic oracle. The expedition was led by a founder, the *oikistes*, acting on the orders of the home city; with the protection of the gods he chose the site, supervised the work of the surveyors and the distribution of land and adapted the constitution of the homeland to fit the new city. Then he became the ruler, often the absolute ruler, and left behind him the memory of a hero; all of this took place in a far-off age when kings and demi-gods still lived amidst a colourful decor of myth and legend. And always, the emigrants took with them fire kindled at the hearth of the motherland.

The proper unfolding of this scenario also calls for another set of characters: the natives might oppose the invader in honourable combat, or be wise enough to submit, or become so dazzled that they offered their king's daughter to the founder. Protis, one of the founders of Massalia (Marseille) in about 600, married Gyptis, daughter of the king of the Segobriges. The Spartan Phalanthes founded Tarentum against the barbarian tribe of the Iapyges (had not the Delphic oracle counselled him to be the "scourge of the Iapyges"?). Setting off from the island of Thera, and guided by Libyan nomads, Battos founded Cyrene in 631, on the harsh North African coast, but on a spot where, wonder of wonders, there was adequate rainfall, or "holes in the sky." The natives also provide scope for the occasional spot of mockery: thus the Carians, in the hinterland of Miletus, are called "barbarians" because of their way of mangling the Greek language—which does at least prove that they spoke it. Of course there are also "noble barbarians" as there would later be "noble savages," for instance on the north shores of the Black Sea where "the Cimmerians, Scythians and Sarmatians are generally more welcoming to the Ionians with their fine wines and beautiful vases."

There are hundreds of such stories, each better than the last, in the writings of Herodotus, Pausanias and a few others. It would be unwise to take them at face value. True, the traditional chronology has often proved correct, but since archaeology has come on to the scene, its findings, and particularly the shards of pottery, have given the lie to certain foundation dates. And since these dates are all interconnected, every change affects the whole chain, so that no one can any longer be sure about the chronology. Of course the language of archaeology needs in its turn to be interpreted. Let us imagine archaeologists, one or two millennia hence, patiently reconstituting the lost past of French-colonized Algeria without any written documents to help them: the capture of Algiers would be as obscure as that of Knossos by the Mycenaeans or the foundation of Tarentum by the Dorians.

For ancient Greece, what was at stake was the initial emergence of civilization as it freed itself from the magma of its "Middle Ages." As the Greeks saw it, everything depended on this moment of liberation.

History has tended to distinguish between two periods of Greek colonization, the first, from 775 to 675, being agricultural, the second, from 675 to 600, essentially commercial. But this is rather too neat an account. In the first place, the Greek adventure did not begin promptly in 776 or 775, the year of the first Olympiad, and there was no sharp boundary between agricultural and commercial colonization. All the more reason for trying to see what happened in the obscure period before the first Olympiad. Such a quest is bound to lead us, by uncertain routes which may be long or very short, to the origins of the movements which impelled the Greeks to leave their various homelands.

In Italy (in the broad sense of the word), there is ample proof of a Mycenaean presence. But as far as we know at present, this took the form of colonization only in the city of Tarentum and its hinterland. In this privileged spot there was even a kind of continuity between Mycenae and the Greek colonial presence.[13] Italy was thus not completely *terra incognita* to the Greeks in the eighth century. In the far west, long before the foundation of Marseille (600), ships from Rhodes had sailed as far as the coasts of Gaul and Spain. This was apparently the origin of Rhode (Rosas), Agathe (Agde) and Rhodanousia at the mouth of the Rhône.[14] But we know little about these settlements.

There is a similar problem, though much more complex, for the Aegean coast of Asia Minor. There are traces of Mycenaean merchants and trading posts all along this coastline. Greek was no doubt spoken in Rhodes, Cos and the nearby islands, as well as in Cilicia and Caria; a Mycenaean settlement existed at Miletus at the end of the Bronze Age. Here, though, as elsewhere, everything clouds over in the twelfth century. Subsequently, Greek refugees reached the eastern shores of the Aegean. Towns grew up, though only small ones: Smyrna around the year 1000, Miletus probably a little earlier. The original Smyrna was surrounded by a wall which according to one expert was "massive and well built," evidence that the city was under threat from without; inside the wall, however, there were only very primitive "curvilinear" houses. It was only towards the middle of the seventh century that everything changed, and very quickly, at least in the "twelve cities" of Ionia, the largest of which, Phocaea and Miletus, were to play a decisive part in colonization both near to home and far afield. In the space of a few decades, they became the most brilliant cities of the Greek world.

However, their modest beginnings imply the existence of some activity in the intermediate area of the Aegean and its islands, all of which were in the hands of the Greeks, from Crete in the south to the Sporades in the north. And they soon settled on the still uncultivated north coast of the Aegean, from the gulf of Thermaikos to the Hellespont. Early Greek culture thus permeated the whole of the Aegean, not particularly strongly, but remaining unchallenged. The "geometric" style of the new civilization emerging on the peninsula has left its mark in many places on the islands and the coasts of Asia Minor. The sanctuary of Apollo on Delos at the heart of the Cyclades, which later shone out like a beacon over the surrounding sea, was already in existence by the eighth century.

Asiatic Greece was thus not really a colonial territory, since it was as old, or nearly as old, as Greece proper, which was coming back to life after the Dorian invasion. Its cities were not "founded" by mother cities on the other side of the Aegean, but grew up independently, in parallel with the cities of the Greek peninsula and the islands. There were similarly mixed populations on either side of the Aegean, with groups of Dorians, Ionians, Aeolians and a few Achaeans. Only gradually did the part of Asia Minor which kept the name of Ionia (Ionia of the twelve cities) come to diverge in its civilization, its way of life and its art from peninsular Greece. And it was later still that the "Ionic" order was distinguished from the Doric order which came into existence on the other side of the Aegean.

In fact Asiatic Greece became prosperous in the course of time only because of its links with the rest of Asia. These links were slow to appear, and when they began to spread southwards in the direction of Syria, it was not so much the Greeks of Asia Minor as the Ionians of Euboea and the islands of the Aegean who were responsible for the new settlements, notably at Al-Mina. Ionia itself probably took no part in this new trade and the orientalization of art and thought that resulted from it. Curiously, it was at Corinth, in about 725 B.C., that this first became apparent in proto-Corinthian pottery. Asiatic Greece, on the other hand, freed itself from the geometric style only towards the middle of the seventh century B.C.

From this point of view, if the historian were granted just one area for which he would be given the complete picture, he would perhaps do well to choose the south coast of Asia Minor as far as the Syrian frontier: it would include Rhodes and Cyprus, former bastions of the prosperity of Mycenae, now its last refuges; Tarsus, which had links with Rhodes and the Cyclades as early as the ninth century; and in particular Al-Mina, a trading post at the mouth of the Orontes, where neo-Hittite Syria reached the sea. This city was discovered by the archaeologists in 1935, and we still do not know its precise foundation date—perhaps the beginning of the eighth century. It was to be a crucially important colony, representing as it did the first opening up of Greece to Syria, Palestine, the neo-Hittite and Aramaean states, Assyria, Urardhu and all the caravan routes of the continental Middle East. The city was moreover largely populated by Phoenicians. It is not therefore surprising that it is increasingly seen as the city where Greece met the east; it was here that the Greeks became acquainted with the Phoenician alphabet, here too that the orientalizing phase of Greek art originated, the first challenge to the geometric style.

More importantly, Al-Mina set an example for others to follow. The Mediterranean with its endless shores was bordered by countries which might be respectively backward, developed, or over-developed for their time; some stood high on the scale of civilization, some very low. But trade could only be really profitable if there was a vigorous and spontaneous electric current passing between high-voltage and low-voltage points. Al-Mina was clearly a high point, a commercial pinnacle, situated as it was on the line linking the still-backward Greece with countries of ancient civilization which had not lost their superiority, though they had lost some of their wealth. A similar high point later on was Naucratis, a Shanghai *avant la lettre* on the Nile Delta, which Psammeticus I ceded to Greek merchants, in particular Ionians. It was founded before 600, probably around 630. It was then that the network of Greek cities, both ancient and modern, really "went live."

Land was of course the basis of everything. At the time when its people began to spread far and wide, Greece was a rather poor agricultural country with an archaic economic system. There was little arable land, and even less of any real quality. As soon as the population grew, the need for internal colonization appeared, but there was little scope for expansion. The pick-axes of the pioneers had to cope with stony ground and knotty tree roots; it was hard to make much of a living out of this marginal land. Try as they might, plough-ing the same land several times over, breaking up the clods with their primitive hoes, they could not coax the soil of Greece into feeding them adequately. In addition, the clearing of the land destabilized the soil, so that a storm was enough to wash it down to the bottom of the hill. The whole of Greece suffered, as it still suffers, from this endemic malady.

The difficulty can easily be restated in social terms. Excessive numbers of poor peasants competing for a meagre living made them easy prey for a few big landowners, turning them into *hectemores*—tenant farmers who had probably to hand over five-sixths of their crop every year—driving them into debt, and eventually making the whole territory "slave land." Eighth-century Greece was already full of peasants on the run; Homer's world is crowded with vagabonds. Hesiod, in *Works and Days*, tells of the endless toil of the peasant, chained to his small patch of land, worn down by bitter quarrels with his neighbours, his family, and the "kings," i.e. the masters in the towns. He could be saved only by the justice of Zeus—or by running away. Otherwise he had to resign himself to being the "nightingale in the talons of the sparrowhawk." Legislators might attempt to improve things; such was the achievement of Solon. But the process would begin again sooner or later, under one form or another.

It is obvious that this situation might give rise to colonial expansion. It gave rise to much else besides: the swollen cities, the hordes of craftsmen, and the wretched fate of the mercenaries, similar to that of the Swiss guards and German mercenaries of the Renaissance. Greek soldiers were selling themselves in Egypt in the sixth century and they were still doing so in the Persian Empire in the fifth century.

But flight could also take the form of a Phoenician-style adventure, and there is every reason to suppose that it did. In those days of rudimentary sailing skills, the peasant could easily become a sailor, and might well possess a boat. In winter, when "the blasts of every wind rage," Hesiod advises his brother Perses, a peasant like him: "do not keep ships on the wine-faced sea, but work the earth assiduously, as I tell you. Pull the ship on to land and pack it with stones all round . . . taking out the plug so that heaven's rains do not cause rot. Lay away all the tackle under lock in your own house, tidily stowing the wings of the seagoing vessel; hang the well-crafted steering-oar up in the smoke; and wait till the time for sailing comes."

Everything thus conspired with the process of pauperization to drive men to distant shores. If Boeotia, Attica and Sparta (except at Tarentum) did not play a major part in the first wave of Greek colonization, it was perhaps because they had not yet exhausted the possibilities of *internal* colonization, because they still had virgin lands to clear and could live on the grain they produced, or in the case of Sparta on grain from nearby Messenia, which they had subdued after a hard struggle. If the cities of Asia Minor or Megara set about exploiting the Black Sea and establishing trading posts there in the sixth century, it was in order to get hold of the grain of the sparsely populated lands of southern Scythia. In the Middle Ages, Genoa applied the same reasoning and came in search of food to the same region.

This grain all had to be paid for, generally with wine and oil—luxury agricultural products—or with manufactured goods. But such exchanges of grain, pottery vases or metals, once they attained a certain volume, could not take place without professional merchants. Almost from the very first wave of emigration then, one must suppose the existence of merchants, commercial calculations, and even colonization motivated by commercial imperatives. Would the Greeks of Chalcis have been impelled in 770 B.C. to settle on the island of Ischia in the bay of Naples by purely agricultural considerations? Such a meagre reward would hardly have justified such a long voyage. It is, in fact, no coincidence that this first observation post (*emporion*) set up by the Greeks beyond the Straits of Messina in the eighth century was a vantage point on the Etruscan sea, within range of Etruscan metal. Metal was a constant concern of the Chalcidians. Similarly the gold of Lydia or Egypt, the silver of Spain and copper ingots had a part to play in the calculations of the first colonizers, whether the Greeks or anyone else.

Can we see Greek expansion from the eighth century to the sixth as a single story? No doubt the cities scattered along the endless sea-coasts did not form a single closed universe. The slow speed of communications and the strength of certain local networks might partially relegate this or that city to the margins of the mainstream circuits. Even so, these circuits existed, and they are the essential element in the "structure" we are trying to reconstruct.

The reader can note the major departure points on the map in Appendix II. Chalcis, Eretria, Megara and Corinth (leaving aside for the moment Miletus and Phocaea) were the first centres of activity in ancient Greece. The central axis of activity in the country ran from the Euripus channel, where Chalcis is situated, to the Saronic Gulf and the isthmus of Corinth, a slim barrier which from the seventh century was crossed by a *diolkos*, a track with man-made grooves (concave rails) and wooden rollers which allowed ships to be hauled across from the Saronic to the Corinthian Gulf. With its two ports, Lechaeum and Cenchreae, Corinth was the end point of this axis towards the west. Athens and Attica were not closely concerned in this gradual colonization process carried out by small groups of explorers.

If one considers the results, one can quite easily distinguish between three zones or rather three types of venture:

1 Those which were very easy (though in the fullness of time neither unimportant nor unproductive)—acquiring lands deserted or only sparsely inhabited and poorly defended.

2 The essential ones—the colonies established in southern Italy (Magna Graecia) and Sicily.

3 The risky all-or-nothing expeditions far to the west. The most important of these was the remarkable creation of Marseille in about 600.

Virtually uninhabited coasts, easy to capture and sometimes even hospitable, included Cyrenaica (which was only settled in one small area); the northern Aegean; and the Black Sea beyond the Hellespont, which was controlled by Miletus from Abydos. On either side of the Bosphorus two Megarian watchposts, Byzantium and Chalcedon, faced one another, but after 650 Miletus was almost the only city to establish trading posts all around the Black Sea, whose stormy waters were "always enveloped in fogs and mists." (To call the sea Pontus Euxinus or "the hospitable sea" was a euphemism.) There the Milesians found precious goods, wood, salt fish, horses, slaves and grain. When Miletus went into decline, Athens took its place on this profitable sea.

In the central part of the Mediterranean, matters were more serious. The failure of the Greeks to make the Inland Sea their own lake was the result of what happened in this area.

At the outset, the sea favoured their ventures towards Italy and Sicily. There is a coastal current running northwards along the Balkan shoreline. Leaving this current behind in the region of Corfu, and if one was prepared to make a direct crossing, it was possible to sail in a day to the Italian coast, there to pick up another current flowing southward. A virtual salt-water river, driving along the coast, it carried ships to the Gulf of Taranto and past the shores of Calabria. From there it was no distance to the Sicilian coast across the Straits of Messina, which were not an insuperable obstacle.

The Greeks were therefore able to settle almost everywhere along a coastal strip from the Gulf of Taranto to the shores of Sicily. It is worth remarking that they were less tempted by the more northerly parts of the Adriatic coast. Corinth occupied Corfu (Corcyra), it is true, conquering this strategic position from the Eretrians; it also seized Apollonia and Epidamnus (Durazzo), two ports sheltered from the severe winter weather by the mountainous coast of Epirus. But there was no attempt (except by the Phocaeans, to whom we shall return) to reach the northern part of the Adriatic, with its many coastal islands to the east and its flat plains and rivers to the west. The piecemeal and apparently haphazard efforts of the Greek cities were above all aimed at finding a route to the west. This did not, however, prevent the colonizers from stopping at times, when it was possible to come to an agreement, whether by peaceful means or by force, with the local populations, Iapyges, Oscans, Sicels or Sicans.

The drive westward with little regard for the intervening places is clearly demonstrated by the chronology provided by both archaeology and tradition. The first Greek colonies were not in Tarentum or Metapontum, Sybaris or Syracuse, but beyond a line running from Tarentum to Syracuse and on the other side of the Straits of Messina, at Pithecusae (Ischia) in about 770. The Chalcidians and other peoples of Euboea had thus immediately embarked on a race to the most distant places. Subsequently this forward position was reinforced locally by the occupation of the islands of Capreae (Capri), Pandateria and Pontia, and by the founding in about 740 of the key city of Cumae (at a date much later than the traditional version, 1052). In the wake of these first settlements, hastily established as far west as possible, came other towns, Naxos (757), Zancle (750), which with Rhegium (c. 740) commanded the Straits of Messina, Syracuse (733), founded by Corinth, and Tarentum (708). The pattern is very like that of the Phoenicians, whose first objective was far-off Spain.

At first things seem to have gone quite smoothly in areas that were either unoccupied or at least not defended by competitors of any consequence. Such rivals only arrived later on to challenge the Greeks for possession of key sites. In the sixth century, the Etruscans were consolidating their positions in Campania: the Greeks went no further than this, and for a long time had access to the wide Tyrrhenian Sea only when their rivals allowed it. There was a division of spoils with the Carthaginians, who kept firm control over western Sicily to the west of a line between Panormus and Motya (being so close, it was unthinkable for Carthage to give up this "bridgehead"). Broadly speaking, the Greeks and the Carthaginians shared occupation of the island from 750 to 650, the former on the east, the latter on the west. But the Greeks' great triumph was to have been the first to seize the hazardous Straits of Messina. It was not a total victory, however, since the Etruscans dominated the Tyrrhenian Sea and the Carthaginians, by clinging on to the narrow, rugged region of western Sicily, kept possession of an essential link in the route leading "by way of the islands" to Spain. In a word, the Greeks had designs on the westward route giving access to metals, but were unable really to secure it.

This did not prevent the colonial Greek cities from flourishing, no doubt because of their extensive and fertile hinterlands. Varro asserts that the grain yield here was a hundred to one. We may remain sceptical, but certainly the threefold triumph of wheat, oil, and wine, in which Diodorus saw the cause of the rapid growth of the Sybarite economy, explains the splendour of these colonial cities.

Their wealth came also from trade and industry, but principally trade, since these cities of the central Mediterranean were above all places of exchange. If Himera and Selinunte minted the first Greek coins in Sicily (Himera in about 570–560) this was because they were the first cities to come into contact with Spanish silver, either via Marseille (founded by the Phocaeans in 600) or perhaps even via trade with Carthage which was a major provider of silver.

At this early stage in their history, most western Greek cities were still closely linked to their mother cities, which housed artisans, carriers and merchants. The products of the industry of the mother cities were a kind of currency which could be invested in the west. Thus it seems *probable* that the fine, multicoloured fabrics of Miletus reached Etruria by way of the land routes over the isthmus, from the Gulf of Taranto to the Tyrrhenian Sea. Sybaris owed part of its wealth to the fact that it directed this mule traffic towards its colony in Laos, on the Tyrrhenian Sea. The road, which was quite a difficult one though it went no higher than a thousand metres, could only be used for lightweight precious goods such as woven cloth.

As for the heavy traffic in pottery, which was carried in the holds of ships, archaeologists can now give us more definite information and even suggest statistics. There was a continuous movement of trade, carrying pots over enormous distances for household or festive use: vases, amphorae, craters, drinking vessels, rhytons, hydriae, aryballoi and even ordinary kitchenware.

And given that there are many different types of pottery, varying according to period and place of origin, and that we sometimes know the trademarks of the workshops and the painters who decorated them, the pieces and fragments unearthed in excavations are valuable evidence for dates. In addition, their immense variety can tell us something about the trade routes and indeed the way this trade altered over time.

If we look at Georges Vallet's 1958 study of Zancle and Rhegium, we can make some general points. Between about 625 and 570, there was an increasing flow of Corinthian pottery, but from 570 to 525 it was the black-varnished pottery of Ionia (particularly Phocaea and Miletus) which dominated the scene, to be ousted in its turn, from about 550, by products from Attica. So we have three ages: the Corinthian, the Ionian, the Attic. The first of these launched a new kind of commerce of a colonial type, like that of early modern Europe. The "crockery" exported to the west by Corinth was the result of mass production and intended to be exchanged for grain which was then traded throughout central Greece by the manufacturing city. This typically colonial trade was designed simply to serve the interests of Corinth, which enjoyed the advantage of its geographical position at the crossroads of the routes through the isthmus. Once Ionia and Attica joined in (the latter before the disasters of 494 and the Persian conquest of Ionia), this colonial trade gave way definitively to an international form of commerce.

If historians have described these exchanges in terms of "accumulation," it is in order to suggest that this economic take-off in the ancient world may already have involved a type of merchant "capitalism," with all the tensions that implies. In 1911, the biggest archaic treasure ever found in the west came to light in Tarentum: over 600 coins together with "six kilograms of unminted silver in the form of cast or hammered plates, and crude, worn coinage cut up beyond recognition, in rods and bars, and a few fragments of silver vases and utensils." It all seems to have been buried around 480, the year of Himera and Salamis. It bears eloquent witness to "accumulation," too eloquent perhaps—today it is suspected that the archaeologists of 1911 may have added a few coins from elsewhere to the collection.[15]

It was in the area beyond Sicily and southern Italy that Greek colonization launched its riskiest ventures, starting in the late seventh century and carrying on into the first half of the sixth century B.C.

There is no need here to pursue the discussion of ancient sources, since Michel Clerc has already done so in his classic study of Marseille from its origins until the fifth century A.D. His conclusions were not invalidated by the 1967 excavations in the area round the Bourse, although these did yield a lot of information about the port of Lacydon (larger than the present-day Vieux-Port), about the stone jetties at which the vessels tied up, the reservoir from which they drew fresh water, and the fortifications of the ancient city.[16]

The founding in about 600 of Massalia (Massilia was the Latin name), where the trade routes up and down the Rhône met the sea-passage to the west, is a sign of the Phocaeans' great boldness. Their city, the largest in Ionia apart from Miletus, grew rapidly at the end of the seventh century and after, until it was taken by the Persians in 549. But all the crucial or easily accessible points on the great map of the western Mediterranean were already taken. As the last comers in the west, the Phocaeans had to travel further than the founders of the Chalcidian or Corinthian cities, beyond Corcyra and Epidamnus, Zancle and Rhegium, beyond Cumae even. They had one trump card: the speed of their ships. Being good sailors like all the Ionians, they had—according to Herodotus—invented a new way of carrying goods, not in roundships powered by sail, but in long *pentecontors* with fifty oarsmen, which the Greeks and other Mediterranean peoples normally used only for warfare. We might see an analogy here with the *galera de mercato* in fifteenth-century Venice, a ship equipped with both sails and oars. In any case, the slim, fast Phocaean cargo ships were unusually capable of defending themselves. We can picture them being used for piracy as well as trade.

Thus the Phocaeans first reached the north of the Adriatic and the city of Adria. It would therefore have been possible for them to make use of the "German isthmus," which lay close to hand. If they chose not to, it was not because they preferred the French isthmus and the Rhône route which the Greek merchants were quick to discover, but because they wanted to sail west towards the Atlantic. Everything suggests, indeed, that Massalia was not the real objective of the Phocaeans and the Greeks of Asia, the Samians and Rhodians. To quote Herodotus literally (I.163), the Phocaeans "opened up the Adriatic, Tyrrhenia [i.e., Etruria], Iberia and Tartessus." Not a word about Marseille. Once again, therefore, it was the silver and copper of Spain which took priority, together with the tin which was already being shipped along the Atlantic coast to Andalusia. We might conclude therefore that Mainake and Hemeroscopion were founded before Massalia. Unfortunately, we know nothing about the former and the latter is regarded as relatively recent by the archaeologists.

Marseille must have gradually put down roots and gained its autonomy. This can only have been consolidated by the fall of Phocaea, which was taken by the Persians in 549 and abandoned by most of its population. A difficult period followed, since the refugees from Phocaea were denied access to Alalia by the Carthaginian and Etruscan navies, while southern Spain was systematically and thoroughly controlled by Carthage.[17] Even so, the Phocaeans had certainly attempted to fight their way to the silver of Spain.

In about 700 B.C., the general renewal of activity had favoured colonization and economic exchanges, to the advantage equally of the Phoenicians, the Carthaginians, the Etruscans and the Greeks. A degree of prosperity opened up new possibilities.

In about 600, events and exchanges seem to gather pace. In a Mediterranean world that was by now thoroughly explored and divided up, the Greek system had reached its zenith with the final ventures from Miletus into the Black Sea and from Phocaea to the western Mediterranean. It was in about 630 that the Egyptian pharaoh ceded the city of Naucratis to Greek merchants, and in about 600 that the Phocaeans founded Marseille at the most distant point of their expeditions to the west.

Naucratis, as we have seen, was a sort of Shanghai, a concession enjoyed by the Asiatic Greeks. The Milesians were there alongside the Aeginetans and large numbers of Greeks from Chios, Rhodes, Tinos, Phocaea, Clazomenae, Halicarnassus and Mytilene. Perhaps the Greeks came to understand there that the Mediterranean belonged to whoever could embrace it from end to end, linking up the *high* point and the *low* point of commerce, Naucratis and Marseille in this case. Those who controlled the two extremities dominated the entire system, and Asiatic Greece thus became the heart of the Greek commercial system.

Not the heart of the Mediterranean, however, since the sea was no one's exclusive property. It had room for three systems which sometimes worked together, but more often competed, using force if necessary.

The most fragile and least impressive network of the three was that of the Etruscans. Even at the time of their victory at Alalia, their commerce did not cover the whole of the Mediterranean. They were a meeting point of east and west, as their prosperity indicates, but they did not create trade links belonging exclusively to them. And in any case their first great disaster, the naval defeat at Cumae (474), dealt them an irreparable blow.

The Phoenician system was altogether more extensive. Phoenicia and Carthage were able to resist everything that fortune threw at them. The crushing defeats suffered at the hands of Assyria and then Nebuchadnezzar did not destroy the Phoenician fleet, which rose from its ashes with the pharaohs of the Saite dynasty; then, in 525, it passed into the service of Persia. Carthage made a similar recovery after the disaster of Himera (480). And so it went on. Nothing seemed able to get the better of this adaptable creature.

We should not therefore be misled by the omnipresence of Greek culture; the Mediterranean never became a "Greek lake." In 525, Egypt escaped Greek control, Cambyses having put a stop to the trading activities of Naucratis. In 494, Ionia, the driving force of the system, was conquered by Persia. Then came the Persian wars, Marathon (490), Salamis (480) and the turbulent glory of Athens. But contrary to what the historians keep saying, the Persian wars were not won by the Greeks; their real conclusion came in 404 with the fall of Athens, which was the work of Persian gold rather than of the Peloponnesian armies. What is more, the gigantic and uninterrupted efforts of Greek industry can be seen as a proof of the difficulty of the situation and the need to overcome obstacles. The emigration of Greek craftsmen and artists, to Etruria for instance, is surely a movement similar to that of the mercenaries making for the Middle East. All this activity led to an inevitable spread of Greek cultural influence, even in Carthage and Carthaginian Spain. But the rival system, that of Carthage, remained undoubtedly the leader in terms of commerce. In addition to Spanish silver, it had African gold.

The sea remained divided then—none of the three systems could gain complete control of it or profit from the advantages which this would have given them. We are a far cry from the triumphant unity of Rome.

CHAPTER SEVEN

The Miracle of Greece

Let us start this chapter by imagining a dialogue between two people, one of whom believes in "the eternal glory of Greece" while the other does not.

The negative view would go something like this: "Why insist so much on the splendour of ancient Greece? It is dazzling only from close quarters. The historian has a duty to stand back and keep some distance from the object of study. A play by Sophocles or Euripides certainly stirs echoes in me, going back to my schooldays, but their world is quite foreign to me. It is not our world. I believe, like Wilamowitz, that we should 'stay inside the Greek world and think in a Greek way about what is Greek'; or as Heidegger said after trying in vain to translate a line by Parmenides, that 'we should allow Greek words to tell us what they have to say in their own language.' Any confusion between present-day western civilization and that of ancient Greece is an anachronistic device, such as one finds in a Giraudoux play. The coherence of the Greek world depended on its being a closed universe. If we try to penetrate it, it will crumble away into dust."

The other speaker, who is perfectly at ease in admiring ancient Greece, and can inhabit it in his mind without feeling a stranger in his own time, would reply, quoting the splendid aphorism of Louis Gernet, " 'There is no history that does not relate to the present.' In other words, ancient Greece is a living presence for us: the Greeks of antiquity can stand for a certain basic humanity which has changed little across the ages. And like the souls of the dead who were brought to life by Odysseus' sacrifices, Greek thought is constantly being reincarnated, transmitted to us. It was to be found in Miletus in the great days of the Ionians; in Athens when Socrates was teaching there; in

Alexandria in Egypt, before the brilliant age of Archimedes in Syracuse; it was still alive in Rome, since the pathetic reduction of Greece to a Roman province in 146 B.C. was in the end a spiritual triumph by the conquered over the conquerors; it was a precious bloom cherished in a hothouse by Byzantium, that second Rome; it flowered once more in the Florence of Lorenzo de' Medici and Pico della Mirandola; and it is still alive today. As Louis Gernet put it, 'It was in Greece that the first framework for philosophical reflection was devised, and it has become commonplace to observe that our approach to the essential problems has changed very little since then.' And perhaps one is saying both too little and too much if one agrees with a modern British historian who has argued that 'the Ionian philosophers blazed the trail, and all science had to do after that was follow it.' "

Nevertheless, what really attaches us to Greek thought is science, reason and our own intellectual pride. Our passions and illusions do the rest. Surely the place that "the Greek miracle" holds in our modern western world results from the need of every civilization or human group to choose its origins, to invent forefathers of whom it can be proud. Belief in this ancestry has become a virtual necessity.

I
GREECE: A LAND OF CITY-STATES

The first embodiment of Greece to be considered takes us from the archaic period (eighth to sixth centuries B.C.) to the classical period (fifth to fourth)—in other words the age of the extraordinary flowering of the Greek city-states. Unique though it was, this age is not without analogies, in particular with the Italian cities of the Renaissance. Like them, the Greek cities were self-governing: archaic and classical Greece was divided up into many political units of small dimensions.

Wherever it took place, the appearance of such autonomous urban centres is only conceivable in the absence of large-scale territorial states, which always have gargantuan appetites for conquest. The Italian cities in their prime in the fourteenth century A.D. would have been unimaginable without the great recessions of the Middle Ages, which dealt a mortal blow to those two political giants, the Germanic Holy Roman Empire and the Papacy as operated by Innocent III. It is my belief that the ancient Greek cities would not have seen the light of day if it had not been for the recession of the twelfth century B.C. They grew up during the dark ages following the Dorian invasion, since what had collapsed with the end of Mycenaean civilization was the palace-centred state, with its mighty rulers and their all-powerful scribes, a greedy state as so many others were in the second millennium B.C.

But these cities which grew up after the storm remained fragile constructs, unprotected against possible threats from the ogre. The ogre for the cities of the Italian Renaissance (although the image does not fit terribly well at first sight) took the form of the little French king Charles VIII when he crossed the Alps in September 1494. For the Greek cities, nemesis might have taken the form of the Persian Empire under the Achaemenids, on whom the sun took a long time to set: it had the requisite monstrous proportions—but in fact this was not to be. The real menace turned out to be the barbarian of Macedonia (at least he spoke Greek!).

Greece was a collection of city-states. In marginal or remote areas like Epirus, Arcadia, Aetolia, or in the more backward north, urban life was probably not very developed. But within the confines of the Greek world proper, the city provided the model, with its petty quarrels, its freedoms, its irreplaceable way of life. This dispersion into small political units seemed logical: for the Greeks it was simply the way things were.

The natural fragmentation of the relief map of Greece, and the small size but large number of plains (20 per cent of the overall surface) seemed to preordain this political crystallization. For Aubrey de Selincourt (*The World of Herodotus*, 1962), Greece was a pattern of islands, whether real islands in the sea or "islands on dry land." Each of the Greek city-states occupied a limited terrain, with a few cultivated fields, two or three areas of grazing land for horses, enough vines and olive-groves to get by, some bare mountain slopes inhabited by herds of goats and sheep, an indented coastline with a harbour, and a city which would before long build ramparts—a little world cut off by both mountains and sea. Yes, Greece was indeed a pattern of islands.

An accident of geography was often enough to alter the balance of power between these tiny units. A few veins of gold and silver were enough to make sea-girt Siphnos a prosperous island; quarries yielding some of the finest marble, and in such quantities that people said it grew again after being extracted, made the fortune of Paros; the intensive traffic of a few ships made Chalcis, Eretria, Megara and Aegina the envy of other towns; the export of pottery vases and olive oil set Athens on the road to greatness in the days of Pisistratus "the cleverest of politicians," "the most republican of tyrants," a sort of forerunner of the enlightened despot.

All things being relative, there were of course some larger units. Sparta (8400 sq km) added to its original territory of Laconia, the land of olive-trees, the neighbouring state of Messenia, a colony in the modern sense of the term, conquered so brutally and exploited so cruelly that a rebellion seemed likely at any moment. Compared to the other city-states, Sparta had a comparatively large area—the first but not the only difference between them. But even this area should not be exaggerated: it was the equivalent of less than two present-day French *départements*, and that included bleak mountains, covered in snow in winter. Another "monster," Athens, covered no more than 2400 sq km—about the size of the Grand Duchy of Luxembourg today. The four plains making up Attica were of modest proportions. Athenians would have had plenty of opportunity to go from Eleusis to Marathon, or from Oropos in the north to Cape Sunion in the south. There overlooking the sea stands the temple of Poseidon, where we know that Plato liked to walk and talk, surrounded by his pupils. When Socrates and Phaedo followed the course of the river Ilissos, which in summer had shrunk to a trickle (taking off their sandals and walking in the stream to cool off), they could leave the Athenian plain before they were aware of it, circle round the back of Mount Hymetus and reach the plain of Mesogea. The distances were all quite small: when smoke rose from the Pnyx to announce the next meeting of the Assembly, the peasant citizen took up his staff and walked into town, summoned by both duty and pleasure.

So Greek cities always had human dimensions, and could be crossed on foot. Most of them had fewer than five thousand citizens. If they had a rich, tranquil and well-balanced hinterland, in theory they could lead an uneventful and contented existence. Sparta tried in vain to maintain a self-contained prosperity of this kind. Thebes, despite the existence of its sturdy cavalry and hoplites, did not go in for military glory (short-lived in the event) until the age of Epaminondas and Pelopidas: the Boeotian plain was simply too prosperous in the area around Lake Copais and its irrigation schemes. And since such things tend to be linked, the Boeotian countryside always followed the development of the Greek world with some delay and at a distance. The fashion for the oriental came late here, and archaic geometrical designs persisted longer than anywhere else, giving its decorative art a certain rustic charm which is missing from the great amphorae and craters of Attica. Cities with less in the way of advantages tended to look outwards. Sooner or later they had to sail the sea, to "marry it" as Venice did in a later age, to enter into conflict with those who stood in their way, and to sail to the ends of the earth. And for good or ill, there was no shortage of this kind of city.

Until the eighth century B.C., we may imagine Greece as a somewhat backward region, such as Thrace or Epirus were even in the classical period, with isolated villages, places of refuge where a still tribal way of life survived, and a few overlords who possessed land, underlings, rights, and in some cases religious privileges. It was something like Arcadia, still in a time-warp even in the age of Pausanias, or like Ithaca under Odysseus, reigned over by farmer-kings who faced unruly challengers, also farmers, while the mass of country people looked on in silence. There were no towns in those days, of course. When the Mycenaean culture collapsed, the old urban superstructure had disappeared almost everywhere.

Time, and favourable circumstances which started things moving again after the eighth century, were required for the city to rise above its rural and quasi-feudal origins. In fact, the critical factor was a very long crisis—economic, social, intellectual and religious; its origins and history were complex and many-sided. The Greek city was a sort of prototype which appears to have developed in the Greek part of Asia Minor a little more rapidly than elsewhere, before spreading to the rest of the Greek world. Since the area covered by Greek influence was a heterogeneous one—Greater Greece was much larger than Greece proper—the geographical explanation often put forward is of only partial value in its uncomplicated determinism. Similarly, economic factors, however important they may appear, can only explain one aspect (a significant one, it is true) of that curious phenomenon, the city-state.

In the first place, the population had grown. As a result, the area of land under cultivation needed to expand and the towns born of unions between villages had to absorb the people whom the countryside could no longer feed, providing a home for any who did not emigrate. At the same time, the new division of labour required more artisans. In the eighth century, metalworking was spreading, and industry was tending to cluster in the poorer district of the towns. Colonization also boosted the general economic advance. The wheels of trade performed miracles, or at any rate changed ways of life.

The most important factor was probably the arrival in the ports of mainland Greece of grain from overseas, either from Greater Greece and Sicily, in which case the distribution centre was Corinth; or from the Black Sea, in which case it was handled by the merchants and ships of Miletus, and later Athens. Even before this, grain had been shipped in from Egypt. This cheap foreign grain was itself a kind of revolution whose meaning is clear. It was a revolution, since imported grain reduced what an economist would today call the activity of the primary sector, never very profitable in itself. With this grain, carried in "hollow ships" to the port of Zea (a section of Piraeus harbour used only by the grain trade), the fields of Attica, even in the time of Pisistratus, could be devoted to more profitable produce such as olives and vines, while its industry could be developed: a process familiar in history. Holland in the seventeenth century A.D. embarked on its golden age only when it started to import Baltic grain in large quantities. That is why the grain trade was revolutionary: it modified the structures of the Greek economy and subsequently those of society. Even a great "feudal" lord, as Louis Gernet would say, would thus become a "gentleman farmer", watching commodity prices on foreign markets.

Two other "accelerators of change" were the development of the alphabet and of currency. The adoption of an alphabet reintroduced writing into a world which had lost it. And once writing was within the grasp of all, it became not only an instrument of command but a tool of trade, of communication and often of demystification. Secret laws became public thanks to the alphabet; and literature began to play the immense role it later assumed.

As for currency, the need for it had been felt before it appeared. There had been a series of primitive forms of money. In the *Iliad* (VI, 236) Diomedes' armour is described as being worth a hundred oxen; while a "woman skilled at doing many tasks" was worth only four (XXIII, 705). Gold ingots were certainly used, as were bronze ingots in the shape of oxhides, though these were less numerous than iron roasting spits (*oboloi*). It was in about 685 B.C. that authentic money (coins made of electrum, a mixture of gold and silver) appeared for the first time in history in Lydia, the rich realm of Croesus; it was in about 625, though the date is disputed, that Aegina minted the first Greek coins, soon to be imitated in all the cities of the Aegean and Phoenicia; and in 592 that Solon, the legislator of Athens, devalued by 33 per cent the Athenian drachma which had previously been aligned on the Aegina standard. So currency manipulation began almost as soon as money was invented. But most specialists think that a true monetary economy was not in place until the fourth century B.C. and the achievements of the Hellenistic period. In the eighth and seventh centuries, this stage was still a long way off.

Nevertheless, throughout the Aegean, things were stirring. Having been long cut off from the eastern world, Greece now made contact with it again through the cities on the Syrian coast, in particular Al-Mina. The luxury of this area dazzled the Greeks, whose way of life was still modest. Along with artefacts from Phoenicia and elsewhere—ivories, bronzes and pottery— Greece began to import a new style of living. Foreign decorative art came as a contrast to the stiff geometrical style. With works of art came fashions, the first elements of Greek science, superstitions, and possibly the beginnings of Dionysiac cults. All round the Aegean, the Greek cities began to grow: tiny independent worlds, basically similar but competing with each other as rivals.

The Greek city-state was a strange little world, very different from the medieval town in western Europe. The latter was quite separate from the countryside: it was self-contained, with political and economic benefits reserved to the privileged townspeople who lived *intra muros.* The Greek *polis* on the other hand, while "linked to an urban centre, was not identical with it." The "citizens" were residents of a territory greater than the city itself, which was only one element in the state, though an important one of course, since everyone made use of its market-place or agora, its citadel as a place of refuge, and its temple devoted to the divine protector of the *polis.* Politically however, it was of a piece with the surrounding territory. Even Corinth, the guardian of the roads across the isthmus, and a major trading and industrial centre, had, "like *all* the Greek city states an economy based on agriculture: the existence of a city was inconceivable without a surrounding territory, the division of which among the citizens was the basis of civic identity" (E. Will).

During the first years of the terrible Peloponnesian War (which began in 431), the Spartans would arrive in serried ranks on the pass above Eleusis every spring, as soon as the anemones were in bloom, ready to attack Attica. According to Pericles' plan of campaign, there was no point in defending the outlying territory which was so regularly invaded. The peasants had to abandon their homes and fields, leaving the invader to enter an empty country-side. The population would take refuge inside Athens and there, from the high walls of the Pelargicon, with nothing more to occupy them, they could watch the enemy arriving in the distance. The city, enclosed within its walls, and linked to the harbour at Piraeus by the Long Wall, was an island, safe from invasion: at this point state and city became one.

The dual nature of the Greek city-state, uniting city and countryside, helps us to understand the probable pattern of its creation. The process began after the Dorian invasion, as soon as peasant life once more picked up the threads of an existence which still survived in the classical period in the form of the religious festivals following on each other's heels all winter, when nature and human hands were resting from their labours. They took the form of feasts, dancing, processions, bonfires, sacrificial holocausts, all very ancient cults attached to the Earth Mother. This peasant society was linked, after the Dorian invasion and possibly even earlier, to a system of clans, patriarchal families known as the *gene*. Each *genos* was a small primitive group, self-sufficient and quarrelsome: the slightest dispute caused conflict between neighbouring clans and in this society without a regular system of justice, the vendetta or law of blood became the code of honour. Each unit had its gods, its pretensions, its myths, its chieftains who boasted of their own exploits or of those of their ancestors who had been the sons of heroes, in other words demi-gods. This all-enveloping mythology is in fact the most irrefutable proof of the ancient nature of the clans.

This all-powerful aristocracy can be glimpsed at the dawn of Greek history. Quite numerous, these clans, the "substantial," "the best," the "well-born" (the *eupatridae* of Attica), derived prestige too from their priestly functions, the wealth of their domains and their many flocks of livestock. Around them gravitated a following of clients, day-labourers and villagers in semi-serfdom. A *genos* or *patria* might join together with other *gene* to form a *phratry* thus uniting several cantons. So the nobles were the first potential basis for the foundation of a state when expanding trade made it desirable or necessary to create one. They would then be the first people to occupy the city, which turned into a useful command post: from here they could survey their land and their peasants from a convenient distance.

A city at its beginnings often had a king, but kingship (*basileia*) was soon powerless when faced with great independent landowners, rival kings themselves. They were the only ones, with their chariots, who could defend the city in time of war. They were the only people with sufficient leisure to devote themselves to public affairs, in which they could also make their own rights prevail. And they also had the power of the priesthood. The rest of the people—the *demos*—was otherwise occupied. So the early elimination of kingship was to the benefit of the patricians. In Athens, the royal power was finally divided among nine magistrates, the archons: the *basileus* who presided at sacrifices; the eponymous archon, the chief magistrate who gave his name to the year; the *polemarchos* who commanded the army; and the six *thesmothetai* who rendered justice. This aristocratic government eventually led to the permanent institution known as the Areopagus, in which the former magistrates took their place.

As always, to govern was to create resentment. It could arise in the first place among the peasants, who were more or less reduced to serfdom by the property rights of the nobles. Then there were the increasing numbers of newcomers to the city, drawn in by the expansion of the economy: there was a sort of "bourgeoisie," if the term is allowable, made up of the new rich, and on the other hand an urban proletariat of *thetes*: paid labourers, impecunious artisans, metics (foreigners) and slaves. The conditions were present, if not for a class struggle, at least for a series of social tensions and hostilities. This crisis was endemic throughout the Greek universe where patterns tended to repeat themselves; political fragmentation did not prevent a strong cultural unity from emerging.

The worst conflict was soon to be that between the city as a collective unit and the aristocracy. For the new kind of city to emerge, it would have to liberate the peasantry, and abolish the religious, legal and political privileges of the "top people." This took a long time and required many compromises, especially in the religious sphere. For the city did not simply represent a new political and geographical order; it was also a meeting of cults and gods, a religious world order which was now to be governed by the collective will rather than by the secret and arbitrary activity of the *gene*. But the latter were not abruptly destituted, as the striking and rather late example of Eleusis demonstrates. Even in Athens, which might seem to us the most revolutionary of cities, to take one example from a hundred, the Eteobutadae retained the privilege of providing the priestess of Athena Polias and the priest of Poseidon Erechtheus. In this way the past and the prestige of the great patrician families were partially maintained under the new dispensation. Athens indeed drew on the lordly culture of the *eupatridae* and assimilated their pride of identity. "The morality of the Greeks was an aristocratic morality," as Louis Gernet put it. Athens was a kind of prefiguration of the aristocratic Polish republic.

The greater involvement of the citizens in the government of their own affairs was nevertheless a major revolution, and one which developed in a climate of tension and anxiety, but also of enthusiasm.

This enthusiasm gave rise to a kind of violent city-centred patriotism. With its manageable compass, its central focus on the *prytaneion*, its agora, its universally recognized laws, and its repeated proclamation of the equality of all citizens, the city was no longer an abstraction. Julien Benda once wrote a book entitled *Histoire des Français dans leur volonté de former une nation* (*History of the French and their Desire to Form a Nation*). Who will give us a history of the ancient Greeks and their desire to create a set of limited political units, of human dimensions? The passionate love they bore their little homelands verged on the pathological, going well beyond the reasonable. They used a term meaning sexual desire, *himeros*, to refer to it: cities might be known as "Salaminos the well-beloved" or Athens "crowned with violets" which all its "lovers" will come to defend at Pericles' call. Nowhere else in world history has this love for the native soil been taken to such extremes, with the result that love could yield only to hatred. A Greek city-state, like an Italian city of the Renaissance, had its *fuorisciti*, the banished, or perhaps one should even say the excommunicated. Exiles were driven by desperation to treason, murder, lies and even, horror of horrors, entering the service of Persia!

The turmoil was not confined to politics. The tumultous return of Dionysiac cults gave rise to a sort of medieval outbreak of flagellation, first of all in the countryside, then overwhelming the cities. Another obsession was that of collective guilt, of the sacrilege which could defile an entire city as the crime of one individual rebounded on all. The Alcmaeonidae, a great patrician family of Athens to which Cleisthenes and Pericles both belonged, were on three occasions banished for having a hand in the assassination of the allies of the usurper Cylon when they had taken refuge by the altars on the Acropolis. The city became quieter only in about 590, when the Cretan Epimenides appeared there as a purifying prophet, able to assuage the gods: he sacrificed black and white ewes to them, as well as "two human victims who apparently volunteered." Sicknesses required healers, thaumaturgi, prophets, tyrants and wise men, who would become social arbitrators (such as Lycurgus, Solon and Cleisthenes) or charlatans who exploited popular credulity. Empedocles of Agrigento, a philosopher born in about 490, "proclaimed himself a god and appeared before the crowd draped in purple and crowned with flowers," practising various kinds of sorcery and resurrecting the dead. In Athens, acording to Herodotus, Pisistratus returned to power for the second time thanks to a certain amount of stage management. A chariot went before him, and in it rode a woman, tall, beautiful and armed from head to foot: Athena in person. That this miracle was believed is a sort of litmus test.

It was also in this period, the so-called pre-Socratic age, that the Philosopher appeared as a figure. The age of the Heroes was followed by the age of the Sages. According to tradition there were seven Sages: Thales of Miletus; Solon of Athens; Periander, the tyrant of Corinth; Cleobulus of Lindos; Bias of Priene; Pittacus of Mytilene and Chilon of Sparta, who embodied the "laconic speech of the Lacedaemonians." But there are plenty of other names on the list of Sages: one Hellenist has counted twenty-two, including Myson of Chen, the obscure or "unknown sage," chosen for his virtuous modesty. All this period is somewhat opaque to us now, but these individuals did exist before being absorbed into a moral legend where they are supposed above all to incarnate the persuasive wisdom of popular sayings: know thyself; nothing in excess; and so on—in other words common-sense mottoes for anxious men in troubled times.

Warfare in the archaic age meant the Athenian *eupatridae* riding out on horseback, or better still in chariots. By the seventh century, the hoplite began to be the regular soldier. The hoplite was a heavy-duty infantryman, equipped with a bronze breastplate, a shield, greaves (*cnemides*) and a long lance which he held in his right hand. He advanced towards the enemy alongside his companions in a solid phalanx: several rows of men shoulder to shoulder, presenting a protective line of shields, like the plates of body armour. The whole troop marched as one man. On the Chigi vase (*c.* 640) we see alongside the hoplites a musician playing a double flute: he is beating time and making the whole phalanx march in step. This discipline was the result of training in the gymnasium. Accordingly, the prime military virtue was not the bravery required to engage in single combat but technical proficiency and self-discipline. War was a kind of game, with its rules and its "ludic aspects." The adversaries would sometimes agree on a pitch for the battle. Such was the conflict in the seventh century B.C. on the island of Euboea between Chalcis and Eretria, and it was from this experience of warfare that the tactics of the hoplites seem to have spread to other Greek cities towards the middle of the century. In Sparta, the young men were divided into two teams to train in one of the Eurotas Islands: the losing side found itself pushed into the sea.

After an age when war was dominated by aristocrats on horseback, the hoplite ushered in the age of the foot-soldier—a revolutionary development, here as everywhere, whether in ancient Greece, in China in the sixth century B.C., or in the Swiss cantons in the sixteenth century A.D. in the days of Charles the Bold. The hoplites, who supplied their own armour and became full citizens, were recruited from the peasants in the countryside surrounding the city. A political and social revolution followed on from this, with only formal divergences from one city-state to another. In Sparta for instance the hoplites made up a professional army known as the Equals. It was in the logic of such development that military society would be integrated in some form into political society, imposing on the latter its own requirements. The Athenian peasant, owner of his own plot of land, his *kleros*, expected the city to respect his rights: it had to protect him, and deliver him from the bonds of debt which attached him to great landowners. The resolution of this difficult problem brought about some new forms of government. Solon's greatest success was the *seisachtheia*, the operation whereby he enabled the peasant literally to "shake off" his burden of debt.

The soldier-citizen had been born. Herodotus and Thucydides compared the Greek soldier, fighting for freedom, to the Persian soldier driven into battle by lashes of the whip. But the peasant-soldier also brought to a city like Athens a certain number of rural prejudices, for instance that toil on the land (and the accompanying leisure, whether that of the great landowner or that of everyone in wintertime) was the only activity really worthy of a man. Any other kind of labour reduced one's status: the artisan, the miner, the merchant or the sailor were social inferiors. Yet trade and industry were expanding: foreigners, slaves and landless peasants had to take on the menial tasks of the city and the port of Piraeus. Some of them made fortunes, others, remaining eternally poor, became the fourth estate of Solon's classification, the *thetes*. But they too would benefit from wars, eventually obtaining basic political rights (that of attending the People's Assembly) in the fifth century.

Their importance was confirmed when Athens, on the eve of the second Persian war, became a maritime power. The silver of the mines of Laurion, only recently discovered, helped build two hundred triremes. They wintered in the naval port of Cantaros in Piraeus; but every spring an army of oarsmen was required to launch them on the sea once more. The trireme was a floating battering ram, designed to strike the flank of the enemy vessel. "As a sailing ship, it had faults; unable to tack, it could only sail with a following wind. So the sail was only an extra form of power and in a naval battle the sail (*akataeion*) was hoisted only in order to escape." The trireme was able to play its role as a warship only when propelled by a mass of human brawn.

Crammed into their vessels, able to stretch out to sleep only when the boat was drawn up on land, the oarsmen had a tough job, so tough that it was later done only by forced labour. Yet in the sixteenth century A.D., in the days of Andrea Doria and Don John of Austria, there were enough poor wretches to provide voluntary labour for the galleys, the *buonavoglie* as they were called in Italy. Poverty must have had the same baleful influence in the days of Pericles, since the oarsmen were free men and were paid wages. And when the Peloponnesian fleet later beat the Athenian navy, it was with crews whom they had been able to levy thanks to Persian gold. But these oarsmen received their share of any booty, so they had the chance to make their fortune, to buy a piece of land and a slave, and aspire eventually to that leisure which in Athens conferred dignity on the individual.

In a word, the phalanx had introduced the peasant to political society, and the oar had brought in the *thetes*, previously more or less untouchables. If Athens adopted these new methods it was perhaps a sign that they were irresistible. Corinth did however oppose this mass phenomenon, and found a different solution to its internal tensions: its agreement with Sparta provided it with a policeman at the gate. At the first sign of trouble, the policeman reported for duty. Athens had chosen democracy instead.

But we should clarify what was meant by this term in antiquity. The reforms of Solon (595) and Cleisthenes (509) had limited the rights of the oligarchs and given pride of place to the powers of the *ekklesia*, the Assembly of citizens meeting on the Pnyx. In the lawcourts of the *heliaia*, citizens were also judges during trials. Except for the *strategoi*, or generals, who were in effective command of the army and were elected, all magistrates were appointed by the drawing of lots. And all citizens, whether they were magistrates, attended the Assembly (from the fourth century), sat in the lawcourts, or went to the amphitheatre, were entitled to draw an allowance. This was the system of citizen-wages. Every citizen was, as we would put it, a state employee and theoretically all-powerful.

But there were limits on this power. The *ekklesia* was obliged to take the advice of the *boule*, a sort of intermediary committee of 500 magistrates of whom fifty (replacing each other by rota every thirty-five days) sat in permanent session. And the prestige of patrician families weighed heavily here. Pericles belonged to the aristocratic dynasty of the Alcmaeonidae. Only after his death did Athenian democracy find its own leaders, of whom the first was Cleon.

Even so, this "democracy" was far from complete. Yes, the citizens had the right, real or imaginary, to be held as absolute equals. But only a few of the men of Attica had the right to the title of citizen. In about 431, there was a citizen class of 172,000, including members of their families, or in other words 40,000 men who were actually citizens out of a total population of 315,000. Democracy was the privilege of this group who stood in authority over a mass of foreigners (metics) and slaves [not to mention women, SR]. The number of slaves went on growing in later centuries. Moreover Athens was able, because of its strength, to exploit its Aegean allies in the Delian League, making them subjects and tributaries. The city also exploited distant markets, by exporting ceramics, fabrics and oil in exchange for the grain it needed to survive.

In short, Athens was a privileged city which oppressed others. Enough at any rate to make us disagree entirely with J.-L. Borges when he writes that "Athens was only a rudimentary version of Paradise." Earthly paradises are always rudimentary, but their gates are not open to all comers.

The universe created by the city controlled the life of its citizens, shaping their thoughts, their actions and their art. This role of matrix operated even in the sphere of philosophy and religion: the way the natural universe, its origins and its equilibrium were understood by philosophers reflected the city and its own particular order.

The decline of the sacrosanct patrician families, allied, as the priest-kings of the past had been, to the dark forces of the supernatural, had returned official religion to the authority of the city, making it an aspect of public affairs. The sacred and the mysterious had been expelled to the margins of society. In the same way, cremation, which had come with the Dorian invasion, had separated the dead from previous forms of ancestor-worship. With the establishment of the earthly city, centred on the agora, and no longer on the sacred

Acropolis (to which Plato wished to return it), religion had become a less constricting garment. Moreover there was no clergy here as there was in Egypt or Babylon: any Greek could officiate as priest and no one was normally appointed permanently to the priesthood. The cities found that this made their tasks considerably easier. They were free to organize festivals, to effect a surface reconciliation between cults which were apparently incompatible, rather as we now organize towns for the safety of pedestrians. Thus Eleusis became the point of departure for the procession of the Panathenians to the Parthenon on the Acropolis, in honour of the official cult of Athena, using the sacred way, with the grooves for the chariots laid down in advance. Being thus linked to the daughter of Zeus, the tutelary goddess of the city, the Eleusinian mysteries became more official, and lost something of their autonomy. The Dionysiac rites became an occasion for theatrical performances, a meeting point between religion and urban life, thus defusing a potentially explosive conflict. Aeschylus, Sophocles and Euripides portrayed in their plays the great figures of Homeric epic, giving the public exactly what it wanted from them—such was the condition of any success.

It was, however, only to be expected that people of sensibility should look beyond these over-consensual cults and their routine rituals for a more authentic religious life. The mysteries, with their purification rituals, the marvellous promise of salvation, and the soul's journey towards a new eternal life exerted a strong attraction. The origins of the Pythagorean revolt are only too comprehensible. Taking refuge in 525 in Croton (a sort of Geneva *avant la lettre*) Pythagoras introduced there a reign of justice in which the essential aim was the salvation of souls, not that of the earthly city. This attitude was regarded as scandalous: the ascetic life and fasting of the Pythagoreans, their attempts to adapt Orphic cults, led all cities to condemn their stance as a kind of dereliction of civic duty, comparable with a little exaggeration to that of a conscientious objector today. There was no one at the time—the sixth century B.C.—capable of seeing the Pythagoreans' embryonic "science," their pursuit of golden numbers and mathematical ratios, as a positive counterweight to the civic ethos. In Athens after the defeat of 404, Socrates was accused of every crime against his fatherland. What did the Athenians wish to punish him for—his friendship with Alcibiades and Critias, opponents of democracy, his pursuit of Orphic and Pythagorean ideas, or even (and this might explain the "Socrates mystery") his position as defender of individual perfection, of an effort which was intrinsically a sin against the collective world of the city-state?

Greek art was gradually locked into the same straitjacket. The art whose original flowering one so admires, freed from imitation of foreigners or from the patronage of the rich, an art which had acquired its own self-confidence, finally entered bag and baggage into the service of the state. The age of Pericles was an age of official art: the workshops, sculptors, stone-masons and foremen were all working for Athens. One cannot complain about this since it bequeathed us the Parthenon. But all official art is already secretly contaminated: it prefers to define its rules and canons and to stick to them, soon degenerating into repetition and pale imitation. By the law which makes classical and romantic movements alternate in turn, Greek art ended up lapsing into the baroque excesses of the Hellenistic style, with a mannerism that was by turns both charming and tragically grandiloquent.

The destiny of Greece was decided by war: first the Persian wars (from 499, the date of the Ionian uprising, to the peace of 450) then the Peloponnesian War (431–404.) Things might have turned out differently in both cases. The handful of Athenian and Plataean hoplites might have been defeated at Marathon (490); the Greek fleet might not have triumphed in 480 in the narrow channel between the island of Salamis and the mainland. Later on, Athens might not have yielded to the sudden passion which drove it to launch the insane Sicilian expedition of 415; and while we are rewriting history, why not imagine that the Athenians might even have won the battle of Syracuse?

But, as we know, Greece was fragmented into a patchwork of independent city-states, all of which were liable to fall prey to their often extreme passions. And these passions were in the end fatal. Was it conceivable that this constellation of autonomous worlds could live in harmony and mutual respect? Aubrey de Selincourt thought so, as he wrote the last pages of his moving and almost always convincing book. But surely this is to ask the impossible. De Selincourt is shocked that one Greek city could set about destroying another, that Croton should destroy Sybaris, or Athens subdue Aegina or Megara. Worse still, Athens first concluded an alliance with the free cities of the Aegean, then in 454 transported to its own city the League's treasure, which had previously been held on Delos, the island of Apollo. Already before this date, Athens had been throwing its weight about. But in 454 any illusions vanished: the allies (*summachoi*) had become subjects (*hupekooi*). It was a betrayal.

This said, and it is all quite true, is it fair to blame Pericles, who was then embarking on a long political career which would end only with his death in 429? The godlike leader certainly did not invent imperialism in general, nor Athenian imperialism in particular. His predecessor Themistocles, creator of the Athenian navy, a regular fighting force, must certainly take some responsibility for that. But historians prefer to put prominent figures in the dock. Everything we have been taught to value about Pericles—his intelligence, his refusal to follow the crowd, his elegance, his eloquence, the quality of his friends, his unusual incorruptibility—all single him out as a good candidate for reappraisal. Of course Pericles had dreamed of Athenian hegemony. According to his friend Anaxagoras, mind (*nous*) rules the world and Athens was to become that mind, guiding the imperfect body of Greek states. This ideal could never be reached without fighting the obscurantism of Sparta, the jealousy of Corinth and the rancours of the allies. Pericles saw this war coming and worked it out in advance: the Athenians should abandon the land and hold on to the sea. The plan brought neither victory nor the salvation of Greece, it is true. But is its author on that account to be held guilty?

To keep the debate brief, let one historian speak as counsel for either side. For René Grousset, who is certainly no grand inquisitor, Pericles could have maintained peace with the complicity of the active and sincere Archidamus, the pro-Athenian king of Sparta, but he deliberately let the occasion slip and chose to go to war. Alfred Weber on the other hand (1935) was perhaps too much the prisoner of a certain German historical literature when he wrote that Pericles took a masterly view of the situation: choosing to fight on sea was the right choice for victory, but the Athenians were simply not up to the grandiose strategy!

My own version would probably disappoint both advocates. It is surely an illusion to believe that great men hold the destiny of the state in their hands, since destiny deals with them as it does with everyone else, and in some ways relieves them of responsibility. It is far from clear that the battle which eventually tore Greece apart was one of those conflicts that might have been avoided with a little common sense and a great deal of magnanimity. A unified Greece was never possible in peace or war. The major explanation of Pericles' action is that Athens had come to assume quite disproportionate importance within the fragile Greek constellation, because of a past which Pericles had inherited and not created. It was the result of a trading combination which brought the city much advantage, since the grain and salt fish of the Black Sea were shipped directly to Athens and this cheap supply of food nourished the expansion of the city, allowed its industries to expand and in particular made possible a capitalism which depended on a low-paid work-force, as it faced growing economic difficulties.

The drama of the Greek city-states was rather like that of the cities of the Italian Renaissance. None of them, not Florence, nor Venice, Genoa or Milan—was able in the end to unify Italy. Athens in 404 opened its gates to Lysander. But neither the victory of anachronistic Sparta, nor the ephemeral rise of Thebes under Epaminondas would throw up any force more capable than Athens of constructing Greek unity. The end-point of the process was the arrival of the great barbarian of Macedonia. His coming had been prepared long before.

II
ALEXANDER'S MISTAKE

The title of this section should not lead the reader to expect a critical analysis of Alexander's Asian campaigns. In his "meteoric" adventure, what happened in the east tends to distract us from what happened—or ought to have happened—in the west. Alexander's great mistake, in my view, was that he failed to recognize the value of the western Mediterranean. He threw himself into a brilliant course of action laid out for him in advance, and which led the other way.

The subjection of Greece to the Macedonian yoke was a consequence of the very expansion of Greek civilization. All the northern fringes of Greek culture—Macedonia, Thrace, Pontus, the Bosphorus and Bithynia—had forged ahead in the fourth century B.C. Macedonia, an inhospitable region, snow-covered in winter, flooded in springtime, with its free peasantry and its warlords accustomed to sorties on horseback, was the one that eventually took the lead. This was logical enough, since the malaise of the Greek city-states had created—as could also be said of fifteenth-century Italy—a cyclonic zone of low pressure, into which currents were drawn from all sides.

Philip II of Macedon (c. 383–336) had turned to his own advantage the squabbles of the Greek cities. They were forced under the Macedonian yoke on the field of Chaeronea in 338. We need not enter into the detail of this familiar story or take sides for or against Demosthenes and Athens. Nor should we mourn too much for the latter: it was spared by the Macedonian conqueror on account of the Athenian fleet with which he hoped to reach the shores of Asia Minor. But Philip never realized his dream, since he was assassinated in 336. His son Alexander, aged twenty, inherited the task. Scarcely pausing to bring under his sway first the Epirots and then the Thebans, whose city he razed to the ground, Alexander crossed the Hellespont in 334, accompanied by the contingents of the pan-Hellenic League as reinforcements.

In that spring of 334, the fortunes of Hellenism from the Spanish coast to the Aegean and the Black Sea were far from being tragic or catastrophic. They were uncertain perhaps, and not particularly promising. Dangers lay around, but none of them was new. Probably Greece itself in the narrow sense was the least healthy of the Hellenic regions.

In the western sea, Greeks and Carthaginians were still skirmishing. They would fight, make a treaty and start again. There was, it is true, a new threat in the form of Rome, which had taken control of rich Campania in 341 and of Latium in 338 and was already looking like a "lair of wolves" waiting to pounce on the rest of Italy. But the Greek cities were not as yet fully aware of this danger.

The other conflict, to the east, was the endemic warfare with the Persian Empire. The Great King controlled the essential sea-crossings between Asia Minor and Egypt. The latter, however reluctantly, was among his most profitable possessions. Since the days of the pharaoh Necho, a "Suez canal" had linked the Red Sea to the Nile. And the gigantic Persian Empire—which it took three months to cross from Sardis to Susa, by the Royal Road—extended to the Indian Ocean from where it imported rare merchandise for the Mediterranean. Indeed, during the tough "nationalist" reign of Artaxerxes III (358–337) the balance of trade had swung against Greece, which had to pay for Persian grain and manufactured goods partly with silver.

Out of lassitude, a sort of peaceful but wary co-existence had developed between the Greeks and the Persians. Greek ships and the Phoenician vessels in the service of Persia had come to observe a sort of *modus vivendi*, with their own reserved areas. And the Persian Empire was routinely recruiting Greek mercenaries. This non-hostile situation might have continued. If we argue with hindsight in terms of "historical" strategy, we can accept that in 334 or so, there were at least two possible options: either the overcrowded Balkan peninsula could have attacked the great Achaemenid Empire in a new Trojan war, this time on a grand scale, or the forces of Greece could have turned instead against Carthage, the Italic peoples and Rome. This would have been a less glorious option: the rich prizes and grand civilizations lay in the Orient. The west, for all the Punic and Greek successes there, did not appeal to the imagination in anything like the same way. But let us allow ourselves to imagine a Greek version of the "prose that was Rome:" Greece would have conquered the entire Mediterranean from east to west, turning it into a Greek lake, instead of the Roman lake it became after a conquest which ran the other way, from west to east.

Thinking of this destiny which never came about, one is tempted to agree with the still stimulating book by Ulrich von Hassel, *Das Drama des Mittelmeers* (1940), which concentrates on the amazing adventures of Pyrrhos of Epirus (let us give him back his Greek name) a couple of generations after the death of Alexander the Great (323).

The king of Epirus had been called on in 280 to help Tarentum. When he arrived there with some thirty thousand men and thirty elephants, he already had an eventful career behind him. A hostage in Alexandria in his youth, he had married an Egyptian princess; then having become ruler of Corcyra (Corfu) and briefly of the whole of Macedonia, he acted as a sort of *condottiere*, ready to go anywhere for money if it suited his fancy or his interest. His elephants created havoc among the Roman legions at Heraclea in the summer of 280; the following year he repeated his exploit at Ausculum, but with more difficulty; in 278 he landed in Sicily, probably the land of his dreams and ambitions and relieved Syracuse from a siege by the Carthaginians; in 277 he entered Agrigento. But Greek Sicily was war-weary. In autumn 276, Pyrrhos returned to Italy; in 275 he was harassed at Beneventum by the Romans, and left the peninsula; and in 272 he met an accidental death in Argos.

Pyrrhos' Italian adventures are trivial compared to the fantastic conquests of Alexander the Great fifty years or so earlier. But in a sense and with hindsight, they provide a verdict on them. Pyrrhos' eventual failure, which stands for the failure of Greece against Rome on the central axis of the sea, was a direct corollary of the "wrong-headed" conquests (as I see it) of the Macedonian Wunderkind. With Alexander, Greece had swung round to face east and south, towards Asia Minor, Syria and Egypt. The last emigration of the Greeks westward—some sixty thousand people apparently in response to a desperate appeal by Timoleon, the ruler who restored the freedom of Syracuse—dates from about 338. Admittedly, Alexander is thought to have contemplated attacking Carthage, which lived in fear of such an assault for years on end. But in 323 Alexander died in Babylon and his empire began to fall apart at once.

What would have happened to Italy if Alexander had ignored Asia and turned his forces on the west? Von Hassel's question is the kind that comes under fire for seeking to rewrite history, but it is tempting all the same to think of Syracuse as the centre of a Greek Empire triumphing over both Rome and Carthage and bequeathing a Greek culture to the west directly, without Rome stepping in to act as intermediary and screen. But the war which never took place was effectively lost. Like it or not, the issue of who was to rule the Mediterranean was already being decided at that point in history in the central area of the sea, between the two basins.

No one has ever satisfactorily explained Alexander's conquest of Persia. It is the apparent ease with which he accomplished it that puzzles one. Neither the familiar claims for the strengths of Macedonia and Greece nor those concerning the weakness or even decay of the Persian Empire are particularly convincing.

The latter had been in existence for a century, but a century is nothing in the lifetime of such an organism. And the monster looked quite healthy, despite a few internal problems. The roads were busy, the administration as efficient as it could be in those far-off days. As regards beliefs, Persia was already tolerant, as Islam was to be in later times. The adventure of the Ten Thousand by no means pointed to any fatal weakness. When Cyrus the Younger tried to dethrone his brother Artaxerxes, the "Ten Thousand" were Greek mercenaries in his service: they were victorious at the battle of Cunaxa (401) but the death of Cyrus on the battlefield cancelled out his triumph. The Greeks then managed to persuade Artaxerxes to withdraw towards the Black Sea: they miraculously escaped the treachery of the Persians, thanks to the energetic action of Xenophon, and finally reached the Bosphorus where they took ship. The episode pointed to internal Persian conflicts and to the success of a group of determined men, but it also revealed the poverty of Greece: it was apparently condemned to export its surplus men, the vagabonds who so worried Isocrates, to the rich state of Persia which could afford to employ them. The episode of the Ten Thousand as told in Xenophon's *Anabasis*, while "an admirable piece of war reporting," is in the end the story of a retreat.

As for the policy of corruption practised in Greece by the *basileis*, the Great Kings, this is evidence neither of strength nor of weakness. It enabled the Persians indirectly to defeat Athens in 404, and they also benefited from their alliance with Sparta to impose the peace of Antalcidas (386) which gave them control of the Greek cities in Asia Minor.

What does all this signify? I would like to point to two explanations, one of them often put forward and obviously carrying some weight, the other virtually unknown, although it was first formulated long ago.

The first stresses the logical connection between the first campaigns of Alexander: in 334 he was victorious at the Granicus, and in 333 in Issus and Tyre, which he captured after a long siege. Then he occupied Egypt without a fight. During these lightning campaigns, the victorious army simply worked its way round the shoreline of the Mediterranean. Thus as if with a surgeon's knife, the huge mass of the Persian Empire was detached from the Mediterranean: its roads were cut, and now led nowhere. The symbol of this surgical operation was the capture and physical and human liquidation of Tyre and Gaza, which had put up a desperate defence but which the conqueror destroyed leaving no stone standing nor defender alive. Without its fleet, the great empire was blind. In 331, after this operation, Alexander fought his way east towards the heart of the Persian Empire. The fate of the empire was sealed on the far side of the Tigris, at the battle of Gaugamela. Completion of the conquest meant pursuing Darius, bringing to heel the satraps east of Iran, and descending upon the Indus—fantastic journeys and difficult feats of prowess; but by 331, the Persian Empire had been brought to its knees.

The second explanation was suggested by E.-F. Gautier in 1930. The strength of Alexander's army (and of the little group of Macedonians who formed his general staff and the core of his companions in fighting, drinking and general roistering) lay in the cavalry. Until then the Greek hoplite, a foot-soldier, had never had the effective protection of a real corps of cavalry. The Persians, who by contrast had excellent horses and horsemen, had had to recruit infantry-men from the other side to protect themselves against Greek incursions. In 334 the army they fielded in the first encounters with Alexander was commanded by a Greek, Memnon, and largely made up of Greek mercenaries fighting as foot-soldiers.

The new element introduced by Alexander, alongside the phalanx, which remained a formidable and respected force, was therefore the corps of cavalry, based on selective horse-breeding and effectively a way of life for the Macedonian warlords. Horses proved to be the ideal war machine to conquer the great expanses of the Persian Empire. In later times, in the days of Crassus, Antony and Trajan, Rome was unable to conquer the Parthians, for want of a genuine cavalry force. We might reflect that the reconquest of the Balkans from the Turks in the eighteenth century A.D. was achieved thanks to the Austrian cavalry, a late development which provided Prince Eugene with the key to victory.

The Persians, of course, had perfectly good cavalry of their own: the Persian nobles were born horsemen. But the Macedonian force had the double advantage of being heavy, well protected and well armed, the cavalrymen wielding both lance and sabre. It was also divided into squadrons; in other words, efficiently commanded. It was this discipline which led to its triumph at the Granicus, Issus and on the Tigris.

Persia was conquered in a rapid movement, just as in the past it had conquered others—Mesopotamia or Egypt. It collapsed after a single campaign, a sort of Blitzkrieg, like a healthy man struck down suddenly by illness in the prime of life. Similar episodes occurred during the Muslim, Mongol and Turkish conquests. On each occasion speed, whether of horses or camels, was a vital factor. We might reflect that in 1940, France, neither a decadent nor a poor nation, was defeated in a lightning campaign by German armoured divisions, the twentieth-century version of cavalry. History is full of "unkind strokes of fate."

On Alexander's death in June 323, his empire fell apart almost at once. It would be a long story to describe what happened to these fragments, Macedonia, Syria under the Seleucids, and Egypt under the Lagids, between this date and the establishment of the Pax Romana.

Apart from political events, there took place what one has to call, for want of a better term, a colonization of the Middle East by the Greeks, as a people and a dominant culture became established there. This colonization, which Rome inherited, lasted about ten centuries, until the Muslim conquests of the seventh century A.D.—which are as hard to understand at first sight as the victory of the "young god" Alexander.

Ten centuries elapsed—in other words, enough to embrace the whole of the known history of France. And yet, "after ten centuries, at one stroke of the Arab scimitar, everything collapsed overnight: Greek language and thought, western patterns of living, everything went up in smoke. On this territory, a thousand years of history were as if they had never been. They had not been sufficient for the west to put down the slightest roots in this oriental soil. The Greek language and social customs had been no more than a layer, a poorly fitting mask. All the Greek cities which had been founded and grown up, from the banks of the Nile to the Hindu Kush, any real or apparent implantation of Greek art and philosophy, all of it had gone with the wind."

Well, perhaps we have to accept that. And looking at it from the other end of history, after the attempts at European colonization on Islamic soil, the historian may conclude that no conquering civilization can ever succeed in countries with a very ancient cultural identity. Impenetrable "walls" prevent acculturation taking place. Perhaps the expansion of civilizations is only possible when they encounter primitive cultures.

It was in order to emphasize this long-term problem that the title of this section referred rather condescendingly to "Alexander's mistake." If Hellenism, with all the vigour and critical mass it possessed at that moment, had turned towards the west and its comparatively unknown lands, might it not have pre-empted the destiny of Rome?

Let us move on several centuries. In 148 B.C., Macedonia had been reduced to a Roman province. Two years later, following agitation from Corinth and the Achaean trouble-makers yet again, Rome intervened, Corinth was razed to the ground, and Greece too was reduced to the status of a province. Only Sparta, Athens and Delphi had the privileged status of federated cities.

This subjugation to Rome was simply one link in a long chain. Syracuse was captured by Marcellus in 212; Tarentum was occupied by Fabius Maximus in 209. And the last stages in this chronology were to be the reduction to the status of Roman provinces of Syria in 63 and Egypt in 31.

By the end of this protracted process, the Greek sphere of influence had been incorporated by Rome into a Mediterranean unit which was for centuries to come to be the basis of Rome's might and its daily existence. Gradually, sooner or later, the men from Italy established their rule, administering and governing, putting an end to the freedoms and turbulence of the old city-states and the pretensions of former kingdoms. The Mediterranean became a calmer place, lulled into somnolence by the benefits and the dangers of the "heavy uniformity of the Pax Romana." Yet at the same time, Greek immigrants flocked to Rome, as the capital of the world was "Hellenized." The vanquished were taking their revenge.

III
GREEK SCIENCE AND THOUGHT
(EIGHTH TO SECOND CENTURIES B.C.)

In what follows, special emphasis will be placed on science, the road to the future which the Greeks so brilliantly opened. But science was part of a greater whole: it was contained and surrounded and transcended by Greek thought in a more general sense, and that in its turn was part of a complex "set of sets": what we would today call Greek civilization. In this galaxy, everything was connected.

But this very coherence is problematic. It is concealed under a great mass of scholarship, and a huge literature, which tackles only one sector at a time. We have many histories of Greek literature (one can still consult with profit that by A. and M. Croiset dating from 1887–93); and there are plenty of histories of philosophy—every generation rewrites this for itself. Histories of Greek art, thanks to today's improved technology, captivate us with their magnificent illustrations; there are some excellent histories of religion, and even histories of everyday life. But what is lacking in the end is an overall work, a comprehensive synthesis—and perhaps it is impossible even to envisage any such, since we cannot yet grasp what its underlying concept would be.

Claude Lévi-Strauss once joked to me that a few minutes' conversation with Plato would tell him more about Greek thought than all the books on his shelves. Well, I am not so sure: to find out about it on the spot would mean a hundred interviews. What one would really like to do is spend a year in Miletus in about 600 B.C., another in Samos in 550 and so on, jumping across time and space. My own preferences go to the early stages of Greek thought—long before Herodotus, Socrates or Phidias, or even Thales of Miletus. Perhaps this is a matter of taste: the great compositions of classical art are not my favourites. But it is also a question of tactics. The most obscure problem about Greek civilization is how did it all begin?

To distinguish between the different periods is of course a necessary step, although a somewhat tedious one. The historian always prefers to divide up the difficulty and find security in what Benjamin Farrington (1965) calls "a kind of scaffolding." He distinguishes between three stages in the general development of Greek science: from 600 to 400 B.C., when for the first time in human history, "a scientific conception of the world and of science was elaborated"; the years from 400 to 320, with Plato and Aristotle, which saw the major flowering of philosophy; and finally the years from 320 to 120, under the patronage of the Ptolemies in the great city of Alexandria in Egypt, when the various branches of the sciences set up their "state of the art" compendia: this was the time of the encyclopedia, the summa and the textbook, the time for final reckonings which is so often a signal that something is coming to an end.

This periodization is debatable of course. The dates chosen (especially the first one: I would myself prefer to take 800 B.C. rather than 600) could be different. But its value lies in setting up an easily understood dialectic from one period to another, which allows us to detect the overall process, with the very beginning, the "Greek spring" so to speak, being in my view the key moment.

The centuries from 800 to 400 saw the rise of the cities and the flowering of art, with a succession of styles: from the geometrical to the orientalizing and the classical; it was the time of grand sculpture and architecture, the time when the Doric and Ionian orders were defined, by the sixth century, to be followed by the Corinthian. And it was also the great age of literature. During these four centuries, every kind of writing appeared and flourished, starting with the epic. First came Homer, then Hesiod; lyric verse was scarcely present at first but reached a pinnacle with Pindar (514–438), by which time we have already reached the fifth century with the aristocratic poet of Thebes and the passionate devotee of Delphi. It was only long after Hesiod that the religious festivals in Athens gave birth to tragedy and comedy, during the reign (glorious in spite of everything) of Pisistratus (560–527).

This order of succession was the regular pattern one finds in many national literatures. In the case of France for instance, our national literature starts more or less with the *Song of Roland,* and our theatre was born out of mysteries and passion plays.

But what does this development tell us? It is at this point that, consciously or not, all commentators begin to introduce value judgements about the merits of Greek art and philosophy. Would Nietzsche have caused such a scandal today as he did in 1871 by pronouncing that the decadence of Greece started at least with Euripides and was clear to see with Socrates? He puts the high point at the moment of the birth of tragedy when Apollo and Dionysus were reconciled: "the Apollonian notion of beauty" which is a clear consciousness, a translation of the "world as it appears" into an aesthetic and rational vision, and the Dionysiac spirit of mystic ecstasy and intoxication, with the orgiastic music of the Bacchanalian choruses overcoming clarity and self-consciousness. But this reconciliation only lasted for a while. In the end, "the ambiguous god of wine and death yielded the stage to Apollo and the triumph of rationality, to theoretical and practical utilitarianism [in other words science] as well as democracy, which was a contemporary phenomenon": these were the "symptoms of [the] ageing" of Greek civilization and for Nietzsche they foreshadowed the depressing spectacle of the modern western world.

The language he used may have aged itself, but not perhaps the idea that Greek thought was most vigorous in its youth. "Everything I write," says Aubrey de Selincourt, "tends to reject the very widespread idea that the pinnacle of Hellenic civilization coincided with the 'Age of Pericles.' Brilliant though that age may have been, I consider it on the contrary to mark the end of many things which were among the most precious characteristics of that remarkable race." I am strongly inclined to share this view. Hence my choices of periodization. I would prefer not to extend the golden age far beyond Herodotus, the extraordinary father of history who was also the founding father of geography and anthropology; and to set aside Thucydides, the scientific historian of the short term, despite his exceptional talents; I would include in those marvellous springtime years (despite a little problem with the chronology) Hippocrates of Cos (?460–?377), the father of scientific medicine, and even Protagoras of Abdera, the first of the Sophists (those travelling orators who claimed to teach the art of government and whom Plato so disliked, but in whom we might detect the very first sociologists, marginal though they were); and I would finally draw a line before Plato and Aristotle. I may be burnt as a heretic for saying so, but in my view by the time they came on the scene, everything worthwhile had been accomplished.

Greece in Asia, where Greek science first began in the sixth century, was closely linked to an Asia Minor which had recovered quickly from the

Scythian and Cimmerian invasions, as well as to neo-Hittite Syria, to Palestine, Egypt, which could be reached by sea, and to Assyria, the new and violent but very lively incarnation of ancient Mesopotamia. Thales of Miletus was reputed, rightly or wrongly, to be the son of a Phoenician woman, and to have travelled in Egypt and Mesopotamia where he learned geometry and astronomy.

These details might not matter if we did not now know for certain that Egypt and Mesopotamia, and before them the varied cultures of the Middle East, already had solid foundations in scientific enquiry. The measuring of fields in Egypt (which had to be done every year after the floods) and the astronomy of the Babylonians, based on a ritual and meticulous observation of the stars and planets, gave rise to substantial progress in both algebra and geometry. We might amuse ourselves by trying to solve the problems which the Egyptians solved, but using other means. What number comes to 19 if you add one seventh to it? answer: $16 + \frac{1}{2} + \frac{1}{8}$ (try it with decimals). Prove that the sides of a hexagon inscribed within a circle are equal to the radius of the circle. A piece of string divided into three parts in the proportions 3, 4 and 5 will form a right-angled triangle. For the value of pi, while they originally adopted 3, which meant identifying the circle with the perimeter of the hexagon, they finally arrived at a pretty close approximation, 3.1604. The Babylonians also resolved problems relating to surface area: given the surface area of 600 units of any size, what is their length and breadth, if their difference, squared and multiplied by 9, is equal to the square of the length? Answer: length 30 by width 20. It is doubtful whether one could arrive unaided at the method of reasoning adopted by the Egyptians or the Babylonians. But the detail of these complex calculations is less important than the knowledge and reasoning lying behind them.

Alongside this early mathematics, there was some pioneering chemistry in Babylon, medicine in Egypt, and astronomy in Mesopotamia, where the sky had been observed for centuries from the ziggurats. The documents amassed there were of great help to Thales and probably enabled him to predict the eclipse of the sun on 28 May 585, fortunately visible from Asia Minor.

In short, the Greek miracle was founded on a solid basis established long before. But Greek science did not simply develop the work of its predecessors. It had to invent a new cast of thought, a new way of asking questions about the world and interpreting observations, and to claim the right to decide between competing explanations. The Greek miracle—which we might identify with the acceptance of the world of hypotheses—was part of the demystification of the sacred which had occurred within the Greek world view. But as in all cases of intellectual innovation—which often scandalize contemporaries—this did not happen overnight or even in a clear and fully conscious manner.

The birth of science obviously involved a whole society and its technology. Egyptian society had been built in the age of bronze and great empires. Greek science was born in the age of iron and city-states.

It was Miletus (rather than Ephesus, although the remarkable philosopher Heraclitus was born in the latter city) that saw the first pioneering form of Greek science. Since the sixth century, the city had had a hundred or so trading posts on the shores of the Black Sea. In Italy it had a powerful colony in Sybaris, which re-exported its industrial merchandise, and it was also present in Egypt in the vital trading centre of Naucratis. So Miletus was an important commercial city, one of the most significant of the Hellenic constellation in the sixth century. Science is always the daughter of leisure, possible only in a society where there are privileged people with free time on their hands, notably in great cities. All the Ionian giants of philosophy—Thales, Anaximander, Anaximenes—are examples of this rule.

Unfortunately we know very little about their work, which is why they are always mentioned in the same breath rather than individually. They were all indeed concerned with attempting to explain the universe, the problem that every civilization encounters from the start. The question has either to be dismissed or answered to the best of one's ability. Egypt and Babylonia handled the question by appealing to miraculous explanations, the gods always being there to back up their reasoning. Ionian "positivism" got rid of the gods, expelling them from the natural world and relying rather on the elements which were thought of as acting in themselves, being *living matter*. For Thales, everything derived from a single principle: Water. After all, the Babylonians used to say that Marduk had drawn mud and earth out of the original mighty waters. "But Thales ignored Marduk and imagined a universe formed out of water by a natural process."

Anaximander's creation hypothesis is better known: he imagined four elements: Earth, Fire, Water and Vapour (not Air as is sometimes said), which were disposed one on top of the other. Fire, on the outside surrounding the rest, made some of the water evaporate, then the earth split apart and turned into wheels of fire. This view is sometimes described as comparing the creation of the world with a blacksmith's forge or a potter's furnace.

In fact Anaximander had a geometric image of the universe. The elements, however they struggled and whatever forms they assumed, had to be in some kind of equilibrium, an "equality of power." All of them derived ultimately from the infinite indeterminate substance which he called *apeiron*, a neutral material from which binary oppositions emerged: dark and light, hot and cold, dry and wet, thick and thin, as well as Water, Vapour and Fire. These elements in turn combined to give rise to living creatures, plants, animals, humans, according to a natural order whereby no one element dominated the others in any form of *dunasteia* or *monarchia*. A doctor and Pythagorean philosopher, Alcmeon, repeated in the early fifth century the image which by then had become commonplace that "health was a balance of powers, *isonomia ton dunameon*, while sickness resulted on the contrary from the domination of one element over the others" (J.-P. Vernant).

In short, this was a view of a cosmos without a hierarchy, where no one element fully obeyed another, a world in which conflicts balanced out, reminding us irresistibly of the social and political structure of the *polis*. Government was no longer in the hands of gods or kings but in the hands of men who had equal rights. Anaximander's universe reflected the idealized equilibrium of the city-state. The world view changed because the world had changed and it became possible to project the everyday world on to the cosmos. J.-P. Vernant sums it up as follows: "When Aristotle defines man as a political animal, he is pointing to something that differentiates Reason in the Greek sense from that of our time. If in his eyes *Homo sapiens* was *Homo politicus*, that was because Reason was itself political in essence."

There is little here of course which relates to the "empirical reasoning" of modern science, based on methodical observation from which the laws of nature can be deduced. But Ionian physics, based on theory rather than on experimental truth, was nevertheless the first step towards modern science, for two reasons. In the first place it was looking for a reasonable explanation and was experimenting with the language of mathematics which is itself a form of rationality. If the earth, in Anaximander's system, was in perfect balance at the centre of the cosmos, and did not need to be supported (by water, as Thales claimed, or by a cushion of air, which was Anaximenes' explanation) that was because it was truly in the centre, and sustained by equal pressure from every quarter.

Secondly, once the gods had vacated the field as the explanation of the universe, every hypothesis could be entertained: humans had become free to seek and imagine; and from now on they would not cease to do so. Anaxagoras of Clazomenae, who apart from his own merits was the man who introduced Milesian thought to Athens (from 460), believed he had confirmed the earthly nature of the stars by studying the huge meteorite which fell at Aigos Potamos in 468 or 467 and which was still being studied in the age of Pausanias.

At the heart of all this, one would like to know more about the obvious role experimental technology must have played in the "new" city of Miletus, whether the furnace or potter's kiln, the trading ship, or the money-changer's shop! One can at least marvel at the first overall map of the Mediterranean drawn up for mariners by Hecateus of Miletus who had sailed in 500 as far as the Pillars of Hercules. All the good fairies stood around the cradle of Greek science. Their gifts were: foreign influence, mathematics, technological experiment, a certain absence of religious constraints and a taste for generalization.

From now on all the Greek thinkers would try to come up with an explanation of the origins of the world, and their solutions followed on and contradicted one another, from one city to the next. Interpreting them is often very difficult. Who would dare say he has understood Heraclitus of Ephesus, poet, prophet, philosopher, and well-deserving of his nickname "the Obscure"? Socrates is supposed to have said that to venture into this deliberately complex thought sytem, one ought to be a "diver of Delos" and have the same agility! What is more, only a few more or less authentic fragments have come down to us, often strangely beautiful in "their oracular brevity, [not unlike] Pascal's *Pensées*." One could wonder for ever, when reading these fragments or the commentaries on them by ancient philosophers and historians of thought, what it was that Heraclitus really thought, or even what direction his thought was taking. Was he a physicist, a mystic, an initiate of the Orphic and Dionysiac mysteries, a logician or a natural philosopher? Every interpretation has been put on his thought.

What is clear, however, is that Heraclitus was searching—in the authentically Milesian way—for a logical interpretation of nature. For him, fire was the key transforming agent, "the lightning that drives the universe": "Fire comes to life by the death of the Earth, and Air by the death of Fire; Water lives by the death of Air and the Earth by the death of Water." "Everything flows" through the metamorphosis of one element into another so that "all becoming is a struggle" and "the world is a harmony of tensions, by turns taut and relaxed, like the strings on a lyre or a bow." This is the language of a visionary. It is not surprising that "the great Heraclitus" was for Nietzsche the symbol of the "Dionysiac profundities."

But Heraclitus believed that everything obeyed an immutable law, by means of which "the ambient milieu is provided" with reason. "There is only one wisdom: to know the Thought which guides all things through the Whole," and he who penetrates the "heart of the universe" will be able to cure the ills of the universe and even the ills of human beings. Surely this idea of a superior law, intelligible to human reason, which the sage must pursue in order to control nature, corresponds fairly precisely to our modern idea of science, the explanation of a world "uniformly constituted for all, not created by any god or man, but which has always existed and always will exist, a fire continually burning, flaring up and dying down in due order."

After about 530, Ionia was no longer prosperous and independent, but the torch which had been lit there had barely died down before it was rekindled elsewhere, in the cities of Sicily and Greater Greece. These were the centres for the parallel endeavours of Pythagoras and the Eleatic School, idealist reactions against Ionian positivism.

Pythagoras was born in c. 582 and left Samos in 532. Fleeing from the Persians, he took refuge at Croton where he became not only the leader of a school of thought but also the leader of a religious sect, whose central concerns were purification and asceticism. His explanation of the origin of the universe—he had his own, needless to say—nevertheless led from Pythagoreanism to that most abstract of sciences, mathematics.

For Pythagoras and his disciples, number was the key to the universe, as Fire had been for Heraclitus. Number had an existence of its own, outwith the human mind, "and everything which can be known," as a fourth-century commentator put it, "possesses a Number, without which it can neither be comprehended nor known." This myth directed the Pythagoreans towards the study of the properties of number: lucky and unlucky numbers, numbers squared and cubed; the miraculous nature of the number 10 which is the sum of the first four numbers 1, 2, 3 and 4. This led them to discover proportions (ratios), arithmetical, geometrical, harmonic; in geometry, "they called the point One, the straight line Two, the plane Three and the solid Four, accord-

Neolithic religion

The Neolithic world honored fertility goddesses, omnipresent goddess-mothers similar to Paleolithic Venuses. These divinities, with strongly emphasized sexual features, are shown standing, sitting, or lying down, with animals or sometimes a child. This goddess-mother from Çatal Höyük, with her hands resting on two beasts, gives birth enthroned.

"King-priest" from southern Mesopotamia, sculpted en ronde-bosse, 3300 B.C. (Paris, Musée du Louvre)

Mesopotamian religions

In Mesopotamian civilizations, the lords of the universe are masculine deities who live and behave as men.

Having offered his statuette to the god, this prayerful Sumerian is assured of sharing the god's eternity. Uruk, end of the 4th millenium B.C. (Baghdad Museum)

This magnificent alabaster statue of the treasurer Ebih-il was dedicated to Ishtar, goddess of war. Mari, c. 2400 B.C. (Paris, Musée du Louvre)

This smiling, strangely human god, called the "god with the golden hand," comes from Elam (southwest Iran). It is a rare example of statuary from Susa from the beginning of the 2nd millennium B.C. Bronze and gold statuette (Paris, Musée du Louvre)

Egyptian religion

In Egypt, the king is a god; until the Fourth Dynasty, the pharaoh is still confused with Horus, the falcon-headed god. Later, the pharaoh would be considered his earthly incarnation. Granite statue, 12th century B.C. (Cairo, National Museum)

The jackal-headed god Anubis appears here in a rite of judgment. The deceased had to pass this test before they could travel to the other world. Alongside Thot, Anubis weighs the heart—representing the conscience of the dead man—which will then be judged by Osiris.

Cycladic religion

The first proto-Greek civilization carried on the older tradition of goddess-mothers, changing them into these strange Cycladic feminine idols. The violin-shaped figures spread beyond the Aegean; they have been found in Sardinia, in Malta, and even in Spain. Marble Cycladic idol from Syros, 3rd millennium B.C. (Athens, Archaeological Museum)

Cretan religion

In Minoan Crete and Mycenean Greece, goddess-mothers were venerated, like this one from 1700–1600 B.C. Snakes symbolizing the powers of earth and fertility wrap around her out-stretched arms. Earthenware statuette. (Knossos, Heraklion Archaeological Museum)

Mycenean religion

Feminine Mycenean idol of the "Psi" type. (Taranto, National Archaeological Museum)

Cypriot religion

The Cypriot populations, whose culture was related to those of Greece, the Balkans, the Syrio-Lebanese coast, and Anatolia, worshipped divinities whose names have mostly been lost. This feminine votive statue in terra-cotta comes from Lapithos, 6th century B.C. (Nicosia, Cypriot Museum)

Gods of Syria and Phoenicia

Syrian religion, like the Phoenician, borrowed widely from the civilizations that met in those countries, the crossroads of the Near East.

This divinity from the Syrian coast was long known as the "lady of Byblos" and shows clear Egyptian-Oriental influence. Bronze and silver, 8th century B.C. (Paris, Musée du Louvre)

This bronze Phoenician statuette, whose face is covered with gold leaf, is from Cádiz, 8th or 7th century B.C. It is a clear adaptation of the Egyptian iconography of the god Ptah. (Madrid, National Archaeological Museum)

Greek religion

Heir to the Cretan and Mycenean religions, Greek religion, which endured for two millennia, passed through many evolutionary phases.

This bronze statue of Zeus, who replaced Poseidon as the most important god of the Greek pantheon, comes from Ugento, around 500 B.C. (Taranto, National Archaeological Museum)

The Ilias Athena, originally from Troy, arrived in Greater Greece with the first Greek colonists. This majestic terra-cotta statue, in a deliberately archaic style, was honored in a sanctuary in Lavinium, and still shows traces of polychrome (5th century).

Maenad decoration in the temple of Portonaccio, Veio, c. 500 B.C. (Rome, National Museum of the Villa Giulia)

Etruscan religion

Unlike Greek and Roman religion, Etruscan religion was revealed by prophetic persons and consigned to books. Its manifestations were very diverse.

The chimera of Arezzo, an ex-voto from the 4th century B.C. Surely one of the most famous objects of Etruscan art, this sculpture was restored by Cellini in the 16th century and has three heads—lion, goat, and snake—like the chimera of legend. (Florence, Archaeological Museum)

Roman religion

Made of loans from Greek, Etruscan, and Oriental religions, the Roman religion recopied those cultures' images. The baroque Vatican Laocöon is a Roman marble copy created in the 2nd century B.C. by Rhodian artists. (Vatican City, Museo Pio Clemento)

After the death of Alexander the Great, the imperial cult spread throughout all the Mediterranean states. In Rome, it became a form of patriotism, consecrating with Augustus an absolute monarchy of divine right. Deification of Emperor Antonius and Empress Faustina. (Vatican Museums)

Other western Mediterranean cultures

Two heads, perhaps representing heroized warriors, attached to different masks, sculpted in a realist manner in the style of the Greek double Hermes. Probably inspired by Hellenistic art, these Celtic sculptures were worshipped in the sanctuary of Roqueperteuse. (Bouches-du-Rhône, France)

An unusual divinity of the Iberian civilization found in La Serreta. It represents a feminine figure seated on a throne nursing two children, with a bird to her left. (Municipal Museum of Alcoy, Spain)

ing to the number of points it took to define each item, a point, a line, an area and a volume." Such reflections even led them to calculate the orbits of the sun and the planets, to account for their real as opposed to their apparent movements, to study acoustics and music, and to assert that the earth was a sphere. Their best-known, though not most important discovery, was what we know as Pythagoras' theorem, according to which, in every right-angled triangle, the square of the hypotenuse is equal to the squares of the other two sides.

But one day the apprentice mathematicians found themselves faced with the enigma of the irrational numbers. A number is irrational in relation to another when it has no common measure with the latter, and no quotient which can be expressed in either a whole number or a fraction. For example: the relation between the diameter of a circle and its circumference is an irrational number. In fact it was the right-angled isosceles triangle which revealed the existence of irrational numbers. Let us suppose that in such an isosceles triangle the two sides of the right angle are one unit long. The hypotenuse will be equal to the square root of 2. This simple answer, which is how we would put it, was not available at the time, but it could easily be demonstrated that the hypotenuse was smaller than 2 (the sum of the two other sides) and larger than 1 so it could not be represented by a whole number. And neither could it be represented by a fraction (this would take longer to demonstrate). It followed that on any given vector, the number of points was not finite, as the Pythagoreans had previously thought: as well as whole numbers, fractions and irrational numbers continued into infinity.

But in that case, reducing the world to numbers can no longer be seen as simplifying its image, if the number of numbers is infinite. "Mathematics was born from Pythagoreanism," one historian concludes, "and like a boomerang, it rebounded on it."

The reaction was not slow to appear, a negation of the Pythagorean view of numbers, from the city of Elea or Velia on the coast of Lucania in the first half of the fifth century. Parmenides (born *c.* 530) centred his enquiries on Being, an overall immutable truth, to be distinguished from opinion, or Non-Being, which was merely the appearance of things. He rejected the "multiple," that is the theories of the Ionians and Pythagoreans, as belonging with appearances—hence the controversy. It was in defence of his master, and in defiance of common sense, that Zeno came up with his famous paradoxes: Achilles can never catch up with the tortoise; the arrow never reaches its destination, etc. It would take too long to explain how these images are both absurd and not absurd. They become almost reasonable if they are viewed as a rejoinder to Pythagorean ideas, an attempt to demonstrate that the latter were absurd. Reasoning in this way about the absurd marks the beginning of logic, or dialectic as Aristotle would call it, and once more the zigzag progress of science benefited.

After this orgy of logic-chopping, we might note the return to the concrete with the experiments of Empedocles of Agrigento (500–430), which demonstrated the role of air, the pressure it exerted and the need to substitute air for vapour among the elements. The same would be true of the arguments of Democritus, who was the first philosopher to speak of tiny invisible particles, or "atoms," or to be precise "the indivisibles." The living architecture of the world was made up of a profusion of atoms rather than a profusion of numbers. In the light of present-day atomic physics and chemistry, his world view, as revealed by a turn of phrase here and there, sometimes seems deceptively modern.

By the fifth century B.C. at any rate, the problem of science was unambiguously posed, while at the same time a conflict arose between pure and applied science.

Socrates and Plato were idealists: their quarry was that timid and elusive bird, the human soul, imprisoned only briefly in the world of men. Science for them was simply a form of meditation, a road towards an eternal and disembodied thought. No one was allowed into Plato's Academy unless he was proficient at geometry. When asked "What does God do all day?" he replied "Geometry." But practical or applied science was anathema to him. In the *Gorgias*, Plato had described the merits of a military engineer: "Yet you despise him and his skill, you call him engineer as an insult, and you would not wish to marry your son to his daughter, nor marry his daughter yourself." When Archytas of Tarentum made wooden doves fly in the air, and became enthusiastic about other mechanical toys, Plato fumed: "He is corrupting geometry . . . stripping it of dignity by forcing it to descend from the immaterial and purely intelligible to corporeal and embodied objects; to make use of vile matter which requires manual labour and is used for servile trades." These are anecdotes but the tale they tell is clear.

This divorce between Greek science and the urge to make mechanical experiments corresponded to a recent change in Greek society. Michel Rostovtzeff noted that "Greek art of the archaic and classical periods never neglected the depiction of trades." Pottery thus offers us a series of tableaux of everyday life, but art would subsequently turn away from "mechanical" subjects, deemed contemptible. "What are known as the mechanical arts," Xenophon tells us, "carry a social stigma and are rightly scorned in our cities."

Public opinion in Athens was unsympathetic to scientific experiment for other reasons. Astronomers and scholars appeared to be men lacking piety, in other words they demystified the heavens and the stars which were traditionally revered as deities. Protagoras was banished, and Anaxagoras put in prison, which he was able to escape only with the help of Pericles himself: but he subsequently left Athens, which was no haven of free thought. Even Socrates thought it was pointless to ask questions about the orbits of stars and the movements of the planets or their causes. It is true that Plato probably helped give astronomy a better name, but only when he came round to the view of his disciples, namely that the observable movements of the planets may seem random (the word planet in Greek means wanderer) but this is only apparent: their real movements are perfectly regular and therefore, like the stars, obey some divine order. Why then condemn astronomy, which was moving away from the tiresome theories of the Pythagoreans and (since "the natural laws were once more subordinate to the authority of divine principles" as Plutarch put it) was returning to its state of innocence? But Plato's approval of astronomy is ambiguous and still disregards the research of the Ionians into *natural* causes which might explain the structure of the universe. The desacralization of the Greek world was thus neither complete nor rapid.

Fifth-century science nevertheless benefited from the fruitful results of thought which turned inwards and not to the outside world. The Platonic distinction between the role of thought and that of perception as instruments of knowledge was to be essential to the future of science. The same was true of the acute sense of mathematical abstraction which brought Platonic philosophy together with pure science. But one cannot altogether escape the impression that at the most creative high point of philosophical thought, the rejection of empirical and experimental science closed off certain paths which had previously been open.

In a sense it was Aristotle who saved for posterity a substantial part of ancient scientific thought. Born in Stagira on the Macedonian coast, the son of a doctor who trained him in medical practice from an early age, Aristotle was then initiated into Pythagorean mathematics and the philosophy of Plato, his *maître à penser*, in Athens. He developed the quasi-theological side of Platonic astronomy, but in the end abandoned mathematics for human science and biology. This odd training explains the encyclopedic nature of his readily comprehensible work, a pedagogical summa which was for centuries to be a source of inspiration for Islam and then the west. Medicine, mathematics, logic, physics, astronomy, natural sciences, political psychology, ethics—all human knowledge was tackled by Aristotle. In the field of zoology he was even an original thinker and in two of his books, the *Mechanics* and the *Meteorology*, he veered towards experimental science. It is true that these works may well be spurious. But the general truth remains that Aristotle definitely moved away from Platonic idealism and poetry. The emphasis was no longer on the soul, that divine spark, but on the human being as a thinking and mortal being, and even on the physiological bases of the movements of the soul, the imagination, the memory and the passions. The Idea no longer had an independent existence apart from its material support.

Finally, Aristotelian physics formed for the first time a coherent system, "a highly elaborated theory even though not mathematically formulated." It was of course a false theory: Aristotle himself was confused by the distinction between natural movements and violent movements. There are natural movements which are perpetual, as he saw it, such as the rotation of the celestial spheres. And since in the order of the cosmos everything had its place, natural movement tended to return it to that place: the stone I hold in my hand, if I drop it, will try to return to the centre of the earth, and will stop on the ground: vapour being lighter than air will float up naturally, and so on. Violent, non-natural movement required traction or propulsion. This might seem logical, except of course that everyday experience tends to contradict it: if a stone is thrown, it shows the anomaly of a mobile object continuing its course without an agent. Aristotle was not troubled by this and explained the anomaly by a reaction of the ambient environment, a whirlwind action which propelled the object onward. "A brilliant explanation," according to A. Koyré, "despite its erroneousness, since it rescued the system; and it was thanks to this that scientific thought managed to survive the vicissitudes of history until the age of Galileo." It would be centuries before the principle of inertia was formulated.

Alexander's conquests led to a prodigious expansion of the Hellenic world. Surveyors, geometers, engineers, geographers and astronomers all benefited from this sudden opening up of great spaces: they now had direct access to Babylonian and Egyptian sources. Greek science now discovered much more about the distances between heavenly bodies, the precession of equinoxes and the geography of distant lands. Should we agree with S. F. Mason (1953) that Alexander's conquests pushed Greek science towards the practical and the applied, as happened to French science after the Napoleonic conquests?

Alexandria, founded by Alexander in 332, became the capital of an independent Egypt in 323. Under Ptolemy I Soter, who reigned until 285, and his son Ptolemy II Philadelphus (282–246) this metropolis upon which the teeming life of Egypt concentrated had soon become the richest, most densely populated and most ethnically varied city in the Mediterranean. The new pharaohs, who were hungry for prestige and sympathetic to the arts and sciences, soon became patrons to scholars from throughout the Ancient World. They created in Alexandria what one might call a Centre for Scientific Research. The dates of the foundation of the museum (the Temple of the Muses) and the libraries are not known for certain. But the resources available (countless books, dissection rooms, zoological and botanical gardens, an observatory) offered scholars both their living expenses and the means to do their research. The museum was a kind of research academy. Everybody who was anybody went to Alexandria, just as in the eighteenth century no European intellectual could afford to ignore Paris.

After Aristotle, Athens still had some fine days ahead of it: it could boast Aristotle's own successors at the Lyceum (Theophrastus, director from 322 to 287, was succeeded by Straton who had spent time in Alexandria); Epicurus; Zeno of Citium, the founder of the Stoic school (born in 335 in Citium in Cyprus, died *c.* 264 in Athens); Pyrrhon of Elis, the earliest of the Sceptics, who came to Athens in 336 and died in about 290. And Rhodes was also a notable centre until about 166, as was Pergamum in Asia Minor. All the same, the critical mass of Hellenic culture and science had emigrated to the new cosmopolitan city of Alexandria.

What is miraculous is that this Alexandrian splendour should have survived at such a high level for two hundred years, two centuries of an intellectual life so rich that its achievements cannot be summed up in a few lines, especially since scientific thought moved away from the traditional syntheses and began to branch out into different sciences. Thinkers were no longer referred to as sages or philosophers, but as mathematicians: Euclid (*c.* 300), Archimedes (287–212), who only passed through Alexandria, if he was there at all; Apollonius of Perge, *c.* 200; grammarians such as Dionysius Thrax, *c.* 290; atomists such as Herophilus and Erasistratus at about the same time; or astronomers, like Aristarchus (310–230), Eratosthenes (273–192) and Hipparchus (*fl.* 125).

This burgeoning of individual sciences corresponded to immense advances in knowledge. After a slow process of maturation, there was an explosion in every sector. Euclid in his *Elements* attempted a systematic presentation of mathematics. Archimedes, alongside bold statements such as "give me a point of leverage and I will lift the world," invented the measurement of the circumference of the circle by approximation: if two polygons are imagined, one inscribed inside the circle and the other outside, and if one then imagines them as having an infinite number of sides which can be measured, sooner or later their perimeters will coincide with the circumference of the circle. He also prefigured infinitesimal calculus. Apollonius of Perge worked on conics. Mechanics was born—Archimedes again—while Aristarchus measured, or tried to measure, the distance between the earth, the moon and the sun, and Eratosthenes measured the terrestrial meridian. Hipparchus was able to predict eclipses. Herophilus in 300 distinguished between veins and arteries, Isistra identified the lymphatic channels. The most sensational of all these achievements was probably that of Aristarchus (*c.* 310–230): according to Archimedes, he pronounced that the earth rotates on its axis in a day and goes round the sun in a year. According to a report by Plutarch, he had to suffer constant insults and narrowly escaped being tried for impiety. These two details may be accurate and may be connected: the notion of the sun being at the centre of the universe was in fact abandoned because it clashed with religious views at the time.

Despite all these achievements, Alexandrian science reached a dead end. The problem about the fate of science during the Roman period has often been posed. Taking my courage in both hands, let me say that the usual answers seem questionable.

My first witness is Robert Oppenheimer, the father of the atom bomb: "If we think of the culture of ancient Greece and the Hellenistic and Roman periods that followed, it seems very odd that the scientific revolution should not have happened there and then." By "scientific revolution" we should understand a full-scale industrial revolution, which did not of course occur until two thousand years later, in the late eighteenth century, starting in England. Were the elements of such a revolution present in Alexandria?

The debate centres on an engineer of genius, Heron of Alexandria, who was active in about 100 B.C. He was the inventor of hundreds of devices and complicated mechanisms, such as a water-bottle with a siphon which could be made to pour or not at will, gearing mechanisms, cogwheels, screws, and a rotating machine powered by steam from a miniature boiler. He also invented an authentic theodolite (called a diopter), and any reader who has ever had to take topographical bearings will recognize the profound simplicity of this invention.

Was there not in all this the promise of a future *applied science*? We can recognize that the use of steam, even to power a toy, was a significant step. But then the steam-engine devised by Denis Papin (A.D. 1681) did not spark off an industrial revolution either: it would take another hundred years before that happened. The technical discovery in itself does not necessarily lead to an industrial revolution. Neither am I convinced by the kind of "endogenic" explanation which suggests that the Alexandrian engineers were frivolous. Louis Rougier has described Heron as "the Vaucanson of Antiquity and not the James Watt." But Vaucanson did more than invent toys: he worked on improvements to techniques of weaving. It has also been suggested (and there is perhaps more truth in this) that the rich "patrons" of Alexandria asked engineers not to perfect working machines, even for use in war (at which, incidentally, they do not seem to have had much success), but rather to provide miraculous tricks to dazzle the faithful in the Graeco-Egyptian cult of Serapis: putting official state science at the service of official state religion, as one historian remarks. Well, possibly: but is that enough to explain the stagnation of technology throughout all the centuries of the Roman period?

Historians have often advanced another answer, taken up by philosophers and experts on technology. Every technological revolution has always been undermined by the existence of slavery, a scourge which spread throughout the ancient world. Athens in the third century became a kind of dormitory town with its great landowners, its workshops, and its slaves who worked both in the fields and the city. From about 166 B.C., Delos became an immense slave market for the entire Orient—a strange destiny for a sacred island. "If Heron of Alexandria did not think of building a steam engine to ease the labour of men," writes Louis Rougier, "it was because slavery existed." This then was "Spartacus' revenge."

No one will deny that a society may be slow to perfect and adopt technologies (even if they are known about) as long as there is no real need for them. This is really the heart of the problem. Was it then the slave-owning mentality, the indifference to the toil of humans working like beasts of burden, that was to blame? It is unlikely that the English and then European industrial revolution, which led to decade upon decade of marked decline in the conditions of the workers, was really inspired by the desire to "relieve human toil." Perhaps on the contrary it had become "profitable" for a given society or group to provide men with the assistance of a machine so that they should produce more, not necessarily by working less or in any better conditions.

Of course, since our views on this are not those of the past, we can hardly avoid feeling rather pleased at "Spartacus' revenge," a sort of restrospective moral victory. Slavery was not only a crime but also a mistake, since it meant that humans were doomed to economic stagnation. But why did the industrial revolution that had not taken place in antiquity not happen in the seventeenth century, in Papin's day? Or perhaps in Renaissance Italy, in Lombardy, where all the scientific conditions seem to have been united? There were no slaves in that society. When in England in the 1780s there really was "take-off," to use the expression popularized by W. W. Rostow, the experience had been preceded by a long-term economic and demographic upturn. The economic fuse was no doubt one of the indispensable factors. Can we imagine retrospectively that this was the missing element in 100 B.C.?

In the preceding pages, I have given prominence to science, which was an essential feature of Hellenistic civilization. But its other features interest us too, for many reasons, among them that Rome was to imitate this late flowering of Greek culture and prolong it by absorbing it into its own civilization.

Athens during this period was certainly not plunged in darkness. It was still a place where one could find the same subtle and delicate sensibility, the same humanization of the countryside, the same monumental splendours, and the same activity in the port of Piraeus. As a university city, Athens attracted plenty of rich young men, and it remained the undeniable capital of philosophical thought. The Academy and the Lyceum still had their scholarchs. As we saw, Theophrastus (322–287) and Straton (387–269) succeeded Aristotle at the Lyceum. Theophrastus' *Characters* achieved lasting popularity, and new and energetic schools of philosophy emerged with Zeno, Epicurus and Pyrrho.

But classical tragedy with its choruses and singing had seen its last days. Travelling players no doubt still performed the plays of Euripides up and down the European and Asiatic regions of Greece. But tragedy was no longer a creative force. The theatre now consisted largely of comedy, which had embarked on a new career, based on everyday stories of Athenian folk. Menander (*c.* 342–*c.* 292), who remained faithful to Athens and resisted the blandishments of Ptolemy Soter, was the acknowledged master of this genre. For a long time all we knew of his writings were a few fragments, or the versions of his plays produced by Plautus and Terence; then in 1959 a complete play, *Dyskolos*, was discovered—a sort of rustic version of Molière's *Misanthrope*.

But Athens was no longer the centre of the Greek universe, which had been hugely expanded by Alexander's conquests. Pergamum, Rhodes, Tarsus, Antioch and above all Alexandria, were its triumphant rivals. In the end, what vanished with the ancient glory of Athens was the predominance of the *polis*, with its popular "open air" literature, intended for the mass of citizens sitting on the steps of the theatre. From now on intellectual life would be dominated by princely courts, libraries and scholars, deliberately restricted circles of specialists, the growing numbers of schools, all anxious to follow new trends, and even a kind of "bourgeoisie" whose existence is explained by the growth of the economy. It was a world with many and various structures.

Greek thought had, however, to confront the native culture of these colonized regions, which remained foreign to it. It was caught up in an imperial mission which obliged it to assert its unity in the face of the other. Thus a common language, a lingua franca or *koine*, tended to replace the dialects. The *koine* was chiefly but not entirely of Attic origin. It was the language of teachers, the virtually unchallenged language of prose writing.

There were other changes too: with the end of public freedoms, eloquence disappeared, logically enough, since there were no crowds to convince by strategems or the power of the word. At most, men were free to offer discreet praise of their masters, or to taste the delights of literary escapism. They could escape into scholarship, history, the imaginary tales which were almost a prototype for the novel, or into the frequently allusive and caricatural playlets known as mimes. Those of the Syracusan Herondas were famous: written in racy verse, they presented sketches of everyday life: a slave-trader explains the irregularity of his accounts to a tribunal, a mother asks the schoolmaster to bring her son into line, a matchmaker bustles about or a shoemaker does the honours of his establishment. The plot doesn't matter: everything is in the skilful dialogue, punctuated with jokes.

Another form of escapism perhaps were the *Epigrams, Idylls* or lovesongs of Theocritus (born in about 300 B.C., probably in Syracuse, before moving to

Cos and eventually Alexandria). He imagines a life far from the city's clutches, among magical landscapes and flute-playing shepherds, poets themselves, who ask the poet as he wanders through the island of Cos: "Where are you going, Similchidas, in the heat of the noonday sun, when even the lizard is sleeping in the dry stone walls and the crested larks, friends of the tombs, have ceased their play?" Another form of escapism was the stylistic originality of the Alexandrian poets, searching for the recondite word, the sibylline allusion known only to initiates within the magic circle.

In art too, this period revealed a new Greece, both romantic and baroque, eager for novelty. The pursuit of the new led in Alexandria, as it did in Pergamum or Rhodes, either to a preference for naturalism (the denial of academic beauty or even of any beauty at all), or to a grandiloquent emotionalism which is reminiscent of what we would call the baroque, or to a rather sugary or precious elegance. The great Greek painting of the late classical era, known to us, alas, only through commentators, and which had already inspired the school of Sicyon and the sculptor Lysippus in about 350, was probably the source of this movement. Indeed, painting continued to enjoy greater prestige than sculpture, and innovation in pictorial composition was as passionate and sophisticated as the stylistic experimentation of the Alexandrian poets. One would like to see some examples of these efforts: a table or a stone floor with a three-dimensional representation of a meal for instance: they may be the origin of some of the fine still lifes one finds in Pompeii.

As at Pompeii, painting and mosaic were the preferred form of decoration in the households of the rich. Alongside traditional religious architecture which drew on both the Ionic and the Doric (though a softened and mellowed kind of Doric), private architecture also developed, as can be seen in the great houses excavated on Delos, with their colonnaded central courtyards, their marble statues, fountains and precious mosaics, and their painted stuccoes. Town planning had also come into being as a conscious art in the fifth century and indeed it was Hippodamus of Miletus, the classical architect of Piraeus, who was claimed as the inspiration of Hellenistic town planning. But the great cities which sprang up so quickly, such as Alexandria, Antioch or Pergamum, helped to set the pattern for an urban order at once functional and aesthetically pleasing.

From our distant vantage point, this rich, teeming civilization of the Hellenistic world seems like a civilization perched on the shoulders of conquered and enslaved peoples—a civilization only precariously balanced. That men should travel from the east to sample this dominant civilization was a sign of its success. People would also come from Africa to Rome, as in later centuries they did to France. But such conquests could not conceal the fact that beneath the surface the languages of the vanquished were still alive: Aramaic for instance was increasingly widely used. And religious life was even more successful at protecting its originality. It even took over some of the Greek cults, which after the disappearance of the religion of the *polis*, were more open than ever to sects and rituals from the east. Perhaps this explains the power of the obstacle against which the effort of the conquerors' civilization, though prolonged over many centuries, would in the end exhaust itself.

CHAPTER EIGHT

The Roman Takeover of the Greater Mediterranean

In its broad outline, the destiny of Rome is devastatingly simple. Viewed from close up, people, events and details complicate the story.

One should above all avoid assuming that this mighty empire came about by some automatic process. The Mediterranean did indeed operate as a mechanism tending to bring together the countries scattered round its immense perimeter. But the sea did not itself spin the web in which it was captured alive.

Rome achieved that particular feat. And Rome might have been well advised to settle for the Mediterranean alone, for the expanse of blue water and the fringe of countries around its shores—to settle for the sun, the vine and the olive-tree. Instead, Rome embarked on a very different course. First Caesar conquered Gaul, then Germanicus took on the great forests of Germania—and subsequently Europe was to lament with him the losses of his legions. Agricola completed the conquest of Britain in A.D. 77–84, and his son-in-law Tacitus set about describing his triumphs. Trajan went in pursuit of Dacian gold and in turn discovered on the banks of the Euphrates how powerless Rome was when faced with the mysterious Asia of the Parthians.

The Roman provinces, where the benefits of the Pax Romana soon became evident, in fact remained fairly remote from the politics of the Capitol, and from the tragedies played out in Rome itself or on the Empire's distant frontiers. The praetorian guard might slaughter one another, the sentries might be facing dramatic alarms along the *limes,* the imperial frontier, but none of that greatly perturbed the stay-at-home provincial. Distance provided him with a comfortable buffer of complacency. But the very fact that the Mediterranean, while in thrall to Rome, was still a living entity with a healthy pulse of its own, meant that all its cultural goods continued to circulate, mingling ideas and beliefs, and bringing about a uniformity in material civilization which has left traces still visible today. The Roman Empire was an area shaped by exchange, a huge echo chamber in which every sound was amplified worldwide; an "accumulation" which would one day turn into a legacy.

The Romanization of the Ancient World, its military and cultural conquest by Rome, is the central focus of Roman history within the Mediterranean. What interests us at this point is the moment when its successes first created the pattern for an universal empire around the shores of the *Mare nostrum.*

I

ROMAN IMPERIALISM

Imperialism is not a word to be uttered lightly. It implies a conscious desire to conquer, and if it is to carry weight in the historical balance, it must lead to some spectacular and enduring achievement. That the word should be applied to Rome—and in antiquity to Rome alone—is the argument of the opening lines of Jérôme Carcopino's magnificent book *The Stages of Roman Imperialism* (1934). One cannot speak in the same way of Athenian or Macedonian imperialism, since both were so short-lived. Athens collapsed in 404 B.C., while Alexander's empire, created almost overnight, fragmented on the conqueror's death. One can however speak of Persian imperialism; and the British Empire can also be clearly identified—both before and after Palmerston, the man who so proudly if anachronistically proclaimed "*Civis romanus sum.*"

If we accept these definitions, there was no Roman imperialism to speak of until perhaps the first or even the second Punic war (218–204 B.C.). The latter marked the critical turning-point, after a series of conquests which were certainly large in scale (covering the whole of Italy!) but not as intentional as might appear in retrospect. It was not until later that Rome assumed its true identity, and embarked on its chosen route.

In the early days of Rome's career, nothing seemed to single out for greatness a town which long lay dormant. There was nothing to distinguish it from the other towns in Latium: Alba Longa (of which it would later be said that it was Rome's *alma mater*); Ardea; Preneste; Lanuvium; Tibur (Tivoli), on its very fertile site; or Lavinium (today Pratica di Mare), a town which according to Roman legend had been founded by Aeneas during his flight from the flames of Troy. In the last-named town, possibly on the archaic altars discovered during the 1960s, "the people venerated the Penates, carried there from Troy, as well as Vesta, goddess of fire and the hearth, a cult of Greek origin, as was that of the Dioscuri, Castor and Pollux."

So we must look beyond the original town, although it is tempting for the historian faced with the Rome of today, a sea of buildings and bustling city life, to imagine the primitive villages which once existed on its sacred hills. It is hard not to feel some tug at the heart when one pictures those first long-ago settlements, consisting of a few hundred shepherds and their families. We must then imagine a town taking shape, founded (or perhaps re-founded) by the Etruscans, when they set out to control the best crossing-place on the Tiber, commanded by the Insula Tiberina. Traditionally the last three kings of Rome were Etruscan: Tarquinius Priscus, Servius Tullius and Tarquinius Superbus.

According to tradition too, Rome rebelled against the latter in 509 B.C. This revolt, which created the Roman Republic, governed by consuls, the Senate and the great patrician families, the patriarchal *gentes*, may in fact have occurred somewhat later, in about 470 B.C. Its significance is still not clear. Did Rome have its own "fifth century" as the historian Jacques Heurgon wondered? The pious fictions of traditional history recount as if they were epic conflicts what were probably minor skirmishes between neighbouring towns, fought with derisory forces. In these obscure times, Rome was allied with the other towns in Latium in the Latin confederation, and the battles, which took place regularly every campaigning season, were little more than internal squabbles over cattle rustling, the ownership of a water source, or a few fields.

The invasion by the Gauls in 390 or 387 B.C. was another matter. But this violent confrontation was also short-lived. Defeated on the banks of the Allia, the Romans were unable to save their city, which fell into the hands of the Senones under Brennus. But the Capitol stood firm, the conquerors retreated and it was soon business as usual in the Latin confederation. The key date must be the collapse of the confederation under pressure from Rome in 338. The Latin cities were subjugated and Rome, now unfettered, was to become ruler of Italy within seventy years, the last date in this sequence being either the fall of Tarentum in 272, or possibly that of Rhegium, another Greek city, in 270. At this point, the conquest of Etruria was complete. Volsinii fell in 265.

The early stages of this irresistible rise to power may perhaps be explained by Rome's association with Campania, in particular with the large city of Capua. This partnership encircled Latium. Capua, the focal point of immigration from the mountains and the countryside, placed at Rome's service a pool of adventurers whose contribution was not negligible. Having a foothold in Campania meant making contact with the Greeks, reaching the sea and benefiting from trade (as some of the earliest coins attest). Even more certainly, it meant a confrontation with the Samnites, the warlike tribes of the Apennines who for more than a hundred years had been terrorizing the rich lowlands.

Rome now embarked on a long and testing struggle, but also enjoyed its first major triumph. By deciding to fight against the mountain people, the city was asserting its leadership over the lowlands, which it helped preserve from harassing threats. Victory was the reward of perseverance, since conflicts broke out several times, in 343–341, 326–304 and 298–290. A war waged in the hills meant that troops were constantly at the mercy of ambushes, supply failures, a missed rendezvous, or the rash overstretching of the marching columns. Indeed, the Roman legions were humiliated at the Caudine Forks in 321. But Rome very quickly learned to use mobile units and to blockade the enemy in the mountain regions (as used to happen in pre-war French North Africa). This was a war of attrition, with each side scoring indirect victories. With the occupation of Apulia in 320 B.C., not only did Rome acquire the last great plain in the peninsula, but also the area into which, in winter, all the herds would come down from the Abruzzi, the very heart of Samnite country.

These were major successes then, but progress was sufficiently slow for the hopes of Rome's enemies to be regularly rekindled. In the end Samnites, Gauls and Etruscans joined forces. But their coalition was defeated by the Roman legions at Sentium in Umbria in 295. The war was now virtually over, with Etruria more or less subjugated, the Po valley reached, and the Adriatic coast occupied. The Greek coastal cities would shortly have fallen too, had it not been for the brilliant rearguard action led by Pyrrhos on behalf of the Tarentines. Once this episode was over, however, the town acknowledged defeat in 272. The Romans soon afterwards occupied Rhegium (Reggio di Calabria) on the Straits of Messina, opposite Sicily.

"Italy," a geographical term originally applied to what we today call Calabria, and later extended to all of southern Italy, would soon come to mean the whole peninsula. Words too can be a form of imperialism.

In this process of conquest, Rome benefited from its central location, which gave it the advantage of overland communications. Roads built outwards from Rome helped to reinforce this natural advantage. In 313 B.C. the censor Appius Claudius opened the Appian Way which ran to Capua and eventually to Brindisi; the Via Salaria and the Via Flaminia ran to the Adriatic, and the Via Cassia crossed Etruria.

Rome also had the good sense, in the light perhaps of its comparative weakness, to treat its conquered peoples leniently, deliberately adopting a policy of patience and to some extent fair dealing. Those populations seen as ethnically and linguistically close to Rome were eventually admitted to full Roman citizenship. Tusculum was the first to receive this privilege from the quasi-legendary dictator Camillus. To those less close, a sort of half-citizenship, under Latin law, was sometimes offered. On the sites of former cities, or on land not yet settled, colonies were created, either Roman (in which case they were peopled with Roman citizens), or Latin (with some autonomy but fewer rights than the former). Another possible status was that of ally, *socius*, with or without treaties granting equal rights.

As I suggested above, though with some hesitation, this might be described as a "fair" policy. But was Roman *bona fides* perhaps a myth invented after the event? Rome certainly made a point of respecting the letter of the treaties, putting morality and legality on its side. But hypocrisy was never entirely absent from a strategy which, after dividing Rome's enemies, now set about devising different levels of status for its new associates.

A central location and a common-sense policy would nevertheless not have amounted to much without the backing of military might. Forged in the course of the Latin wars, the Roman legion was the instrument of victory. The first citizens belonging to the five "Servian" *classes* fought in the heavy armour of the Greek hoplites: helmet, breastplate and round shield; other *classes* adopted lighter armour, with pectorals instead of breastplates, and long oval shields. Legionaries with low incomes, and therefore poorly equipped, had been granted pay since the siege of Veii (Isola Farnese). The Roman foot-soldier borrowed from the Samnites the use of the javelin (*pilum*, a long slender blade set in a wooden shaft). The practice became established of disposing the legionaries according to social status. The most lightly armed, the mis-leadingly named *hastati* (misleading because in fact they did not carry spears) formed the front lines; then came the *principes* and finally the *triarii*, a reserve army of heavy infantry in the third line. This order was more flexible than that adopted by the Greeks. Roman soldiers did not fight in close formation: a gap separated each man from his neighbour and successive lines were drawn up in quincunxes, so that in retreat one line could fill the gaps in another without difficulty. Discipline was strict, even though this was not a regular army. Every night, the men had to pitch camp to protect themselves against surprise attacks. Cavalrymen were as a rule supplied by the allies, but were few in number.

Finally and significantly, Rome benefited from division in the enemy ranks: internal quarrels kept Alexander's successors, the Greek kings, at a dis-tance, and the Carthaginians and Greeks were at each other's throats in Sicily, oblivious to the world around. Rome took advantage of these distractions to embark on the conquest of Italy, patiently weaving its web, and constantly repairing any damage. In the end, it emerged strong and self-confident, a match for the Greeks and Carthage, greedily eying Sicily across the Straits of Messina and beyond it the rest of the Mediterranean, to which the island held the key.

With the three Punic wars (264–241, 218–202 and 148–146 B.C.) Rome and Carthage became locked into a Hundred Years War. Control of the Mediter-ranean at once became the issue in a contest which would end only with the death of one of the adversaries. When Rome took Rhegium in 270, the Carthaginians placed a garrison across the water in Messina. The two politi-cal monsters—on one hand Italy, united from the Po valley to the Gulf of Tarentum; on the other North Africa, from northern Cyrenaica to present-day Morocco, backed up by southern Spain—eyed each other across the narrow straits. They were well-matched adversaries, capable in fact of com-ing to terms, as earlier treaties had demonstrated. It would, moreover, be inaccurate to describe their confrontation as one between a sort of gadfly (Carthage, the maritime power) and the heavy-footed soldier (the Roman legions). Carthage was no less expert than Rome at building roads and bridges, and its agriculture was well developed, while Rome had been inter-ested in the Mediterranean since well before 264 B.C. It had had dealings with the cities of Greater Greece, and merchant shipping was active along Italian coasts.

As for Rome's fleet, the normal components, triremes and quinqueremes, long vessels with three or five stepped rows of oarsmen, took only a short time to build. In 260, at the outset of the wars, Rome launched a fleet of 100 quinqueremes and thirty triremes, plus some other ships, all in the space of sixty days; in 254, the Romans launched 220 vessels in six months. We need not take these figures quite literally perhaps, but the ships were certainly assembled very rapidly, probably too quickly for their quality not to suffer, as had already been the case in Greece. As a result, these navies did not last long, sometimes only the space of a single campaign.

Early in the war, some sources report, the Italian shipyards had copied a Carthaginian quinquereme which had fallen into Roman hands. That is not impossible. The quinquereme was a monstrous ship, developed in Cyprus or Phoenicia before Alexander's campaigns. Of the western Greek cities, only Syracuse had built quinqueremes. But it was child's play to copy the design. Supplies of timber were no problem for Rome: the peninsula still had many forests. The Greeks in the Gulf of Tarentum had timber for boatbuilding delivered from the Sila massif in Bruttium. The Romans had it floated down the Tiber to Ostia. In this respect, Carthage was at a disadvantage, since it had to look to Sardinia for timber supplies.

These longships might be easy to build but they were costly to operate, particularly since they could be used only on calm summer seas and over short distances, such as between Italy, Sicily, Malta, the Lipari Islands, the Egadi Islands and the nearest points on the North African coast. What was more, they required huge numbers of men: sailors, oarsmen, soldiers—as many as four hundred in each ship, according to Polybius. Overall, this was an extraordinarily expensive war: with both sides equally committed, it was bound to become a matter of attrition.

In 264 B.C., Rome had effortlessly occupied Messina, having been called upon by the then rulers of the city, the Mamertines, a rather remarkable band of adventurers who had betrayed the Carthaginian garrison. After imposing a peace settlement on Hieron of Syracuse, the Romans began the siege of the western cities: Agrigentum fell during the winter of 263–262, and 25,000 captives were sold into slavery. In 254, almost ten years later, it was the turn of Panormus (Palermo), another Carthaginian stronghold: here 10,000 of the inhabitants were reduced to slavery. At sea, in 260, one Roman fleet was defeated off the Lipari Islands, but a second one, under the command of the consul C. Duilius Nepos, was victorious off Mylae (Milazzo), thanks to the grappling irons and boarding planks which the Roman sailors used against the enemy. The Carthaginian vessels, which were easier to manoeuvre, were thus cheated of their advantage and boarded by force: the naval battle became hand-to-hand combat, just as if it were being fought on land (and this was to be the rule for centuries to come, in encounters between galleys). From now on, Rome felt sufficiently confident to confront Carthaginian vessels along the African coast. In 256, an expeditionary force was landed on Cape Bon. It wintered in Tunis, but was crushed the following year: the unfortunate commander was the consul Atilius Regulus.

The tide did not yet turn in Carthage's favour. However, the city had found in Hamilcar Barca a commander of genius, who had dug himself in on two fortified and impregnable mountain tops in Sicily: Mount Heircte, near Palermo, and Mount Eryx near Drepanon (Trapani). His troops launched raid after raid, and the Punic ships also engaged in some fruitful piracy. This low-key war worked against Rome's interests. The Republic lost 700 ships to storms, pirates and the enemy navy. Carthage now launched a massive fleet, but Romans and Greeks combined in a stupendous effort and crushed it in 240 off the Aegates Insulae (Egadi), off the western tip of Sicily.

The disaster brought Hanno and the peace party to power in Carthage. Rome was able to impose draconian peace terms. Sicily was now in Roman hands and Rome took immediate advantage of Carthage's grave internal problems to lay hands on Sardinia and Corsica. Weakened by an uprising in Libya and a savage revolt by its own mercenaries (who were owed large sums in back pay), Carthage was obliged to accept Rome's conditions; it managed to retain the rights only to levy soldiers and load grain in Italy.

After the Sicilian disaster, however, and the crushing of the mercenaries' revolt in 238, Hamilcar Barca had gone to Spain with the remnants of his army in 237. Thus began the conquest of Spain, effected by the powerful and proud Barca dynasty. The operation meant capturing the Guadalquivir valley and the high plain of Castulo, forcing a passage to the Mediterranean (the later route of the Via Augusta) and establishing a stronghold in eastern Spain where New Carthage (Cartagena) was founded by Hamilcar's son-in-law, Hasdrubal. In *c.* 225, Rome made the Carthaginians promise not to cross the Ebro or disturb the Roman colonies which had been settled from Marseille along what is now the littoral of Catalonia. But the occupation of the Iberian peninsula along its two major axes, the Guadalquivir and the eastern seaboard, gave Carthage direct access to the precious Spanish silver mines and the possibility of cornering their production. A few years later the mint in Cartagena was turning out 300 silver pounds a day. In Carthage itself, beautiful coins stamped with fine images of animals—horses and elephants—testify to this age of prosperity.

Hamilcar had, however, been killed in 231, in an encounter with local forces. Ten years later Hasdrubal was assassinated. His nephew Hannibal, son of Hamilcar, was acclaimed commander of the army: a breathtaking career was about to begin.

Neither Rome nor Carthage had in fact abandoned the struggle. Each side spied on the other, fearing its might. Rome had to deal with severe unrest in Sardinia and Corsica, where the local tribes were as recalcitrant as the Samnites. There was an even graver threat in northern Italy, where, after some inconclusive campaigning, Rome had struck at the Gauls in 225. Six years later, the Latin colonies of Piacenza and Cremona were founded, but these were fragile outposts. The colonies themselves provoked the uprising of the Boii. And all the while, war was once more brewing between Rome and Carthage.

Which would strike first? Hannibal, who had taken Saguntum and crossed the Ebro in April 218? Or the Roman fleet stationed at Lilybaeum, which, after a pre-emptive occupation of Malta, was preparing to sail to Africa? In September 218, Hannibal crossed the Alps—his exact route is still unknown—and descended with fewer than 30,000 men into the Po Valley. In December that year, he was victorious in the battle of the Ticino. In January 217, on a snowy day, he triumphed at Trebbia; on 23 June, he crushed a Roman army at Lake Trasimene in Etruria. Then, although delayed by the tactics of the dictator Fabius Cunctator, he had the good fortune to win his greatest victory yet, at the battle of Cannae on 2 August 216. But for reasons that remain obscure (not enough men, not enough siege equipment?) he failed to march on Rome, lingering among the fleshpots of Capua, that other Rome, which had "abandoned itself" to him. The following years brought him some successes (he held Tarentum from 213 to 209), but once hemmed in in southern Italy, he was not well supported by Carthage. The defeat on the banks of the Metaurus in 207 of his brother Hasdrubal, who was bringing substantial reinforcements from Spain, sealed his fate.

Taking refuge in Bruttium (Upper Calabria) he remained there for years, his escape route cut off by Roman legions, just as his father had been cornered on the slopes of Mount Eryx. Rome meanwhile struck a series of telling blows: Cartagena was taken in 209 and Scipio landed in Africa. Hannibal was recalled and the battle of Zama (202) finally marked the end of the second Punic war.

The conflict which broke out for the third time in 148 B.C., ending two years later with the destruction of Carthage, raises too many questions not to have become the subject of fierce polemic.

The key witness in the case is one of the best historians to have come out of Greece, Polybius. Born in Megalopolis in Arcadia in 210 or 205 B.C., he was still only a child at the time of the battle of Zama (202) but he witnessed the fall of Carthage in 146 at the side of his friend P. Cornelius Scipio Aemilianus. It was a strange twist of fate for this son of an influential politician of Megalopolis. In his youth, he had campaigned against Rome and for the freedom of the Hellenes, along with Philopoemen, "last of the Greeks." It was as a result of this that Polybius had arrived in Rome in 167 as one of the thousand Achaean hostages deported to Italy after Pydna. But this exiled rebel was not only captured but captivated by the great city where he lived for sixteen years, being a frequent guest at the house of the Scipio family, whose devoted friend he became.

His *Histories* provide a narrative of events from 264, the date of the outbreak of the first Punic war (which figures in the introduction) to the catastrophe of 146. The account is all the more valuable, firstly since this well-informed writer was a man of great intelligence, anxious to take the broad view, and secondly since his experiences in Greece had led him to reflect on the phenomenon of Roman expansion. For him, the triumph of Rome was somehow decreed by destiny, the result of a kind of law of nature. So instead of opposing it, it would be more sensible to associate the destiny of Greece with it. He tried to convince both his compatriots and the Scipios, descendants of a glorious dynasty which was moreover already converted to Greek culture and its teachings.

Polybius' work concentrates therefore on explanations for Rome's imperial destiny. Among today's western historians, with their increased sensitivity to the evils of imperialism and unjust wars, the debate is seen more in terms of apportioning responsibility for the long conflict from which Rome emerged thoroughly transformed. If the collapse of earlier agreements in 218 was Hannibal's doing, was Carthage thereby guilty of starting the war? Was Roman imperialism merely a reply to Carthaginian imperialism? Let us agree with Polybius that by laying siege to Saguntum, in an area from which his treaty with Rome ought really to have excluded him, Hannibal know-ingly provided a *casus belli*. But the Barca dynasty did not represent the whole of Carthage; while for all the prudence of Roman policy, there had been hawks in Rome pressing for action since before the first Punic war. Was the fleet assembled at Lilybaeum there for purely defensive purposes? If it had set sail before Hannibal had attacked, would Rome then be the guilty party? In any case, war was nothing new in 218, it was simply breaking out afresh. When the Romans occupied Messina in 264, they had done so in spite of their treaty of friendship signed with Carthage in 306. In short, is it reasonable to single out any one act of hostility as carrying unilateral respon-sibility, when this conflict was so clearly predestined on the map of the known world?

We may conclude that the sea was simply not big enough to hold both Rome and Carthage: that they were on an inevitable collision course, fuelled by mutual distrust. The Barca dynasty, who seem to have hesitated, might possibly have consented to remain masters of Spain, without further aggres-sion, if Rome had been willing to live with that. For Hannibal, the war was a risky, even a desperate throw of the dice. It was a miracle that his family in Spain had succeeded, in the short space of fifteen years, in creating an army of 60–70,000 men. But Rome had more than twice as many at its command. To dispatch the Punic army overland to distant Italy was an act of folly. Before it ever got there, it had lost half its men. After Trebbia, Hannibal's soldiers had had to take to the hills to escape, ending up strung out along thirty kilometres or so of difficult mountain passes in the Apennines.

Hannibal had counted on a simultaneous uprising against Rome by the imperfectly subjugated Italian peninsula. He was right about the Celts, but almost entirely wrong about the Etruscans, the Samnites and above all the Greeks, who in the end preferred Rome to their long-standing enemy, Carthage. There was secession in Tarentum and Syracuse, it is true, and Han-nibal had a master-plan which involved bringing in Macedonia under Philip V. But the latter's army did not even reach the Adriatic.

Hannibal's only hope lay in the comparative lack of experience of the Roman leadership. Unfamiliar with the Greek style of warfare employed by Hannibal, the Romans only slowly shed their old-fashioned ways, in some kind of "psychological about-turn" which may have been the secret of their revival. Rome thus gradually created its own form of "modern" warfare, one that was not simply imitated from the Greeks, since it was based on far more solid foundations than Hannibal's strategy—which was in the end that of a brilliant *condottiere*. Rome refused to engage in the Hellenistic form of sportsmanship which meant that after suffering a single defeat, one immediately conceded victory without further resistance.

After the second Punic war, Carthage had been stripped of everything, even Africa. Its territory now stopped at the Numidian frontier; its currency (50,000 talents in reparations exacted over fifty years) and its fleet seemed to be irremediably stricken. Yet it continued to trade, developing its rich resources of vines and olives. Its agricultural exports were detrimental to the interests of the large Italian landowners, while its capacity for renewal revived all the old Roman fears: *delenda est Carthago*.

A war between Carthage and Massinissa, the Numidian king, provided the pretext for a Roman expeditionary force. It encountered fierce resistance, but Carthage eventually succumbed to the legions of Scipio Aemilianus (Africanus). The city was burnt, razed to the ground and the salt of sterility scattered over its smoking ruins. A quarter of a century later, Caius Gracchus set about restoring the stricken city, which once again flourished in the time of Caesar and Augustus. But Roman Carthage would never remotely resemble the astonishing Punic capital of old.

As early as 200 B.C., after the battle of Zama, it was predictable that Rome would probably capture the eastern sector of the Mediterranean. Being dependent on the sea, this zone was likely to fall into the hands of any power with maritime supremacy. All the great cities of the east were seaports: Alexandria in Egypt; Rhodes, at the time an unrivalled trade and financial centre, where money was cheap to borrow, 8 per cent compared to 24 per cent in Alexandria; Antioch, a caravan city but only a short distance from the coast, and thus able to attract the Seleucid Empire westwards; Pergamum, which with Byzantium stood guard over the Bosphorus; Corinth, still an important centre; and Athens, soon to become so once more. In the west by contrast, the sea was controlled by a single city which wielded enormous power once Carthage had been eliminated.

The outcome was the welding together of the eastern and western basins of the sea, two independent universes as a rule oblivious of each other. It is true that the welding process—in other words the formation of the Roman

Empire—was to call for a sequence of events which hardly strikes one as logical. If the operation proved so troublesome, perhaps it was less "natural" than it might seem in retrospect? It certainly took time. The first blow struck for Roman expansion, the outbreak of the second Macedonian war, occurred in 200; the last came in 61 (the conquest of Syria) and 31 (the late, or rather postponed reduction of Egypt to the status of a Roman province). From 200 to 31 B.C., from Scipio Africanus to Augustus, the chronological span is almost two centuries.

This slow pace, indicative of delays of other kinds, is probably explained in fact by the difficulty Rome was experiencing in becoming the economic centre of the sea. The threads of a Mediterranean-wide network did not automatically come together around Rome. Delos was transformed by Roman policy in 167 into a free market for slaves and wheat, in competition with Rhodes, but Italian businessmen did not appear there in any numbers before 125 or even 100. The port of Puteoli near Naples, intended for the Levant trade, did not become prosperous until the late second century B.C. And it was not until Attalus III, king of Pergamum, bequeathed his kingdom to Rome in 133 B.C. (the future province of Asia was created in 129) that the predatory *publicani* (tax-farmers) descended on it like vultures. So it should not be assumed that the Mediterranean was quickly unified to Rome's advantage. We should not set too much store by such scraps of information as the odd shipment of wheat from Egypt to Rome in 210, or from North Africa to the Aegean in the 170s, or the spread of piracy in the Levantine seas early in the second century, corresponding to increased recruitment of slaves for Italian buyers.

In general, it is true that from west to east, from Rome to the Parthian kingdom of Bactria, price fluctuations, credit rate changes, financial trends and even social disruption (according to F. M. Heichelheim), tended to echo one another over an increasingly wide area. But this was only a very general tendency. Different economic situations prevailed, even in neighbouring areas: what happened to Syria under Antiochus III was not the same thing as the violent deterioration of Egypt under Ptolemy. And if an overall pattern was eventually to dominate the Mediterranean economy, our best guess is that this did not happen before 170, 150 or even 130 B.C.

In about 200 B.C., the Hellenistic world, i.e. the eastern Mediterranean under Greek domination, was neither a house threatened with ruin, nor the glorious realm described by U. Kahrstedt. It certainly possessed the best institutions, combining despotism and "enlightenment," the comparative independence of the city-states and the advantages of vast territorial kingdoms. It is also true that a money economy was thriving within it, and that it enjoyed immense accumulated wealth, a high standard of living and a densely settled population. But to say that it was on the verge of being the promised land, in other words a form of capitalism about to take industrial form, and moving away from a slave-based regime, is much more doubtful. It is also far from clear that the non-achievement of such an industrial revolution is to be laid at the door of the Roman "barbarians," even if they did indeed bring with them much destruction, torture and pillage.

The division of Alexander the Great's inheritance among three powers, Syria, Egypt and Macedonia, led almost immediately to a series of wars, punctuated by short-lived alliances and unprecedented violence of the worst kind, namely civil war. In the early third century B.C., some kind of balance between on the one hand the weighty power of Egypt and on the other the fast-expanding cities of Rhodes, Miletus and Ephesus, and the revival of commerce in the trading posts on the Black Sea had probably created a thriving north-south axis. Taking advantage of the divisions of the "big three," lesser states had then sprung up, such as the kingdoms of Pergamum, Bithynia, Pontus, Armenia and Bactria, alongside brilliant cities like Rhodes and the clusters of towns in Crete and Cilicia, where piracy flourished. But by the end of the third century, Egypt's power had suffered serious damage, both internally and externally: externally as a result of the crisis brought by the second Punic war, which *may* have slowed down silver shipments eastwards and which certainly deprived Egypt of the immense markets of Italy, Sicily and Carthage itself; and internally, since Egypt's victory over Syria at Raphia had been achieved only with the help of native Egyptian levies (i.e. troops that were not Greek). As a result, internal disturbances (national, colonial, even racial) convulsed Egypt, which now became the "sick man" of the Middle East. This weakness and the consequent power vacuum encouraged an aggressive policy by Philip V of Macedonia and Antiochus III, one characterized by hasty and ruthless offensives.

This situation explains *to some extent* the short-term brutality employed by Rome. Roman policy took advantage of having only two great powers to deal with in the Near East (Macedonia and Syria, both of them fragile) in order to eliminate as quickly as possible the potential danger they represented.

The origins of the second Macedonian war, 200–197, in which Rome became embroiled when the Punic war was scarcely over, remain obscure. It seems unlikely that the Senate simply took fright at the improvised alliance between Philip V and Antiochus III, or that the urgent, desperate embassies from Pergamum, Rhodes and Athens were sufficient motive to send armies out into a distant conflict which could easily have been avoided, since Macedonia was trying hard not to infringe the clauses of the 205 treaty binding it to Rome. The question is better understood from the viewpoint of Roman politics: the imperialism which had flexed its muscles during the struggle with Carthage was gaining strength. The major actors of the first Macedonian war, P. Sulpicius Gallus or M. Valerius Laevinus, were not alone in wishing to return to the fray. A kind of "military professionalism" had come into being, in which the lure of spoils, an obsessive desire for glory and the consequences of over-investment in the military all played their part. All wars that come to an end raise the problem of demobilization, and Rome had plenty of soldiers for whom it was hard to find suitable employment.

The legions, excellently commanded and trained for "modern" warfare, were an irresistible force, particularly since the eastern powers, failing to learn from past experience, did not update their armies. Perhaps it is always the fate of highly civilized countries to be a war or two behind their less refined opponents. At Cynoscephalae, Philip V's army was made to look somewhat ridiculous. Macedonia was cut down to size on this occasion and underwent another humiliation: Flaminius' proclamation of Greek independence at the Isthmian Games of 196 gave back the Greeks their freedom, including that of indulging in petty squabbles. In 194, the legions left the Balkans. After so much pillage, extortion and killing, who would now dare rise against Rome? Then in 190, backed by the Pergamenes and Rhodes, the Scipios triumphed at Magnesia ad Sipylum over the much larger army of Antiochus III, driving that magnificent and ambitious "Sun King" back across the Taurus.

Some twenty years later in 167, Rome had a similar walkover against Perseus, successor to Philip. V. L. Aemilius Paulus, the son of the consul defeated at Cannae, provided another demonstration of unfailing Roman superiority, on the field of Pydna. His triumph back in Rome displayed untold riches, the spoils of quite atrocious pillage. This time, the Macedonian monarchy and indeed Macedonia itself were wiped from the land of the living.

———

Such a Blitzkrieg with its attendant looting was possible only because of a degree of economic prosperity. A vanquished power had to have enough resources to recover, before it was worthwhile for warfare and looting to start up again. This was what happened in the first third of the second century B.C. The economic climate remained favourable, any damage or financial losses were quickly made good and war indemnities, however crippling, were paid. Even Egypt, which had witnessed some frightening devaluations of the order of ten to one, and had had to issue copper currency, managed to recover after this bloodletting.

After 170, however, came a recession. Wheat prices were catastrophic, the standard of living fell and social unrest spread like leprosy, reaching even the distant conquerors, Rome and Italy. It must be conceded that politics was partly responsible for this sequence of upheavals. But the economic downturn also played a part. War became even more savage. Macedonia rose up and was promptly reduced to a Roman province; the policeman had come to stay (148 B.C.). When Greece rebelled in turn, it was savagely punished and an example was made by destroying Corinth, almost gratuitously, in the very year of the sack of Carthage. Greece too was reduced to being a Roman province in 146, and when Attalus died, his kingdom was bequeathed to Rome, becoming the province of Asia in 129.

Everywhere, the whole length of the sea, civil wars, so-called "social" i.e. confederate wars, or tribal wars broke out one after another, seeming to provoke each other into existence. The revolt of the Celtiberians in Spain which started in 154 did not end until 133, with the horrific siege of Numantia. In North Africa, the war against Jugurtha began in 109 and had repercussions in Rome itself in 102 and 101. The Cimbri and Teutons invaded Provence and even northern Italy; in 91, the revolt of Italy, another confederate war, brought Rome almost to the brink of ruin. Finally, savage internal power struggles were by this time almost unremitting. How in the circumstances was it possible to conquer and hold the entire Mediterranean world?

Taking advantage of the conflicts tearing Rome apart—first the "social" war then in 88 the first victories of Sulla, whose army reached the city itself—Mithridates, king of Pontus, was for several years the instigator of a striking revenge movement against Rome, applauded throughout the east. In 88, at his bidding, a general war, the Pontic uprising, broke out and swept through the province of Asia. Cities opened their gates to him and resident Romans were massacred (a total of 80,000, it was said). Gathering force, the wave of rebellion crossed the Aegean: the Romans of Delos were murdered. From Macedonia, an invading force reached Thessaly. Central Greece and Athens itself were up in arms.

Rome had a delayed reaction. The repression, led by Sulla, was marked by the recapture of Athens and the city was harshly dealt with. But other concerns prevented Sulla from pursuing his trajectory further. The route to world dominion lay elsewhere, in Rome itself, and he signed in haste the botched peace of Dardanos in 83. So the disturbances in the east continued. Even the fierce campaigns of Lucullus did not bring about pacification. That would be achieved only later and without much merit, during Pompey's easy excursion. In 63, the old king of Pontus, abandoned by all, had one of his bodyguards run him through with a sword. Two years later, Syria became a Roman province.

But Rome's revived fortunes are probably to be accounted for by the upward movement of the economy, as a result of which the tide had turned once more in Rome's favour, possibly in Sulla's time, and certainly by the time of Caesar. The east would have been thoroughly subdued and order would have reigned, had quarrels in Rome itself not taken a tragic turn.

These quarrels, culminating in the triumph of Augustus in 31 B.C., lasted an entire century. Historians have studied in minute detail, with great erudition and endless debate, this eventful and dramatic period of Roman history, horribly monotonous as it was, and with human villainy constantly on display. In the struggle for power, every contender, however different in origin, had hands stained with blood and filth. In the end, they became indistinguishable.

More generous souls—can we call them pure?—such as the Gracchi, first Tiberius and then Caius, dreamed of renewing Rome, building up once more a class of small landowners. But they did not last long against their own caste, the *nobilitas*, which monopolized power, reigned supreme in the Senate and was the source of all patronage. Neither of the illustrious brothers was saved by the sacrosanct function of tribune of the plebs, which each held in turn. The first was assassinated in 133, the second in 123.

Marius, born near Arpinium, was a *novus homo*, and it was the people's party, the Roman plebs supported by the *equites*, which carried him to his first consulate in 107 B.C. He had come to prominence in the Jugurthan wars and having ousted his patron, Metellus, achieved victory over the Numidian king in 105. If the age of Marius was eventful, with the rebellions he encouraged until his death in 86, it is not that there was some historical logic at work, still less was it the result of skill on the part of Marius, who was a brave soldier but a short-sighted politician; nor was it even because of pressure of popular feeling. The plebeians of Rome, living in some leisure and on state charity, were quite incapable of setting up a democracy.

In fact, ancient Roman society had lost its stability. The ruling class, the *nobilitas*, made up of patricians and plebs ennobled through officeholding, was still *in situ*. But around Rome and throughout Italy, there was no longer that numerous population of small landowners who were by turns peasants then soldiers. The urban plebs were partly a product of this disintegration. Alongside the *nobilitas*, which clung to its office, controlled the Senate, gave out pro-magistrates' posts and owned huge estates worked by slave labour, especially in the rich Campania, lived a bourgeoisie composed of financier-*equites* and tax farmers, and this class constituted an increasing threat, with its new taste for conspicuous consumption. In short, a sick society was collapsing from below, rendering both power and institutions fragile.

The essential symptom, which can stand for many others, was the transformation of the army: once a citizen-army, then a professional army, it was recruited from now on among the poor, the have-nots, the *capite censi*, men from the lowest classes, *infra classem*. They quickly became masters of the situation, pushing their commanders to take power, the latter being fairly unburdened by anything we might term sincere political convictions. In 100, Marius's army crushed the popular party, deemed guilty of having revived the project of agrarian laws favoured by the Gracchi, and of stirring up the city's population.

Sulla too was an army man, receiving power from its hands on his return from the Levant in 82. His victory, followed by appalling repression, led to a dictatorship. Was this an eastern-type despotism? Not really, since Sulla abdicated in 79 and the conflict resumed, first between Pompey and Caesar, then between Antony and Octavian. No monarchy had been created by Julius Caesar, who was murdered in the Ides of March conspiracy in 44. But one was set up after the particularly dramatic conflict between Antony and Octavian.

This latter conflict had indeed brought to the surface the latent antagonism between east and west, as if everything was starting again from scratch, or as if the Levant was becoming capable by some miracle of regaining its former prosperity. Was this reality or illusion? Octavian, the future emperor Augustus, embodied the unitary vision of Julius Caesar, the desire to unite an almost consolidated west to an east as yet incomplete and unconsolidated, reaching beyond the Euphrates, which he deemed a frontier too close for comfort. Antony and Cleopatra, driven by circumstances, also dreamed of an east unified for their advantage. Might this dream, which foundered abruptly at Actium in 33, have led to the creating of a Byzantine Empire centuries ahead of its time? Some historians think so (and so did Pascal). But this may be taking too literally propaganda put about by Augustus, since the "Egyptian" episode was a convenient component in his plans to establish and enforce a strong central power on a new formula. After all if Antony had won, he too would have created a Roman Empire.

Augustus' achievement was that in taking over the legacy of Caesar, he adapted it and concealed its most glaring ambitions. Caesar's prudent successor, the first Roman emperor, was considered a saviour by the entire Mediterranean, masters and slaves alike (not just by Virgil and the friends of Maecenas). The gifts he brought with him were above all peace (*ubique pax* was his motto), respect for individuals, and a social order—and these things mattered greatly after so many years of tumult, especially the last few, when tensions had reached an all-time peak.

II

ROME BEYOND THE MEDITERRANEAN

In the end, Roman imperialism simply ran out of steam. The key period, from this point of view, was the reign of the emperor Hadrian (A.D. 117–138). By this time, the outline of the Empire represented an immense ellipse around the Mediterranean, stretching far beyond it in some directions, running closer to its shores in others, but with the sea providing the basic shape: essentially the Roman Empire was the land surrounding the *Mare nostrum*.

To the south and east, the Empire was protected by desert wastes, the Sahara and the Syrian desert. Danger lurked only beyond the empty spaces of Syria, with the arrival of the Parthians, first the Arsacids then the Sassanids, who revived Iran, that never-entirely-vanquished heart of the Persian Empire.

But the Parthians long remained a distant hornets' nest—troublesome only if disturbed on their home ground. And this "anti-Empire" did not interfere with the routes bringing silk, drugs and spices to Rome, since the Romans had access to the Red Sea and thereby to merchandise from the monsoon coast of the Indian Ocean. It was in the north, on the European frontier, that Rome felt most threatened. The Empire included Italy, Spain and the Balkans, but in order to secure the frontiers of these "continents," especially the last, it was drawn into controlling the waters bounding them—the Black Sea (Pontus Euxinus), the Danube and the Rhine—and therefore to venture into uncharted lands, sometimes almost uninhabited, where everything was different: population, climate, crops, vegetation, rivers and seas.

Was this constant outward expansion really necessary? When the Empire finally gave up the struggle, was it out of resignation or because it had tailored its desires to what could be accomplished with the means to hand? This enormous human entity—enormous for the time that is (50 million souls at least)—spread over an area which was also enormous. In an age when distance was a formidable obstacle, it could not count on being protected by the rather flimsy envelope of the Empire's frontiers within which it was more or less enclosed. The further the distance from the Mediterranean, the less protected one was, as the supply lines were stretched to their utmost, across desert or ocean wastes, or the almost empty expanses of primitive countries like Germania. The maintenance of the frontier posts alone was a masterpiece of organization in the face of harassment, and had constantly to be undertaken. Fifty million souls, working, tilling the soil, forging metals and weaving cloth, seafaring and leading their pack-animals, offered an endless challenge to the soldier. Would the protection of the frontiers have been possible at all without the enrolment of barbarian auxiliaries, the Palmyrian archers or the fair-haired foot-soldiers from Germania?

Before the Empire had even come into being, the problem had arisen years before, with the scare caused by the Cimbri and Teutons: the most damaging threat to the Mediterranean complex before the Germanic invasions of the fifth century.

In about 120 B.C., a human tide (made up of Cimbri in the north and Teutons in the south) had started to flow out of the Jutland peninsula: in its steady advance, this tide of men, women and children encountered the living obstacle of other peoples, whom it attacked or raided as it went, bringing some of them south with it. Within ten years, in its quest for land, this flood had reached the banks of the Danube, south of present-day Moravia. Moving along the Alps and harassing the Romans, it appeared in the Jura mountains in 109. Four years later, it was in the Toulouse area. The Cimbri then pressed on into Spain, before returning and once more joining up with the Teutons in what is now Belgium. Combining forces, they then headed for Italy. The Teutons, having won a battle at Orange, eventually selected Provence for themselves, while the Cimbri turned towards Helvetia and the Brenner Pass. Their joint goal was the northern part of the Italian peninsula, a region still fragile a century after Hannibal's invasion. As for Provence, the Provincia, which had been a Roman possession only since 120, it was at this time a mere strip of territory along the seaboard.

Marius, whom Rome had equipped only with inexperienced legions, arrived at Aquae Sextiae (Aix-en-Provence) to encounter the Teutons. They took no notice of him and kept heading eastwards en route for the promised land. For six days, they marched past the Roman camp, jeering and promising "to call on the soldiers' wives in Rome, insolently asking whether they had any messages for them." But Marius caught up with the horde and massacred men, women and children, taking a rumoured 300,000 prisoners. This figure, though probably inflated, nevertheless gives some idea of the size of the invasion. The following year, on 3 July 101, at Vercelli, Marius met the Cimbri who had crossed over via the Brenner and then moved west across northern Italy, instead of marching on Rome. Another victory for his army flooded the Roman market with slaves.

The episode left nightmare memories, however, not only for Gaul, but for Italy, which had seen the barbarians at the gate. The "Cimbrian terror," a horrific legend, was to survive even longer than Rome itself.

Compared to the Germanic world, seething with upheavals and disturbances, Gaul looked like a rich prize or prey. Comparatively rich and populous (with perhaps 12 to 15 million inhabitants), endowed with a fertile countryside, thick forests, many towns, and flourishing industries (wool, leather and metal-working), Gaul was divided among rival peoples, great territorial tribes. Hence its political weakness, which was to have dramatic consequences.

Rome feared that in this state Gaul might be an attractive destination for the overspill population of Germania and since it was ill prepared to resist, would channel it south to the Mediterranean, as in the days of the Celtic invasions. Indeed Celts and Germans were much the same thing in the eyes of the Romans, with the latter possibly appearing even more savage than the former. The security of Italy, in short, required that the lid be kept on Gaul, and the question must have arisen very soon of occupying *Gallia comata*, "long-haired Gaul," (as opposed to *Gallia togata*, "toga-clad Gaul," the Provincia and future Narbonnaise). What was more, the merchants of Italy, the *negotiatores*, were interested in the Gallic market, where their goods were increasingly finding buyers. "Amphorae of Italian wine are found in about 100 B.C. as far north as Chateaumaillant" in the present-day *département* of the Cher, and even further afield. Military ambitions for a glorious conquest did the rest.

In April 59 B.C., the Roman Senate, caught up in the intrigues of the triumvirs (Pompey, Caesar and Crassus), conferred on Caesar an exceptional command, in Illyria and Cisalpine Gaul; later adding to it Transalpine Gaul. Was there an ulterior motive here? In appointing him to strengthen the security of the Alps, a formidable barrier, but full of potential entry-points and under threat from northern tribes, did the *patres conscripti* hope that *Gallia comata* would prove to be a dangerous, even mortal trap for an ambitious general like Caesar? If they did, they certainly miscalculated. Caesar's pretext for action was provided by the migration of the Helvetii westwards in the spring of 58. Weary of being harassed by the Germans, they sought refuge in Gaul. "Turning aside from guarding the Alps, Caesar marched on the Rhône, and Gaul thereby became a battlefield." In fact, Caesar also had to play politics between the rival powers and mutual fears of the Gallic tribes; he had to deceive the Helvetii the better to surprise them, and seize this excuse for moving north. In the event, everything worked out as planned, one deliberate action leading to the next, and all calculated in advance. Caesar drove back the Helvetii at Bibracte, and in the same year he expelled Ariovistus's Suevi from Alsace. He was thus able to establish himself in Gaul under the guise of protecting it.[1]

Was the entire episode driven by Caius Julius Caesar's personal ambition? Undoubtedly he saw in this adventure an opportunity for personal glory, political power, and a means of restoring his family wealth, latterly eaten into by "insane demagogic expense." The fact that he was remarkably intelligent and clear-sighted only makes matters worse. But it is also true that Gaul was a self-designated prey, thanks to its political weakness and lack of organization. If Gaul was not to be Roman, it might well have become Germanic, with the threat of invading hordes, first the Helvetii, then the Suevi—and who knew what might follow? The return to the nightmare scenario of the Cimbri and Teutons would almost certainly have stung Rome into action. So there might have been another conquest in any case. In short, Caesar himself was dependent on a predestined set of circumstances, going far beyond his personal history. Gaul was conquered so that it would provide an effective and permanent barrier between Rome and the Germanic threat.

A map of Caesar's campaigns spells out only too clearly what took place during these dark years, punctuated by sieges and long periods of waiting, over an immense geographical area where even the rapidly marching legions could not overcome distance. We cannot here follow it in the detail to be found in the victorious bulletins Caesar sent to Rome, the city he could not forget, where his "alter ego" Publius Clodius was still active.

His conquest of Gaul between 58 and 54 was a series of easy victories, methodically executed. A bloody furrow opened up in the flesh and landscape of the Gauls. In 58, the Helvetii were crushed at Bibracte, and the Suevi at Mulhouse. In 57, the legions struck at the Belgic tribes, pushing on towards the Scheldt and Meuse. In 56, after crossing the scrubland of Armorica, the Roman army beat the Veneti, triumphing over their solidly built ships. In the same year, Aquitaine was seized, west of the Provincia. The ring-fence cutting off Gaul from any contact with either Britain or the lands across the Rhine was traced in the form of an open wound which would not heal. To keep it active, Caesar needed only to cross the Channel twice, in 55 and 54, and the Rhine twice, in 55 and 53.

It has been argued that these expeditions were unnecessary. In fact Caesar was less concerned with victory in Germania or Britain than with the situation in Gaul, which he intended to tame and accustom to Roman rule. But in 54, 53 and 52 and 51, being confined from outside, Gaul exploded from within. The rebellion started in the Massif Central, which the conquerors had bypassed without entering. Vercingetorix led this heroic resistance, beating the Amiens legion back to Sens, and inflicting defeat on the Romans at Gergovia. Then the tide turned and the Gallic force besieged in Alesia capitulated at the end of September 52. They had watched horrorstruck as the Roman army encircled them as if by magic with its war machines, earthworks, palisades, circumvallations, and lines of stakes in the earth. It was a textbook demonstration, using quite simple methods, of the Romans' technical superiority, the fruit of iron discipline.

In conclusion, then, if the greatest event in Roman history was undoubtedly the conquest of the Mediterranean, the second was the conquest of Gaul, the bringing to heel of a huge living entity. Gaul contained perhaps three times the population of the whole of Italy, and Rome would frequently depend on this mass of men who entered its service.

But could Gaul protect itself sufficiently to assuage Rome's anxieties? Caesar may have thought so, being lulled into complacency by his two easy sorties across the Rhine. Both times he found himself in an empty landscape, deliberately abandoned by its inhabitants. He failed to recognize the "extraordinary fecundity" of Germania.

This error inspired a plan devised by Augustus at the end of his life: to move the Empire's frontiers up to the Elbe and Moldau rivers, stopping at the division between east and west Germans, on a line which the natural frontier of the Danube would extend to the Black Sea. The middle and lower Danube frontiers were the first to be fortified. Then in 12 B.C., Augustus' stepson, Drusus, undertook by both land and sea the conquest of western Germania, from the Rhine to the Elbe. The conquest was completed in 7 B.C. by his brother Tiberius. But sixteen years later, in A.D. 9, the Cherusci rose up and Varus' legions were destroyed in the Teutoburger Wald by Arminius.

This unprecedented disaster had far-reaching repercussions, out of proportion perhaps to the event, during which everything was against the legionaries: betrayal by allied troops, torrential rain, cumbersome baggage trains, and marshy ground where the soldiers had to fight knee-deep in mud. And indeed Germanicus Caesar, son of Drusus, adoptive son of Tiberius, and successor to Augustus, rapidly turned the situation around, restoring the prestige of Rome and burying the remains of Varus' companions, with full honours. Notwithstanding which, Tiberius called back the adventurous prince, "warning him in incessant letters," Tacitus reports, "to come back and celebrate the triumph as arranged; there had been enough successes and adventures." Tiberius then imposed his "short-sighted policy." Roman forces were evacuated from Germania, and Germanicus, after duly getting his triumph, was sent in despair to the eastern Empire where he died prematurely, possibly at the hands of an assassin.

So the limit of the Empire was more or less fixed along the 2000 kilometres of the Rhine and Danube. When subsequently it was massively reinforced in the important buffer zone of the Agri Decumates (Ten Cantons), Rome was implicitly recognizing, indeed virtually creating, a long-term enemy. The Empire had encircled Germania.

After the rational prudence of Augustus, and the suspicious and edgy prudence of Tiberius, Trajan was to display much audacity, inexperience, enthusiasm and desire for fame in embarking upon the superhuman task of conquest in which he was to find both death and glory. When he succeeded Nerva in A.D. 98, Trajan already had a long military career behind him. Born in Italica in Spain in 52, he was the first provincial to be raised to the imperial throne. He would indeed give the Empire a new lustre, a second youth.

When Trajan consolidated the Rhine frontier, creating towns (Xanten and Nijmegen), and building roads through the sensitive zone of the Agri Decumates, he was merely taking essential routine precautions, since the frontier had constantly to be maintained, like the hull of a ship. But his intervention against the Dacians and their king Decebalus in 101–7 was a new development. The annexation of Dacia (present-day Transylvania, Wallachia and Moldavia) and its transformation into an imperial province provided an advance bastion for the Danube. Rome would set up thriving colonies here, recruited mainly in the east, but Latin was the lingua franca of this new world, which would prove a durable creation. A further advantage was the existence in Dacia of mines of precious metal, and "Dacian gold" financed some of the great public works of the reign, the most famous of which was Trajan's forum with the celebrated column.

But the most significant campaigns were those of 114 and 117 against the Parthians. The bend in the Euphrates, Mesopotamia and beyond it Iran, were weak points in the Roman armour. The disaster which had befallen Crassus at Carrhae in 53, and Antony's defeat ("a retreat from Moscow" as Guglielmo Ferrero called it) were sinister precedents. Yet the Parthian Empire, divided against itself and troubled by bitter disputes on its frontiers, was not at first sight an over-formidable enemy.

In 114, Trajan landed at Antioch and marched into Armenia. From this stronghold, he sent his legions in 115 to Mesopotamia, seizing most of it. The following year, he took Ctesiphon on the Tigris and Seleucia on the Euphrates, then reached the Persian Gulf to the south. The Parthian king Chosroes had fled, so Trajan thought that by selecting a successor he had won the war. But hardly had he left when revolt flared up almost everywhere. Only the Greek population, small in number, had welcomed the invader, the Iranians were indifferent, and the Jews and Arabs were violently opposed to Rome. Chosroes reappeared near Ctesiphon. Discouraged, Trajan turned for home. In August 117, he died at Selinno in Cilicia.

The expedition had ended in failure. Rome had encountered not so much obstacles posed by nature or destiny, as the limits of its own intelligence, or experience. In the attempt to conquer Asia, the Romans did not make use of the weapon which had taken Alexander to the banks of the Indus, namely cavalry. It was on horseback too that Antiochus III had launched his *anabasis* from 212 to 202 B.C., succeeding in turn in reaching the Indus. Trajan thought he could simply surprise Mesopotamia by going via the mountains of Armenia—the kind of ruse a Spanish or Samnite peasant might imagine.

In short, Rome had not displayed any very great audacity or ingenuity either in Germania, where success would probably have required control of the Baltic and North Sea, or in the Euphrates valley, the vast expanses of which could be crossed with ease only on horseback. Fallout from this failure was to affect the first steps taken by Hadrian (117–38). Trajan's successor spent most of his reign visiting and reinforcing his frontiers. The first thing he did was to evacuate the provinces created by Trajan beyond the Euphrates. The reaction to this common-sense policy was the conspiracy of 118 which ended in the execution of Trajan's generals, Cornelius Palma and Lucius Quietus. All imperialist expansion ceased forthwith. The Empire had reached its definitive outline: it would now shelter behind a miniature version of the Great Wall of China. Rome had stopped devouring territory.

This halt was called for internal rather than external reasons, as if suddenly Rome had lost the appetite for expansion. If "optimism and nationalist sentiment died with Trajan," as J.-L. Lauguer puts it, one should not hold Hadrian responsible. The new regime suited the Empire, since it proved durable, becoming established in what one might call a monotonous and unexciting routine, but also bringing the Pax Romana, an unrivalled benefit. And if the whole edifice remained intact for so long, was it simply because of the solidity of the wood, earth and stone of the Roman defence works, the efficiency of its roads, the remarkable organization of a well-disciplined, well-trained and enthusiastic army, itself anxious to deploy its variously recruited men and the social mobility it represented? Once the price of Rome's own security had been estimated and paid by the praetorian cohorts, the Empire still needed to deploy about thirty legions along the endless perimeter of the fortified frontiers, perhaps as many as 300,000 men, a figure at once enormous and derisory. Did the solidity of the Empire not also depend therefore on the simple fact that Hadrian's forced retreat, and Antoninus' immobilism, were matched by the complicity and agreement of the population outside the Empire's frontiers?

Later on, when the great steppes began to see the stirrings of unrest once more, as restlessness in the far east drove the Parthians westwards from 162 and the Germans from 168, the *limes* quickly turned out to be powerless against this human tide, and the Empire lost the initiative for centuries to come, to the advantage of the primitive populations which surrounded and harassed it. Rome's defence became now more than ever a question of resources, of the quality of its men and their intelligence. It had to face ten, twenty, a hundred problems at once, all without any real solution—or rather requiring a miracle, a providential saviour such as Diocletian (245–313).

But saviours often die in the attempt. From then on, a tragic landscape formed the backcloth of the Empire as, assailed from without and within, wounded and bleeding, it still clung to life.

III
A MEDITERRANEAN CIVILIZATION: ROME'S REAL ACHIEVEMENT

With Rome victorious, the Mediterranean continued to be true to its own identity. That meant diversity over time and place, and a wealth of different colours, for in this sea of age-old riches, nothing ever disappeared without trace: sooner or later everything surfaced once more. But at the same time, the *Mare nostrum*, as centuries of the Pax Romana encouraged trade between regions, also displayed a certain unity in style and life. This civilization, as it became established, would become one of the most outstanding in human history.

The chief feature of this civilization was the Latin language, and with it the Latin religion, and Roman style of life. These gained ground without difficulty once the legions had prepared the way by conquest, for example in North

Africa until the time of Septimius Severus (193–211); in Dacia after Trajan's brutal triumphs; in Gaul until the first century A.D., though with some curious reversals: "worship of Mars outstripped Mercury in the Narbonnaise and eliminated him altogether in Aquitaine proper, whereas Mercury drove out Mars in the east and overtook him in the militarized zone of the Agri Decumates."

But there were also counter-currents dictated by obstinate loyalties, by the refusal to come into line, whether in Syria with the revival of pre-Hellenic cults, or in Gaul with the spread of Druid religions, which escaped Roman vigilance. And what is one to say of the strong cult of Mithras, which reached Italy and Rome itself, having spread through the soldiers' camps; or of St. Paul, defending Christianity in Athens in front of the Areopagus? These were part of a deep-seated refusal to bend the knee. The east remained faithful to its ancient languages; Greek constantly and successfully challenged the supremacy of Latin. Indeed this was the essential imbalance in the cultural life of the vast sea.

A shared civilization was more easily assimilated when it came to the details of material life. The Cisalpine hood, the *poenula*, was worn in Rome as well as in colder countries; Italian wine seduced the Gauls; while the braces, breeches and woven goods of Gaul were exported over the Alps; the Greek *pallium*, a garment consisting simply of a broad length of woollen cloth passed over the shoulder and secured at the waist, became the preferred garb of many Romans, especially philosophers; Tiberius when in exile in Rhodes wore one all the time. Cooks exchanged recipes and spices, gardeners exchanged seeds, cuttings and grafts. The sea had long made such voyages possible, but with the unlimited authority of the Empire, barriers fell and transfers happened more quickly.

In a short and stimulating article writen in 1940, Lucien Febvre imagined how surprised Herodotus, "the father of history," would be, if he could see the Mediterranean peasants of the twentieth century. Pliny the Elder, who lived only a few centuries later than Herodotus (A.D. 23–79), would not have been so astonished.

Still, even Pliny had never seen the eucalyptus (a nineteenth-century arrival from Australia) or the plants imported after the discovery of America: sweet peppers, aubergines and tomatoes, the ubiquitous Barbary fig, maize, tobacco and many ornamental flowers. He did know, because he had reflected upon it, that plants and cuttings can travel and that they had certainly spread through the Mediterranean. Things usually moved from east to west. So we read in Pliny that "the cherry tree did not exist in Italy before the victory of Lucullus over Mithridates [73 B.C.]. He brought the first one from the Black Sea and in a hundred and twenty years it had crossed the ocean and even reached Britannia." Still in Pliny's time, peach- and apricot-trees had just arrived in Italy, the former probably originating in China and coming via Asia Minor, the latter from Turkestan. Walnut- and almond-trees from the east had only recently arrived. The quince, no doubt an earlier arrival, had come from Crete. The chestnut was a fairly late gift from Asia Minor. Cato the Elder (234–149 B.C.) does not mention it.

Of all these travellers, the three oldest, which we imagine to be rooted since the beginning of time on the shores of Mediterranean, are wheat (and its related cereals), vines and olive-trees. A native of Arabia and Asia Minor, the olive-tree was probably carried westward by the Phoenicians and Greeks, and the Romans completed the work of diffusion. "Today," Pliny writes, "it has crossed the Alps and reached the centre of Gaul and Spain," that is, it had already passed its optimum geographical habitat. It was even reported to have been tried in England!

Vines too were planted everywhere, despite rain, wind and frost, since the first far-off times when planters took an interest in *lambrusco,* a wild vine with fruit containing but little sugar, probably originating in Transylvania. The determination of the peasant vinegrower, the different tastes of drinkers, and the minute variations of soil and microclimate led to the creation of hundreds of varieties of vine in the Mediterranean. There were many ways of growing them: on stakes, left to trail on the ground, or trained up trees, such as elms or even the tall poplars of Campania. Pliny provides an endless list of varieties of vine and the way to grow them, as well as an already quite impressive list of fine wines. He is equally eloquent about types of wheat, their specific weight and flour content, or the value to men and animals alike of barley, oats, rye, beans and chick peas.

Oil, wine, cereals and pulses—between them they provided virtually the entire basic daily fare of the inhabitants of the Mediterranean. To complete the picture, we have only to include flocks of sheep, coming down the mountains in winter in southern Italy to make Tarentum a wool town, and some characteristic plants such as box, sad cypress, Pluto's funereal tree, and toxic *taxus,* poisonous yew, "hardly green, frail and sad"—and we could almost be standing at Pliny's side, surveying the classical landscape of the hills and plains of the Mediterranean. Like him, we might—and why not?—prefer to all the perfumes of Egypt and Araby the intoxicating scent of olive-trees in flower and the wild roses of Campania.

This geography helps explain many things: the Roman world was based on an agricultural economy governed by principles which would remain in force for many hundreds of years, until the industrial revolution of the nineteenth century. The division of the economy into sectors delegated to poorer regions the task of producing grain, while allowing the richer ones the benefits of vines, olives and livestock. Here originated the split between advanced economies, such as Italy, and backward ones like North Africa or Pannonia, the latter, however, being better balanced and less vulnerable than the former. In any given zone, the landscape might be closer to one or other of these poles and a dividing line separated what cannot quite be called a developed economy from an under-developed one. The line did not become sharply drawn, and then not always, until industry, capitalism and growing population provided the impetus, that is until a free market became established.

The Empire was characterized by its towns and cities: both the older ones, which continued to exist on their ancient sites and, like the Greek cities, set Rome an example with their developed urban culture and its refinements, and the new towns, most of them founded in the western Empire, often far from the Mediterranean. Brought into being by a Roman power which shaped them in its own image, they provided the means of transplanting to far-flung places a series of cultural goods, always identifiably the same. Set down in the midst of often primitive local peoples, they marked the staging-posts of a civilization of self-promotion and assimilation. That is one reason why these towns were all so alike, faithfully corresponding to a model which hardly changed over time and place. What towns could have been more "Roman" in character than the military and trading cities along the Rhine-Danube axis?

Every Roman town depended on stone-built roads, intended for pack animals and soldiers laden with their impedimenta. Each road, on arriving at its destination, led straight into the city from the countryside which surrounded it on all sides like a sea. Neither Pompeii in Campania, nor Timgad in Numidia had suburbs, such as one regularly finds around medieval cities, with their slums, flea-infested inns, workshops for noisy or malodorous trades, sheds for carts, and stables for post-horses. Indeed, there was hardly any wheeled traffic on Roman roads, and no post-horses except for imperial messengers, while urban manufacture had not yet spread outside the city centre. The trades could all be found inside the city, sometimes grouped by street: bakers, barbers, weavers, innkeepers. In Pompeii, the taverns were rather like "modern snack bars, where customers could be served instant food, and where the rooms were often hired by the hour." We would not have felt lost looking in at a Roman bakery: the equipment and working practices have come down to us through the ages. The Roman smithy could still be seen not long ago in any French village, with its furnace, bellows, pincers to hold red-hot iron, and anvil. The fulling basin or the shears of the cloth-cutter look exactly the same in Roman sculptures and in medieval paintings.

Similar reflections come to mind if one contemplates the Romans' lifting gear, pulleys and cranes; their methods of quarrying stone and the stone lathes used to finish cylindrical columns; or their brick walls built exactly like those of today. However, baked brick was not in general use in Greece until the third century B.C., reaching Rome a couple of hundred years later. It was a costly building material, and its use indicates a certain rise in living standards.

The major innovation in this field, starting about 200 B.C., was the technology of concrete. What the Romans called *opus caementicium* was originally a simple mixture of sand, lime and stone chips. Later on, the lime was replaced either with *pozzolana*, volcanic ash from Pozzuoli, which gave good hydraulic concrete, or crushed brick dust, which produced the reddish mortar so typical of many imperial buildings. Left to harden in moulds made of planks, this concrete mixture, which was waterproof, enabled the Romans to build quickly and cheaply major buildings of previously unheard-of design, with arches and vaults bigger than any earlier architects had managed. When the moulds were taken away, this early "industrial" material could be faced with stone, stucco, mosaic or even brick, to give it a more noble appearance: it certainly played an important role in the building of the many city centres of the Roman Empire.

The plan of these city centres was virtually identical in all cases. Around the forum, a rectangular space paved with large flagstones, would stand the temple of the three gods of the Capitol: Jupiter, Juno and Minerva; then would come the curia, or local senate (the decurions were the city's senators and the *duumviri* its consuls), the basilica, which might have a colonnade, where lawsuits were heard and where strollers could seek shelter on rainy days, though they could also find cover under the portico surrounding the forum. The forum was always a market place, even when there were other markets near by, and was periodically appropriated by peasants selling fruit, vegetables, poultry or lambs. Other buildings always to be found close to the centre included theatres, amphitheatres, circuses, latrines and baths. Baths in particular took up an immense amount of space. Under the Empire, they were "the cafés and clubs of Roman cities," the place to go at the end of the day. Finally there were the triumphal arches, monumental gates, libraries, and the aqueducts vital for the massive water consumption of the city-dwellers. This completes the list of features found in all Roman cities, according to an almost invariable plan.

There were a few exceptions: Leptis Magna had a forum outside the town; Arles had a portico underneath the forum, which was built on top of it, as if on pillars. Timgad put its "Capitol" outside its walls. These anomalies, dictated by the expansion of the city or the peculiarities of the site, did not affect the basic plan, which we find endlessly repeated. New towns were usually built by the labour of soldiers and local inhabitants, workers who were more numerous than they were expert. The idea was to have a simple design and work quickly. Starting from the centre, the future forum, a north-south line was drawn, the *cardo*, and an east-west line, the *decumanus*: they met at right angles in the forum, providing the median axes along which the city would be built. In Lutetia (now Paris), the forum of the small open town on the left bank of the Seine was underneath the present-day rue Soufflot, the *cardo* ran along the rue Saint-Jacques, the baths were on the site of the Musée de Cluny and the Collège de France, and a semi-amphitheatre stood on the site today known as the Arènes de Lutèce.

Of course these elements had themselves travelled a good distance before being assembled to make up the composite model of the Roman city. The forum was a version of the Greek agora, as was the portico. The theatre too was Greek in origin, although Rome altered it considerably. The basilica came from Greece as well: Cato the Elder probably built the first one in Rome, the Basilica Porcia. The Roman temple borrowed much from Greece at first, via the Etruscan temple. The amphitheatres (where gladiatorial combats or *venatio* with wild beasts took place) were probably of Campanian origin, while the thermal baths were also probably from pre-Roman southern Italy.

In short, Rome took a great deal from elsewhere—which is not to say that it was inferior. It borrowed much and gave much back, as all long-lasting civilizations do, and as indeed Greece had done.

Rome was thus at the head of a federation of towns and cities, each handling its own affairs, while overall control was vested in Rome.

Prospering until about the second or third century A.D., these cities thereafter fell upon hard times. If we accept the pessimistic but probably accurate view of Ferdinand Lot, they were not inhabited by sufficiently large populations. Rome, Alexandria, and possibly Antioch, were the only large cities of the Empire until the rise of Constantinople. Networks of second-rank towns were conspicuous by their absence. Timgad was the only town for miles around, but it had merely fifteen thousand inhabitants at most. What was more, while the town acted as political centre and market place for the local countryside, the town-country relationship was not mutual. In other words, the town did not fulfil for its region that manufacturing role which would later enable the economy of medieval Europe to take off. Should we blame the great estates and their workshops, where labour was carried out by slaves or "colonists," small farmers already chained to the land? Was it because the known sources of energy were not systematically used? Or was it simply that the depressing economic situation was more to blame than structural features for the stagnation and then decay of the towns?

The impression that the towns' destiny was linked to that of the Empire is not inaccurate. The Empire had long enabled them to rise. It had created a vast economic area, or at any rate made it possible to operate within it; it had promoted a monetary economy of sorts, which increased trade, and a form of capitalism, limited perhaps but already in possession of the essential elements, all in fact inherited from the Hellenistic world, such as merchant guilds, and quoted prices on the exchange (the forum at Rome). Alongside the *mercatores* or merchants there were already bankers (*argentarii*) who offered credit, the *proscriptio*, a sort of cheque, and the *permutatio*, a kind of transfer. But these modern terms may give a misleading image of an economy which was very quickly to be caught in the lethal toils of the state, even before the downturn of the last centuries of the Empire.

As a centre of power and wealth, Rome was effortlessly attracting the changing trends in philosophy and the arts well before the battle of Actium and the triumph of Augustus: this had started to happen with the arrival in the victorious city of the earliest Greek immigrants, merchants, artisans, intellectuals looking for work, political exiles or even slaves, reputedly more quick-witted than their masters. The Hellenization of Rome had been going on for hundreds of years. Greek gradually became the second language of cultivated men, as French was in Enlightenment Europe—with the difference that the primacy of Greek lasted centuries rather than a mere hundred years.

It is true that sometimes the culture transmitted by the Greeks was of such high quality that the pupil was not able to surpass the master or even to reach the same level. This was unfortunately true of science, which would advance no further than the point at which the Greeks had left it. It is also generally true of philosophy, the crowning glory of Greek thought. Rome slowly absorbed its lessons, though not without some resistance. The Roman authorities even expelled philosophers on several occasions. But under the protection of a few high-ranking families, the philosophers were finally able to bring to Rome some portion of Greek thought after the troubled years following Alexander's death (323 B.C.). All the same, if Epicureanism inspired Lucretius (99–55 B.C.) and if Stoicism was destined for a remarkable future, culminating in Marcus Aurelius, can one really speak of an original Latin philosophy? Many historians of ideas have emphatically denied this, considering that both Cicero and Seneca simply plagiarized their predecessors.

Greek art, which had previously only reached Rome indirectly, via Etruria and Campania, truly came as a revelation in the second century B.C., following the capture of the Sicilian cities, the eastern campaigns and the reduction of Greece to a Roman province (146 B.C.). From then on, as wealth and luxury developed in Rome, Greek culture, of which only philosophy had hitherto affected a few patrician families, transformed the very arts of living in Rome. Artists from Greece or the Greek-influenced Middle East flocked in, entering the service of a newly rich but not particularly well-informed Roman clientele, anxious to gain social advantage by collecting works of art about which it knew little, to decorate houses and villas.[2] With the healthy appetite of a young civilization, Rome absorbed everything indiscriminately: the great historical compositions of Pergamum, the affected and extravagant baroque of Alexandria, the cold beauties of neo-Atticism and even the greatest masterpieces of the Greek classical era. Originals and copies of sculptures (the latter turned out at an industrial pace in Athens for the west) flowed into Italy and piled up in dealers' yards. Cicero requested some "bas-reliefs for his villa in Tusculum" from his wealthy friend Atticus in Athens, who also sent Pompey statues for his theatre, the first stone-built theatre to be constructed in Rome (55 B.C.). A few years later, when the temple of Apollo was rebuilt early in the reign of Augustus, it was on a Hellenistic model: the statues and paintings with which it was decorated, all Greek, turned it into a veritable museum. In 1907, the so-called *Mahdia* wreck, a Roman cargo ship from about this period, was discovered off the Tunisian coast: its cargo included sixty columns (probably brand-new ones), as well as statuettes, bas-reliefs, bronze and marble sculptures, including several unquestionable masterpieces.

Such works of art were imitated of course by the Italian and Greek artisans working throughout the Italian peninsula. And even when there was a strong input of originality from Rome—in the taste for realistic detail, for lifelike portraiture, landscape and still life—the original spark must have come from the east.

But no civilization can live entirely off foreign imports. At the time it became the capital of a newly available Hellenism, which it copied with enthusiasm, Rome was already a society with deep-seated traditions of its own. Even if the Romans appeared to be abandoning their past, to Cato's despair, their ancient taste still led them to make certain choices, the significance of which would become clearer in the long run, when Rome's admiration for all things Greek was no longer tinged with a sense of inferiority.

Moreover, some things were a matter of necessity. After Actium, the need for buildings became urgent, new sites opening up as fast as old ones were completed. Rome began to see the arrival of a swelling stream of immigrant populations, out of all proportion to that of the Greek cities, except Alexandria. Town planning created its own problems. It is not surprising if the domain in which Rome most rapidly developed its own personality was architecture.

Sulla, Pompey, Caesar and Augustus all played some part in this building programme. Agrippa rebuilt the city's drainage system and water supply; Augustus built two or three new aqueducts, and added to Caesar's existing forum a new one, separated by a wall from the Suburra district on the Esquiline, the haunt of actors, gladiators, hustlers and beggars. By so doing, he was separating the official city, with its marble-clad walls (imitated from the Greeks in the second century B.C., and quarried in Carrara) from the old more disreputable city, built in the ancient materials of lath and plaster, and repeatedly ravaged by fire. Countless new buildings followed: fora, basilicas, baths, theatres, circuses, temples, palaces and tenements.

Roman architecture absorbed and adapted all the means and elements then known. Doric, Ionian and Corinthian columns were all present, but in modified form: the Doric, simplified and given a plinth, became known as Tuscan; the order known as composite combined the acanthus leaves of the Corinthian with the scrolls of the Ionian. But the most impressive aspect of Roman architecture was the functional art of its engineers. Using concrete as a building material, Roman engineers were responsible for building marvellous bridges and aqueducts, with arches and domes everywhere, barrel-vaulting and groynes, which freed architects from the constraints of load-bearing pillars and columns, and made possible the huge internal spaces required by the large numbers of city-dwellers. Rome's grandiose style came into being almost of its own accord.

The Colosseum, begun by Vespasian and finished by his son Domitian, is a fitting symbol of that grandeur. It set new records for the time, measuring 188 metres by 156, with a circumference of 527; the height of the outer wall was 48 metres, and a further storey made of wood could be added; some 50–80,000 spectators could be accommodated around the vast internal arena of 80 by 54 metres. Its name came from the Colossus, a statue of Nero, over 30 metres high, depicted as the sun god. The Colossus was eventually taken down but its name remained in the Colosseum—itself a colossus of a kind. Throughout the Empire, there were numerous huge amphitheatres: at Italica in Spain (156 by 154 metres); and a whole series in France: Autun, 154 by 130; Poitiers, 138 by 115; Limoges, 137 by 113; Arles, 136 by 108; Tours, 135 by 120; Bordeaux, 132 by 103; Nîmes, 131 by 100.

In the domains of painting and sculpture, Roman art slowly distinguished itself from its Greek models. Greek artists were too numerous for local taste to emerge immediately. It was easier to find outside Rome. There was indeed a popular art—R. Bianchi Bandinelli has described it as "plebeian"—an art not so much Roman as south Italian, which was to contribute something distinctive to Rome. This was a sturdy, realistic kind of art, depicting people and things with verisimilitude: to make a rather far-fetched comparison, it was rather like the French art of the Loire valley before it was confronted with the sophisticated and noble art of the Renaissance. Native art would in time assert itself, one might almost say take its revenge against foreign influence, but the process would be a slow and gradual one.

Thus was created that composite art, the early "Roman" style, a precocious example of which is provided by the sculptures on the altar of Domitius Ahenobarbus (between 115 and 70 B.C.). These combined mythological compositions of Greek inspiration with scenes treated much more realistically. However, Rome's official art long retained traces of foreign influence. We should not forget that the *Laocoön* in the Vatican Museum, the work of sculptors from Rhodes, excited enormous admiration among the Romans, including Pliny the Elder. The statue of Augustus, known as the *Porta Prima*, superimposes the emperor's head and breastplate on to the Greek torso of Polycletes' *Doryphorus*. The panels of the *Ara Pacis* (decreed in 13 B.C., this altar to peace was put up four years later on the Field of Mars) were almost entirely by Greek artists.

It is in the domestic art of the portrait that one finds Roman art par excellence. This has often been traced to Rome's Etruscan origins and it is true that a certain *verismo* is to be found in the bronze and terracotta statues of ancient Etruria. But it is even more closely linked to the Roman tradition of the *jus imaginis*, a privilege of the patrician families. Polybius noted in some detail the sight, strange to his eyes, of the funeral rites of the *nobilitas* and the role played in them by the *imago*, the wax mask of the departed which rich families preserved, a tradition linked to ancestor worship. "When an illustrious relative dies, the masks are carried in procession to the funeral. Selected individuals who in height and external appearance most closely resemble the originals put them on their faces, and wear 'pretextual' togas if the dead man was a consol or praetor, purple togas if he was a censor, and gold-embroidered togas if he was awarded a triumph." These fragile wax death-masks were later replaced by stone or bronze busts of remarkable realism. Greek influence occasionally introduced a more pretentious note, but the Roman portrait, whether sculpted or painted, retained from its age-old tradition a very great expressive force and was always comparatively sober in style. There was a marked contrast in Augustus' day between this simple beauty and the virtuoso examples of official art, based on imitation of Greek models.

It would be some time before imperial art no longer consisted of "cultural borrowing, but of assimilated features transformed into a new culture." R. Bianchi Bandinelli has contrasted the age of Augustus with an "age of Trajan," roughly from Nero to Marcus Aurelius, marked by passion and romanticism. For the first time, foreign borrowings and the native spirit of Rome were combined and balanced. Pergamum was a precursor of the sculptures on Trajan's column, but one can detect a new style, spirit and themes in the countless details incorporated into the frieze, two hundred metres long, which runs round the whole length of the column, telling the long story of Trajan's two victorious campaigns against the Dacians in A.D. 101–2 and 106–7. The scenes depicted are realistic, even gruesome in places. War is shown with its many dead, while the enemy is nevertheless treated with respect and shown to be scoring blows as well. Other novelties were the recognition (though can we be sure of this?) of the atrocities committed, and the entry into a work of art of the everyday actors in a great adventure: the soldiers, carters and bridge-builders. For the first time in Roman history, its anonymous heroes were being honoured.

The visual arts travel with ease from one civilization or country to another. Europe might have been divided into two by the Reformation but it was united by one artistic movement, the baroque. Literature on the other hand is tied to particular nations and therefore cannot avoid being *sui generis*.

Rome had a literary tradition well before Augustus. It seems to have had a sudden flowering then, but on closer inspection, writes Pierre Grimal, "the literary maturity of the Augustans can be seen to date rather from the crisis which preceded his reign." Nevertheless, Augustus and in particular the patron and *eques* Maecenas strongly influenced the literature of their time, both by their politics and in their personal taste. Maecenas was himself a poet, tempted by hermeticism and preciosity; Augustus' intellectual enthusiasm is undeniable. It might also be argued that literary consciousness identified itself with the new regime: the Augustan age saw the end of the civil wars, and a new sense of security and confidence in Roman "virtue." During these years, Rome witnessed a revolution of the mind that could, despite the anachronism, be described as nationalist. *Mutatis mutandis*, this was not unlike a stronger version of the French Renaissance as represented by Du Bellay and Ronsard. As opposed to the Hellenistic east, attractive yet unsettling, which had still been the model of the young poets of the Neoteroi circle in the days of Catullus (87–54 B.C.), there was now a reassertion of western values, those of Rome and traditional Italy. Careful preparation of public opinion also played a part: Rome, having acquired material superiority, now aspired to other kinds of greatness.

Augustus, like the Greek rulers, was a "providential prince." He may truly have imagined that he could rival Pericles and Athens, possessing as he did a quasi-religious sense of the grandeur and mission of Rome. It is this, more even than the influence of Maecenas, which gives its special character to the works of Virgil, Livy, Horace, possibly even Propertius. Virgil, who had always been a "Caesarist," naturally enlisted on the side of the young Octavian. He was simply continuing his lifelong itinerary then, rather than flattering the emperor, when in 29 B.C. he began the *Aeneid*. This work was still unfinished when he died, ten years later: in Virgil's own eyes it was imperfect and he begged in vain that it should be destroyed after his death. Rome now had its own Homeric epic, a monument to its glory and to that of Augustus who, since he claimed descent via the Julian line from Aeneas himself and therefore from Venus, was marked out by destiny to rule the Empire. There would also soon be a history of the city of Rome, from the pen of Livy (59 B.C.–A.D. 17) whose whole-hearted patriotism delivered even more than had been asked of him. His history, despite an honest attempt to look critically at his sources, remains a hymn to the grandeur of Rome. The teachers in the schools of the Empire nevertheless long preferred to these paeans of praise the more dry and terse prose of Sallust (85–35 B.C.), author of the *Jugurthan War* and the *Catiline Conspiracy*.

The other writers mentioned were not so committed to the state. Like Catullus and Tibullus, Propertius was mainly known for the poems addressed to his beloved Cynthia. But his *Elegies* written at the end of his life draw on the old legends of Rome: Tarpeia and the Trojan ancestors of the *gens Julia* appear, as well as young Roman women who conformed more closely than Cynthia to the reform in morals which Augustus sought to impose. Horace too followed a cautious line. Sensitive about his origins (he was the son of a freed slave) he was no less so about his past: in 42 B.C., in Macedonia, he had served in the army of the republican rebels, Brutus and Cassius. And he also valued his independence, living on his Sabine estate near Tibur, aloof from the temptations if not the rewards of the great. But he too received official commissions, writing the words of the hymn sung to celebrate the Secular Games in 17 B.C. When he died, aged 57, a few weeks after Maecenas (in 8 B.C.), he was buried alongside his friend.

Other writers were frankly recalcitrant towards the powers that be. They included the writer of elegies Tibullus, and most notably Ovid (43 B.C.–A.D. 17), who consciously returned to the Alexandrian inspiration of the Neoteroi. His daring poetry, humour and erotic verse, which made him the favourite poet of the courtesans and idlers of Rome, led to his banishment by Augustus. He composed his *Tristia* and *Pontics* at Tomes in Mesia on the distant shores of the Black Sea, and it was there that he died, still in exile.

It would be difficult to claim for literature what Bandinelli claims for the visual arts, namely that the age of Trajan was a time of greatness. Instead of the giants of the Augustan age, one would have to champion those of the next century: Quintilian, Lucan, Persius, Martial—which seems paradoxical—but also Tacitus, Seneca and Petronius, which is defensible enough. If we were to listen to the brilliant essayist Emil Ludwig, however, "everything that made the Romans great had already been produced by the Republic." And that would mean going back to Cicero and Terence or to Plautus (whom Horace detested). Historical judgements depend on individual taste.

Troubles were on the horizon well before the death of Marcus Aurelius; they were to punctuate the long and war-tormented reign of this philosopher-emperor. Frontier security, internal peace and the balance of power between the different provinces had all started to deteriorate. Prey to economic recession and monetary turmoil, Rome was ceasing to be the centre of the universe. The east was acquiring its liberty: its religions and ways of thought were encroaching violently upon the Roman tradition. The principate, as Augustus and the Antonines had conceived of it, was looking like an outdated form of prudent government. Bureaucracy had increased and the imperial power was sliding towards "the practices of oriental despotism": in his cruel folly, Commodus tried to have himself venerated as the god Hercules. He was the first emperor to call himself "king of the world and servant of divinity." Septimius Severus, of African and possibly Carthaginian origin, carried this transformation even further.

This mutation of society and civilization under the last of the Antonines was reflected in the arts. The change is clear, though not easy to interpret. It can be traced in the sudden, almost total disappearance of mural painting and in the striking contrast between the bas-reliefs on Trajan's column and those on the column of Marcus Aurelius. While the former obey a unitary conception and chronological order, the latter carvings present events in a confusing mélange, with different styles of workmanship: the battles against the Marcomanni, the Dacians, the Cottians and the Quadi are shown as the scenes of various miracles—thunderbolts, or torrential rain which saved the legionaries from thirst while drowning their enemies. This was an art which set out to make an impression rather than to record, and in so doing appealed to popular taste. Amedeo Mauri, the art historian, has suggested that the freedom of a certain kind of painting in Pompeii and elsewhere at the same time is not unlike the advertising hoardings of today.

Another change was that the provincial arts regained a degree of autonomy. Septimius Severus' triumphal arch at Leptis Magna already foreshadows the art of Byzantium. At Palmyra and Doura, a marginal art was emerging, a kind of cross between the Greek and the Mesopotamian. In its preference for the abstract, it has a kind of primitivism about it. These are fleeting glimpses of what was to come, and we can make sense of them only because we know the inexorable outcome of this story. Although everywhere the overall "Roman Empire" style, which had already become over-familiar, was tending to break down under pressure from local originality, this ubiquitous style was still strong enough to re-assert itself in certain circumstances. It can be seen under Gallianus (253–68), the friend of Plotinus, and under Diocletian (284–313), in the baths he had built in Rome or the palace he had built at Spalato. In short, there were many signs that that times were changing, but we are still a long way from Byzantium or from the Dark Ages.

And Rome went on creating ever-larger cities, turning them into capitals: Trèves/Trier, Milan, Salonika, Nicomedia. Literature too continued to flourish. Let us be bold enough to say that Ammianus Marcelinus (320–90) was the equal of Livy; that Ausonius of Bordeaux was a poet of true worth, that the literature of Christianity was extremely important, that the encouragement of education which was so evident in these difficult centuries certainly counted for something. Above all, there is the extraordinary success story of Roman law, which has remained in evidence to the present day.

One would quickly get lost in abstruse explanations if one were to open one of the admirable textbooks on Roman law we have today, to look up the meaning of simple terms like consent, obligation, contracts, property; or if one were to try to understand how law followed the complex history of a society, adapting to it while adapting that society in turn. In his work on the institutions of antiquity (1967) Jean Gaudemet studied the evolution of Roman life in the light of this dialectic between society and law. He paints three successive pictures, first Rome under the Republic, then the Rome of the First Empire, followed by the Rome of the Late Empire—the last of these being the key period. The Roman law of the Theodosian Codex (438) and the Justinian Codex (527) to be followed by the *Digest*, the *Institutes* and the *Novelles*, came at the end of a very long period of evolution, with various inherited factors superimposed on one another. Roman law was built up slowly, day by day, based on usage and custom, the *senatus-consultes*, the edicts of magistrates, the imperial "Constitutions," jurisprudence, and doctrines developed by legal experts.

The role of the legal experts, the jurists, who acted as legal advisers and barristers, was the most original feature of this complex construction. Without a doubt, Rome's intelligence and genius came into its own in this area. The metropolis could not maintain contact with its Empire—the rest of Italy, the provinces, the cities—without the legal regulations essential to the maintenance of political, social and economic order. The body of law could only increase over the ages. The great legal thinkers able to handle this vast mass of rules did not appear until a fairly late stage. Sabinus and Proculus were contemporaries of Tiberius; Gaius, whose *Institutiones* were discovered in 1816 by Niebuhr in a Verona palimpsest, lived in the age of Hadrian and Marcus Aurelius; while Pomponius, another famous jurist, was his contemporary. As for law schools, they appeared in the Late Empire, in Rome, Constantinople and Beirut, which played a leading role in the fifth century: the law school there would preserve Roman law, enabling the renaissance under Justinian to take place.

So Roman law stood firm until the last days of Rome or even longer. "When one considers how Roman law and institutions survived Rome's political dominion," writes Jean Gaudemet, "the idea of the decline and fall of the empire becomes quite meaningless." Rome certainly did not die in its entirety. The whole of the west was shaped by Roman survivals.

The old notions of the decline and fall of Rome are certainly open to debate. The Empire, although reported to be dying, survived its internal quarrels and the extravagance of its masters. There was no more gold or silver, the economy fell back into a pre-monetary state, yet life went on. There was no longer a disciplined army, as one after another the frontiers collapsed and the barbarians poured in, penetrating deep into Roman territory. Yet there were still soldiers prepared to die for Rome along the Rhine, outside Milan, on the banks of the Danube or in the valley of the Euphrates, fighting a new and formidable enemy, the Sassanid Persians, after 227. Even the building sites remained busy: Rome's colossal ramparts were built under Aurelian in 272. From 324, Constantine started to build his new capital at Constantinople, inaugurating it in 330. If we are looking for a symbolic event, here is one indeed. This gigantic torch would send its light down the centuries to come.

This was no hastily constructed city, built in a day: it was a second Rome, an act of incalculable consequences, the more so since it was linked to the emperor's conversion to Christianity. By this act the destiny of both the Mediterranean and the Empire took the path which would lead to the eventual survival and longevity of Byzantium—something which Constantine in the course of his actions probably neither realized nor desired, for he had certainly not chosen the new capital to escape the structures of pagan Rome. Since the days of Diocletian and the tetrarchy, few emperors had had the time to stay long in Rome. In his new capital, Constantine was within reach of the Danube and the Euphrates, fragile gates on which the barbarians were constantly hammering.

But it is Constantinople's future that we in the west find so fascinating, since our own history is as it were prefigured there. Who could fail to be interested in the prodigious seismic change produced by the triumph of Christianity? In the event it triumphed only after centuries of deep trouble. But it was carried on the violent groundswell of a deep-seated revolution—not an exclusively spiritual one—which had developed slowly from the second century.

It was between 162 and 168, in the early reign of Marcus Aurelius (161–80), that the foreign situation so comprehensively deteriorated. The intellectual, moral and religious crisis of the Empire followed almost immediately. Although the tolerant paganism of Rome with its thousands of gods might still be alive and in reasonable health throughout the Empire, and although the cult of the emperor was still strong, broadly corresponding to a form of patriotism, it seems certain that paganism could not truly satisfy either the masses or the elites. The latter looked to philosophy for their salvation, the former yearned for more accessible gods, for more tangible consolations. There could be no greater consolation than the belief in life after death. It is not without significance that "in the second century burial became more frequent than cremation, whereas in previous centuries the proportions were the other way round. . . . The form of burial which left the dead person's body as it had been in life is not unconnected to the spread of belief in an after-life, in eternal salvation and the possible resurrection of the body" (E. Albertini).

Here there was a connecting thread. Although sociological and geographical differences can be seen, revealing a variety of responses according to class and region, the question being asked was everywhere the same. Rich and poor were troubled by the same anguish. The renewal of Greek philosophy in Rome is significant. The Cynics (Demetrius and Oenomaos), those strange philosophers who claimed to be messengers from Zeus, became travelling preachers. Neoplatonism took over from both Epicureanism and Stoicism. The most important of its interpreters was Plotinus (205–70), a Greek, born in Egypt. At the age of forty, he settled in Rome and opened a school which enjoyed huge success. His philosophy took Plato as its starting point but sought to reconcile all the various strands of contemporary thought in a single mystical urge.

More disturbing signs pointed to the depth of the crisis. There was a proliferation of thaumaturgi and miracle-workers, such as Apollonius of Tyana, who died in Rome in 97, but whose life with its marvels provided Philostratus (d. about 275) with enough material for a novel. His hero preached the cult of the sun, performed miracles, halted epidemics and healed the sick. The success of this book was a symptom of the times, and it would be outdone later. To influence mortals was one thing: to influence the life of the gods was another—and this was what theurgy claimed to do, providing a field day for charlatans and illuminati.

Such a climate explains the growing prestige in the west of eastern cults: the cults of Isis, Cybele, Attis, Mithras, and before long the religion of Christianity, quickly gained ground. The soldiers who travelled throughout the Empire played a part in this spread of religions, as did the eastern merchants, the *Syri*, Jews and Syrians, who were present everywhere. But the emperor and his entourage carried enormous weight in this process. Neither Cybele nor Mithras and the bloody baptisms of his cult would have been so widespread had it not been that certain emperors looked on them with favour.

This was equally true of Christianity, which was for a long time persecuted by Rome. Without Constantine's conversion, what would have become of it? "Let us imagine that the king of France decided to convert to Protestantism, the religion of a small minority of his subjects," writes Ferdinand Lot. "Fired with pious zeal against 'idolatry', he would have destroyed or allowed to fall into ruin all the most venerated sanctuaries of the kingdom, the abbey at Saint-Denis, Reims cathedral, the crown of thorns, the Sainte-Chapelle. That still only gives a faint idea of the frenzy that took hold of the Roman emperors of the fourth century."

But the Christian religion did not become the state religion without coming to some arrangement with the politics, society and even the civilization of Rome. The civilization of the Roman Mediterranean was taken over by the young forces of Christianity. As a result, it had to accept many compromises, fundamental and structural ones. And it is in this shape, and carrying this mixed message, that the civilization of antiquity has come down to us.

Editor's note: This work, which covers such a long chronological span, has no overall conclusion. This might seem rather surprising: the reason is that it was originally conceived as the first volume in a collection (see the prefaces above) and would have led directly into the next volume, by another historian, which was to be devoted to Byzantium. Fernand Braudel therefore planned his conclusion so that it would fit the introduction of the following volume. When the collection was cancelled, it was left as we have it here.

Appendix I

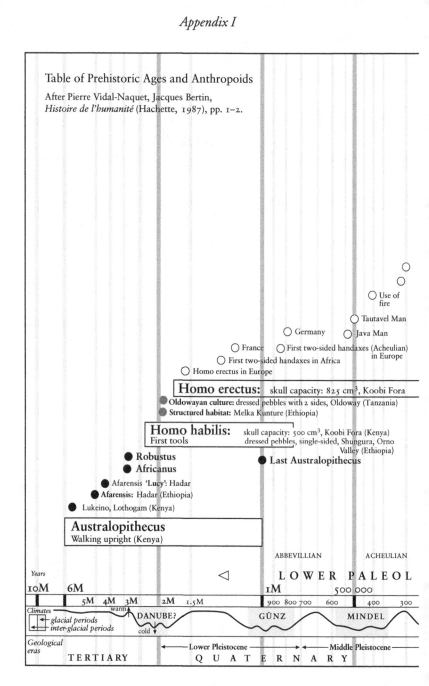

Table of Prehistoric Ages and Anthropoids

After Pierre Vidal-Naquet, Jacques Bertin,
Histoire de l'humanité (Hachette, 1987), pp. 1–2.

○

○

○ Use of
fire

○ Tautavel Man

○ Germany   ○ Java Man

○ France   ○ First two-sided handaxes (Acheulian)
○ First two-sided handaxes in Africa   in Europe
○ Homo erectus in Europe

Homo erectus: skull capacity: 825 cm³, Koobi Fora

● **Oldowayan culture:** dressed pebbles with 2 sides, Oldoway (Tanzania)
● **Structured habitat:** Melka Kunture (Ethiopia)

Homo habilis: skull capacity: 500 cm³, Koobi Fora (Kenya)
First tools   dressed pebbles, single-sided, Shungura, Orno
Valley (Ethiopia)

● **Robustus**   ● **Last Australopithecus**
● **Africanus**

● Afarensis 'Lucy': Hadar
● **Afarensis:** Hadar (Ethiopia)

● Lukeino, Lothogam (Kenya)

Australopithecus
Walking upright (Kenya)

ABBEVILLIAN   ACHEULIAN

Years   ◁   **L O W E R   P A L E O L**

10M   6M   **1M**   500 000

5M 4M 3M   2M   1.5M   900 800 700   600   400   300

Climates
warm
↤ *glacial periods*   DANUBE?   GÜNZ   MINDEL
↤ *inter-glacial periods*   cold

*Geological
eras*   ◀——— Lower Pleistocene ———▶ ◀— Middle Pleistocene ———
T E R T I A R Y   **Q U A T E R N A R Y**

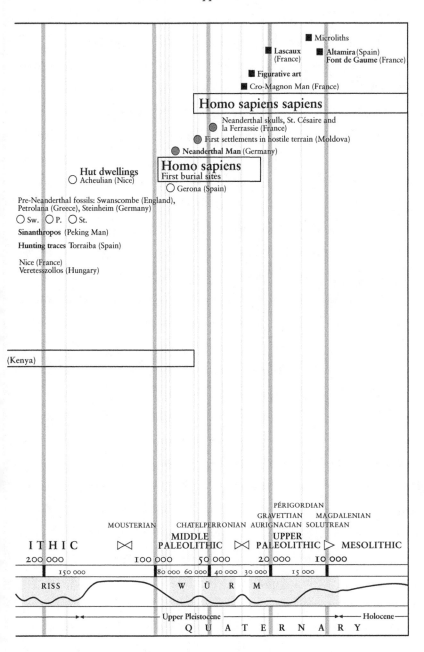

Appendix II

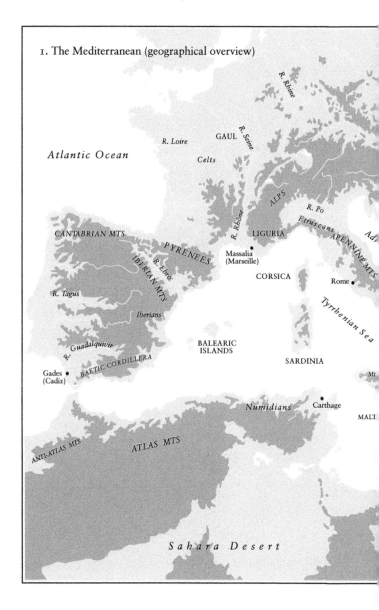

1. The Mediterranean (geographical overview)

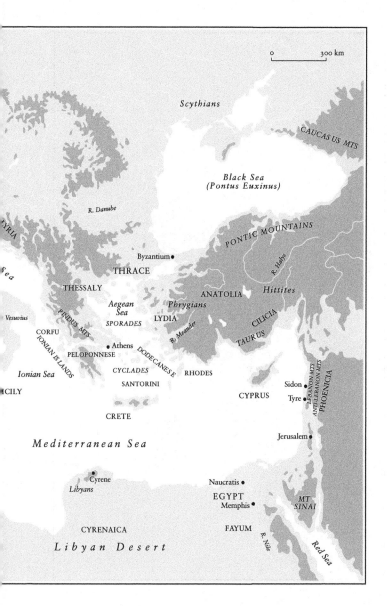

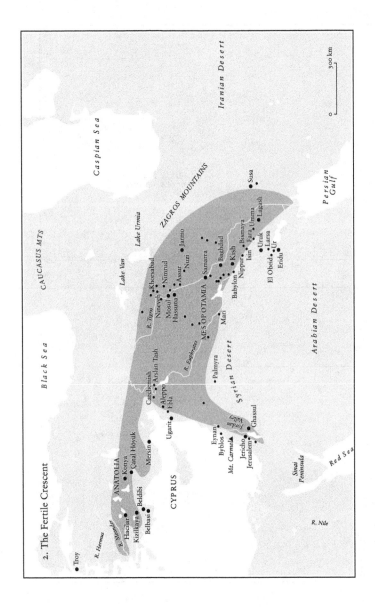

2. The Fertile Crescent

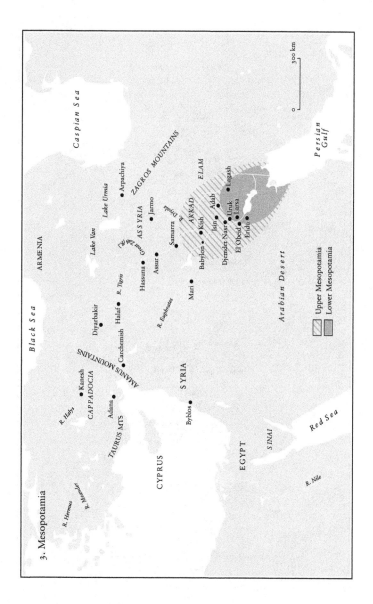

3. Mesopotamia

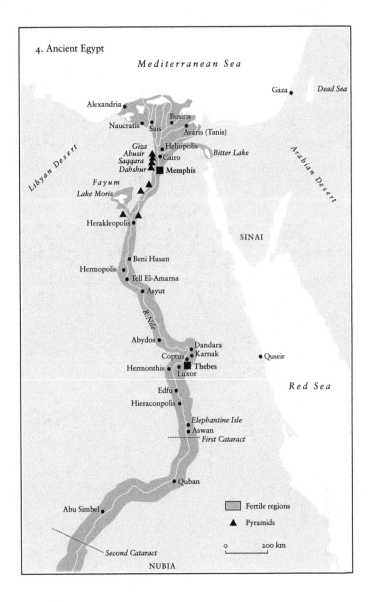

4. Ancient Egypt

Mediterranean Sea

Gaza   *Dead Sea*

Alexandria

Busiris

Naucratis   Sais   Avaris (Tanis)

Libyan Desert

Giza   Heliopolis
Abusir   *Bitter Lake*
Saqqara   Cairo
Dahshur   ■ Memphis

Arabian Desert

Fayum
Lake Moris

Herakleopolis

SINAI

Beni Hasan

Hermopolis   Tell El-Amarna

Asyut

R. Nile

Abydos   Dandara

Coptus   Karnak   Quseir

Hermonthis   ■ Thebes
Luxor

Red Sea

Edfu

Hieraconpolis

Elephantine Isle
Aswan
---- *First Cataract*

Quban

Abu Simbel

☐ Fertile regions

▲ Pyramids

0   200 km

---- *Second Cataract*

NUBIA

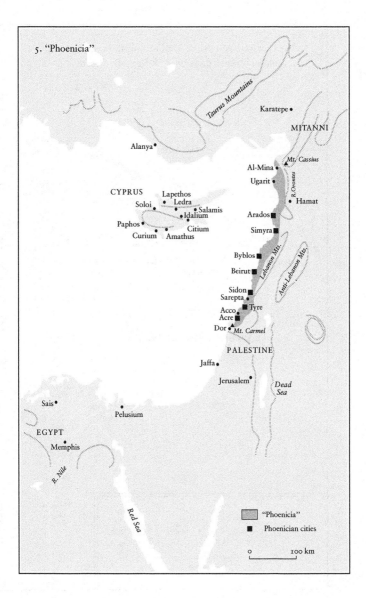

5. "Phoenicia"

Taurus Mountains

Karatepe •

MITANNI

Alanya •

Al-Mina • ▲ *Mt. Cassius*

Ugarit •

CYPRUS   Lapethos

Soloi •   Ledra

Salamis

Paphos •   Idalium   • Citium

Curium •   Amathus

R. Orontes

Hamat •

Arados ■

Simyra ■

Byblos ■

Lebanon Mts.   *Anti-Lebanon Mts.*

Beirut ■

Sidon •

Sarepta ■ Tyre

Acco

Acre ■

Dor • ▲ *Mt. Carmel*

PALESTINE

Jaffa •

Jerusalem •   *Dead Sea*

Sais •

Pelusium •

EGYPT

Memphis •

R. Nile

Red Sea

▨   "Phoenicia"

■   Phoenician cities

o |———————| 100 km

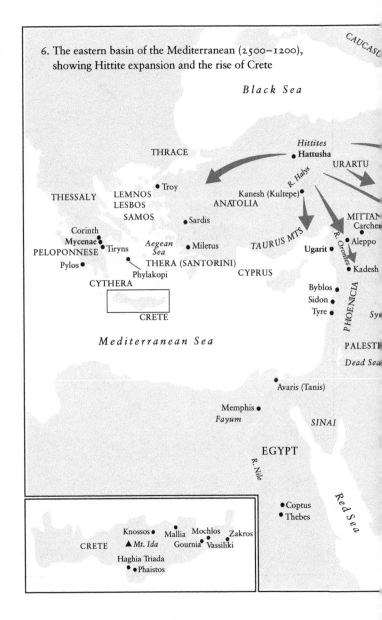

6. The eastern basin of the Mediterranean (2500–1200), showing Hittite expansion and the rise of Crete

Black Sea

CAUCASU

THRACE

Hittites
Hattusha

URARTU

THESSALY

LEMNOS
LESBOS

SAMOS

Troy

R. Halys

Kanesh (Kultepe)

ANATOLIA

Sardis

MITTAN
Carche

Corinth
Mycenae
PELOPONNESE Tiryns

Aegean Sea

Miletus

TAURUS MTS

Ugarit

R. Orontes

Aleppo

Pylos

THERA (SANTORINI)

Phylakopi

CYPRUS

Kadesh

CYTHERA

Byblos

Sidon

Tyre

PHOENICIA

Sy

CRETE

Mediterranean Sea

PALESTI

Dead Sea

Avaris (Tanis)

Memphis
Fayum

SINAI

EGYPT

R. Nile

Red Sea

Coptus
Thebes

Knossos
▲ *Mt. Ida*

Mallia
Gournia

Mochlos
Vassiliki

Zakros

CRETE

Haghia Triada
Phaistos

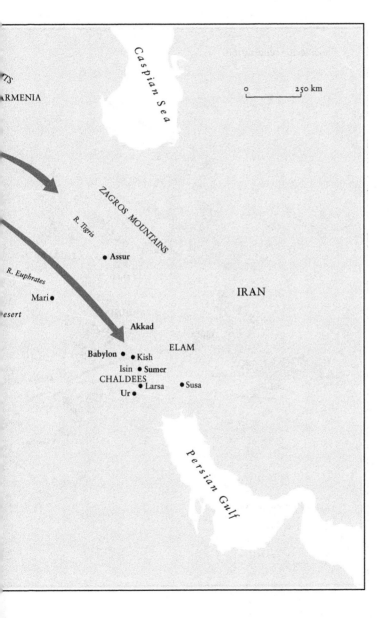

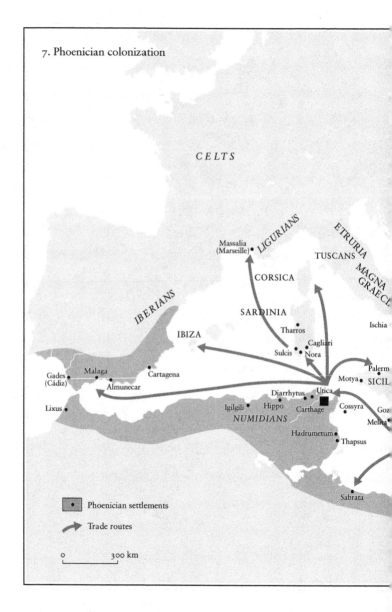

7. Phoenician colonization

CELTS

LIGURIANS

ETRURIA

TUSCANS

MAGNA GRAECI

Massalia
(Marseille)

CORSICA

SARDINIA

IBERIANS

Tharros

Ischia

IBIZA

Cagliari

Sulcis • Nora

Gades
(Cádiz)

Malaga

Cartagena

Palerm

Motya • SICIL

Almunecar

Diarrhytus • Utica

Lixus

Igilgili • Hippo

Carthage

Cossyra

Goz

NUMIDIANS

Melit

Hadrumetum

Thapsus

Sabrata

▪ Phoenician settlements

Trade routes

0 — 300 km

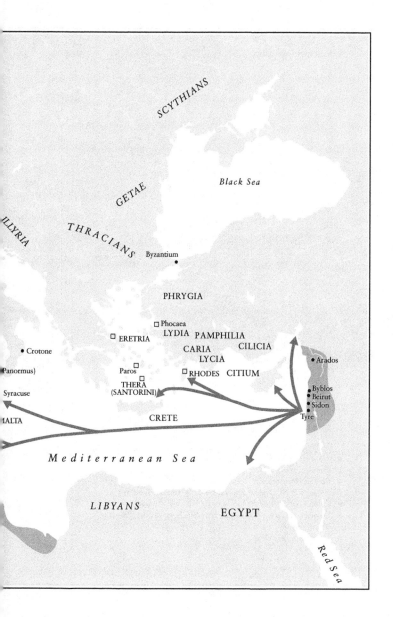

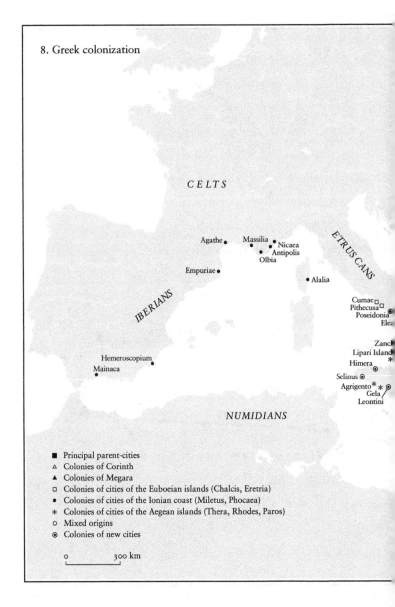

8. Greek colonization

CELTS

Agathe •   • Massilia
       •   Nicaea
       • Antipolis
     Olbia

Empuriae •

ETRUSCANS

• Alalia

IBERIANS

Cumae ▫
Pithecusa ▫ ◉
   Poseidonia
     Elea

Zancl
Lipari Island
Himera ◉   *
Selinus ◉
Agrigento * * ◉
     Gela
     Leontini

Hemeroscopium •
Mainaca •

NUMIDIANS

■   Principal parent-cities
△   Colonies of Corinth
▲   Colonies of Megara
▫   Colonies of cities of the Euboeian islands (Chalcis, Eretria)
•   Colonies of cities of the Ionian coast (Miletus, Phocaea)
*   Colonies of cities of the Aegean islands (Thera, Rhodes, Paros)
○   Mixed origins
◉   Colonies of new cities

○   300 km

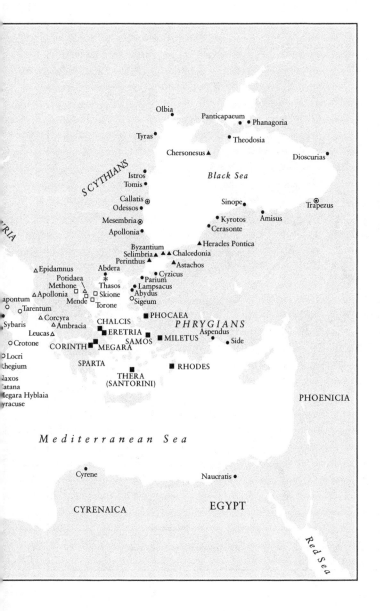

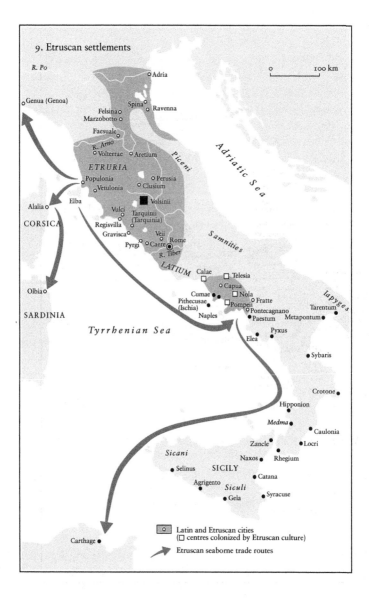

9. Etruscan settlements

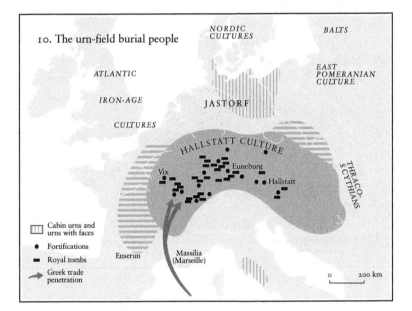

10. The urn-field burial people

NORDIC CULTURES

BALTS

ATLANTIC

EAST POMERANIAN CULTURE

IRON-AGE

JASTORF

CULTURES

HALLSTATT CULTURE

Vix

Euneburg

Hallstatt

THRACO-SCYTHIANS

Cabin urns and urns with faces

Fortifications

Royal tombs

Greek trade penetration

Enserun

Massilia (Marseille)

0   200 km

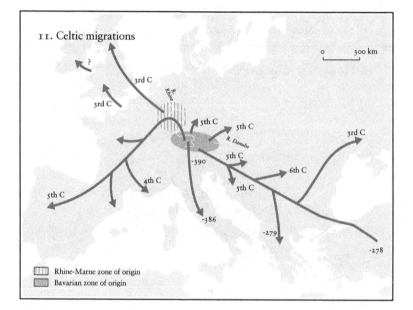

11. Celtic migrations

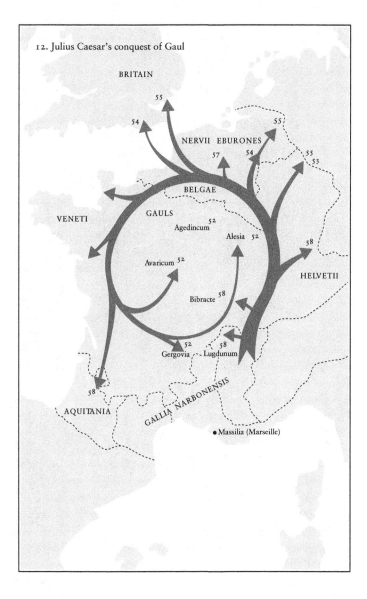

12. Julius Caesar's conquest of Gaul

BRITAIN

55

54

NERVII EBURONES

55

57 54 55
53

BELGAE

VENETI

GAULS

52
Agedincum

Alesia 52

58

Avaricum 52

HELVETII

Bibracte 58

52 58
Gergovia Lugdunum

58

AQUITANIA

GALLIA NARBONENSIS

• Massilia (Marseille)

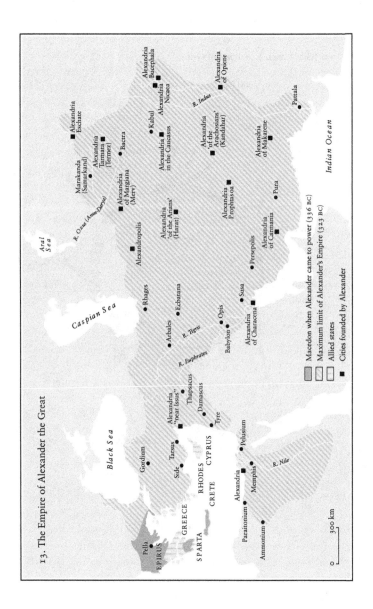

13. The Empire of Alexander the Great

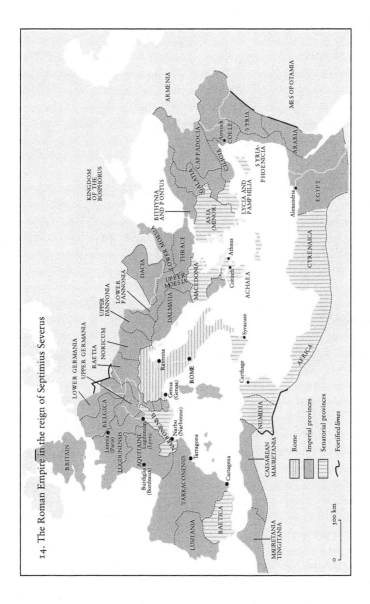

14. The Roman Empire in the reign of Septimius Severus

Notes

Editors' Foreword to the French Edition

1. Françoise Gaultier, Chief Curator in the Department of Greek, Etruscan and Roman Antiquities at the Louvre, read the sections on the Etruscans, and Jean-Louis Huot, Professor at the University of Paris I, read the sections on the eastern Mediterranean.

CHAPTER TWO
The Long March to Civilization

1. Today one would put it at between one and two, or even three million years. The oldest carved tools (found in Africa) are about two and a half million years old. (JG)

2. There is now reason to think that the Paleolithic goes back over two million years. (JG)

3. Today the Middle Paleolithic is regarded as starting in about 200,000 B.C. and ending in about 35,000. It was thought to last only about 40,000 years at the time Braudel was writing. (JG)

4. We know now that this is not the case. Sardinia was settled in the thirteenth millennium B.C. and Corsica in the eleventh. But it also seems possible that a much older population could have inhabited these islands (witness the "Paleolithic" artefacts of Sardinia, and the hearth in a cave at Coscia in Corsica which has been attributed to Neanderthal man). (JG)

5. The figure is now thought to be 200,000 years B.C. (JG)

6. Neanderthal man is nowadays considered to have been a *sapiens*. He is described as *Homo sapiens neandertalis*, to distinguish him from *Homo sapiens sapiens*, who would eliminate him during the transition between the Middle and Upper Paleolithic ages. (JG)

7. Their arguments have been confirmed in recent years: it is no longer suggested that the Mesolithic was marked by hardship and backwardness: on the contrary, the development and exploitation of the forests made possible the establishment of "progressive" cultures, as Braudel himself notes below. (JG)

8. The term "town" should be used with caution: large villages of Neolithic times were not necessarily towns with all that the term implies: administration, centralized functions, specialized artisans, often in their own districts, monuments created for purposes of prestige or identity, etc. The figure of 2000 inhabitants is not known with certainty. (JG)

Notes

9. As with Jericho, the term "town" is controversial. (JG)

10. It is now thought that the cattle of Çatal Höyük were only in the process of being domesticated. The chronology of the appearance of domestic cattle in the Middle East is still a matter of debate. (JG)

CHAPTER THREE
A Twofold Birth

1. They are now thought to date from about 4000 B.C. (JG)

2. They have now been excavated at the Aetokremnos site on the Akrotiri peninsula. (JG)

3. The cardial culture is now thought, according to "calibrated" dating methods, to date from the sixth millennium B.C. (JG)

4. Today the date is put at about 2500 B.C. (JG)

5. If the boats drawn at Tarxien are contemporary with the temple, they must date from the third millennium B.C. The suggestion of contacts with the Aegean in the second millennium is therefore anachronistic as far as these images are concerned. (JG)

6. Fernand Braudel thought that the megalith/Earth-Mother/metal-working complex was all part of the same culture and diffused from the eastern Mediterranean. This combination is no longer regarded as valid (cf. Jean Guilaine, *La Mer partagée. La Méditerranée avant l'écriture 7000–2000 avant J.-C.*, Paris, 1994). The sequence is now thought to have been as follows: (1) the first agricultural societies and their religions (eighth to seventh millennia B.C. in the Middle East, sixth millennium in the west); (2) the megaliths: the oldest ones are in the west and date from about 4500 B.C.; (3) metal-working: this developed earliest in Anatolia and southeast Europe (in about 5000 to 4500 B.C.) and later in the west (*c.* 3500–3000 B.C.). (JG)

7. Carbon dating has now provided a much earlier date for the megaliths of the west, especially those on the Atlantic coast. Megalithic culture was a Neolithic phenomenon and had no connection with metal-working in these western regions. (JG)

8. Since 1969, it has become possible to date many megaliths. The ones in the west seem to be completely unconnected with those in the Mediterranean. It seems that the phenomenon could be the result of either contacts or convergence, varying from case to case. (JG)

9. The desertion of the Hal Tarxien temple is now dated to about 2500 B.C. It is not clear that the temple was destroyed. (JG)

10. Here again, the dating has been completely modified since 1969. Traces of Paleolithic settlement have been found in Sardinia dating from the thirteenth millennium (the Corbeddu cave) and dates even further back are possible. In the sixth millennium B.C., Neolithic settlers colonized Corsica, Sardinia and other regions of the western Mediterranean. (JG)

11. These lines were written at a time when it was customary to telescope the chronology of these phenomena. The much longer chronology favoured today allows us to date the cult of Ozieri to the fourth millennium B.C., the dolmen tombs to the third, the "tombs of the giants" to the second, and the *nuraghi* villages to sometime after 1500 B.C., with rebuilding going on down to Roman times. (JG)

12. This view according to which the megaliths spread west from the Mediterranean is no longer tenable. The oldest dolmens on the Iberian peninsula are those on the Atlantic coast, not those on the Mediterranean side. The megalith phenomenon appears to have been partly created in the west. (JG)

13. There is no evidence of the links between these invaders and the megaliths, or of any eastern influence. More generally, the comparison with the Aegean is misleading. (JG)

14. That is precisely what has been discovered, with the help of carbon dating. Some of these phenomena have even been found to be older still, going back to the fifth millennium B.C. (JG)

15. These migrations are disputed today. (JG)

CHAPTER FOUR

Centuries of Unity: The Seas of the Levant 2500–1200 B.C.

1. The announcement was premature: the script of the Indus valley has still not been deciphered. (PR, 1996)

2. This explanation is no longer accepted. On the crisis of the twelfth century B.C., see W. A. Ward and M. S. Joukovsky, *The Crisis Years: The 12th Century B.C.: From beyond the Danube to the Tigris*, Dubuque, 1992. (PR)

3. On Crete and the "disaster" of Thera and its consequences, see the more nuanced views taken today in R. Treuil et al., *Les Civilisations égéennes du Néolithique et de l'Âge du Bronze*, Paris, 1989. (PR)

4. This hypothesis is today discredited. (PR)

5. Minoan ships did not in fact reach Malta, Sicily or southern Italy, but Mycenaean ships did. (PR)

6. On the Peoples of the Sea, see above, note 2. (PR)

7. There is even more scepticism on this point today. (PR)

8. But we now know that life started up again there on a smaller scale and that the sites were not really abandoned until the end of the twelfth century. (PR)

CHAPTER FIVE

All Change: The Twelfth to the Eighth Centuries B.C.

1. Rather than "Phoenicia," it would be more accurate to say "the Phoenician cities." (PR)

2. On these "invasions" see the more recent work in P. Brun and C. Mordant, eds., *Le Groupe Rhin-Suisse-France orientale et la notion des Champs d'Urnes*, Nemours, 1988. (PR)

CHAPTER SIX

Colonization: The Discovery of the Mediterranean "Far West"
in the Tenth to Sixth Centuries B.C.

1. Corinth was not the only city concerned. Other cities founded colonies: Chalcis, Megara, Sparta, Colophon, Paros, Miletus and Phocaea, as the author himself points out below. (PR)

2. Nowadays, it is well established that there were several centres of production. Cf. J. Winter in *Iraq*, 43, 1981, pp. 101–30. (PR)

3. As in all the other Phoenician sites in the western Mediterranean. (PR)

4. See J. Desanges, *Recherches sur l'activité des Méditerranéens aux confins d'Afrique*, Rome, 1978. (PR)

5. Nowadays it is not thought that the Phoenicians were the first people to mine metal in Sardinia. See Michel Gras, "Trafics tyrrhéniens archaïques," *BEFAR*, 258, Rome, 1985. (PR)

6. In fact, Greeks from Euboea were already navigating in the western Mediterranean from the eighth century B.C. (PR)

7. We would not be so certain of this today: a few instances have been found at Sarepta. (PR)

8. On the Phoenicians and in particular on the *tophet* and Carthage see Michel Gras, Pierre Rouillard and Javier Teixidor, *L'Univers phénicien*, Paris, 1995, 2nd edition. (PR)

9. Nowadays the theory that the Etruscans arrived by emigration is in fact being ousted by the notion of an indigenous formation. See D. Briquel, *Les Étrusques*, Paris 1993 and the catalogue of the exhibition *Les Étrusques et l'Europe*, Paris, 1992. (PR)

10. These excavations have now been carried out and the results published by A. Pontrandolfo and A. Rouveret, *Le Tombe dipinte di Paestum*, Modena, 1992. (PR)

11. In fact Villanovan culture has already been attested in Campania in the ninth and eighth centuries B.C. (PR)

12. The same is true of the Po valley as of Campania (see previous note). (PR)

13. It is no longer thought that there was any continuity between Mycenae and Greek colonial culture, rather there appears to have been a hiatus. (PR)

14. It is now thought that there were only a few voyages at this period, and we do not know at all who was responsible for them. (PR)

15. On Greek colonization in general, see *Les Grecs et l'Occident*, Paris, 1995 and J.-L. Lamboley, *Les Grecs d'Occident. La période archaïque*, Paris 1996. (PR)

16. On Marseille, see "Marseille grecque et la Gaule," *Études des Massalictes*, 3, Aix-en-Provence, 1992. (PR)

17. Nowadays this point is not accepted. Until the Barcides went to Spain, the Carthaginians had little presence there. (PR)

CHAPTER EIGHT

The Roman Takeover of the Greater Mediterranean

1. On the Roman conquest of Gaul, see the critical view of C. Goudineau, *César et la Gaule*, Paris, 1990. (PR)

2. For a full discussion, see *L'Art décoratif à Rome à la fin de la République et au début du Principat*, Rome, 1981. (PR)

Bibliography

Because of the unfinished nature of the French text, references were incomplete, usually consisting only of an author's name and sometimes a date. The list of titles cited here has been compiled by the translator from the British Library Catalogue to 1975 as being the most likely references, but it cannot be regarded as definitive or complete.

Albertini, E., *L'Empire romain* (Paris, Alcan, 1929)

Albright, William Foxwell, *The Archaeology of Palestine and the Bible* (New York, Fleming Revell, 1932)

Aldred, Cyril, *The Development of Ancient Egyptian Art from 3200 to 1315 B.C.* (London, Tiranti, 1952)

Bailloud, G., with P. M. de Boofzheim, *Les Civilisations néolithiques de la France dans leur contexte européen* (Paris, Picard, 1955)

Balout, Lionel, *Préhistoire de l'Afrique du Nord* (Paris, Arts et Métiers Graphiques, 1955)

Benda, Julien, *Esquisse d'une histoire des Français dans leur volonté de former une nation* (Paris, Gallimard, 1932)

Bérard, Victor, *Les Phéniciens et l'Odyssée* (Paris, A. Colin, 1902–3)

Bianchi Bandinelli, Ranuccio, *Storicità dell'arte classica* (Florence, Sansoni, 1943)

Bittel, Kurt, *Die Ruinen von Bogazköy* (Berlin, De Gruyter, 1937)

Bloch, Raymond, *Les Étrusques* (Paris, PUF, 1954)

L'Art et la civilisation étrusques (Paris, Plon, 1955)

Bordes, François, *Les Limons quaternaires du bassin de la Seine* (Paris, Masson, 1954)

Typologie du paléolithique ancien et moyen (Bordeaux, Univ. de Bordeaux, 1961)

The Old Stone Age, tr. J. Anderson (London, Weidenfeld & Nicolson, 1968)

Boule, Marcelin, *Fossil Men: elements of human paleontology*, tr. J. and J. Ritchie (Edinburgh, Oliver & Boyd, 1923)

Bourdier, Franck, *Préhistoire de France* (Paris, Nouvelle bibliothèque scientifique, 1967)

Breuil, Henri, *Les Hommes de la pierre ancienne* (Paris, Bibliothèque scientifique, 1959)

The Men of the Old Stone Age, Paleolithic and Mesolithic, tr. B. Rafter (London, Harrap, 1965)

Carcopino, Jérôme, *Les Étapes de l'impérialisme romain* (Paris, 1961)

Carpenter, Rhys, *Beyond the Pillars of Hercules: the classical world seen through the eyes of its discoverers* (New York, Delacorte Press, 1966)

Bibliography

Ceram, C. W., *The World of Archaeology* (London, Collins, 1968)

Cintas, Pierre, "Fouilles puniques à Tipasa," *Revue africaine* (Algiers, 1949)

Childe, Gordon, *The Bronze Age* (Cambridge, Cambridge University Press, 1930)

Coon, Carleton Steven, *The Origin of Races* (London, Cape, 1963)

Croiset, Alfred and Maurice, *Histoire de la littérature grecque* (Paris, 1887–93)

Desborough, Vincent, *The Last Mycenaeans and Their Successors: an archaeological survey c. 1200–1000 B.C.* (Oxford, Clarendon Press, 1964)

Dussaud, René, *Les Civilisations pré-helleniques dans le bassin de la Mer d'Égée* (Paris, 1914)

Effenterre, Henri van, *La Crète et le monde grec* (Paris, Bibliothèque des Écoles Françaises d'Athènes et de Rome, 1948)

Evans, John Davies, *The Prehistoric Antiquities of the Maltese Islands: a survey* (London, Athlone Press, 1971)

Malta (London, Thames & Hudson, 1950)

Farrington, Benjamin, *Aristotle, Founder of Scientific Philosophy* (London, Weidenfeld & Nicolson, 1965)

Gaudemet, Jean, *Institutions de l'antiquité* (Paris, 1967)

Gautier, Emile-Félix, *Le Passé de l'Afrique du Nord* (Paris, Payot, 1964)

Gernet, Louis, *Droit et pré-droit en Grèce ancienne* (Paris, Année sociologique, 1948–9)

Anthropologie de la Grèce antique (Paris, 1968)

Grenier, Albert, *Les Religions étrusque et romaine* (Paris, 1948)

Grimal, Pierre, *Dans les pas des Césars* (Paris, 1955)

La Vie à Rome dans l'antiquité (Paris, PUF, 1972)

Grousset, René, *De la Grèce à la Chine* (Monaco, 1948)

L'Empire des Steppes (Paris, 1939)

Heichelheim, F. M., *A History of the Roman People* (Englewood Cliffs, Prentice-Hall, 1962)

An Ancient Economic History, tr. Stevens (Leiden, Sijthoff, 1958)

Heurgon, Jacques, *La Vie quotidienne des Étrusques* (Paris, Hachette, 1962)

Daily Life of the Etruscans, tr. J. Kirkup (London, Weidenfeld & Nicolson, 1964)

Hrozny, Bedrich (Frédéric), *Code hittite, transcription et traduction française* (Paris, 1922)

Hubert, Henri, *Les Celtes depuis l'époque de la Tène et la civilisation celtique* (Paris, 1932)

The Greatness and Decline of the Celts, ed. M. Mauss (London, Kegan Paul, 1934)

Kirk, G. E., *A Short History of the Middle East* (London, Methuen, 1948)

Koyré, Alexandre, *Etudes d'histoire de la pensée scientifique* (Paris, Cahiers des Annales 19, 1961)

Kramer, Samuel Noah, *History Begins at Sumer* (London, Thames & Hudson, 1958)

Lévi-Strauss, Claude, *Tristes tropiques*, tr. J. and D. Weightman (London, Cape, 1973)

Lot, Ferdinand, *La Fin du monde antique et le début du moyen âge* (Paris, 1927)

Lucas, J. V., *The End of Atlantis* (London, 1969)

Ludwig, Emil, *On Mediterranean Shores* (*Am Mittelmeer*), tr. E. Paul (Boston, Little, Brown, 1929)

Mason, Stephen Finney, *A History of the Sciences: main currents of scientific thought* (London, Routledge and Kegan Paul, 1953)

Meyer, Eduard, *Geschichte des Altertums* (Basel, 1953–8)

Morenz, S., *Egyptian Religion* (*Ägyptische Religion*, 1960), tr. A. Keep (London, Methuen, 1973)

Moscati, Sabatino, *Il Mondo dei Fenici* (Milan, 1966)

The World of the Phoenicians, tr. A. Hamilton (London, Weidenfeld and Nicolson, 1968)

Nougier, Louis René, *Géographie humaine préhistorique* (Paris, 1959)

Oppenheimer, J. Robert, *Science and the Common Understanding*, Reith Lectures (London, Oxford University Press, 1953)

Bibliography

Picard, G. "A travers les musées et sites de l'Afrique du Nord," *Revue archéologique*, 6, 25 (1947)

Piganiol, A., *Essai sur les origines de Rome* (Paris, 1917)

Planhol, X. de, *De la plaine pamphylienne aux lacs pisidans. Nomadisme et vie paysanne* (Paris, 1958)

Posener, G., *Dictionnaire de la civilisation égyptienne* (Paris, 1959)

    A Dictionary of Egyptian Civilization, tr. A. McFarlane (London, Methuen, 1962)

Przyluski, Jean, *L'Évolution humaine* (Paris, 1942)

Rougier, Louis, *Le Génie de l'Occident. Essai sur la formation d'une mentalité* (Paris, Laffont, 1969)

Schaeffer, Claude, *Mission de Ras-Shamra* (Paris, 1936)

Seele, Keith and Steindorff, Georg, *When Egypt Ruled the East* (London, 1957)

Selincourt, Aubrey de, *The World of Herodotus* (London, Secker & Warburg, 1962)

Smith, William S., *Interconnections in the Ancient Near East: a study of the relationships between the arts of Egypt, the Aegean and Western Asia* (New Haven, Yale University Press, 1965)

Stekelis, Moshe, *Les Monuments mégalithiques de Palestine* (Paris, 1935)

Vallet, Georges, *Rhégion et Zancle. Histoire, commerce et civilisation des cités chalcidiennes du détroit de Messine* (Paris, 1958)

Varagnac, André and Deroloz, R., *Les Celtes et les Germains* (Paris, 1965)

Vernant, J.-P., *Les Origines de la pensée grecque* (Paris, 1962)

Vieyra, Maurice, *Les Assyriens* (Paris, 1961)

Vita-Finzi, Claudio, *The Mediterranean Valleys* (Cambridge, Cambridge University Press, 1969)

Weber, Alfred, *Kulturgeschichte als Kultursoziologie* (Leiden, 1935)

Wilamowitz-Moellendorf, Ulrich von, *Griechische Verskunst* (Berlin, 1921)

Will, Edouard et al., *Korinthiaka. Recherches sur l'histoire et la civilisation de Corinthe des origines aux guerres médiques* (Paris, 1955)

Translator's Note

As this is the last of the full-length books by Fernand Braudel to be translated into English, I would like to put on record my thanks to the people who have regularly helped and advised me over the years, for those translations with which I have been associated. (Some of his books have been ably translated by other hands, notably Miriam Kochan, Sarah Matthews and Richard Mayne.) I would therefore particularly like to thank Madame Paule Braudel for all her kindness and expertise; Richard Ollard, whose encyclopedic knowledge and generosity have been available since the earliest days and who has read over the manuscript of the present work; Stuart Proffitt, who is an editor in a million; Douglas Matthews, who has expertly compiled several of the indexes; and Peter France, who has always been there, but has offered help well beyond the call of duty in this last volume. Most translations are to some extent team efforts, but for any mistakes and shortcomings in the final text, I am solely responsible.

Siân Reynolds

Index

Abbeville period, 21, 22
Abraham, 199
Abruzzi, 6
Achaeans, 120, 124, 141, 153, 154, 169, 280
Achaemenids, 229, 245
Achilles, 171, 259
Achytus, 260
Adad, 143
Adonis, 197
Adriatic Sea, 26
Aegean Sea, 26, 80–5, 89, 92, 109–11, 114,
    179; climate in, 151; early peoples of, 120;
    Greek colonization around, 214–15; schism
    between Middle East and, 96; spread of
    Cretan influence around, 115, 120–1, 127
Aemilianus, Scipio, 195
Aemilius Paulus, V. L., 285
Aeneas, 273, 309
Aeschylus, 241
Aeteo-Cretans, 150
Aetesian winds, 8, 151
Afanasievo civilization, 139
Agamemnon, 86
Agathocles, 199
agriculture, 11, 12, 17–18, 36, 48, 78;
    Carthaginian, 191, 196; climate and, 8–10,
    24; on Crete, 109; currency and, 100;
    Etruscan, 204, 205; Greek, 120, 214,
    216–18, 221; iron and, 171; megaliths and,
    87; Mesopotamian, 50–2, 56–7, 138;

origins of, 37–44; Roman, 298–300; trade
    and, 232
Agrippa, 305
Ahijjiva, 154
Ahiram, 173
Akhenaten, 131–3
Akkadians, 72, 105, 107, 129, 136, 137, 145;
    language of, 62, 65, 142, 146
Al-Mina, 216
Albertini, E., 313
Albright, W. F., 161, 181
Alcaeus, 9
Alcibiades, 241
Alcmaenoidae, 236, 240
Alcmeon, 256
Aldred, Cyril, 68–9
Alesia, siege of, 293
Alexander the Great, 80, 153, 165, 177, 182,
    194, 195, 229, 244–50, 263, 267, 272, 276,
    277, 284, 296, 304
Alexandria, 252, 262–5, 267, 268; Rome and,
    282, 305
Alin, Per, 149
Alishar, 96
Almagro Basch, Martin, 92
alphabet, 172–5, 216, 232
Alps, 4, 6
Amazon basin, tribes of, 33, 35, 39
Amenhotep, 69
Amenophis III, 102, 131

Index

Amenophis IV, 102, 107, 133

American Indians, 77

Ammenemes I, 107

Ammon, temple of, 50

Amon Râ, 68, 70

Amorites, 107, 145

Amosis, 121

Anatolia, 5, 58, 109–11, 128; agrarian culture of, 39–40, 42–5; Cimmerian invasion of, 163; copper mining in, 98, 99, 101; Hittites in, 141, 143, 149, 152; Phrygians in, 160; Scythian invasion of, 163

Anaxagoras, 243, 257, 261

Anaximander, 255–6

Anaximenes, 255

Andronova civilization, 139

animals: climate change and, 24–5; on Crete, 109; culture and abundance of, 35–6; depicted in prehistoric art, 31–2, 34; domestication of, 36, 40–2, 50, 56–8, 139, 144, 167, 338n10; Egyptian, 53; in Mediterranean Sea, 12–13; nomadism and, 138, 139; sacred, 124; of steppes, 139–40, 164

Antiochus III, king of Syria, 283–5, 296

Antoninus, 297

Antony, Marc, 249, 288, 295

Anu, 73

Apennines, 4, 6, 206

Apollo, 198, 210, 215, 253; temple of, 304

Apollonius of Perege, 263

Apollonius of Tyana, 314

Appian, 186, 196

Appius Claudius, 275

Apulians, 6

Aquae Sextiae, battle of, 291

Arabian desert, 144

Arabs, 137–8, 145, 146, 249–50, 296; Spain invaded by, 191

Aramaeans, 145–6, 160, 161; Greeks and, 216; Phoenicians and, 183

Aratos (author), 187

archaeology, 18–19

Archidamus, 243

Archimedes, 228, 263, 264

Archimedes screw, 54

architecture, 128–9; Carthaginian, 188, 193, 194, 196; Greek, 252, 268; Hittite, 143; Roman, 301–2, 305–6; see also palaces

Areopagus, 235

Argos, 113, 120–2; see also Mycenae

Ariovistus, 292

Aristarchus, 264

Aristophanes, 9

Aristotle, 195, 252, 253, 256, 260–3, 266

arithmetic, 65

Armana style, 130–4

Arminius, 294

Arsacids, 289

art, 106, 155; Aegean, 109–10; Carthaginian, 193–4; Cretan, 115, 125–7, 129–32; Egyptian, 50, 53, 58; Etruscan, 204, 210–11; Greek, 193–4, 210, 216, 233, 242, 251–3, 260–1, 268, 304–7; Hittite, 143; Paleolithic, 24, 25, 30–5; Phoenician, 184; Roman, 305–8, 310–11; sacred, 45; Scythian, 164; Syrian, 132

Artaxerxes III, 245, 247

Aryans, 136

Asclepios, 197, 198

Assurbanipal, 84, 155, 162, 189

Assyria, 72, 74, 106, 107, 129, 137, 142, 148; Cimmerian invasion of, 163; Greece and, 216, 254; Iron Age in, 171; Phoenicians and, 184, 189, 225; Scythians and, 163, 165; warfare of, 144, 156, 161–2

Astarte, 133, 197, 198, 200

Astrabad, 96

astronomy, 254, 261–4

Athena, 237, 241

Athens, 83, 116, 122, 219, 225, 227, 230, 257, 260–1, 263; art of, 242; Carthage and, 195; collapse of, 272; economy of, 232; government of, 235–40; Macedonia and, 245; Mycenaean, 149; Persia and, 248; religion in, 241; Rome and, 250, 282, 287; Scythians in, 164; slavery in, 265; theatre in, 266–7; warfare of, 233–4, 237–9, 242–4

Atlantic depressions, 8, 24

Atlantis, legend of, 119

Atlas Mountains, 4

Attalus III, king of Pergamum, 283, 285

Attica, 217, 219, 222

Atticus, 304

Attila, 163

Attis, cult of, 314

Augustine, St., 191

Augustus, 208, 282, 283, 287–9, 294, 295, 304, 305, 307–10

Aurelian, 312

Index

Aurignac period, 25, 26, 29, 31
Ausonius of Bordeaux, 311
Australopithecus, 19–20
autochthonous theory, 201, 203
Aztecs, 179

Baal, 132, 133, 143, 197–9
Babylonia, 57, 99, 105–7, 114, 124, 161, 189;
    Assyrian attack on, 161–2; economy of,
    101; Hittites and, 137, 142; migration to,
    136; number system of, 65; religion of, 72,
    73, 241, 255; river craft of, 74; science of,
    254, 263; Semitic peoples in, 146
Bactria, 284
Baetic Cordillera, 4
Bahrain, copper mining in, 101
Bailloud, G., 93
Balearic islands, 87, 91, 186–7
Balkan Mountains, 4
Barca dynasty, 281
Barcidae family, 198
Barnett, R. D., 184
barter, 192
Basch, Almagro, 171
Battos, 213
beauty, ideas of, 31
Beduin, 144
Belgic tribes, 293
Benda, Julien, 236
Benjaminites, 145
Bérard, Victor, 180
Bes, 70
Bianchi Baninelli, R., 306, 307
Bias, 237
Bible, the, 51, 154, 187, 197; Exodus, 119;
    Ezekial, 183, 187; Genesis, 71; Isaiah, 162
Bibracte, battle of, 292, 293
Bithynia, 284
bitumen, 188
Black Sea, 26, 179
Bloch, Raymond, 201
boats: Egyptian, 76–7; Mesopotamian,
    74–6; sea-going, *see* ships, sea-going
Boeotica, 217
Boii, 279
Book of the Dead, Egyptian, 134
books, Etruscan, 209
Bordes, F., 29

Borges, J.-L., 240
Boule, Marcelin, 28
Boyans, 169
brachycephalic peoples, 51
Brennus, 273
Breuil, Abbé, 23, 77
Britain, 168; megaliths of, 86, 87, 93;
    Roman, 299; *see also* Cassiterides
British Empire, 272
British Museum, 49, 76
Brittany, megaliths of, 86, 87, 92
Bronze Age, 20, 60–1, 87, 89, 96, 147, 184,
    255; on Crete, 109, 113; end of, 156, 167,
    168, 171, 214; in Egypt, 102; human
    migration during, 134–41; trade during,
    96–9; writing systems of, 172
Brutus, 309
burial chambers, 86, 88, 90
Bushmen, 29
Byzantium, 282, 289, 311, 313

Caesar, Julius, 98, 169, 170, 282, 287–9,
    292–3, 305
Cagliari, museum of, 181
Camares style pottery, 120
camels, 138
Camillus, 275
Campanians, 6
Canaanites, 79, 83, 130, 145, 146, 160, 182–3,
    197; African, 191; alphabet of, 172; religion
    of, 199
Cannae, battle of, 279, 285
"Capua tile," 200
Cappadocia, 61, 129; migration to, 136
carbon dating, 19, 38
Carcopino, Jérôme, 272
Carmel, Mount, 25
Carpenter, Rhys, 119, 151, 171
Carians, 213
Carrhae, battle of, 295
Carthage, 8, 90, 91, 166, 177, 186, 188–99,
    224, 225, 247, 284; Africa and, 190–1, 195;
    economy of, 192–4, 199; Etruscans and,
    206; fall of, 195, 280, 282, 285; founding
    of, 181, 182, 203; government of, 195;
    Greece and, 221, 224, 245, 246, 276;
    religion of, 194, 197–200; Rome and,
    276–82, 285; ships of, 187

Index

Caspian Sea, 26
Cassite language, 62
Cassiterides, 190, 192, 195
Cassius, 309
Çatal Höyük (Anatolia), 39, 40, 42–6, 57, 125; temple at, 5, 44, 45
Cato the Elder, 195, 299, 302, 305
Catullus, 308, 309
Caucasus Mountains, 4, 136
cave-paintings, 24, 25, 31–3, 77
Celtiberians, 286
Celts, 86, 168–70, 207, 281, 292
Ceram, C. W., 18
ceramics, see pottery
Chaeronea, battle of, 244
Chalcidians, 218, 220; alphabet of, 173
chariots, 140, 142, 166, 170
Charles the Bold, 238
Charles VIII, King of France, 229
Cheops, 107
Chephren, 107
Cherusci, 294
Chicago Museum, 76
Chigi vase, 237
Childe, Gordon, 37, 61
Chilon, 237
China, 48, 102, 103, 164; money in, 192; timber in, 60
Chosroes, 295–6
Christianity, 298, 313, 314; literature of, 311
Chusor, 198
Cicero, 209, 304, 310
Cilicia, 136, 284; Cimmerian invasion of, 163
Cimbri, 286, 290–1
Cimmerians, 140, 163, 165, 170, 213, 254
Cintas, Pierre, 181, 188–90
Clacton period, 21
Cleisthenes, 236, 239
Cleobulus, 237
Cleon, 240
Cleopatra, 289
Clerc, Michel, 223
climate, 8–10; changes in, 23–27, 151–3, 155
Clodius, Publius, 293
cloth, see weaving
colonization, 177, 179–225; by Etruscans, 199–212; by Greeks, 212–24, 231, 249–50; by Phoenicians, 180–99

Colosseum, 306
Commodus, 310
conjoncture, 103–6
Constantine, 312–14
Constantinople, 312–13
Coon, S., 29
copper, 60–1, 87, 91, 98; smelting of, 96
Corinth, 193, 215, 218–20, 222, 232, 233, 243; Etruscans and, 210; Roman conquest of, 250, 282, 285; Sparta and, 239
Cornelius Scipio Aemilianus, P., 280
Corsica, 23, 26, 89, 194, 278, 279, 337n4, 338n10
cosmopolitanism, 106, 127–30, 143
Cottians, 310
Coulanges, Fustel de, 17
Crassus, 249, 292, 295
cremation, 168, 190, 240
Crete, 5, 7, 19, 25, 57, 77, 82, 94, 95, 106, 108–32, 137, 144, 146, 177, 184, 284; art of, 115, 125–7; chariots in, 140; cosmopolitanism of, 127–30; economy of, 98, 114–17; Egypt and, 130–2; expansionist boom on, 112; fall of Mycenaean civilization on, 149–50; geography of, 108–9; Hellenistic, 116, 215; Hyksos and, 104; maritime shipping of, 79–81, 83, 85; Mycenaean conquest of, 113, 115, 117, 119–12, 130; natural disasters on, 117–19; pottery of, 56, 109, 111–12, 117, 120; religion of, 124–6, 132; ships of, 186; urbanization of, 113–15; writing in, 63, 108, 123, 124
Critias, 241
Cro-Magnon, 28, 29, 52
Croesus, 232
Croiset, A. and M., 251
cromlechs, 86
Cumae, battle of, 194, 207, 225
Cunaxa, battle of, 247
cuneiform script, 62, 65, 172; deciphering of, 95
currency, see money
Cybele, cult of, 314
Cyclades, 15, 82, 90, 92, 109, 115, 120, 137, 215, 216
Cyclops, 5
Cylon, 236
Cynics, 313

Cyprus, 15, 25, 77, 82, 94, 109, 137, 152; Assyrian conquest of, 189; copper mining in, 102; Crete and, 112, 115–17; Greece and, 216; metal-working in, 97; Museum of, 180–1; Mycenae and, 121; Phoenicians and, 184–7; pottery of, 127
Cyrus the Younger, 247

Dacians, 295, 298, 307, 310
Dagon, 198
Dananiyim, 150, 154
Darius, 80, 192, 194, 248
dead: burial of, 28, 41, 190 (*see also* burial chambers; tombs); cremation of, 168, 190, 240; Roman funeral rites, 307
Dead Sea, 41–2, 78, 136, 188
Decebalus, 295
Delian League, 240, 242
Delphic oracle, 212, 213
Demetrius, 313
democracy, Athenian, 239–40
Democritus, 260
Demosthenes, 245
demotic script, 62
Desborough, Vincent, 150–1
deserts: nomads of, 138–9; Semitic peoples of, 144–6; *see also* Sahara
Diocletian, 297, 311, 313
Diodorus of Sicily, 188, 201, 221
Diomedes, 232
Dionysiac cults, 233, 236, 241, 253, 257, 258
Dionysius Thrax, 263
Diver, Tomb of the, 204
dolichocephalic peoples, 51
dolmens, 86, 90, 92
Domitian, 306
Dorians, 147, 148, 150, 152–3, 155, 160, 215, 229, 234, 240
drama, Greek, 252, 266–7
Dravidian language, 95
dromedaries, 138, 144
drought, 8, 24, 53, 147, 148, 151–3
Druid religions, 86, 298
Drusus, 294
Du Bellay, Guillaume, 308
Duilius Nepos, C., 278
Dzungarian gate, 138

earthquakes, 5, 10, 118, 148–9
Eberhardt, Isabelle, 9
Effenterre, H. van, 114
Egypt, 8, 17, 18, 39, 46–50, 52–71, 74, 94, 109, 124, 127, 169, 177, 188, 255, 284; Alexander's occupation of, 248; Armana style in, 130–4; art of, 50, 53, 58, 211; Assyrian attack on, 162, 189; Atlantis legend in, 119; Carthage and, 193; chariots in, 140; Cimmerians and, 165; climate change in, 151; comparative fortunes of Mesopotamia and, 107; cosmopolitan culture of, 106; Crete and, 111–13, 115–17, 128–32; decline of, 146, 156, 159, 160, 162; domesticated animals in, 56; economy of, 98, 100–6; escape of Jews from, 119; Etruscans and, 202; glass production in, 185; Greece and, 155, 200, 216, 217, 224, 228, 232, 252, 254, 255 (*see also* Alexandria); Herodotus in, 164; Hittites in, 142, 143; Iron Age in, 171; irrigation in, 54; under Lagides, 249; Libyan mercenaries in, 166; maritime shipping of, 78–81, 83, 85; metal-working in, 60–1, 96–7; migration to, 135, 137, 141; Mycenae and, 121, 122; numbering system in, 63, 65; and Peoples of the Sea, 147, 153–5; Persian conquest of, 194, 245, 248; Phoenicians and, 182–4, 186; political unification of, 67–9; pottery in, 55–6; religion of, 66, 68, 70–3, 124, 125, 132–4, 198, 241, 255; river traffic in, 76–7; Rome and, 250, 283, 286; science of, 254, 263; Scythians and, 163–4; Semitic peoples in, 144, 173; social organization of, 69–71; timber in, 59–60; Troy and, 110; urban culture of, 65–7; warfare of, 144; weaving in, 58; writing in, 62–3, 65, 172
El, 197
Elamite language, 62
elephants, 24, 25
Empedocles, 5, 236–7, 260
England, industrial revolution in, 264, 266
Enki, 73
Enlil, 72, 73
Epaminondas, 230, 244
Epicurianism, 304, 314

Index

Epicurus, 263, 266
Epimenides, 236
Erasistratus, 263
Eratosthenes, 264
Eretrians, 220
erosion, 11
Eshmun, 197, 198
Etna, Mount, 5
Etruscans, 5, 6, 129, 153, 177, 179, 180, 186,
    199–212, 224–5, 273, 274, 307; alphabet
    of, 173; Carthage and, 193, 194; decline
    of, 206–8; Greeks and, 218, 220, 221,
    224; language of, 200–3; Phoenicians and,
    189; religion of, 198, 200–3, 208–9; Rome
    and, 281; tombs of, 184, 201–4, 207,
    209–12
Euboeans, 173, 237
Euclid, 263, 264
Euphrates River, 10, 47, 53; boats on, 74; see
    also Mesopotamia
Euripides, 227, 241, 253, 266
Evans, Arthur, 95, 98, 114
Evans, J. D., 88
evolution, human, 19–20, 24, 27–30

Fabius Conctator, 279
Fabius Maximus, 250
farming, see agriculture
Farrington, Benjamin, 252
fashions: Carthaginian, 191; Greek, 233;
    Hittite, 143; Kassite, 137; Phoenician, 184;
    Roman, 298
Fayoum, Lake, 53
Febvre, Lucien, 298
Ferrero, Guglielmo, 295
Fertile Crescent, 39–40, 50, 58, 146; copper
    smelting in, 96; Hittites in, 142; Semitic
    peoples in, 146
feudalism, 142
fire, production of, 28
fisheries, 193
Flaminus, 285
floods, 9, 52; of Nile, 53–4, 67, 70
France: Indo-European invasion of, 168;
    literature of, 252; Napoleonic, 263;
    Renaissance, 308; see also Gaul
frescoes, see art

Gaius, 312
Galatians, see Celts
Gallianus, 311
Gallic Wars, 169
Gantija, temple of, 88
Gaudemet, Jean, 311, 312
Gaugamela, battle of, 248
Gaul, 298, 299; Caesar's conquest of,
    291–4
Gauls, 273, 274, 279; see also Celts
Gautier, E.-F., 191, 248
gazelles, 24, 25
geography: climate change and, 152; human
    migration and, 134–41, 165–7; of Rome,
    298–300; of Greece, 229–31
geological revolution, 26–27
Gergovia, battle of, 293
Germanicus, 294
Germans, 137, 150, 170, 290–5, 297
Gernet, Louis, 227, 232, 235
Gibraltar, Strait of, 26
Gilgamesh, 59, 66, 73
glaciation, see Ice Ages
glassware, 185
Glotz, Gustave, 95
Gobi Desert, 138
gods, see religion
gold, 61, 102, 121, 188, 192, 225
Gorgons, 164
Gracchi, 282, 287, 288
Gravettian period, 29, 30, 32, 125
Great Mogul, 179
Greco, El, 9
Greece, 8, 13, 110, 111, 127, 160, 165, 184, 194,
    227–69, 299; Achaean arrival in, 120, 141;
    agriculture in, 78; alphabet in, 172, 173,
    200, 232; art of, 193–4, 210, 216, 233, 242,
    251–3, 260–1, 268, 304–7; Carthage and,
    193–5, 278; Cimmerian invasion of, 163;
    city-states of, 114, 233–44 (see also Athens;
    Corinth; Sparta; Thebes); civilization of,
    251–69; climate of, 151–2; colonization by,
    177, 179–81, 212–25, 231, 249–50; crema-
    tion practiced in, 190; Crete and, 109;
    currency in, 100, 232; dark age of, 155,
    229; Dorian invasion of, 147, 148, 150,
    152–3, 155, 215, 229, 234, 240; economy of,
    192, 231–3, 284; Egypt and, 62, 102;

Index

Etruscans and, 201–9; geography of, 229–31; government in, 234–6; irrigation machine use in, 54; Macedonian conquest of, 244–50; maritime shipping of, 79, 80–4, 186, 187; migration to, 135; Mycenaean, 105, 122, 149; Neolithic, 40; Paleolithic, 23; Phoenicians and, 189; pottery of, 186; religion of, 57, 197–9, 208–9, 212, 234–7, 240–1, 251; rise of civilization of, 177; Rome and, 250–1, 274, 276, 277, 280, 285–7, 302–5, 313; schism between Middle East and, 96; Scythian art influenced by, 164; warfare in, 237–9, 276 (*see also specific wars*)

Greek language, 120, 123, 213, 227, 267, 298, 304

Grenier, Albert, 200

Grimal, Pierre, 308

Grousset, René, 243

Guanches, 29

Gudea, 59

Guti, 107

Gutu, 136

Gyptis, 213

Hacheptsut, 79

Hacilar, 39, 40, 45, 46

Hadrian, 289, 296–7, 312

Hagiar Kim, temple of, 88

Halaf culture, 51

Hallstatt civilization, 168–70

Hal Saflieni, catacombs of, 88

Hal Tarxien, temple of, 80, 84, 88–9

Hamilcar, 194, 278, 279

Hammurabi, 65, 73, 75, 99, 100, 105–7, 128, 137, 145

Haneans, 145

Hannibal, 194, 279–81, 291

Hanno, 187, 190, 278

Hasan Dag, 5

Hasdrubal, 278, 279

Hassel, Ulrich von, 246, 247

Hassuna culture, 51

Hathor, 70, 133

Hatti Empire, *see* Hittites

Haunebu, 121

Hebrews, 146, 154, 160–1; alphabet of, 173;

Phoenicians and, 183; sacrifice practiced by, 199; *see also* Jews

Hecateus, 257

Hector, 110

Hegel, Georg Wilhelm Friedrich, 177

Heichelheim, F. M., 156, 283

Heidegger, Martin, 227

Helladic civilizations, 109

Helvetii, 169, 292, 293

Heraclidae, 152–3

Heraclitus, 255, 257–8

Herakles, 109, 198, 208

Herculaneum, 5

Hercules, 310

Hermes, 208

Herodotus, 79, 163–6, 202, 213, 223, 238, 251, 253, 298

Heron, 265

Herondas, 267

Herophilus, 263, 264

Hesiod, 9, 12, 217, 252

Heurgon, Jacques, 202, 208, 273

hieratic script, 62; numbers in, 63, 65

hieroglyphics, 62–3, 112, 172

Hieron of Syracuse, 207, 277

Himeria, battle of, 194

Himilco, 190

Hipparchus, 264

Hippocrates, 253

Hippodamus, 268

hippopotami, 24, 25

Hiram, king of Tyre, 183

Hittites, 5, 81, 83, 105, 107, 111, 130, 132, 137, 141–4, 156, 162, 170, 202; chariots of, 140; fall of, 147–9, 152, 154, 160, 171; Hyksos and, 104; language of, 62, 95, 146; neo-, 216, 254; palace economy of, 98; Phoenicians and, 183, 184

Holy Roman Empire, 228

Homer, 15, 184, 185, 217, 252

Hominoidae, 19

Homo erectus, 19

Homo sapiens, 21, 28–9, 37, 337n6

Hood, Sinclair, 150

hoplites, 237–8, 248, 275

Horace, 8, 208, 308–10

horses, 138–40; military use of, 144–5, 163, 164, 248–9

Horus, 63, *illus. 64*, 68, 70
hot springs, 5
Hottentots, 29
Hrozny, Bedrich, 95
Hubert, Henri, 169
human migrations, geography of, 134–41, 165–67
human sacrifices, 199
Huns, 163
Hurrians, 136, 140, 143, 160
Hyksos, 49, 104, 107, 115, 121, 141, 142, 166, 183

Iapyges, 213, 220
Ice Ages, 23–5, 28, 35; sea level and, 26
ideograms, 62
imperialism, Roman, 272–89
Inanna, 57, 73
Incas, 179
Indo-Europeans, 139–41, 172, 191; and fall of Mycenaean civilization, 150; invasion of Europe by, 167–8, 170; languages of, 95, 108, 120, 141; *see also specific peoples*
Indus River, 10, 48; language of civilization of, 95
industrial revolution, 264, 266, 300
inlandsis, 24
Innocent III, Pope, 228
Inuit, 28, 29
Ionians, 215, 216, 222–5, 227, 228, 255–7, 259
Ireland, 87
Iron Age, 156, 162, 168, 170–1, 255
irrigation, artificial, 10, 48; Egyptian, 54; Mesopotamian, 50–2, 54
Isaac, 199
Ishtar, 73, 198
Isis, 70; cult of, 314
Islam, 247, 262
Isocrates, 247
Israel, 160, 161, 199
Isthmian Games, 285
Italy, 284; Cimbri and Teutons in, 291; Etruscans in, 184, 199, 201–9; Greeks in, 214, 219–22, 255; Indo-European invasion of, 168; Mycenaeans in, 214; Renaissance, 228, 229, 236, 243, 266; Roman unification of, 272–5

Jarmo, 40–1, 46, 57
Jemdet Nasr period, 55, 110
Jericho, 40, 41, 46
Jerusalem, temple of, 160
Jews, 119, 160–1, 296, 314; *see also* Hebrews
Judah, 160, 161
Jugurtha, 286, 288
Juno, 200, 301
Jupiter, 301
Justinian, 312
Justinian Codex, 311

Kahrstedt, U., 284
Karnak, temple of Ammon at, 50
karum (merchants' community), 101
Kassites, 105–7, 136–7
Keynes, J. M., 70
Kirk, G. E., 82, 83
Knossos, palace of, 98, 113–18, 122, 123, 125
Knumhotep, 144
Koyré, A., 262
Krakatoa, 118, 119
Kültepe, 96

Lagash, 107
Lagerie man, 28–9
Lagides, 249
language: Akkadian, 62, 65, 142, 146; Greek, 120, 123, 213, 227, 267, 298, 304; Indo-European, 95, 108, 120, 141, 167–8; Latin, 207, 297, 298; origins of, 33, 35; writing and, 62, 95
Larsa dynasty, 105, 107
La Tène civilization, 168–70
Latin language, 207, 297, 298
Lauguer, J.-L., 296
law, Roman, 311–12
League of Twelve Peoples, 204–6
Lebanon, 39, 49, 70; and cosmopolitan culture, 106; forests of, 59, 76, 78; menhirs of, 88; mountains of, 136
Leptolithic Age, 22
Levallois period, 21, 25, 28
Levant, 95–6, 179; Bronze Age trade and, 96–9; Greece and, 215–16; Hyksos and, 104; Rome and, 282–3, 288–9; shipping

and, 80–5; *see also* Crete; Egypt;
Mesopotamia
Lévi-Strauss, Claude, 39, 251
Libby, William F., 19
Libyans, 153, 166, 195, 213
Ligurians, 168
Li Muri, tombs of, 90
Linear A, 108, 172
Linear B, 63, 123, 124, 172
Lions, Gulf of, 26
Lipari archipelago, 5, 85
literature; Greek, 252, 267; Roman, 308–11
Livy, 308, 309, 311
Lot, Ferdinand, 17, 303, 314
Louwites, 111
Lucan, 309
Luce, J. V., 119
Lucius Quietus, 296
Lucretius, 304
Lucullus, 287, 298
Ludwig, Emil, 310
Lugalzaggisi, 112
Luvians, 141
Lycurgus, 236
Lydia, 160, 232; Cimmerian invasion of, 163
Lysander, 244
Lysippus, 268

Macedonia, 110, 150, 152, 153, 229, 244–50,
281, 283–6, 309
Maecenas, 208, 289, 308, 309
Magdalenian period, 29, 31, 35–7
Magna Graecia, 219
Mago dynasty, 194, 196
Maïkop, 96
malaria, 11–12
Malta, 25, 110, 186; megaliths on, 87–91, 93;
ships landing at, 80, 84–5, 115
mammoths, 25, 27
Manchuria, steppes of, 138
Marathon, battle of, 194, 242
Marcellus, 250
Marcleinus, Ammianus, 311
Marcomaanni, 310
Marcus Aurelius, 304, 307, 310, 312, 313
Mardu, 72
Marduk, 57, 162, 255

Marinatos, Spyridon, 80, 81, 118
Marius, 288, 291
Marseille, 213, 219, 222–4
Martial, 309
Martonne, Emmanuel de, 166
Mason, S. F., 263
Massalia, *see* Marseille
mathematics, 254, 258–9, 261, 262, 264
matriarchal societies, 57
Mayas, 179
Mauri, Amedeo, 310
Medes, 162, 164, 165
Medici, Lorenzo de', 228
medicine: Egyptian, 254; Greek, 253, 255, 264
Medinet Habu, temple of, 184
Mediterranean Sea: animal and plant life in,
12–13; autonomous areas of, 14; climate of,
8–10; first mariners on, 77–8; geological
history of, 3–7; at heart of ancient world,
15–16; Sahara and, 7–8; waterways
running down to, 10–12
megaliths, 85–94, 338*nn7, 8, 12, 13*; Maltese,
88–9; Sardinian, 89–91; sea passages and,
87–8; Spanish, 91–2, 110
Megiddo, battle of, 183
Melkart, 189, 197, 198
Melos, 115
Memnon, 248
Menander, 267
Menelaus, 185
Menes-Harmer, 18, 50, 64, 67
menhirs, 86, 88, 92
Menrva, 208
Mesolithic Age, 20, 22, 35–6, 39, 43; art of, 33
Mesopotamia, 8, 17, 39, 46–61, 71–6, 169,
177; agriculture in, 56–7, 138; bronze
metallurgy in, 96–7; chariots in, 140;
comparative fortunes of Egypt and, 107;
cosmopolitan culture of, 106; Crete and,
112, 113, 116, 128, 129; decline of, 146, 156,
159, 160, 162; domesticated animals in, 56;
economy of, 98–102, 105, 106; glass
production in, 185; Hittites in, 142, 143;
Iron Age in, 171; irrigation in, 50–2, 54;
metal-working in, 60–1; migration to,
135–8, 140; Persian conquest of, 249;
Phoenicians and, 184; pottery in, 51, 54–5,
130–1; religion of, 71–2, 124, 125, 132, 143,

198, 202; river traffic in, 74–6; Roman
invasion of, 295–6; science of, 254; Semitic
peoples in, 144–6; timber in, 59; Troy and,
110; urban culture of, 65–7, 72; weaving
in, 58–9; writing in, 63, 65
metal-working, 57, 60–1, 96–8, 167;
    Carthage and, 192–3; on Crete, 109, 117;
    Greeks and, 218, 231; Hittite, 142; Hur-
    rian, 136, 160; megaliths and, 87, 91, 93;
    Phoenician, 161, 184–5; in Troy, 110
Metellus, 288
Meyer, Eduard, 85, 180
Mgarr, temples of, 88
microliths, 22
Miletus, 214, 232
Millares, Los, archaeological site, 91, 92
Minerva, 301
Minoan Crete, *see* Crete
Miocene era, 20
Mithras, cult of, 298, 314
Mithridates, king of Pontus, 286, 287, 298
Mittani state, 102, 106, 136, 142
Mnaidra, temple of, 88
money: in Carthage, 192, 279; development
    of, 49; Greek, 221, 222, 232; in
    Mesopotamia, 99–101
Mongolia, steppes of, 138
monotheism, 124–5
monsoons, 24
Morenz, S., 68
Moscati, Sabatino, 181, 192
Moth, 198
mountain-dwellers, 135–7
mountains, 4–7
Mousterian period, 21, 25
Mulhouse, battle of, 293
Mycenae, 92, 131, 137, 216; chariots in, 140;
    Crete conquered by, 113, 115, 117, 119–12,
    130; fall of, 147, 149–55, 181, 229; Greece
    controlled by, 105, 111; Italy and, 214;
    pottery of, 56, 185; ships of, 81, 83, 85, 186;
    tombs of, 86; writing in, 63
Mykerinos, 107
Myson, 237

Nahal Mishmar cave, 61
Narmer, 112; Palette of, 50, 63, *illus. 64*, 67

Natufian culture, 41–2
Naucratis, 16, 224
navigation, 120, 187; *see also* ships, sea-going
Nazar, B., 181
Neanderthals, 21, 22, 27–8, 33, 337*nn4, 6*
Nebuchadnezzar, 189, 225
Necho, 80, 190, 245
Negro peoples, 52; Paleolithic, 29
Neolithic Age, 11, 19, 20, 109, 111, 166, 167,
    338*n7*; agrarian civilization of, 37–46;
    climate change in, 24; domestication of
    animals in, 36, 56; maritime shipping in,
    78; religion in, 57, 124, 125
Neoplatonism, 314
Neoteroi, 308, 309
Nero, 306, 307
Nerva, 296
Niebuhr, Barthold Georg, 312
Nietzsche, Friedrich, 253, 258
Nile River, 10, 11, 47, 98, 105; Delta of, 53;
    flooding of, 53–4, 67, 70; traffic on,
    76–80; *see also* Egypt
"Ninevite V" pottery style, 55
Nineveh, palace of, 83
nobilitas, 287–8
nomes (rural districts), 66, 67
nomads, 138–41, 144–6; warlike, 162–5
noria (irrigation machine), 54
Nougier, R.-L., 29
Nubia, 133; gold mining in, 102
Numantia, siege of, 286
numbers, 63, 65
Numidians, 190, 282, 288
nuraghi (towers), 90

Odysseus, 116, 227, 231
Octavian, *see* Augustus
Oenomaos, 313
oikistes, 212
Olympiad, first, 214
ornaments, 22
orogenesis, 4
Orphic cults, 241, 257
Oscans, 205, 207, 220
Osiris, 70
Ovid, 309
Ozieria, tombs of, 90, 91, 338*n11*

Index

Paestum, sarcophagus of, 204

"palace economy," 97–8

palaces: Assyrian, 161, 162; Cretan, 98, 113–18, 122, 128, 146

Paleolithic Age, 20–3, 36, 58, 77, 337nn2–4, 338n10; art of, 30–5; climate change in, 24, 26; human evolution in, 27–30

Paleozoic era, 4, 11, 18–19, 140

Palestine, 25, 39, 94, 145, 146, 154; Crete and, 112; Greece and, 216, 254; Hyksos in, 142; menhirs of, 88; metal-working in, 97; Mycenae and, 122; Scythian invasion of, 163

Palma, Cornelius, 296

Palmerston, Lord, 272

pan-Hellenic League, 245

Papin, Denis, 265, 266

Parmenides, 227, 259

Parthians, 289–90, 295, 297

Pascal, Blaise, 257, 289

pastoral peoples, 36, 139

patriarchal societies, 57

Patroclus, 171, 185

Paul, St., 298

Pausanias, 213, 231, 257

Pax Romana, 14, 249, 251, 296, 297

Pebble Culture, 21

Pegasus, 164

Pelasgians, 120

Pelopidas, 230

Peloponnese, 6

Peloponnesian war, 225, 233, 239, 242

penguins, giant, 25

Peoples of the Sea, 96, 135, 137, 146–56, 159, 170–1, 202; climate change and, 151–5; and collapse of Hittite Empire, 147–9; and end of Mycenaean civilization, 149–51; Phoenicians and, 181–3

"Perugia cippus," 201

Pergamum, 284

Periander, 237

Pericles, 14, 115, 233, 236, 240, 242, 243, 253, 260–1, 308

Persepolis, 51

Perses, 217

Perseus, 285

Persia, 54, 100, 102, 162, 194, 272, 289; Achaemenid, 177; Alexander's conquest of, 247–9; cavalry of, 165; economy of, 192; Greece and, 217, 229, 242, 245, 258; Iona conquered by, 222–5; warfare in, 238

Persius, 309

Petronius, 310

Phaedo, 230

Phalanthes, 213

pharoahs, 67–9

Phidias, 251

Philip II of Macedonia, 244–5

Philip IV of Macedonia, 284

Philip V of Macedonia, 281, 285

Philistines, 146, 154, 160, 161, 171, 183

Philopoemen, 280

philosophy, Greek, 194, 252, 253, 255, 304, 313; see also specific philosophers

Philostratus, 314

Phocaeans, 194, 206, 214, 220, 223–4

Phoenicians, 7, 79, 80, 82–4, 94, 155, 159–61, 166, 299; alphabet of, 172, 173; colonization by, 177, 179–88, 220, 224–5 (see also Carthage); currency of, 232; Etruscans and, 203, 210; Greece and, 216, 233, 254; Persia and, 245; religion of, 197, 198, 208; warships of, illus. 176

phonograms, 62

Phrygia, 148, 160; alphabet of, 173; Cimmerian invasion of, 163

Phylakopi, 115

physics, Aristotelian, 262

Pico della Mirandola, Conte Giovanni, 228

pictograms, 62

Piganiol, A., 203

Pillars of Hercules, 4

Pindar, 252

Pirenne, Henri, 17

Pisisratus, 232, 237, 252

pitch, 188

Pithecanthropus, 19, 28

Pittacus, 237

Plato, 10, 119, 151, 230, 241, 251–3, 260–2, 314

Plautus, 310

plebeians, Roman, 287–8

Pliny the Elder, 181, 188, 298–9, 307

Pliny the Younger, 204

Pliocene era, 20

Plotinus, 311, 314

plough, development of, 49, 56–7

Plutarch, 261, 264
polar shift, 27
polis, Greek, 233, 256, 267
Polybius, 169, 277, 280, 307
Polycletes, 307
Pompeii, 5, 268, 300–301, 310
Pompey, 287, 288, 292, 304, 305
Pomponius, 312
Pontic uprising, 286–7
Pontus Armenia, 284
Porsenna, king of Clusium, 207
Poseidon, temple of, 230
Posener, G., 69
pottery, 39–43, 45, 78, 155; Cappadocian,
   129; Corinthian, 193, 215, 222; Cretan, 56,
   109, 111–12, 117, 120; Dorian, 153; Egypt-
   ian, 55–6; glazes for, 185; Greek, 206,
   210, 213, 221–2, 261; Hittite, 143;
   Mesopotamian, 51, 54–5, 130–1; Myce-
   naean, 85, 122, 149; of Cyprus, 127;
   Phoenician, 185–6; ships depicted on, 82,
   83; Trojan, 110
Po valley, 6, 26, 206
Prautus, 267
Priam, 110, 129
Proculus, 312
Propertius, 308, 309
Protagoras, 253, 261
Protis, 213
Proto-Neolithic Age, 39
Przyluski, Jean, 31, 57
Psammeticus, 163–4, 216
Ptah, 70
Ptolemies, 195, 252, 263, 267, 283
Punic language, 191
Punic wars, 272, 276–82, 284, 285
Purasati, 154
Pustratta, Emperor, 102
Pydna, battle of, 285
Pyramids, Texts of the, 68
Pyrrhon, 263, 266
Pyrrhos, 246, 274
Pythagorus and Pythagoreans, 194, 241, 256,
   258–62

Qadesh, battle of, 140, 142
Quadi, 310

Quarternary era, 20, 23
Quintilian, 309

Râ, 68
races, human, 28–9
radio-carbon dating, 19, 38
rainfall, 9–10, 12; during Ice Ages, 24
Ramses II, 68, 107
Ramses III, 68, 153–5, 183, 184
Red Sea, 78–9, 98, 102, 135, 136
Reformation, 308
Regulus Attilius, 278
reindeer, 24–5, 35–6
Rekmire, 122
religion, 132; agriculture and, 57; Carthagin-
   ian, 194, 197–200; Christian, 298, 311, 313,
   314; Cretan, 124–6, 132; Druid, 298;
   Egyptian, 66, 68, 70–1, 133–4, 255;
   Etruscan, 200–3, 208–9; Greek, 57, 197–9,
   208–9, 212, 234–7, 240–1, 251, 258, 264;
   Hittite, 143; megaliths and, 85–94;
   Mesopotamian, 71–3; Neolithic, 45;
   Paleolithic, 31, 45; Roman, 298, 313
Rhodes, 15, 109, 115, 116, 121, 137, 152, 214,
   216, 263
Rif Mountains, 4
rituals, 28, 31
rock formations, 4
roe deer, 25
Rome, 6, 11, 90, 168, 169, 177, 225, 245, 249,
   271–314; brutality of, 284–5; Carthage and,
   188, 193–7, 199, 276–82; and Christianity,
   312–14; civilization of, 297–311; civil wars
   in, 286–7; decline and fall of, 312; Etruscans
   and, 202, 205–9; fall of, 17, 191; Germanic
   invasions of, 137, 150; Greece and, 228, 246,
   250–1, 266, 283–4; Iron Age in, 171; laws of,
   311–12; Levant conquered by, 282–3; livestock as currency in, 100; beyond Mediterranean, 289–97; religion of, 197, 208–9;
   science and, 264–5; threat of Cimbri and
   Teutons to, 290–1; and unification of Italy,
   272–5; warfare of, 249, 275–6
Ronsard, Pierre, 308
Rostovtzeff, Michel, 260–1
Rostow, W. W., 266
Rougier, Louis, 265

Sabinus, 312
sacrifices, 202; human, 199, 236
Sahara, 7–8, 24, 52, 135, 138, 139, 166, 289
sahels, 7, 8
Sahura, 60, 78
Saint-Acheul period, 21, 22
Saite period, 104, 225
Salamis, battle of, 83, 194
Sallust, 309
Samarra culture, 51
Samnites, 205, 274, 281
Santorini, *see* Thera
Saqqarah, 78; tombs of, 53
Sardinia, 23, 25, 26, 94, 110, 153, 186, 278, 279, 337n4, 338n10; bronzes of, 127; megaliths on, 87, 89–91; Phoenician colonization of, 181, 188, 193
Sargon, 60, 67, 72, 99, 145
Sarmatians, 213
Sassanids, 289, 312
Schaeffer, Claude A., 5, 93, 148–9
Schliemann, Heinrich, 110, 129
science, Greek, 233, 241, 251–69
Scipio, 279
Scipio Africanus, 205, 282, 283
Scipios, 285
sculpture, *see* art
Scythians, 140, 163–5, 170, 213, 218, 254
sea level, changes in, 26
seafaring peoples, *see* Peoples of the Sea
sea trenches, 4
Secular Games, 309
sedimentation, 11
Seele, Keith, 49
Seleucids, 249, 282
Selincourt, Aubrey de, 229, 242, 253
Semites, 72, 129, 144–6; languages of, 172, 173; religions of, 198, 199; *see also specific peoples*
Seneca, 304, 310
Sennacherib, 83
Senones, 273
Sentium, battle of, 274
Serapis, cult of, 265
Servius Tullius, 273
Sesostris II, 107
Seth, 70
Severus, Septimius, 298, 310

shaduf (irrigation machine), 54
Shamash, 99, 100
ships, sea-going, 77–8, 98, 155; Carthaginian, 190, 277; Cretan, 115, 116; Egyptian, 78–80; Greek, 217, 223, 238–9; of Levant, 80–5; megaliths and, 87–8; Phoenician, 186–7; Roman, 277
Sicans, 220
Sicels, 220
Sicily, 14–15, 25, 26, 115, 186–8, 193, 276, 284; Carthage and, 192, 195; Greece and, 219–22, 232, 246, 258; Rome and, 278; tombs on, 89
Sicyon, school of, 268
Silius Italicus, 198
silver, 100–2, 188, 192, 221, 222, 225, 278–9
Sinai, copper mining in, 102
Sinouhe, 71
sirocco, 8
slavery: in Carthage, 195; in Egypt, 69–70; in Greece, 217, 240, 265–6; in Rome, 277
Smith, W. S., 106, 127, 130, 157, 204
smiths, 60–1, 87
snow, 9
Socrates, 227, 230, 241, 251, 253, 257, 260, 261
Solomon, 98, 160, 183, 187
Solon, 151, 217, 232, 236–8, 239
Solutré period, 27, 29, 30, 35
Sophists, 253
Sophocles, 227, 241
Spain, 33, 34, 94; Carthage and, 192–4, 225, 278–9; Greece and, 223; megaliths in, 91–2, 110; North Africa and, 191; Phoenicians in, 181; Rome and, 286
Sparta, 83, 153, 217–18, 230; colonies of, 213, 217, 230; Corinth and, 239; Persia and, 248; Rome and, 250; warfare of, 233, 238, 243, 244
Stekelis, M., 88
steppes, 138–41, 166; horsemen of, 162–5
Stoicism, 263, 304, 314
stone tools, *see* tool-making
Stonehenge, 86, 93
stoneware, Egyptian, 55, 112
storms, 9–10; during ice ages, 24
Strabo (author), 84, 187
Straton, 263, 266

Index

Stromboli, Mount, 5

Suevi, 292, 293

Suez, isthmus of, 26

Sulla, 286, 287, 288, 305

Sulpicius Gallus, P., 285

Sumerians, 18, 49, 51–2, 57, 60, 72, 107, 129; boats used by, 75; cities of, 66, 114; currency used by, 100; number system in, 65; writing in, 62, 63

Suppiluliuma II, 148

Suteans, 145

Syracuse, 195, 199, 207, 227, 247, 277; battle of, 242, 246; Roman conquest of, 250

Syria, 7, 39, 49, 59, 71, 107, 114, 132, 133, 137, 284; alphabet invented in, 172; and cosmopolitan culture, 106; copper mining in, 102; Crete and, 111, 112, 115, 116, 127, 130; desert of, 138, 144, 145; Egypt and, 60, 142; Greece and, 155; Greece and, 216, 233, 254; Hyksos and, 104; maritime shipping of, 78–80, 83, 85; megaliths and, 92; migration to, 136; Mycenae and, 122; Neolithic, 42, 43; Peoples of the Sea in, 154, 155; Phoenicians and, 183, 184; religion of, 143; Rome and, 250, 283, 285, 287, 289, 298, 314; Scythian invasion of, 163; under Seleucids, 249; writing in, 65

Syros, 109, 129

Tacitus, 294, 310

Tages, 209

Takla-Makan, desert of, 138

talayots (towers), 91

Tanit, 194, 198–9

Tarquinius Priscus, 273

Tarquinius Superbus, 273

Taurus Mountains, 4, 61, 78, 101, 136

tax system, Egyptian, 70

technology, 264–5; Roman, 300–302

Telemachus, 6

Ten Thousand, 247

Tepe Hissar, 96

Terence, 267, 310

Tertiary era, 4

Tethys, 4

Teutons, 286, 290–1

textiles, *see* weaving

Thales, 237, 251, 254–6

thaumaturgy, 314

Thebes, 230, 244, 245; necropolis of, 69

Themistocles, 243

Theocritus, 267–8

Theodosian Codex, 311

Theophrastus, 263, 266

Thera, 5; explosion of, 118–19, 123, 152

Thessaly, 109, 152

Thoth, 70

Thucydides, 83, 238

Tiamat, 57

Tiberius, 294, 295, 298, 312

Tibullus, 309

Ticino, battle of the, 279

tidal waves, 118

Tiglath Pileser I, 146

Tigris River, 47, 53; boats on, 74, 84; *see also* Mesopotamia

timber, 59–60, 84

Timoleon, 246

tin, 97, 98

Tinia, 208

tombs, 93, 150; Carthaginian, 191; Egyptian, 112, 129–31; Etruscan, 184, 201–4, 207, 209–12; Mycenaean, 121, 122; Sardinian, 90; Sicilian, 89; Spanish, 91–2; *see also* burial chambers

tool-making, 19–22, 25, 28–30, 166; agriculture and, 38; decoration and, 32; iron and, 171

torque-wearers, 93–4, 167

town planning, 268, 305

trade, 48, 137, 161; on Black Sea, 284; breakdown of, 155–6; Bronze Age, 96–9; Carthaginian, 192, 193; colonization and, 179, 180, 182; and cosmopolitan culture, 106; Cretan, 112, 114–17, 121, 127; Egyptian, 5, 59, 78–80, 102; Etruscan, 206, 210; Greek, 214, 221–2, 231–2, 245; Mesopotamian, 59, 61, 101; Mycenaean, 121; overland, 144, 166; Phoenician, 184–9; urban cultures and, 65

Trajan, 249, 295–6, 298, 307, 309, 310

Tripolye civilization, 139, 170

Trojan war, 122, 153

Troy, 96, 109, 110, 122, 129, 273

Turms, 208

Tuscany, 204–5

Tutankhamun, 79, 97, 171, 184, 185

Index

Tutmosis I, 131
Tutmosis III, 50, 56, 102

Uenamun, 159
Umbrians, 168
Ur, 105, 107
Urardhu, 160, 161; Cimmerian invasion of, 163; Greeks and, 216
urn people, 168, 170, 203
Uruk, 107; pottery of, 54–5
Usatovo civilization, 139

Valerius Laevinus, M., 285
Vallet, Georges, 222
Varagnac, André, 169
Varro, 221
Varus, 294
vegetation, 12–13, 298–300; climate change and, 25
Vegoia, 209
Veneti, 293
Ventris, Michael, 108
Venuses, Paleolithic, 30, 45, 125
Vercelli, battle of, 291
Vercingetorix, 293
Vernant, J.-P., 256
Vertumnus, 209
Vespian, 306
Vesuvius, Mount, 5
Vieyra, Maurice, 54
Villanovans, 168, 203, 210
Villefranche period, 23
Virgil, 5, 12, 208, 289, 308–9
Vita-Finzi, Claudio, 10
volcanoes, 5, 10, 118–19

wall-painting, see art
waterways, 10–12; and changes in sea level, 26
weaving, 57–9; Carthaginian, 193; Greek, 221; Phoenician, 184
Weber, Alfred, 18, 26, 70, 243
Weber, Max, 199
Werth, Emile, 37
wheel: arrival on Crete of, 112, 116; development of, 49; potter's, 54–6
Wilamowitz-Moellendorf, Ulrich von, 227
Will, E., 233
winds, 8, 151
wood: boats built of, 76; economic role of, 59–60
Woolner, Diana, 80, 85
writing, 17, 18, 20, 49, 61–5; disappearance of, 153, 155; Egyptian, 62–3, illus. 64; see also alphabet
Würm Ice Age, 24, 28

Xenophon, 247, 261
Xerxes, 194

Yakimlu, king of Arados, 189

Zagreb, museum of, 200
Zagros Mountains, 39, 50, 136–7
Zama, battle of, 190, 280, 282
Zeeland, 87
Zeno, 259, 263, 266
Zeus, 9, 109, 124, 208, 217, 241, 313
Zimri Lim, palace of, 128, 129